MARY TUDOR

The White Queen

MARY TUDOR
The White Queen

WALTER C. RICHARDSON

UNIVERSITY OF WASHINGTON PRESS

SEATTLE AND LONDON

Published by the University of Washington Press 1970
Library of Congress Catalog Card Number 68-11050
Printed in Great Britain

To Anna

PREFACE

THE purpose of this biography is to rescue a minor Tudor character from the curious combination of fact and fiction that has previously enveloped her, and present instead a clear-cut picture of one whose historical position in the complicated diplomacy of the sixteenth century has never been properly assessed. Though more romantic than that of many, her life is not untypical of other princesses of her time, who played important, if small, parts in its history. Mary Tudor was the favorite sister of a dominant monarch, Henry VIII, and her family characteristics are apparent in everything she did. A colorful figure in a colorful age, Mary adds another chapter, however brief, to the Tudor record.

Evidence does not exist for either a detailed account of all her activities or a full reconstruction of her personal life; yet such as there is, when considered in the light of contemporary events, gives abundant proof of her imprint upon the early Renaissance society of which she was so much a product. The records concerning her, while widely scattered, are quite extensive, and in a study such as this the type and variety of both primary and secondary sources present the perennial problem of documentation. When the sources are so varied and innumerable, should the text be overburdened with exhaustive references? Some types of historical study require minute citations; others do not. This is a case in point. The life of Mary Tudor is neither controversial nor of dynamic political significance. Believing that readers will find more value in a straightforward narrative account than in one encumbered by the usual research apparatus, I have deliberately eliminated footnotes and the other impedimenta normally included in historical biographies. Those who desire a reading acquaintance with the sources used will find ample guidance in the Bibliography, which though indicative is in no sense complete. Except for occasional instances where the original form is retained for effect, quotations are reproduced in modern spelling and punctuation.

In conclusion, it is a pleasure to acknowledge my appreciation to the University Council on Research of the Louisiana State University for a generous subvention that enabled me to continue my researches abroad for a longer period than would otherwise have been possible.

Likewise, to the many individuals who contributed generously of their time and knowledge toward the completion of the manuscript, my indebtedness is great: the officials of the Print Room and the Manuscript Division of the British Museum; Mr. Roy Strong of the National Portrait Gallery, for making available to me his vast fund of information on sixteenth-century portraiture; and the librarians and staff of my own university.

Finally, I should like to express my thanks to the private owners and institutions who granted permission to reproduce the portraits and illustrations presented in the text. Full acknowledgments are given in the list of Illustrations.

Baton Rouge, La.
September, 1968

WALTER C. RICHARDSON

CONTENTS

x Contents

ILLUSTRATIONS

Eighth Henry ruling this land,
   He had a sister fair,
That was the widow'd Queen of France,
   Enrich'd with virtues rare;
And being come to England's Court,
   She oft beheld a knight,
Charles Brandon nam'd, in whose fair eyes,
   She chiefly took delight.

And noting in her princely mind,
   His gallant sweet behaviour,
She daily drew him by degrees,
   Still more and more in favour:
Which he perceiving, courteous knight,
   Found fitting time and place,
And thus in amorous sort began,
   His love-suit to her grace:

I am at love, fair queen, said he,
   Sweet, let your love incline,
That by your grace Charles Brandon may
   On earth be made divine:
If worthless I might worthy be
   To have so good a lot,
To please your highness in true love
   My fancy doubteth not.

Or if that gentry might convey
   So great a grace to me,
I can maintain the same by birth,
   Being come of good degree.
If wealth you think be all my want,
   Your highness hath great store,
And my supplement shall be love;
   What can you wish for more?

It hath been known when hearty love
   Did tie the true-love knot,
Though now if gold and silver want,

The marriage proveth not.
The goodly queen hereat did blush,
   But made a dumb reply;
Which he imagin'd what she meant,
   And kiss'd her reverently.

Brandon (quoth she) I greater am,
   Than would I were for thee,
But can as little master love,
   As them of low degree.
My father was a king, and so
   A king my husband was,
My brother is the like, and he
   Will say I do transgress.

But let him say what pleaseth him,
   His liking I'll forego,
And chuse a love to please myself,
   Though all the world say no :
If plowmen make their marriages,
   As best contents their mind,
Why should not princes of estate
   The like contentment find?

But tell me, Brandon, am I not
   More forward than beseems?
Yet blame me not for love, I love
   Where best my fancy deems.
And long may live (quoth he) to love,
   Nor longer live may I
Than when I love your royal grace,
   And then disgraced die.

But if I do deserve your love,
   My mind desires dispatch,
For many are the eyes in court,
   That on your beauty watch :
But am not I, sweet lady, now
   More forward than behoves?
Yet for my heart, forgive my tongue,
   That speaketh for him that loves.

The queen and this brave gentleman
   Together both did wed,

And after sought the king's good-will,
    And of their wishes sped :
For Brandon soon was made a duke,
    And graced so in court,
And who but he did flaunt it forth
    Amongst the noblest sort.

And so from princely Brandon's line,
    And Mary did proceed
The noble race of Suffolk's house,
    As after did succeed :
And whose high blood the lady Jane,
    Lord Guildford Dudley's wife,
Came by descent, who, with her lord,
    In London lost her life.

                                        The Suffolk Garland

MARY TUDOR

The White Queen

PROLOGUE

THE exact date of birth of Mary Tudor, Henry VII's fifth child, was unrecorded. Although the subject of considerable past speculation, the actual date has never been positively determined, hinging as it does upon a few scraps of inconclusive evidence. Nor is accuracy significant except in relation to her age in 1514, when after the repudiation of the Castilian marriage contract her engagement to the King of France was announced. In justifying this reversal of policy to the Pope, Henry VIII explained that his sister was only thirteen in 1508 at the time of her betrothal to the nine-year-old Prince Charles of Castile. He was right about the boy's age, and, if his statement about Mary is correct, she was born in 1495. Other testimony suggests the eighteenth of March, probably at Westminster, although that is another point on which all the Henrician chroniclers are silent. The Perkin Warbeck rebellion and the disturbances in Ireland that year overshadowed everything else; rebel executions in January and February were followed by Warbeck's landing in Kent during the summer and the siege of Waterford in Munster soon afterward, but by the year's end his Irish supporters had been subdued and brought to 'whole and perfect obedience.' With the Tudor throne still insecure and the succession depending on male heirs, another female child born of the royal purple was comparatively unimportant.

Fresh dangers marked the outset of each successive year as plot and counterplot unfolded. Before Warbeck was apprehended and finally hanged at Tyburn, other Yorkist conspiracies ripened, burst, and spent their force: traitors were reported, infamy avenged. At the gallows and on the block treasonable heads fell, while here and there in London familiar stocks exposed treacherous culprits to the derision of the populace. Neither the rich nor the mighty escaped; even the Lord Chamberlain, Sir William Stanley, shared the fate of every supporter of the losing cause. In an age of violence and political unrest, strong men breathed rebellion and dared to challenge the new order at the risk of their lives. Accustomed to this though he was, chronicler Edward Hall observed that a great many people had been either born 'in the womb of continued dissension, or nourished with the milk or sucking the paps of civil sedition.'

As threats persisted, so did executions. In turn, a Scottish border raid was repulsed and an uprising in Cornwall ruthlessly crushed at Blackheath. Reprisals followed. Visitors to the capital during the summer of 1497 met the blind gaze of dead eyes in grisly heads perched on London Bridge. Two had belonged to lawyer Flamank and Michael Joseph the blacksmith, leaders of the Cornish revolt, whose dismembered bodies, hanged, drawn, and quartered, had been publicly displayed as a gruesome warning to others. Over nine thousand pounds in fines was collected from the rebels, causing foreigners to acknowledge that a shrewd sovereign could make a financial profit from adversity; but the resistance that for a few years was so rampant slowly dwindled. Before the end of the century, the last of the imposters, Frank Wilford, was hanged and quartered as a traitor. Late in November of 1499 a final batch of conspirators was executed, among them the hapless young Earl of Warwick, whose only offence was a direct claim to the throne. With his death the Yorkist cause was lost.

For the most part Henry VII's household of the late nineties was unaffected by this political instability. In the capable hands of Mary's grandmother, Lady Margaret Beaufort, Countess of Richmond, who ruled her son's court and his family, life flowed on at an even tenor, undisturbed by the alarms and reports of local insurrections daily besetting the Council. Under her charge discipline and austerity directed the ménage. The boy pretender, Lambert Simnel, scullion turned king's falconer, whose capture at Stoke-on-Trent had cost England two thousand loyal subjects, was there, a living reminder of Yorkist foolhardiness. From the example of such unfortunates as he Mary must have realized at quite at an early age that the lives of children of royalty, or even those who professed royalty, were not governed by the normal standards of lesser folk. As a child she also met another hapless victim, Lady Catherine Gordon, who came as a stranger to the Court in 1497. She was the Scottish wife of Warbeck, for whose imposture she too had to suffer the brand of disloyalty, and her position after capture was almost as anomalous as his. She was first held captive until all doubt of her possible pregnancy was removed, lest a child be born outside England to inherit its father's pretensions. Thus introduced into English society, she was honorably treated, after her husband's execution becoming a lady-in-waiting to the Queen, and it was in this capacity that Mary knew her. In court circles treasonable connections did not necessarily stigmatize a social career, and Lady Catherine had married again three times before her death in 1537.

Some people shape history to their own ends; others become its driftwood, running with the current, and in their aimless course find an ease of living impossible for the strong. Prey to environment, they are drawn willy-nilly to every maelstrom. As a young girl Mary was one of these, if her formative years are viewed in the light of the political era in which she lived. Caught in the upsurge of Tudor diplomacy, she rose to queenly heights immediately, with neither personal effort nor volition. She was dynastically eligible for a matrimonial alliance between England and any of her Continental neighbors, and for years her marriage was the principal issue in treaty negotiations, first with the Netherlands and later with France. Her father's plans for her ended in failure, but Henry VIII was more successful. In 1514, when he was seeking peace with the French King, then widowed and vulnerable, his sister was exactly the right inducement.

European politics during Mary's lifetime was dominated by the rivalry of France, the Holy Roman Empire, and Spain, with insular England seeking to maintain a balance of power among the three. For the first fifteen years of his reign Henry VII had little time for foreign affairs; since wresting the throne from the Yorkist king, Richard III, at Bosworth Field in 1485, he was too preoccupied in securing his position against pretenders to give attention to much else. His objectives were direct and practical: keep England out of war, extend her trade, and forestall any Continental support of her rebels. After the turn of the century, however, when the domestic crisis had been resolved, he devoted more and more effort to arranging strategic marriage treaties as a means of increasing England's influence and prestige abroad. Through his two elder children, Arthur and Margaret, he was able to make alliances with Spain and Scotland, but the former was jeopardized by the death of Prince Arthur in 1502. Unless Arthur's widow, Catherine of Aragon, daughter of Ferdinand and Isabella of Spain, could be detained in England and married to her brother-in-law, the future Henry VIII, England stood to lose a valuable ally. Continuation of accord with Spain, therefore, became paramount in English diplomacy. Before his death in 1509 Henry VII achieved his goal: not only was the marriage between Henry and Catherine agreed to, but Mary was betrothed to Prince

Charles of Castile, Ferdinand's grandson, further strengthening
Anglo-Spanish understanding.

With Henry VIII the caution and wisdom of age were abandoned
for the adventurism of youth; the policy of nonintervention in
European politics gradually gave way to involvement, as the new
King sought to match skills with the veteran rulers on the Continent.
However, he adhered to his father's commitments by marrying
Catherine and renewing negotiations for the fulfillment of Mary's
marriage contract. Having cast his lot with Spain in the struggle for
European domination, which since 1494 had centered in Italy, he
joined his father-in-law and the Pope in a Holy League to check
France. Betrayed by them in the war that followed, Henry retaliated
by making a separate peace treaty with France in which Mary's
marriage to Louis XII was stipulated.

In all this England was dealing with experienced adversaries, heads
of powerful states to whom intrigue and diplomatic finesse were
almost second nature. Among them were a number who at one time
or another strongly influenced the pattern of Mary's life: two successive kings of France, Louis XII and Francis I; Ferdinand the
Catholic, King of Aragon; and Maximilian of Austria, Holy Roman
Emperor since 1493 and head of the House of Hapsburg. Son of
Emperor Frederick III, Maximilian first married Mary of Burgundy,
who as daughter of Charles the Bold inherited both Burgundy and
the Netherlands, and after her death Bianca Maria Sforza of Milan.
By his first wife he had two children, Philip, Archduke of Austria,
who came to be known as Philip the Handsome, and Margaret, who
after 1507 ruled as Regent of the Netherlands, or the Low Countries.
Both France and Spain had been consolidated, France by Louis XI
and Charles VIII before Louis XII came to the throne in 1498, and
Spain under the joint rule of King Ferdinand of Aragon and Queen
Isabella of Castile after their marriage in 1469. Germany, on the
contrary, had attained neither centralization nor national unity. As
Emperor of that anomalous 'empire' in central Europe, known since
the tenth century as the Holy Roman Empire, Maximilian ruled
over a conglomeration of more than three hundred separate states
and territories, often called the many Germanies. He early allied
himself with Spain by marrying his son Philip to Joanna, the
second daughter of Ferdinand and Isabella, in October of 1496,
and his daughter Margaret to their only son, Don Juan, the following year. Philip took his wife to the Netherlands, and in 1500

their eldest son Charles was born in the ancient Flemish town of Ghent.

This infant Prince, heir to the world's largest empire, was obviously the prize matrimonial attraction of the age. Sovereigns with marriageable daughters foresaw with greed that this scion of Europe's two greatest dynasties would ultimately combine the power of both. Even his titles as a child, Archduke of Austria, Duke of Luxemburg, and Prince of Castile, pointed to his illustrious future. Only the rapidity with which he would inherit his birthright could not be anticipated. On his father's death, Charles, at the age of six, came into possession of the lands of the House of Burgundy, including the several provinces then known as the Low Countries (*les pays de pardeça*), which not long thereafter were also called the Netherlands. In 1515 he was declared of age and took over the administration of the Netherlands from his aunt Margaret, the Archduchess of Austria. Though his mother Joanna was still living, her mental derangement prevented her from assuming control of Castile, which she had inherited from Isabella. Accordingly, Ferdinand ruled in her name until his death in 1516, when Charles became also King of both Castile and Aragon, uniting the rule in one person. Three years later when his grandfather Maximilian died, he was elected to succeed him as Holy Roman Emperor on June 28, 1519, at the age of nineteen.

The young Emperor was catapulted into a position of leadership second to none in Europe. His Hapsburg possessions encompassed Germany, Austria, the Netherlands, and the Free County of Burgundy or Franche-Comté; from his Spanish grandparents he became ruler of Spain, her overseas colonies, and Aragonese acquisitions in the Italian peninsula. Such was to be the power of Prince Charles of Castile, Mary's betrothed for almost six years. When they finally met in 1520, long after her second marriage, he was Emperor and she Duchess of Suffolk.

As the younger sister of Henry VIII, Mary Tudor has never existed in the popular mind as more than a shadowy figure, veiled in a mist of Tudor fact and fiction. Her familiar name is confused with that of her niece, 'Bloody Mary,' Queen of England, or with her other illustrious kinswoman, Mary Stuart, Queen of Scots. To historians, she is the unimportant member of an important royal family, significant only in relation to the international events in which she briefly took part. When in 1514 her marriage treaty with Prince Charles was repudiated, the resultant shift in foreign policy drastically altered her future, taking her to Paris instead of to the Court at Malines in the Low Countries, where as Regent, Margaret of Austria still had custody of the Prince. Marriage to Louis XII brought three months of glory, until his death flung her into the discard of widowed queens. Then for a time she emerges as a tragic human figure seeking desperately for help in a foreign land. Instead of a lifetime role as Queen of France or Queen Mother, she was again subject to the designs of conniving monarchs, as both Henry VIII and Francis I sought to profit from her plight by forcing her into another advantageous political marriage. Her irresolution, though natural enough, was short-lived, and within weeks the dominant Tudor spirit reappeared. Deliberately defying her brother she secretly married his best friend, her own countryman Charles Brandon, Duke of Suffolk, then a temporary ambassador at the French capital; but Henry's hard-won forgiveness and her public wedding at Greenwich upon her return to England were hollow victories, and historically her short spectacular career was finished. Her position as Duchess was of no particular interest to annalists and, except for periodic appearances at Court, the details of her private life are unrecorded. Even her death attracted no attention in the capitals of Europe. In the tempest of Reformation politics Mary Tudor had no part, and when two decades later in 1553 she was recalled to memory, it was impersonally as grandmother of the unhappy Lady Jane Grey.

Obviously Mary's life could never have been altogether of her own making, but it was by no means entirely circumscribed. In marrying Brandon without Henry's consent, she did so in full knowledge that they both risked possible poverty, exile, or death from their obdurate sovereign. As it was, her headstrong action incurred no personal regrets, though it was to bring some long and lean years of responsibility and disappointment. Never one to challenge the old or fight the new, she met problems as they arose, not always patiently but usually without open rebellion. When at Court she insisted upon receiving her due as Queen Dowager of France: periodically she demanded attendance there, living in the royal household during the social season, though sometimes having to finance it out of her own pocket. She persuaded Henry VIII that her presence at the Field of Cloth of Gold was indispensable to its success, and she made the most of her opportunities as Duchess, forging a place for herself in the hearts of the rural people of Suffolk as well as in the social life of the county. In everything she did Mary was a

Tudor, as ruthless in her smaller orbit as was Henry in his. Whether by weeping, threatening, cajoling, or charming, she expected to have her own way with people, sharing a family trait that refused to accept rebuff. Though tolerating country life she missed the brilliance of regular court society denied her by her second marriage, probably never quite forgetting that she had once been the pampered consort of a reigning monarch. Yet in spite of these frustrations the years with Brandon were not unrewarding. She had a dependable husband, the King's favorite, whose success in politics and war was the envy of the Council, children to comfort and please her, and a peaceful if not exciting life in Suffolk. She fared better than most royal ladies of the sixteenth century, finding in love and marriage a degree of happiness denied to the majority of them.

In contrast to the careers of the other Tudors hers was neither long nor eventful. For a time after her marriage to Brandon she appeared regularly at court functions, but Henry's irascibility and growing distrust of people led to recurrent estrangements. When not absent on matters of state or foreign missions, her husband was frequently occupied with social activities from which Mary was excluded, much of his time being given to jousting, tilting, and gaming with the King. Most of her later years were spent at their country houses in East Anglia, especially at Westhorpe near Botesdale, Suffolk, where she died in 1533 at the age of thirty-eight. Her mother had died at the same age. It was not particularly young for a generation whose women were considered old at forty and whose life expectancy was less than thirty. Despite the few who died young like Henry Fitzroy, Prince Arthur, and Edward VI, the Tudors survived well. Mary's father and sister both lived to be fifty-two, and her two grandmothers, Elizabeth Woodville and Margaret Beaufort, fifty-six and sixty-eight, respectively. Her namesake, Queen Mary, died at forty-two, Henry VIII at fifty-five, and Elizabeth, who cheated at everything, won life's gamble by a broad margin, being the first English sovereign to attain seventy. Firsts came naturally to the Tudors.

The early sixteenth century was a time of momentous change. Transformation was visible everywhere, in challenging new ideas and the metamorphosis of social patterns, every phase of the slow past giving way to the volatile present. Exuberance, excess, and Rabelaisian appreciation of the physical and the grotesque characterized the England of the twenties and thirties, revealing in its state of flux a world of divergent contrasts. Side by side with the evils of enclosures, rising prices, and the prevailing misery of the masses, greater opportunities for all classes were ushering in a society which was to spearhead the Elizabethan Renaissance. Pride in things English increased, self-confidence manifesting itself in national arrogance and ostentation. It is against this kaleidoscope that Mary's life must be interpreted.

CHAPTER ONE

The English Princess

Adieu my daughter Mary, bright of hue,
God make you virtuous, wise and fortunate.

Thomas More, 'Lamentation' (on the death of
Queen Elizabeth, mother of Mary)

DURING the first year of his reign Henry VII married Elizabeth of York, the eldest surviving child of Edward IV, thereby uniting in the Tudor line the rival houses of York and Lancaster. Mary Tudor was their third daughter, born at a time when England was still seething with the rebellious unrest of those who continued to conspire for Yorkist restoration. Abroad, the new monarchy lacked effective support, as yet not strong enough to take an active part in European politics. To a rising dynasty the birth of even a female child was welcome. For England it both strengthened the succession and provided Henry with another girl to use in matrimonial alliance with a foreign power.

If Mary's childhood was unspectacular it cannot have been dull. An intermittent procession of curious visitors came to see and admire the royal children, who caught fleeting glimpses of the world of ceremonial function and entertainment outside their own small sphere on their journeys with the King's household from one residence to another. Their most permanent home was Westminster Palace, long the seat of government, but the Court frequently moved to London either at Baynard's Castle or the Tower, or down river to Greenwich or Eltham. Less often it traveled up the Thames to Sheen or Windsor, and occasionally went as far as the royal manor of Woodstock in Oxfordshire, but far the commonest excursion for the children was by river from Richmond to Greenwich in the Queen's barge. Decorated in green and white, it was rowed by twenty-one or more liveried oarsmen, each of whom was paid eightpence for the trip.

Most of the major national events of Mary's earliest years were not likely to excite a child whose experience was circumscribed by nursery and schoolroom. She was too young to remember the London celebration of 1497 when her father received the Cap and Sword from Pope Alexander VI, and flaming fires throughout the city heralded him as 'Protector and Defender of the Church of Christ.' It is impossible to know how much she may have seen of the interesting comings and goings of the Court, but she might have been at Eltham in 1502 when the three strange men dressed in skins were brought to the King from the 'Newe Found Ile Land,' who, as described by an unknown London chronicler, ate raw flesh and spoke such a peculiar language 'that no man could understand them.'

In appearance Mary was like her mother, the fair, blue-eyed Elizabeth, who by all contemporary accounts was the loveliest of the Yorkist women. She inherited her fragile beauty and delicacy of feature, but the striking characteristic of them both was their profusion of golden hair, which in Mary had a dominant reddish tinge; she also had her mother's height, rather above the average for women of that period. There the resemblance ended. From her father's side came the Tudor traits of impatience, stubbornness, arrogance, and quick temper, though both her sense of duty and will to dominate were acquired as much from training as from birth. With little of their typically coarse humor, she yet shared the inclination of all her family to extreme likes and dislikes, loved magnificence as much as they, and had a Tudor desire to impress that was too strong to curb. The thrill of possession and display remained with her to the end, as important to the woman as it had been to the child.

Elizabeth of York died six years before Henry VII, worn down by the repeated strain of childbirth. She had known and performed her duty as Queen without resentment, giving England eight children, three of whom lived to survive her. Two of them, Edmund and Catherine, died during their first year, Elizabeth lived to be only three, and the eldest, Arthur, died at fifteen. Mary's dearest playmates, Margaret and Henry, were her seniors by six and four years respectively, but he was her favorite even in childhood, and his affection for his younger sister was noticeable throughout her life. A man of violent emotions, Henry had many headstrong attachments, but it is doubtful if he ever really loved anyone quite as selflessly as he did her.

1 Mary Tudor, Duchess of Suffolk, *c.* 1530
by Johannes Corvus

2 Richmond Palace, fronting the River Thames, as built by Henry VII. From an old drawing,
engraved by J. Basire, 1765

3   Mary Tudor (?) as a young girl, by an unknown artist

Mary's parents seem to have had deep affection for their children, though scant time to devote to them, especially the girls. In a monarch's household where the position of royal offspring was consonant with their prospects of succession, it was the sons who were spoiled, a tendency which became more pronounced in new dynasties where the very insecurity of the throne produced undue solicitude for the welfare and education of male heirs. Mary could never have become the idol of the Court living in the shadow of two elder brothers. As heir apparent Arthur was the most pampered; when he died in 1502, Henry, already a confident, blustering boy, stepped easily into his brother's place. It was not until after Margaret's proxy marriage to James IV and her departure for Scotland in the summer of 1503 that Mary, then the only princess at Court, began to come into her birthright.

As with most children of contemporary reigning families, the details of her nursery years are little known. Theirs was a practical, routine world whose daily happenings were unrecorded, with only a few staid entries in the expense accounts of expenditures on their behalf to offer glimpses of it. Deliveries from the Great Wardrobe indicate that the Tudor children were in most respects well cared for. Such commonplace items as blankets, cushions, carpets, bearhides, bedding, napkins, handkerchiefs of Holland linen, and articles of clothing were provided regularly, with occasional reference made to ribbons of colored silk or gold for the princesses. As Prince of Wales, Arthur early was given his own household, as was Henry later, but the girls were not so indulged. The King being thrifty in all domestic spending, his wife and daughters were familiar with the virtue of self-denial. As her allowance from Henry for public charity was small, the Queen herself economized scrupulously in her private household that she might give more liberally to the poor and needy; yet her frugality has undoubtedly been exaggerated. Though money was not wasted, none was in want, and nothing suggests that Elizabeth or her children were conscious of deprivation.

Mary received her share of baubles and new clothes, but contemporary fashion dictated that they be the same as those of grown women, which restricted freedom of movement and discouraged energetic exercise. Her baby clothes were of stiff silk and damask covering her from chin to toes; looking like a little old woman at the age of three or four, she wore voluminous long-sleeved dresses and full kirtles of tight-fitting bodices and ankle-length skirts, to modern

B

eyes more suited to an audience chamber than a playroom. As a further frustration, a long, gold, chain necklace and a close cap were customary for formal occasions. Considering the stereotyped education that went with such conventional dress, it would seem that young princesses of the late fifteenth and early sixteenth centuries had none of the healthy fun and active games of children of the middle and lower classes. It is doubtful if they did.

Black is a somber color for a child of two; yet in 1497 Mary wore gowns of black satin and velvet, bordered in ermine or mink, and belted with heavy dark ribbon. Her wardrobe that year included linen smocks, kirtles of black damask, hose, and eight pairs of soled shoes. By 1499 she had graduated to purple tinsel satin and blue velvet, with kirtles of tawny, crimson, and green. Night kerchiefs are listed, and after she was eight, nightgowns or 'rails,' suggesting that smaller children may have slept naked. Her personal wants were ministered to more by her grandmother, Margaret, Countess of Richmond, than by her mother, who was too busy with both public and household duties to supervise the needs of her children. Among all the records mentioning Elizabeth of York the sole links connecting her with her daughter are two entries among the Queen's privy purse expenses for the year 1502. One is a papal pardon granted to Mary during the Jubilee of the previous year, for which the sum of 12d. was allowed; the other a payment of 12s. 8d. to a tailor for making her a gown of black satin, plus an additional 3d. for hemming a kirtle. At the same time he was paid 8d. for mending dresses for her maid of honor, Jane Popincourt, and a shilling for making two linen petticoats for the Queen.

For the most part public amusements were denied the children, although they may have sometimes surreptitiously watched the dancers, players, and itinerant performers who entertained the Court, and heard the music of the minstrels and musicians. On occasion as Mary grew older she was allowed to watch ceremonial parades, when the streets were lined with people in fantastic garb, or to gaze at ghostly white-clad figures marching by torchlight, silhouetted against the night. The High Masses and extravagant feasting of Christmas were succeeded by an exhilerating week of pleasure, culminating in the giving of New Year's gifts, but prior to 1500 Mary's participation is nowhere mentioned.

Two episodes at the end of the century must have been dramatic enough to impress themselves on Mary's childish memory. The first was a disaster of late December, 1497, when the old Palace of Sheen mysteriously burned to the ground, only a small part of it surviving. On the south bank of the Thames some nine miles up river from the Tower, this palace was a favorite residence of Henry VII and one almost as dear to his family. Formerly a hunting lodge, anciently known as the 'Shining Palace,' it had more than once been rebuilt in the course of centuries. Henry had repaired and embellished it and had added gardens, warrens, and an adjacent meadow to accommodate the royal deer of 'New Park.' As the eldest, Arthur had the most memories of this house, among them the long series of jousts and pageants held there during May of 1492 when he had been proclaimed Regent of all England while his father was away fighting the French War. The children were all young enough in 1497 to be spellbound by the spectacle of smoke and flame pushing back the night shadows. The family was at Sheen for Christmas with most of the Court, but apparently no lives were lost. While the damage was estimated at over sixty thousand ducats, it was reported in Italy that the loss was considered of little consequence since it was unconnected with the Yorkist conspiracies. Henry VII immediately envisaged rebuilding the palace 'all in stone and much finer than before.'

Only two and a half years old when the fire occurred, Mary could not have remembered the simple beauty of the old palace, its brick gateway adorned by a white greyhound and a red dragon. As a young girl she would probably have been less impressed by it than by the magnificent new palace, the phoenix rising from the flames, which is described in a manuscript of 1503 as an earthly paradise. Henry was a builder as well as a statesman, and the burning of the original manor house gave him an excuse to erect a Renaissance monument in its place, his contribution to the architecture of the new age. A showpiece, it possessed courtyard, fountain, gardens, playing fields, and spectacular weathervanes topping its fourteen turrets, from the largest of which was a peaceful view of river and water-meadows. Henry's treasured achievement was named Richmond after the earldom whose title he had inherited from his father. Fittingly it was there a few years later that he died. Mary was to become very familiar with this house whose 'mighty brick wall' and massive gates, double-timbered with 'heart of oak stuck full of nails, wrought and thick and crossed with bars of iron,' had given Henry VII the privacy he wanted. Before Wolsey acquired it in 1527 its solidity, 'vaned and bent with towers,' had endeared it to all who had lived there.

After the fire the royal nursery moved to Eltham, where Mary received most of her early education. There in the late spring or early summer of 1499 her second memorable experience occurred when she met Erasmus, later to be so intimately associated with the growing humanism of the English Renaissance. He had been persuaded to come to England by William Blount, Lord Mountjoy, a former pupil of his in Paris; while staying at Mountjoy's house in Greenwich he was visited by Thomas More, who took him to Eltham Palace nearby to see the King's children. They were all there, Erasmus writes, except Arthur, who by that time had his own household elsewhere. His account of the meeting is interesting in that it gives both his impression of the future Henry VIII, and a definite assertion of Mary's age which must have come from More:

> When we came into the hall, attendants not only of the palace, but also of Mountjoy's household, were all assembled. In the midst stood Prince Henry, now nine years old, and having already something of royalty in his demeanour in which there was a certain dignity combined with singular courtesy. On his right was Margaret, about eleven years of age, afterwards married to James, King of Scots; and on his left played Mary, a child of four. Edmund was an infant in arms. . . .

Erasmus then went to London to write, at Prince Henry's request, a panegyrical poem in praise of England, which he presented to the boy with a respectful dedication. Obviously predisposed towards his new home, he was in high spirits, immensely pleased with his English reception. His correspondence indicates that he had fallen in love with everything he encountered, the countryside, the court artists and musicians, the unexpected scholarship of the universities, and the various men of letters who had befriended him. He was most charmed by the people themselves, whom he found frank, unsophisticated, and good-natured, and was delighted with the natural liveliness, affability, and beautiful complexions of English girls. 'Divinely pretty,' he described them, 'soft, pleasant, gentle and charming as the Muses.' Erasmus had discovered in what was to become for him almost a second home, rewards more satisfying than the 'mountains of gold' promised in recognition of his talents.

In November, 1498, Mary received her first proposal of marriage, if an overture for political alliance involving a dynastic union can be so described. This offer came from Milan, whose duke, Ludovico Sforza, Il Moro, requested her hand for his son, Massimiliano, the Count of Pavia. An Anglo-Milanese alliance would then have been most advantageous to Il Moro, since Italy was under threat of another French invasion by Louis XII, who had just acceded to the throne and was preparing to make good his claim to Milan. In order to strengthen friendly relations with the King of England, the Duke instructed his ambassador to attempt a threefold mission: assistance against France, the Order of the Garter for himself, and a wife for his eldest son, who was about Mary's age.

It was a preposterous request, one which can be explained only by the dire straits in which the Duke found himself. At that moment the unscrupulous Sforza, far from being the favored 'Son of Fortune' he was sometimes called by admirers, was desperately seeking support north of the Alps and hoped that England would be flattered by an alliance with one of the richest states in Italy. His envoy, Raimondo de Soncino, was less sanguine, suspecting that the British would in the end be motivated by their liking for French gold. He was as much aware as was Henry that England's diplomatic position had changed appreciably in recent years; by 1498 the English King had taken stock of his own assets and become increasingly less impressed by the arrogance of others.

Henry's refusal was courteous but firm. Sforza was informed that the first two requests were impossible, in view of the fact that England and France were at peace. Louis XII had already been admitted to the Order of the Garter, originally the badge and first order of King Arthur, he explained, and 'the knights of old who bore this badge swore to be friends of friends and foes of foes'; therefore it followed that no enemy of the French monarch could be eligible for membership. Henry expressed regret. As for the third request, under no circumstances would he consider betrothing his daughter, who was only three years old, for another four years. If when she reached a marriageable age his friend the Duke should still be interested, he promised then to give the matter every consideration. Henry enjoyed prevarication as much as he hated to make an emphatic denial to any offer which might conceivably be useful in the future. It remained for the ambassador to tell Sforza that he had almost abandoned hope of receiving any reply at all from the English king, having waited forty days before even being granted audience.

Prince Arthur's proxy marriage to Catherine of Aragon took place the following May, the first of the series of interminable matrimonial projects in which eventually all the Tudor children were involved; but it can have meant nothing to his sisters beyond the novelty of having a sister-in-law from distant Spain. Formal negotiations for this alliance had been under way since March, 1488, and after eleven years it was at last to be realized. Catherine was expected in England sometime during the summer of 1500, when Arthur would have been approaching fourteen, but various obstacles delayed her departure for another year.

She arrived in early October, 1501, amid the general rejoicings of both nobility and gentry, who outdid themselves in the enthusiasm of their welcome. Catherine's entry into London was met everywhere by gay pageants and fine music. The streets were decked with draperies of cloth of gold and silver, velvets, and beautiful satins; triumphal arches soared overhead, and red wine flowed from the conduits below. Mary must have watched with the wide-eyed interest of a child of six, intrigued with the foreign fashions and perhaps astonished at Catherine's riding a mule, Spanish style, in 'rich apparel,' with 'a little hat fashioned like a Cardinal's.'

The marriage was solemnized with magnificence at St. Paul's on Sunday, the fourteenth of the following month. After the ceremony the Prince and his wife, 'both lusty and amorous,' went to a feast 'yet not so sumptuous as populous, nor yet so populous as delicate, nor so delicate as of all things abundant.' Every variety of diversion celebrated the wedding: public games, masques, dances, feasting, all climaxed by a great tournament, and an elaborate banquet and pageant in Westminster Hall where scions of all the nobility flaunted their waxing prosperity. Prince Henry, already an incorrigible exhibitionist, led his sister Margaret to the floor for a special dance and 'perceiving himself to be accombred with his clothes, suddenly cast off his gown and danced in his jacket.' This was probably the first occasion of its kind at which Mary was present, one for which she was given two new dresses. Both were of velvet trimmed with fur, one russet, the other crimson, with a green satin kirtle and a pair of matching sleeves. Her sister wore cloth of gold; six years older than Mary and by then engaged to the King of Scotland, she had a grander position to maintain. Mary's grandmother, the Countess of Richmond, wept at the wedding, which John Fisher, Bishop of Rochester, found characteristic of her: 'Either she was in sorrow by reason of present adversities,' he wrote, 'or else when she was in prosperity she was in dread of the adversity to come.'

The triumph of the couple was short-lived. After less than five months Arthur contracted the sweating sickness that was sweeping the West Country in 1502 and, weakened by chronic consumption, died. His widow, a bewildered girl of sixteen, alone and friendless in a foreign land, was retired to the solitude of Durham House to wait helplessly while others planned her future.

The news of Arthur's death, received late one night at Greenwich, was a great blow to his father. Of his children, two had died in infancy; Edmund, his third son, had been buried less than two years before, and now his eldest. Cause of death in the sixteenth century was always problematical; many were taken by the mysterious sweating sickness, others sickened and died for no known reason, or wasted away, it was sometimes said, of melancholy. Arthur's health had been of concern even before his last illness; he had always been puny and the Council had warned against the young couple's cohabitation in his weak and sickly condition. Henry may have felt himself responsible by having pushed the boy into too early a marriage, and was perhaps voicing this qualm when he told Ferdinand that he had risked his son's health for the love he bore Catherine. The touching description of his sorrow, written by an unknown contemporary, presents a grief-stricken, emotional Henry, quite unlike the cold, calculating sovereign so frequently depicted by later historians. Wishing to share his sorrow with the Queen, he called her to his chamber that they might take 'the painful news together.' Comfortingly she urged him to occupy his mind with other things, the weal of the realm, himself, his other three children, and to remember that at thirty-five she could still give him other sons. After supporting her husband, she broke down completely in the privacy of her own room, 'so sorrowful of the heart, that those that were about her were fain to send for the King to comfort her.' It was his turn to console, to remind her of her own wise counsel, and putting their trust in God's mercy, mutually to thank Him for their surviving son. However exaggerated this account, it suggests a closeness of understanding between them not altogether common to the age. Neither tenderness nor compassion was among the usual ingredients of a royal marriage.

Arthur's funeral was prolonged and expensive as befitted the heir to the throne. On a cold rainy day in late April the long procession wended its serpentine way from Ludlow Castle to Bewdley, and thence to Worcester Cathedral for the funeral service and burial. The staffs and rods of the Prince's household were broken and cast into the grave as the coffin was lowered, 'a piteous sight' to behold.

For Mary, the gloom of death was relieved by the prospect of her sister's marriage to James IV of Scotland. Henry had always considered amicable relations with England's neighbor to the north to be vital to his foreign policy; since the Scottish king was unmarried, a general treaty of friendship, accompanied by a marriage alliance, might ensure permanent peace between the two countries. Scotland's support of Warbeck had prompted Henry to make overtures as early as 1495 when Margaret was only five, but negotiations were not completed until early in 1502 after a papal dispensation had freed them from their prohibited degree of consanguinity. The proxy marriage was solemnized at Richmond immediately, with Mary and her companions in attendance. That afternoon they watched Charles Brandon distinguish himself in the jousts, probably one of his first public appearances, and after nightfall fires were lit in the City and wine was distributed to the populace. On the fourteenth of March the people of London learned from a royal proclamation that peace with Scotland had been established 'for evermore.' Though Margaret was not to be delivered to her husband until the following year, Henry was impatient of delay, probably anxious lest James change his mind, and either return to his old ally, France, or in restless lust find himself a new mistress. Margaret reluctantly bid her father and grandmother goodbye at Colly Weston, and rode forth for Scotland, an apprehensive child, to meet her future. Such misgivings as she had must have been allayed by the magnificence of her wedding to the King of Scotland on August 8, 1503, at Holyrood Chapel.

The thistle and the rose were joined for better or for worse. A 'goodly pair,' it was said; a fruitful union too, but it brought to England, to Margaret, and to her immediate descendants, nothing but trouble. She was plump and pretty then, clear-skinned and golden-haired, but such beauty as she had faded with her youth; selfishness and morbid anxiety left their mark on her, Tudor passion apparent in a 'great twang of her brother's temper.' Five days of revelry and £2,200 of good marriage wine could not guarantee happiness in her new kingdom to Margaret Tudor.

Elizabeth of York did not live to witness her elder daughter's departure for turbulent Scotland. Gentle and serene, she died on

February 11, 1503, at the Tower, where she had been lying in child-bed since Candlemas after giving birth to her last child. The baby was named Catherine after the Queen's younger sister, Lady Courtenay, but failed to survive her mother. After lying in state, her body was carried through London to Westminster for burial. Mourned by all, her death elicited a special tribute from Polydore Vergil: 'She was a woman of such character that it would be hard to judge whether she displayed more of majesty and dignity in her life than wisdom and moderation.' In London alone 636 Masses were said for the repose of her soul.

There is no mention of Mary's attendance at her mother's funeral. She seems to have received mourning clothes with the rest of the family, but they were soon rejected for dresses of a brighter color. Within four months she was in blue damask edged in velvet, white stockings, and tawny silk ribbons.

CHAPTER TWO

Education and Training

*The whole World was made for man, but the twelfth part
of man for Woman: Man is the whole World, and the
breath of God; Woman the rib and crooked piece of man.*

Sir Thomas Browne, *Religio Medici*

THOUGH the Tudor nursery did from time to time move to some
other royal residence, its permanent home seems to have been
Eltham Palace in Kent. The main buildings of the original quad-
rangle, surrounded by wall and moat, had been rebuilt by Edward
IV, and in the early sixteenth century contained family apartments,
chapel, great hall, courtyard, and the more recent addition of a
tilting ground. Convenient to London but in rural surroundings, it
was an ideal place for the children to live a healthy country life away
from the impure air of the city and the distractions of Court. Here
strict family supervision was exchanged for the more indulgent one
of teachers. The head governess was efficient Elizabeth Denton, who
eventually left the nursery to become lady-in-waiting to the Queen;
she was succeeded by Anne Cromer, about whom practically nothing
is known either then or later.

At about five or six years of age Mary was given her own staff of
attendants, among them a physician, wardrobe keeper, schoolmaster,
and gentlewomen of the chamber. Her entourage cannot have been
very large since she had no allocation for a separate establishment.
After Arthur's death Catherine was granted £100 a month for herself and the expenses of her entire household, inadequate for her
needs though by no means a miserly appropriation when measured
in terms of contemporary purchasing power. Arthur's household
allocation had been only £666 a year prior to his becoming Prince of
Wales in 1490. While Catherine's expenses were far greater than
hers, Mary's position as younger daughter was in other ways not

dissimilar to her sister-in-law's. In describing Catherine's residence at Westminster during the autumn of 1504 the Spanish ambassador, Roderigo de Puebla, noted that the King had ordered Princess Mary to be attended in the same way as the Princess of Wales.

Like all royal children Mary was taught Latin, French, music, and composition; she learned dancing and the embroidery at which all the Tudor women seemed to excel, and probably plain sewing as well. Since knowledge of French was essential, it was taught to the royal children from an early age. By 1498 a 'French maiden,' very likely the Jane Popincourt who was to scandalize the Court some fifteen years later as the Duc de Longueville's mistress, had been appointed as playmate and companion to the two princesses, presumably to teach them French by the painless method of daily conversation. In Mary's case it seems to have been an effective introduction to the language, complete mastery being furthered by regular tutoring as she grew older. In 1512 John Palsgrave was engaged to perfect her French before her departure for the Continent, and when she finally left for Paris in 1514 Mary was fluent both in the language and in the French manners that she had learned with it.

Most court children became infected with some of the pride and vanity of their elders, and Mary was inevitably influenced to some extent by all the traits, good and bad, of her associates, in a society of which Jane Popincourt and Catherine of Aragon represented opposite poles. Princesses were likely to have more cultural and intellectual instruction than their ladies-in-waiting, but to share their training in practical housekeeping. The Countess of Richmond probably insisted that Mary acquire command of household administration, and may herself have passed on to her granddaughter some of her own proficiency as an amateur apothecary, a skill so vital to the chatelaine of a great house. The social graces and accomplishments of her society, dancing, cards, participation in court masques, table etiquette, polite conversation, and decorous manners had all to be mastered. Mary grew up to be well-balanced and cultivated, possessing probably some superficial knowledge of the humanities, especially belles-lettres. Apparently she had the eagerness and aptitude for learning noticeable in all the Tudors, though she was never offered the superior training from which her nieces, Mary and Elizabeth, profited so conspicuously.

Since her earliest tutors, if she had any separate ones of her own, are unknown, it may be assumed that she was taught to read and write with the others of the royal nursery. Then, as today, children were habitually instructed in groups rather than individually, even among royalty; in this educators had the support of the great Spanish authority, Juan Luis Vives, who maintained that it was 'not good to be taught alone.' If Mary was taught with her brothers and sisters, she learned from such distinguished men as Giles D'Ewes, Bernard André, Thomas Linacre, and the aggressive extrovert John Skelton, and studied music under skilled court musicians, perhaps the unidentifiable Giles the Lutist, 'Watt the Luter,' or 'the Welsh harpist.' Her excellence in music points to both natural aptitude and expert direction.

Princesses were never subjected to the rigorous intellectual disciplines imposed on princes, most of whom were overeducated, with a breadth and exactitude of knowledge rarely achieved by their sisters. In varying degrees the Tudor children were all endowed with unusual intelligence; when pushed to the limit of their capacities the results could be quite extraordinary. Arthur and Henry were precocious boys. It was said that the former, after six years of intensive study under the blind poet and historiographer André, showed amazing development. He was familiar with the grammarians Guarinus, Perottus, Pomponius, Sulpitius, Gellius, and Valla; had read Homer, Vergil, Lucan, Silius, Plautus, and Terence; and was conversant with the orations of Cicero and Quintilian. Nor had the historians been neglected, for the works of Valerius Maximus, Sallust, Eusebius, Pliny, Suetonius, Livy, Caesar, and Thucydides were listed among his readings. Before Arthur was sixteen his tutor, André, could 'boldly affirm' that he had 'either committed to memory or read with his own eyes, and cleaved with his own fingers' these various collections of knowledge.

After Arthur's death Henry VII was more than ever solicitous of his surviving son's health and training. Writing back to Spain in 1504 Fernando, Duke of Estrada, observed that it was 'quite wonderful' how much the King loved Prince Henry and how concerned he was with his education. Wise and attentive in everything, he neglected none of his parental duties, the Duke explained, adding that there could be no better school in the world than the society of such a father as the King.

Prince Henry showed even greater promise during adolescence than had Arthur, his precocity being more noticeable because it adorned a graceful, robust body. His classical education had followed the same course, though as younger brother his brilliance had been less publicized. Probably acquainted with such scientific knowledge as was then available, he displayed according to some a 'remarkable docility for mathematics'; well versed in Latin and French long before he became king, he also found time during the eventful years of his marriage to Catherine to learn Spanish and at least a smattering of Italian. Tall and strong at seventeen, with the bodily strength of his maternal grandfather Edward IV, he was a natural athlete, expert at archery and tennis, and able at the hunt or tournament to ride and tilt with the skill of a veteran. He was an enthusiastic and accomplished dancer, finding in dancing an outlet for his energy, spirits, and exhibitionism. Prince Henry kept this interest until infirmity forbade it, and continually encouraged introduction to the English Court of new forms of dance from the Continent. As a musician he was player, singer, and composer, and some of his songs have survived the centuries and are still known today. The concentrated energies of his teachers were not wasted. Skelton, the poet laureate, boasted that it was he who had given his royal pupil 'drink of the sugred well' and acquaintance with 'the Muses nine.' In this young man scholars found personification of the Renaissance ideal of an educated prince: one who combined beauty, chivalry, and culture, with intelligence, godliness, and scholarship.

Though not intellectually trained himself Henry VII respected learning in others, and must have allowed his cultural tastes to be guided by them. If not a connoisseur of the beautiful he was a connoisseur of the expensive, and spent money freely on buildings, jewels, extravagant hospitality, and magnificent clothes, all of which were rapidly becoming Renaissance status symbols. Mary grew up surrounded by fine things: 'There is no country in the world where Queens live with greater pomp than in England, where they have as many court officers as the King,' said ambassador Puebla, while on another occasion he expressed surprise at finding thirty-two ladies, all 'very magnificent and in splendid style,' in attendance upon Mary's mother when he called to see her unexpectedly. Not only the King but other members of his family employed minstrels, since appreciation and knowledge of music was integral to the new emphasis on culture. Under Henry VIII the musical personnel of the King's chapel, numbering 114, cost almost 2,000 pounds annually, and helped to turn the Tudor Court into the musical capital of Europe. Henry VII was ostentatiously hospitable, sometimes entertaining to dinner between six and seven hundred at a time, at an estimated cost of about fourteen thousand pounds per year. To visiting ambassadors whose reports were descriptively detailed, his audiences were no less imposing: 'The King received him in a small hall, hung with very handsome tapestry, leaning against a tall gilt chair, covered with cloth of gold,' related the Venetian Andrea Trevisano. 'His Majesty wore a violet-coloured gown, lined with cloth of gold, and a collar of many jewels, and on his cap was a large diamond and a most beautiful pearl.'

Domestically the King's mother, the Countess of Richmond, was the principal power at Court, rigidly enforcing the regulations and rules of conduct which she prescribed for everyone. Tall, stern, and proud, she was Queen Mother in fact as well as in name. Like her modern counterpart, the late Queen Dowager Mary of Teck, she put king and country before everything else, though unlike her, duty never built a barrier between her and her son. The words of the present Duke of Windsor describing his mother's attitude towards the crown, might well have been written by Henry VII: 'To my Mother the Monarchy was something sacred and the sovereign a personage apart.'

As a patroness of the arts the Countess of Richmond knew intimately all the foremost intellectuals of England and from them absorbed a deep appreciation of learning. Although for a woman of the fifteenth century her education had been unusually thorough, she was a student and translator rather than a scholar. Apart from French her training in languages, if indeed she ever had any, was rudimentary. Like her son's, her Latin appears to have been slight, neither of them having gone much beyond the religious services they had learned to recite. More than once the King was embarrassed by his inability to understand the Latin discourses and orations of ambassadors, always dependent upon his ministers for interpretation and reply. Aware of this deficiency in himself he was resolved that his sons should not suffer from the same handicap.

In the royal nursery and school also, the governing influence was Lady Margaret, who superintended her grandchildren's activities, selected their attendants, and chose such social relaxation as they were permitted to have. Earlier she had been responsible for bringing up the daughters of Edward IV, and had at one time maintained a kind of household school, customary then, for 'certain young gentlemen of her finding' under the Oxford-trained Maurice Westbury.

Mary and her sister must have felt the effect of her calm, effortless dignity and high standard of morality, profiting, with John Fisher, as much from her example of 'great virtue' as from the practical instruction she gave them.

During Mary's lifetime many treatises on the education of male youth were written by humanistic scholars like Erasmus, More, William Lily, Sir John Cheke, Richard Hyrde, Sir Thomas Elyot, and Roger Ascham. Theories of female psychology and education had received little attention before 1523, when Vives came to England after completing his *De Institutione Feminae Christianae*, dedicated to Queen Catherine; about the same time he prepared a plan for the training of her daughter, *De Ratione Studii Puerilis*; Thomas Linacre also wrote a *Rudimenta Grammatica* for her. The few treatises available before then set forth ideals of feminine behavior no longer compatible with Renaissance thought. Those in English, among them the famous *Ancren Riwle* of the High Middle Ages and the later *Garmond of Gude Ladeis* by the Scottish schoolmaster of Dunfermline Abbey, Robert Henryson, no longer presented acceptable patterns of conduct for the awakening Englishwoman, who, refusing any more to abide by chastity alone, demanded more from life than home, family, and salvation after death.

Vives did not sanction purely secular education for girls, seeing in religious training a safeguard against the temptations of physical pleasures. Such diversions, for example, as new and unconventional dances which permitted embraces or any form of bodily contact were strictly taboo :

> And the mind set upon learning and wisdom shall not only abhor from foul lust . . . but also it shall leave all such light and trifling pleasures wherein the light fantasies of maids have delight, as songs, dances, and such other wanton and peevish plays. 'A woman,' saith Plutarch, 'given unto learning will never delight in dancing.' But here, peradventure, a man would ask, 'What learning a woman be set unto; and what shall she study?' I have told you, the study of wisdom : that which doth instruct their manners and inform their living and teacheth them the way of good and holy life.

To contemporary thinkers any pattern for the education of women must be totally dissimilar to that of men, but what form the difference should take was a subject of some controversy. Most Renaissance theorists dismissed outright the idea that women had need for more than moral and domestic education, and those who condescended to study the matter were by no means positive that intellectual training was even desirable for the weaker sex. Hyrde probably voiced a general misgiving in stating that it was a dangerous innovation, subject to serious consequences. Frail by nature and 'inclined of their own courage unto vice,' he declared, they were susceptible to every novelty. In reading they would choose what was sweet to the ear rather than wholesome to the mind, and classical literature 'would of likelihood both inflame their stomachs a great deal more to that vice, that men say they be too much given unto of their own nature already, and instruct them also with more subtlety and conveyance, to set forward and accomplish their forward intent and purpose.' In contrast, Vives, in full sympathy with women's advancement in the Renaissance atmosphere of Spain, advocated study for girls in ethics, Latin, and Greek, without neglecting altogether the traditional forms of music and dancing, and the domesticity which were their customary fare. He was brought to England by Catherine, who had been reared in the Castilian Court where 'little girls sucked in Latin with their mother's milk.' Vives paid her a true compliment when he said of her: 'this woman had dusked the brightness of the heroes. . . .' Having loved literature from childhood, Catherine was determined that her own daughter should have a liberal and advanced education.

Growing up at a time when by English convention woman's place was still in the home, her chief function that of child-bearing, Mary was less educationally favored. The medieval concept of woman's inherent inferiority still lingered in the attitude that she existed for the male, around whom her whole life revolved. Her first duty as a child was to obey her father, as an adult to love and obey her husband, ready and willing to execute his bidding. A wife belonged solely to her mate in thought as in desire, but shameless carnality was a masculine vice, to which she must submit with patience and forbearance but with no lust of her own. What woman wanted weakness in a man? 'Serve then your lion,' admonished Erasmus, 'accommodating yourself to his manners, avoiding exasperating his wrath. Think within yourself, where you are the lion, I am the lioness; where you are master, I am mistress.' Obviously agreeable to men was Gratian's *Decretum* that since 'the husband is the head of the wife, while the man's head is Christ, every wife who is not subject to her husband, that is to her head, is guilty of the same

offence as the man is when he is not subject unto Christ his head.'
Even the enlightened More in his *Utopia* accepted the medieval
premise that husbands were pre-eminent. Wives ministered to their
husbands, children to their parents; both disciplinary punishment of
wives and chastisement of children were condoned in the model
state. To Renaissance theologians women possessed the same satanic
influence that Eve held for the age of Chrysostom; ubiquitous, she
was 'a necessary evil, a natural temptation, a desirable calamity, a
domestic peril, a deadly fascination, a painted ill.' In his blast *Against
the Monstrous Regiment of Women*, John Knox denounced her new
dominance as 'repugnant to nature, contrary to God, and . . . the
subversion of good order and of all equity and justice.' Women were
by nature 'weak, frail, impatient, feeble and foolish,' he wrote, 'and
experience hath declared them to be unconstant, variable, cruel and
void of the spirit of counsel and regimen.' Even in 1595 churchmen
at Wittenberg were questioning whether or not women were, after
all, human beings, their only place in society being possibly one of
adornment, for their very inconstancy, their fickle weakness, their
charm and their folly were not unlike 'divers sorts of meat minced
together in one dish.' At almost the same time John Donne was
writing that within or without matrimony 'variety made of the
female the most delightful thing in the world.' By the end of the
sixteenth century she had become man's indispensable companion.
Eloquent in her defense, Robert Greene writes in *Orpharion*:

> Women are sweets that salve men's sorest ills,
> Women are Saints, their virtues are so rare:
> Obedient souls that seek to please men's wills,
> Such love with faith, such jewels women are.

Earlier in the century individuals had rebelled against the inferior
position assigned to women. Louise of Savoy was not alone in pro-
moting equality of education for the sexes and in practising it among
her own children. Some royal daughters learned Latin as well as
French. Mary Stuart and Elizabeth I both became proficient in it,
and in time Elizabeth with her classical background, came to be
considered the educational criterion of English women. But such
'topsyturvydom' in education, as Erasmus called it, was slow to be
accepted in less exalted circles, where a precocious girl was still urged
to turn her mind to spiritual things and to prepare herself practically for wifedom, suckling being more important than letters: 'The

mother feeds, the father instructs.' Daughters of the English nobility, frequently farmed out to prominent households where they might associate with their social inferiors, continued to be nourished on such commoner fare. Young noblemen did not want more book-learning in a wife than they themselves had; modesty, silence, piety, and virtue were her most desirable attributes. Serious studies like serious pleasures were not for women. Englishmen of Mary's genera-tion were much in agreement with Jean Bouchet: 'From a braying mule and a girl who speaks Latin, good Lord, deliver us.'

Girls were exhorted to the strictest sexual morality, especially when living at one of the European courts, those 'seats of Satan' where their virginity was constantly beseiged. Spiritually uplifting reading programs were prescribed as occupation, in the hope that they would keep the devil at bay. The Scriptures, the Church Fathers, Plato, the Christian poets, and other works recommended for their alleged wisdom and virtue, were read, and for the less cultivated, devotional manuals in English were available. Copybooks into which selected passages from standard Greek and Roman authors were transcribed by students served as moral guides, as also did the *Adages* and *Familiar Colloquies* of Erasmus. Even in privileged families, history and oratory might be prohibited to women and poetry con-sidered suspect. They must be exposed to nothing that could suggest immoderation or rouse their physical instincts.

Vives insisted that above all girls be reserved and temperate, if not absolutely abstemious: 'I would rather see a girl deaf or blind than thus over-stimulated to pleasure.' Her earliest teaching was to love good, hate evil, and embrace chastity, for 'there is nothing that Our Lord delighteth more in than virgins.' Every woman must go to her husband on her wedding night *virgo intacta*, and her previous chastity was, therefore, of supreme importance. Deprived of it she could not easily aspire to an honorable marriage, her only hope for a meaningful life. St. Jerome had proclaimed that God could do any-thing but restore virginity. When compared with chastity, beauty and wealth paled into insignificance.

The suggestion that Mary's best-known descendant, Lady Jane Grey, inherited her aptitude for learning from her, is true only in so far as that above-average intelligence was a Tudor trait. The story of Roger Ascham's delight in finding the thirteen-year-old Jane pouring over Plato's *Phaedo* while her less intellectual parents were out hunting is exaggerated. The child's comments on the harshness of being so relentlessly hounded to greater attainment is nearer the truth, though her mother may have been more ruthless than most. Mary had never been disciplined to such a sustained routine of study. Later, however, Hyrde noted how much she had profited from the Latin tongue. The implication is misleading; her intellectual attainments were almost negligible. She knew nothing of theology or politics, nor did she ever pay the slightest attention to the affairs of state or the challenging religious problems with which her husband was so constantly concerned. It was only culturally that she showed any particular ability. At the French Court where aesthetic sensibility was more appreciated than in England, this quality of hers won immediate admiration.

CHAPTER THREE

Mary, Princess of Castile

> A contract of eternal bond of love,
> Confirmed by mutual joinder of your hands,
> Attested by the holy close of lips,
> Strengthen'd by interchangement of your rings;
> And all the ceremony of this compact
> Seal'd in my function by my testimony.

William Shakespeare, *Twelfth Night,* V.1

MARY'S education was interrupted in 1508 by her betrothal and proxy marriage to Prince Charles of Castile, son of Philip of Burgundy and Joanna of Spain, which took place after over eight years of difficult bargaining with first his father and, after Philip's death in 1506, with his grandfather and *de facto* guardian, Maximilian, head of the Holy Roman Empire. Owing to Charles's youth, consummation of the union was postponed for another four years, after which the Princess was to be delivered to her husband at the Court of his aunt Margaret, Regent of the Netherlands. For England the contract was almost as good as fulfilled; the years before her departure from England would be busy ones for Mary, devoted to instruction and education in preparation for her new life.

By the time the wedding was solemnized the English Court was infected with some of the spirit of the occasion, exchanging initial suspicion for enthusiasm; even the Imperial ambassadors, after parleys with the King during ten days of lavish hospitality, were impressed with their mission. Something positive was sensed in Henry VII's unusual expenditure, his reluctance to spend good money without tangible return being a byword. At Richmond Palace where the royal family was in residence, arrangements for the ceremony were complete, and in the reaches beyond the palace and on into London activity spread as everyone prepared for the popular celebration that was the invariable accompaniment to an important national event.

Mary was eager as any girl of thirteen to reach out for the boundless future. None could then predict what it would hold for her, but even though young and uninitiated in the hazards of dynastic entanglements, she herself could not have been unaware of the political imponderables surrounding them. There could be no certainty that the vows to be so solemnly taken would be kept or that all the commitments in the marriage treaty would be honored when the time came for consummation of the contract. Although Mary knew this and realized that ultimate bedding did not follow preliminary trothplight as night does day, there was still the exciting reality of the present in which she was being married to a future sovereign of accepted promise. Once betrothed, Mary attained maturity with both its responsibilities and apprehensions, and by the standards of her century became a woman. Before noon on Sunday, December 17, 1508, she pledged her troth to Charles in the expectation of becoming his wife in body as well as in name a few years later.

Across the Channel the European scene was again shifting, a change from which England hoped to benefit. If the machinations of the Emperor were successful, Charles and Mary might before long be installed as rulers of Castile. In north Italy Louis XII had already re-established French ascendancy and only the previous week had joined Spain and the Empire in the League of Cambrai, sponsored by the fighting Pope Julius II, for the spoliation of Venice. Commited to Maximilian, Henry VII now had a stake in his enterprise; accompanying his younger daughter would go a substantial loan for its furtherance. Though Henry was an opportunist, he was not a man to be hurried into action. In failing health, he must have realized that he might not live to see the fruition of his carefully made plans, but he could not have foreseen that the vagaries of European diplomacy would eventually carry his youngest to Louis XII and not to Charles.

Mary hardly looked her thirteen years, but her natural dignity and courtesy belied the slender figure they adorned. Neither still a child nor yet a woman, her gravity, politeness, and royal bearing, inculcated by those who knew the proper demeanor of a princess, could spontaneously dissolve into temper or laughter; despite the disciplines of education and the accompanying mental attitude which made most royal children seem prematurely old, Mary was still far from being grown-up, a fact which her father fully understood. Insistent that she be used to promote his political designs, he had been equally insistent that the date for consummation of her marriage should remain indefinite. In maintaining that she was still too young for the pitfalls of childbirth, he showed a perception of the evils of early marriage shared by too few of his contemporaries.

This betrothal had been long in the making. As far back as 1496 the commercial treaty known as the *Intercursus Magnus* had begun negotiations for free trade between England and the Netherlands, to be followed four years later by a general renewal of amity during Henry VII's meeting with Philip at Calais. Not the least of Henry's objectives was the furtherance of closer commercial ties which might more easily resolve future controversies between English and Dutch merchants, and friendly overtures from Philip prompted him to pursue this aim. Banquets and other fashionable forms of festivity marked the English entertainment of the Archduke of Austria during this first of a series of meetings, after which diplomatic fencing gave way to the proper business of practical settlement. In early June, 1500, the treaty of friendship was verbally reaffirmed and a twofold marriage projected: five-year-old Mary was pledged to four-month-old Charles, then Philip's youngest, while Eleanor, his first-born, was promised to Mary's brother Henry, Duke of York. To the King it mattered little that the agreement was vague; a start had been made, to be followed in time by something more definite. With mutual cooperation declared, the conference ended, and Henry was back in London by June 17, after an absence of six weeks. Suspicion had ostensibly been forgotten.

The understanding did not last long. By prevailing standards of statecraft, diplomatic promises were kept only until something better presented itself, and Philip had no scruples in repudiating his; within two years Charles was espoused to Claude of France, the infant daughter of Louis XII. Since Louis had no sons, this heiress, destined to inherit through her mother the Duchy of Brittany, was a better match than the Princess Mary, who had no such anticipated heritage to dangle before the eyes of prospective suitors. So the treaty which had been presumed to settle her future was nullified. Mary was free again. No further steps were taken by either party until 1506 when sheer luck offered Henry a chance to renew negotiations. En route for Spain in January of that year, contrary winds unexpectedly carried Philip and Joanna to England at a time when Philip was

rather amenable to a fresh alliance. Louis XII had just renounced
the marriage agreement between Claude and Charles, as specified no
fewer than five consecutive times, by bestowing her on Francis of
Angoulême, heir presumptive to the throne of France. Meanwhile
Philip's own star had risen appreciably with the death of his mother-
in-law, Isabella of Castile; he was not only Lord of the Netherlands
and Burgundy, but by virtue of his wife, King of Castile as well.
Potentially a more important figure than his father in European
affairs, had he lived longer he might have risen to the eminence
attained by his son. Henry had more reason than ever to woo him,
and here was opportunity to press for a *rapprochement.*

For once behaving impeccably, Philip notified the King of his
forced landing in England and sought hospitality at the English
Court, as etiquette required. While irritated at the unexpected though
unavoidable delay, he was prepared to play the role of distinguished
guest as graciously as possible. Less concerned with time than her
husband, Joanna should have been delighted with the prospect of
seeing her younger sister Catherine again, but she appears to have
been apathetic and unconcerned. They had not met since August,
1496, when she had been shipped off to Flanders to begin the most
tragic of all the unhappy careers of her family.

All that happened during the following weeks is not recorded.
Apparently Prince Henry was sent to Winchester at the head of a
delegation of nobles to welcome the royal guests and escort them to
London. Meanwhile unstinted preparations were being made for their
reception, which Philip had hoped would be as brief and simple as
possible. Arriving on January 31, he was hurried from London to
Windsor and later to Richmond for what proved to be a full three
months of enforced holiday. Although the parties and feasts were
more than he had bargained for, he had little choice but to accept
them and be unwillingly impressed by them. This was not difficult
even for Philip, since the English had outdone themselves both in
manners and magnificence. Unlike his children and grandchildren
Henry VII was not naturally adept at gracious hospitality, but he
had risen to this occasion. A man of deliberate action who injected
into all public affairs something of the studied determination that
characterized his private life, he was well aware that it was to his
own advantage to let the Archduke himself observe the wealth and
grandeur of his English ally.

Just outside Windsor Castle Philip and his party were met by

King Henry and the Duke of Buckingham, with an entourage of over five hundred attendants, each 'most gorgeously appareled and richly mounted.' Little is known of the style maintained in the Windsor household at this time, but it cannot have been meager; the royal visitors were housed in 'a most honourable fashion,' according to an eye witness account, in a private suite of rooms. There were seven chambers in all, 'hanged with cloth of arras wrought with gold as thick as could be,' and as for the beds of state, 'no king christened can show such three.' The version of the reception by an anonymous English herald substantiates other descriptions of its brilliance :

> To write of the great rich cupboard which continually stood in the great hall with all gilt plate, or of the great and rich beds of estate, hangings of rich cloth of gold, or of the rich and sumptuous cloths of arras with divers cloths of estate both of the king's lodging and in the king of Castile's lodging, so many chambers, hall, chapel, closet, galleries, with other lodgings so richly and very well appointed, with divers other things, that I suffice nor cannot discern, and as I suppose few or none that were there that ever saw castle or other lodging in all things so well and richly appointed, and the great continual fair open household, so many noblemen so well appointed, and with so short warning heretofore as I think hath not been seen.

Restless though he was Philip must have been as struck with this excessive display as with the pageants, jousts, and extravaganzas in his honor, but he could not have mistaken Henry's intention : the scene was being set for fresh political discussions, and the pace would not relax until a preliminary treaty had been signed. Joanna arrived at Windsor on the tenth of February, after which the Court went to Richmond for another burst of social activity.

Mary and Catherine enjoyed the 'great cheer' brought by the royal visitors, according to chronicler Wriothesley. Neither girl had received much attention in recent years, the one because of her youth, the other because of her awkward position as the untimely widow of Prince Arthur. Detained in England a virtual prisoner, Catherine was entirely dependent upon the whim of her father-in-law to make her future queen of the realm. The two girls, despite discrepancy in age, had been naturally drawn together. As the youngest child since the death of her brother Edmund in 1500, Mary had been overshadowed by her dominant sister Margaret and her extrovert brother Henry, but the former had been Queen of Scotland for three years by this time, while as heir apparent the latter was rapidly passing out of her life. She had found in this grave unaffected daughter of Spain a confidential companion and friend. In spite of the ten years' difference in age, not only had mutual interest and position thrown them together, but perhaps also unconscious recognition that each was a foil to the other. Youthfully wise at barely twenty-one, prematurely poised and earnest, Catherine needed the light relief of Mary's merriment and impetuosity. The pair of them must have looked forward to the arrival of the Castilian King and Queen, Catherine because it meant a sisterly reunion, and Mary because reconciliation with Philip might renew her engagement to his son. Joanna arrived in time for the festivities she found so tedious and watched without interest the dancing exhibition of the princesses during the first evening's entertainment. Afterwards Mary danced for Philip, who kissed her in reward; sitting with her father and his guests under the canopy of state, she later demonstrated her skill on the lute and clavichord. The visitors praised her, delighted and surprised at so much talent in so young a girl.

On the previous morning, as an expression of friendship, the Archduke had been ceremoniously invested with the Order of the Garter, whose foundation in the fourteenth century has been styled by a modern historian 'the most brilliant inspiration of the Age of Chivalry.' As Windsor had originally been intended by Edward III as the home of the order, this newest Garter feast was held there. Not to be outdone, Philip returned the compliment by bestowing upon the Prince of Wales the illustrious Golden Fleece, an honorable Burgundian order of knighthood, equally exclusive if less ancient that the English one. These acts were mere gestures of good will, but before the day was over definite commitments had followed. The Treaty of Windsor of February 9, 1506, was under the circumstances as much as either party expected.

In fact two separate agreements were reached in this formal renewal of Anglo-Burgundian friendship. The first bound them politically in defensive and offensive cooperation : each promised military aid to the other, in England's case against French designs without and Yorkist pretentions within; in Burgundy's, assistance in Castile if circumstances so demanded. Both pledged themselves to renounce all rebels who had sought refuge in their territories, with immediate surrender of them upon demand. The latter concession was most timely, since Philip's continued protection of the adventurer Edmund de la Pole was causing Henry no little embarrassment. The eldest surviving son of the second Duke of Suffolk, John de la Pole, and Elizabeth of York, sister of Edward IV, he was by rank and Yorkist connections a powerful claimant to the throne, who, since 1498, had been prowling around Europe seeking aid for his dynastic ambitions from any source available. Although his peerage had been reduced to an earldom, he had assumed arbitrarily his father's title, as did his younger brother Richard, who, after Edmund's eventual execution in 1513, took up the Yorkist cause, soliciting in both France and the Empire military as well as financial aid for an invasion of England. Whether or not Henry VII detained the Archduke deliberately until Edmund de la Pole was in his possession is problematical, but the fact remains that Suffolk was handed over and lodged in the Tower before Philip's departure from England.

The second compact was in the form of a marriage treaty, the final portion of which was not completed until March, after Maximilian's approval had been obtained. This proposed the marriage of Mary's father, Henry VII, and Philip's sister, Margaret of Savoy, whose dowry and jointure were agreed upon. It was probably at this time that renewal of the agreement between Charles and Mary was reconsidered, but no written contract materialized until the following year.

In the end England was to be disappointed in both these unions, but the good will established produced another significant development. Persistent tariff wars during recent months demanded that strained trade relations across the Channel be improved, and once closer amity had been established, Henry requested a settlement of these commercial disputes. The agreement was worked out later, but Philip had granted the desired concessions before leaving England. The treaty, not inappropriately called by Bacon *Intercursus Malus*, was signed on April 30, 1506, a week after the Archduke's departure. The adjustments were favorable to the English but unacceptable to the Dutch, who deferred ratification until after Philip's death when the settlement was revised under terms agreeable to both countries.

Meanwhile Philip was finding his prolonged stay with the English more pleasant than he had suspected. Gregarious and athletic by nature, he seems to have enjoyed the hunting, jousting, and drinking, content to tarry at another's expense until his fleet was re-

assembled and the weather propitious for sailing. After over a fortnight at Windsor he joined Henry and the ladies at Richmond,
ostensibly to admire the new palace. There, according to Edward
Hall, 'were many feats of arms proved both at the tilt and at the
tourney and at the barriers.' It was a week before he could leave to
rejoin his armada at Falmouth, and not until the twenty-third of
April, after ninety-seven days in England, did he finally set sail for
Spain carrying with him memories of wearisome deliberations, questionable contracts, and Henry's exorbitant hospitality.

In diplomacy there is no real denouement. Principals die, conditions change; progress painfully won can quickly be lost by for-
tuitous circumstance. Realizing this Henry redoubled his efforts to
crown his recent achievement by closer alliance with both Ferdinand
and Maximilian. While speaking grandly of the 'true perpetual
friendship . . . between the Empire of Rome, the Kingdom of Castile,
Flanders, and Brabant, and the Kingdom of England,' he knew full
well that without supporting action these were idle empty words.
He had got De la Pole back, it is true, but the solemn promise of a
double marriage with the House of Hapsburg could easily be disregarded. Matrimonial pacts were not marriages, and while his own
chance with the Duchess Margaret looked slender, the Spanish
match of the Prince of Wales and Catherine was also far from fulfillment. The essential link in this diplomatic chain might well be
the union of Mary and Charles, given the consent of the boy's
grandfathers and satisfactory terms. Henry had from the beginning
been 'much taken' with the idea, seeing in it a master stroke, an
alliance that might become, in Bacon's appraisal, 'the greatest marriage of Christendom, and for that it took hold of both allies.'

Plans for completion and ratification of all the alliances went on
in 1507 and 1508, despite fluctuating Continental politics. The unexpected death of Philip in the autumn of 1506 had brought further
complications, and from that point forward English success depended
solely upon the cooperation of the slippery Maximilian and his
talented daughter Margaret. None was more conscious of this than
Henry. To him strong dynastic unions yielded enduring results in
state policy that political alignment alone seldom did, and this conviction directed the program by which he hoped to achieve family
stability. Determined to execute these designs successfully before his
death, Henry spent much of his last energy in their behalf.

When it became obvious that Margaret would have no part in her father's schemes, Henry began concentrating on confirmation of the pact for Mary's marriage. Maximilian was willing to promise almost anything to prevent England from turning to France or Spain, even had his need for money not predisposed him towards any suggestion that might prove financially profitable. A new treaty was, therefore, signed at Calais in late December, 1507, which in addition to provisions for mutual aid in the event of war, clinched Mary's betrothal to Charles.

The treaty of 'perpetual peace' was specific enough to satisfy even the English. The espousals were scheduled for the following Easter or earlier, with the final marriage to follow not later than forty days after Charles's fourteenth birthday. Mary's dowry was set at 250,000 gold crowns, her jointure of towns to be the same as that of her great-aunt Margaret, the late Yorkist Dowager Duchess of Burgundy, and in view of the tender age of the couple, heavy bonds were exchanged to guarantee execution of the contract. When news of the signing reached England Henry was full of 'high contentment,' and on Christmas Day he commanded London and other cities of the realm to join him in 'all possible demonstrations' that the world might know 'what gladness and rejoicing is generally taken and made.' Obediently they announced the good news, the capital as the sovereign city and 'seemliest in sight' taking the lead: bells rang out, and bonfires summoned townspeople to gather round free hogsheads of wine.

After much time and labor 'this great and honourable marriage' was at last in sight. Confidence in it led Henry, with understandable pride, to boast that he had built 'a wall of brass' about his kingdom, which 'is now environed, and in manner, closed on every side with mighty princes our good sons, friends, confederates, and allies.'

Henry had hoped for early fulfillment of the contract but Maximilian prevaricated, still flirting with the French. Months passed in futile talk during which the treaty remained unconfirmed. In the end a promised loan of 100,000 crowns convinced the Emperor that his bread was buttered on the English side. A commission was dispatched to England in the autumn of 1508 for exchange of ratifications preliminary to solemnization of the marriage, but not before Henry had sent over a special emissary to prod Maximilian into action.

All was friendship for the time being, as elaborate preparations were made in London. Arriving at Dover on the first of December the Imperial ambassadors journeyed, via Canterbury, slowly up to London with their English escort, receiving generous gifts and expressions of welcome all along the way. Their audience with the King at Greenwich was particularly imposing, they observed, for with him and his ministers were the Prince of Wales, at least a dozen bishops, and 'the greater part of the princes and leading men of the kingdom.' Their letters report that everyone treated them most graciously, especially the King, and that they could not adequately describe 'the honour and the reception which he gave us,' than which 'nothing could have been better.' The distinguished embassy of eight was headed by the Sieur de Berghes, one of the greatest lords of northern Brabant and chamberlain of the Emperor, who was to act as proxy for Prince Charles. His colleagues too had been carefully chosen, indicating the significance attached to the mission.

Ten days later Mary was married. A vivid description of the ceremony and the festivities that followed it has come down from the pen of the Brescian Pietro Carmeliano, poet and Latin secretary to Henry VII. The King welcomed foreign humanists to England, in their varying capacities using the talents of all artists and scholars who came to serve the crown, each 'as may become me best, in field, in town, in Court, or anywhere.' Carmeliano's tract, *Solennes ceremoniae et triumphi*, performed just such a practical service; it was persuasive enough in both content and style, even in Castilian translation, to impress the King of Aragon and the Spanish nobility with the emerging greatness of England, whose 'honour is in such wise now enhaunced that all Christian regions pursue unto thee [Henry VII] for alliance, confederation, and amity.' Whether Henry actually intended to seize the Spanish possessions of his future son-in-law or not, Ferdinand was apprehensive; the English ambassador in Spain stated that he was 'sore displeased' with the marriage.

The Archbishop of Canterbury began the ceremony with a polished address in Latin on the dignity of Holy Matrimony and the significance of a union from which so 'many great and notable effects' could spring. Reply to his speech on Charles's behalf was made by Jean de Sauvaige, President of Flanders, who eulogized similarly. The oratory over, Berghes joined the Princess on the dais under a canopy of cloth of gold, and avowing the loyalty and undying affection of her absent bridegroom he formally recited his authority to represent the Prince in the vows to be taken. Then, her hand in his, he solemnly repeated the matrimonial formula, *per verba de praesenti*, which though read as if it were his own composition had long before been 'substantially devised' and 'put in writing.'

Knowing every step of the often-rehearsed ritual, Mary did not forget her lines despite the fact that she had 'no manner of person to rehearse the words of matrimony to her uttered.' Unhesitatingly she took Lord Berghes by the hand—the tract makes a point of her dignified behavior—and declared her vows with 'sad and princely countenance,' speaking 'perfectly and distinctly in the French tongue.' The assembly was impressed by such fluency in a child, for she neither paused nor faltered during her recital. Carmeliano observes that the surprise of the spectators was exceeded only by their joy: in 'extreme content and gladness the tears passed out of their eyes.'

The espousal contract used in the ceremony, one recognized by both church and state, was a covenant of betrothal and marriage to follow. Indissoluble in character and equal to marriage under the law, it was a public exchange of vows commonly known as 'hand-fasting' in which the couple were united by 'making fast the hands,' accompanied by the seal of a kiss. Between commoners a proxy was seldom employed, but in royal marriages the use of one was customary. There were two types of recognized contract, *per verba de futuro* and *per verba de praesenti*, depending upon the tense of the verb used in the promise. In the former wedlock was solemnly pledged by the phrase 'I will' or 'I shall take thee to my wife or husband,' but fulfillment of the vows was not obligatory. When given publicly it was a convenient announcement of future intent, not a true marriage. Ordinarily this form was used when the parties were so young that the date of consummation had to remain indefinite. In contrast, the *de praesenti* contract was pronounced in the present tense, making it more final and obligatory. As expressed by the heroine of John Webster's tragedy *The Duchess of Malfi*, the pact was considered binding: 'I have heard lawyers say, a contract in a chamber *Per verba de praesenti* is absolute marriage.'

In both cases cohabitation sealed the union. The troth which Mary plighted was of a standard contemporary pattern:

I, Mary, by you, John, Lord of Berghes, commissary and procurator of the most high and puissant Prince Charles, by the grace of God Prince of Spain, Archduke of Austria, and Duke of Burgundy, hereby through his commission and special procuration presently read, explained and announced, sufficiently constituted and ordained, through your mediation and signifying this to me, do accept the said Lord Charles to be my husband and spouse, and consent to receive him as my husband and spouse. And to him and to you for him, I promise that henceforth, during my natural life, I will have, hold, and repute him as my husband and spouse; and hereby I plight my troth to him and to you for him.

Then putting a gold ring on her middle finger, the proxy 'in reverent manner' kissed her. Mary was married, *de praesenti*, in lawful consent to a boy she had never seen. The ritual ended with the court musicians playing for 'a good space upon their instruments,' in honor of that 'noble act and triumph.' On its conclusion 'all the lords, ladies, and nobles hearing and seeing the premises, then and there were desired to bear witness thereunto.' As the music re-echoing through the hall died away, the company moved to the royal chapel for Mass.

The Mass was followed by a banquet, and the banquet by the first of a series of jousts. Mary and her friends watched it from the 'richly hanged and appointed' gallery where the official party had assembled to praise, criticize, or laugh at the exploits and outfits of the contestants. The sports continued for three days, with feasting, music, and dancing in the evenings, climaxed by a great tournament on the last day. That night the people of London participated in the merry-making with bells and bonfires.

Two particular events highlighted the week. By request of the Emperor the absent Charles was honored as his father had been by membership in the Order of the Garter, a gesture of fatherly good will on Henry's part; from the Netherlands came expressions of friendship and a stilted letter in Charles's name stating his satisfaction with his new bride, thereby observing ritual courtesy. In the early sixteenth century diplomacy was a game played by set rules which became increasingly more formal as Renaissance ceremonial intensified. With Charles's letter, to be presented to Mary at one of the banquets, came 'three goodly and right rich' jewels, which to her at least were more than mere tokens of esteem. A balas ruby, pale rose-red, garnished with pearls came from Margaret, and from Maximilian a brooch of one large diamond and an oriental ruby surrounded by pearls. Charles himself had sent a more intimate gift, a ring monogrammed with the letter 'K' for 'Karolus' surrounded by diamonds and pearls. Almost two decades later, during which time he had jilted ten women, he married Isabella of Portugal. The inscription on Mary's ring, engraved so many years earlier, was an ironic reminder of his promise to her : *Maria optimam partem elegit que non auferetur ab ea* ('Mary has chosen the best part, which will not be taken away from her').

Among the inventoried jewels received was one which the delegation immediately gave to Henry as part collateral for his loan to the Emperor. This unusual ornament, the 'Rich Lilly,' or *Fleur-de-lis*, is listed by Rymer as an arrangement of gold and precious stones weighing 211½ ounces. Years later when Henry VIII returned it to the Empire as partial security for France after the peace of Cambrai in August, 1529, it was described as being so large and heavy that it seemed 'a horse-load' to carry; Francis I, upon the restoration of his two sons who had been held captive by the Emperor, agreed to turn over Genoa and Asti to him and recall his troops from Italy. The jewel was delivered to Charles V the following year.

Their assignment over, the ambassadors departed, loaded with 'marvellous great and honourable gifts.' Their mission had bred satisfaction for both governments; Maximilian had secured his loan, and Henry had gained a long-sought Hapsburg alliance. Carmeliano lauded it as a triumph for English diplomacy :

Rejoice, England, and to thy most noble victorious and fortunate sovereign lord and King give honour, praise and thanks. . . . Thy flourishing red rose be so planted and spread in the highest imperial gardens and houses of power and honour that by such spectous [sic] buds and branches as by God's grace shall proceed of them, all Christian regions shall hereafter be united and allied unto thee, which honour till now thou couldst never attain.

4   Charles, Prince of Castile, as a boy. From the bust attributed to Conrad Meit

5 Mary's 'Spouselles.' From Petrus Carmelianus, *Solennes ceremoniae et triumphi*

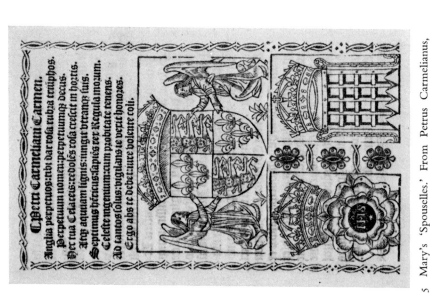

6 The Tower of London, at the time of Henry VII

CHAPTER FOUR

Marriage and Politics

Who knows not how to dissemble knows not how to reign.

Polyglot of Foreign Proverbs

THOUGH Henry VII was dominated by dynastic ambition, his European policy was deliberate and cautious. To him as to his son shrewd alliances were important guarantees of peace and security, and they both recognized their implicit possibilities. Enthusiastic and inexperienced Henry VIII was to learn diplomacy painfully, but his father, a master dissembler, was a born politician; even when marriage plans failed to materialize, England acquired prestige from powerful if impermanent alignments. Henry VII's whole life was motivated by intrigue of one kind or another, and like Maximilian, he thrived on it. Before 1500 domestic conspiracy and rebellion had left little time for more than brief sallies into foreign fields, but during the next few years his position changed rapidly. Economically the country prospered: commerce flourished, and with its extension national credit was established. Significant gains in Tudor wealth and power brought new recognition to the government, while in the practical world of power politics English gold supported aspirations abroad. Everywhere England's reputation was steadily increasing. During the Yorkist-Lancastrian conflict of the fifteenth century she had not been a power to be reckoned with by Continental neighbors, but her new stability was not to be overlooked, and the changed situation was producing overtures from those who had earlier ignored her.

In an age when political marriages were common features of diplomacy, Henry VII was determined to profit from his natural assets, union of families constituting a potentially strong political tie. It was said of the Austrian Hapsburgs that they had won more success and territory by marriage than by aggression: 'Let others wage wars: thou, happy Austria, wed!' Nor had Maximilian ever forgotten that injunction. Twice widowed, he was ready to consider a third marriage despite his avowed disinclination for it. The summer of 1515 found him at fifty-six still 'fickle and inconstant,' if Pope Julius II is to be believed, flirting with the little Princess of Hungary who had not even reached the tender age of marriageability. Irrespective of years or debility, remarriage was expected of widowed monarchs.

No enterprising sovereign could afford to remain single for long, much less permit his children to do so, and each Tudor child was called upon to contribute to the success of state policy. It was the alliance implicit in the marriage that was sought: royal sons and daughters learned from babyhood that they were valuable diplomatically, and that their duty and future lay in marrying to their country's best advantage. 'The best way to hold your kingdom together is by making use of your own children,' Charles V told his son in 1548, 'for this you will have to have more children and must contract a new marriage.' Henry VII obviously acted on the same assumption; his matrimonial schemes for himself though varying in practicability, far from being fantastic were in the best tradition of the age.

From the time of her first marriage proposal at the age of three, Mary's suitors were either encouraged or rejected on the basis of state policy. Neither her immaturity nor the personal suitability of a prospective husband was a primary consideration. In a century when health and happiness seldom determined marriage agreements her father's solicitude for her welfare was unusual, but it carried little weight where the main concern was dynastic. Political alliances and matrimonial contracts went hand in hand, and if personal happiness attended them it was an unearned blessing to which only the commonalty had any right. Catherine's father had Aragonese interests more in mind than hers when he wrote that marriage was the greatest comfort in the world, for God favored good husbands and wives; he added that a successful marriage 'is not only an excellent thing in itself but also the source of all other kinds of happiness,' both political and individual. 'Common people may look for handsome wives,' said Ferdinand, 'but princes do not marry for love; they take wives only to beget children.' Royal marriages were made to serve the needs of nations at a time when for most families mar-

riage was a business transaction entered into for its mutual suitability and profit.

Princesses were sometimes betrothed almost as soon as they were
born, and as nothing personal was implied by the haggling over their
ultimate disposal, they probably regarded it as a necessary ingredient
of their careers. When a woman's only function was to bear children
her youth was precious, and few were 'over-wearied with years'
when they wed; to be mature and still single was to be unwanted.
Margaret Tudor was a wife at thirteen; at fourteen Margaret Beaufort was both a mother and a widow. Soon after her second marriage
Mary stood as godmother in the Great Hall at Greenwich Palace to
witness the betrothal of her two-year-old niece, Mary, whose baby
finger was encircled by a large diamond ring. Far away her princely
groom, the infant Dauphin of France, slept peacefully in his cradle;
he was still younger than she. She was to be engaged many times
before she became Queen of England and chose Philip II of Spain as
her consort, and among her suitors was her eventual father-in-law,
the Emperor Charles V, who repudiated her with as little compunc-
tion as he had her aunt.

From the time of Mary's birth Henry VII's plans for his daughters
were synonymous with his ambitions for England, Margaret having
already been offered to James IV as a prelude to better relations with
Scotland. Closer entente with the Netherlands was vital to general
expansion of European trade, and again the simplest approach was
through marriage. Meanwhile he assiduously cultivated both Burgundy and Spain, as early as 1488 having taken the primary step
down the circuitous road that was to bring Catherine of Aragon to
England, first as Princess of Wales and then as Queen. The standard
of political morality in Europe at this time was at such a low ebb
as to be virtually unprincipled: typical was the series of pledges and
understandings during the Anglo-Burgundian bargaining over the
betrothal of Mary and Charles of Castile, which culminated in their
proxy marriage in 1508; but diplomatic seesawing over its consummation continued until Mary's repudiation of the contract in 1514.
Before this wearisome episode was over, Germany, Spain, and eventually France had also become entangled in it.

A definite promise in one direction did not, however, preclude the
consideration of any other likely offers that might meanwhile present
themselves. In fact, it strengthened Henry's position to be weighing
several matrimonial possibilities one against the other, since Mary's

betrothal to Charles would probably materialize sooner if it were known that her hand was being sought elsewhere. This motivated his encouragement of the rumor that Emmanuel the Fortunate, King of Portugal, had requested Mary as a wife for his son Prince John, heir apparent to the throne; the report may even have originated in England at Henry's instigation, for Thomas Lopez, the Portuguese ambassador wrote to his master in October, 1505, saying that the King personally had told him of it, adding that the English sovereign would make his choice for his daughter 'where best he may.' Lopez was skeptical, experience having taught him that in matters of expedience truth sat lightly on rulers.

Jockeying for the most profitable disposal of his children was not Henry's only preoccupation; since his wife's death in 1503 he was himself eligible for remarriage. He had long before taken the precaution through the Papacy of providing for the succession by a later wife, should Elizabeth have proved barren, and though the papal bull had been an unnecessary safeguard, he was too careful a man to disregard any eventuality or forfeit any opportunity that his widowed state might present. The King's quest for a new wife and a new alliance was a political one of the kind he loved, and despite failing health, he pursued it with enthusiasm. Historians have interpreted his efforts as the senile folly of an old man, but they shocked no one at the time. Ferdinand of Castile had set an example when within a year after the death of Isabella, hoping for a male heir, he had taken a young bride though his own youth was long since spent. To resolute dynasts procreation was more than a pleasure; it was a necessity that only the feckless ignored.

Exigency dictated Henry's preference: so long as the outcome of Prince Henry's and Mary's marriages remained uncertain he was inclined to look first either to Spain or the Empire for himself. The most obvious lady was Maximilian's daughter, Margaret of Austria, widow of Philibert II of Savoy, but the European scene was constantly changing and Henry's interests veered with it. The Spanish princesses were not to be ignored: by Philip of Burgundy's death his widow Joanna was free to remarry, as was her younger sister Catherine, the widowed Princess of Wales. Though the latter's projected marriage with Prince Henry had scarcely progressed, Henry VII was loth to relinquish what had been a cherished objective for so long. In spite of this the idea of marrying her himself was provocative enough for tentative investigation; it would achieve the same ends, plus the distinct advantage of freeing his son to make a profitable marriage alliance elsewhere. In addition to acquiring the balance of her dowry, still partially unpaid, Henry did not find her unattractive; slightly under eighteen, she was the right age for child-bearing, and with only one surviving son he had need for more male children. Though ailing, at forty-six he was still able to beget, and Catherine was already conveniently in England and available. He might combine the satisfaction of another son for himself with Spanish support for the marriage of Mary and Charles. Neither Catherine nor her parents seem to have considered the idea repugnant; for a man to marry his daughter-in-law was the least censurable of courtly conduct in the sixteenth century. But it was not to be. Spain had other plans.

Neither were the eligible French princesses to be discounted; either of Louis XII's little girls, Claude and Renée, would do for his son, leaving the indomitable Duchess of Savoy or her daughter for himself. Widowed at twenty by the death of the Count of Angoulême, the ruthless and self-seeking Duchess Louise was a prize for any man who could control her; a still greater attraction was her daughter Marguerite d'Angoulême, later the celebrated Queen of Navarre, whose promise even as a child had impressed the French Court. Born in 1492, the year that brought Columbus fame, she was to sail more troubled waters than he. When wooed by England, first for Arthur and then for Prince Henry, she already possessed an individuality and intellectual forwardness rare among girls of her generation. Described by English ambassadors as 'très belle et saige,' she was as decorative as the flower whose name she bore and as naturally hardy. Never conventionally pretty, like Mary Tudor she early acquired an appealing sensitivity and gentleness. When the King himself sought her hand Marguerite was a striking girl of thirteen, large for her age, physically robust and temperamentally pliant enough to be molded to a man's will.

By the summer of 1505 Henry VII was becoming increasingly skeptical about the materialization of a matrimonial alliance with Spain. It is not surprising, therefore, to find him turning to France with various proposals: Marguerite or her mother for himself, the former for his son, or possibly Mary's betrothal to the twelve-year-old heir presumptive, Francis of Angoulême. While it was reported that he was making great efforts for the latter marriage, the principal bid seems to have been for himself. He desired most to marry Mademoiselle Marguerite, according to ambassador Lord Herbert, 'both on account of her proximity of lineage to the king, who is the prince he loves most in the world, but also for the great goodness and virtues which he has understood to be in the said lady.' An overture of this kind was made chiefly to test the worth of 'the good and true fraternity and alliance existing between the two princes,' and in the light of subsequent events it is obvious that Henry did not then intend any reversal of policy; nor was Louis XII taken in though he expressed perfect willingness to draw up a contract. A few months later, in May, 1506, his elder daughter Claude was betrothed to Francis, and about the same time a closer understanding between France and Spain developed. Rebuff was part of matrimonial diplomacy; unimpressed by the suggested settlement of 200,000 crowns accompanying it, Marguerite bluntly refused Henry's proposal, dismissing his avowal that he preferred her to all others in the world. 'What!' she is said to have exclaimed, 'they wanted to carry her off to a distant country where a foreign tongue was talked, and to marry her to a King? and what a King! old, decrepit! Francis was to be a king one day; could she not find a husband young, rich and noble, without crossing the seas?'

Another eligible lady was Ferdinand's niece, the twenty-seven-year-old Queen of Naples; hard to please for a man of fifty, Henry declared that he would not have this Joanna of Naples for all the treasures of the world unless she were beautiful. Puebla, through whom most of the advances were made, told Ferdinand that the English King would not commit himself without first having a reliable description of her from his own ambassadors, 'the English thinking so much as they do about personal appearance.'

Puebla was right: Henry was chancing none of the personal regrets that his son was to experience thirty-five years later upon first beholding his fourth Queen, the 'Flanders Mare.' In 1505 envoys were sent to Valencia where the Neapolitan Queen lived with her mother of the same name and title, to investigate her at first hand. They were solemnly instructed to judge her qualities under no fewer than twenty-four items, for the King 'meant to find all things in one woman.' This stress upon her appearance led Henry's biographer, Bacon, to observe that such amorous interest on the King's part was more fitting for a young man than for one of his maturity. Her age, weight, stature, and general physical features, her speech, posture, deportment, mannerisms, and personality were recorded, as were her education, habits, companions, and the nature and excellence of her household. The envoys particularly emphasized the 'clearness of her skin,' the 'colours of her hair,' the 'condition of her breath,' any 'sickness of her nativity, deformity or blemish in her body,' the 'fashion of her nose,' her 'breasts and paps, whether they be big or small,' and 'specially to mark the favour of her visage, whether she be painted or not, and whether it be fat or lean, sharp or round, and whether her countenance be cheerful and amiable, frowning or melancholy, stedfast or light, or blushing in communication.' Finally, and this was no afterthought, they were to discover what land and property she was expected to inherit and to appraise its value.

The answers were mostly satisfactory. Joanna was of indefinite size, medium height, fair-skinned and without pimples, possessing an amiable, cheerful face. In appearance she was presentable: brown hair, greyish eyes, clean teeth well set, with sweet breath and passionate lips. Inclined toward heaviness, she nevertheless had a 'very good compass'; though her breasts were 'somewhat great' they were offset by a comely neck. She spoke Spanish and Italian, understood something of Latin and French, but knew no English. In conversation she was deliberate and discreet, 'not having many words nor moving countenance, but full stedfast,' as a good wife should, 'with no high speech, and after the manner of that country with a noble gravity, and not too bold but somewhat shamefacedly womanly.' She drank water and occasionally wine, but, and this should have pleased the English, she was 'a good feeder, and eateth well her meat twice on a day.' These specifications were officially presented to the King and Council in one of the most remarkable documents in diplomatic history.

It would have been enough for most men, but Henry trusted no one, and wishing to see for himself he hired a competent artist to paint a portrait of her, but here the Queen demurred; nor did it matter, for the sudden death of Philip of Burgundy introduced another far more eligible lady, his widow Joanna, the new Queen of Castile. Both Henry and the Queen of Naples were relieved—he because her income was less than he had hoped, she because she preferred a younger husband of her own choosing.

Two events had precipitated a radical change in the Spanish scene within a short space of time: the death of Joanna's mother Isabella on the twenty-sixth of November, 1504, and that of her husband two years later. The earlier deaths of her brother, the Infante Juan, and her elder sister had made Joanna heiress apparent, not only of Castile and Aragon, but of the entire Spanish empire. Unexpectedly widowed at twenty-five, overnight she became the most marriageable woman in Europe, her only drawback being questionable sanity. On the assumption that she was unfit to rule, her father claimed the regency of Castile for her son Charles, but Ferdinand himself was fifty-four and precariously situated in relation to the succession. In the shape of a new husband for Joanna, an enterprising son-in-law could be either a help to him or a great hindrance, according to how patiently he awaited her inheritance. For Henry VII it was too challenging an opportunity to be overlooked: if he married Joanna the union of Charles and Mary would be assured, and that between Prince Henry and Catherine made considerably more probable. Such was the reasoning that prompted him to contemplate spending his remaining years with a mad woman, a prospect which he chivalrously avowed filled him with 'rapturous joy.'

Married at seventeen to the conceited sophisticate, Philip the Handsome of Burgundy, the high-strung Joanna had had more than her share of tribulation. She was passionately in love with her husband, who proved as faithless in marriage as he was irresolute in politics; distress and anxiety over his philandering, coupled with the strain of childbirth, early took their toll. Her reason began to fail after the birth of her second child in 1503 when she became 'subject to sudden attacks,' acting as 'one distraught.' Thereafter fits of hysteria were so recurrent that both her mother and her cavalier husband treated her as insane whether she was or not. The tragedy of Philip's death during her sixth pregnancy increased her morbidity to such an extreme that she refused to permit his burial, taking the beloved corpse in a leaden coffin wherever she went lest she miss the day which her deranged mind had set for his resurrection. The seriousness of Joanna's insanity, however, varied with the motives of those describing it, and though she was known for years to her countrymen as 'La Loca' or 'Jeanne la Folle,' her mental condition was almost certainly exaggerated.

Henry's interest in her rested on two suppositions: that by marrying her he might gain control of her kingdom, and his apparent belief that she was still able to bear children; but he needed confirmation of both points before attempting to persuade Ferdinand into agreement. Catherine was prevailed upon to write to her father in support of Henry's suit, emphasizing the great and enduring affec-

tion which he had for her sister. In London, Puebla, who acted as
spokesman for both powers, accepted the marriage offer as sincere.
Writing during the spring of 1507 he told Ferdinand that Joanna
'would soon recover her reason if wedded to the King of England,'
for there was no one in the whole world who would be 'so good a
husband to the Queen of Castile' as he, 'be she sane or crazy,' adding
that 'if her infirmity should prove incurable, it would be no incon-
venience if she were to live here [in England]. For it seems to me
that they do not much mind her infirmity, since I told them it does
not prevent her from bearing children.' In the autumn he reiterated
that the marriage was earnestly desired in England by both King
and Council, 'even if worse things were said of the insanity of the
daughter of your Highness.' As a manifest of his good intentions
Henry had expressed himself willing to go to Spain and woo Joanna,
and Puebla was convinced that as a husband he would be 'a model
of filial affection.'

Protracted though it was this particular courtship was bound to
miscarry; as Joanna's condition deteriorated, it became obvious that
immediate marriage was out of the question. English efforts were
increasingly being directed towards Germany and the Low Countries,
and her negotiations with Spain eventually collapsed in favor of a
general European coalition, the Treaty of Cambrai closing an un-
worthy chapter in Anglo-Spanish relations.

Even when wooing Joanna of Castile Henry had never renounced
the idea of a double marriage with Burgundy, under consideration
since 1506 and first suggested much earlier. Impecunious Maximilian
was receptive to any financially promising proposal, and as a suitor
Henry was no less mercenary; though the fiction of personal desire
was always maintained superficially, everyone including Margaret
knew that it was not she who was desired 'more than anyone in the
world' but her dowry. In spite of their mutual and well-deserved distrust, it would have been a profitable alliance for both monarchs. The
chief obstacle was the Archduchess herself. Margaret was plainly not
interested. A mature woman in her late twenties, twice married, and
Regent of the Netherlands in her own right, she was no longer to
be bartered away at her father's whim.

Margaret's life had not been easy. Motherless when barely old
enough to speak, at three she was betrothed to Charles, Dauphin of
France. Gratified by this connection, Maximilian immediately dispatched her to France to spend her childhood at Amboise being

groomed for her future position as queen and mother, but in less than a decade her world order had collapsed. Ignominiously she was sent home, repudiated in favor of 'la petite Brette,' Anne of Brittany, who at fourteen had briefly become 'Queen of the Romans' by proxy marriage to Margaret's own father. Though her pride must have suffered, the mortification lay in the loss of a throne rather than a husband; she was to acquire the latter soon enough in the precocious Infante Juan, Prince of Castile and Aragon. Juan was a passionate, virile youth who found the physical delights of marriage too much for his years. Moderation might have stayed his tragic death of the pestilence a few months later, for it was admitted that his body had been weakened by sexual overindulgence, but moderation was not characteristic of the age. His mother, Isabella, though apparently warned in ample time, refused to intervene on the grounds that it would be thwarting God's will; it was thought by some that she valued an heir more than her son's health. The baby which Margaret carried did not live: at eighteen she was a childless widow, and the responsibility for uniting the two kingdoms was transferred to the shoulders of her brother and sister-in-law.

Not long after, in 1501, she married Philibert II, Duke of Savoy, only to be widowed a second time after a few happy years. She returned to Brabant at twenty-four, sadder and wiser, to establish a distinguished court at Malines where she dedicated herself to ruling the Low Countries and bringing up her nephew Charles and his three sisters. Born a Fleming, a Fleming she would die. State policy dictated another marriage, but to the end, with remarkable tact and cleverness, Margaret successfully evaded it.

While Maximilian was welcoming Henry VII as Margaret's third husband, she was insisting upon rejection of all offers, 'be the suitor never so virtuous, rich, gifted or well-born.' She countered all persuasions with her own determined arguments: she was fated to be unhappy in marriage; the proposed dowry was too generous; the treaty itself was one-sided, favoring England more than the Netherlands; even that she feared a childless union. Undaunted, Henry pressed his suit with renewed vigor, dispatching two embassies to the Netherlands in 1508. In the earlier of these Thomas Wolsey made his first bid for notice by accomplishing the entire mission there and back in under seventy hours, displaying the efficiency for which he was to be famous. It was his initiation into the subtleties of diplomatic equivocality: 'There is here so much inconstancy, mutability, and little regard of promises and causes, that in their appointments there is little trust or surety; for things surely determined to be done one day are changed and altered the next,' he reported. It would seem that Henry's patient 'love and kindness,' used 'in the tracting of our said marriage hitherto' was of no avail. Resolved to be put off and 'abused' no longer, he instructed Wolsey to insist on 'a final answer at this time without any further delays.'

Henry's primary objective was not so much the hand of Margaret for himself, as fulfillment of the longstanding agreement for marriage between Mary and Charles. With Prince Henry's marriage to Catherine by this time assured, the second union would reinforce England's alliance with Spain. If Henry VII was criticized for his own efforts to remarry, his failure may have prompted the criticism. Had he succeeded in doing so effectively it would have been hailed as a diplomatic victory.

CHAPTER FIVE

Transition

> O, wonder!
> How many goodly creatures are there here!
> How beauteous mankind is! O brave new world,
> That hath such people in't!

Shakespeare, *The Tempest,* V.1

HER father's death was a turning point in Mary's life. With Henry VIII's accession, overnight she assumed a newly significant place in court society as the King's attractive unmarried sister. While Henry VII lived, thrift and political expediency dominated the social calendar; when he entertained without regard for expense it had been as a calculated investment. Not so with his son, whose extravagance expressed irrepressible *joie de vivre* and who was devoted to nothing more ulterior than a single-minded determination to enjoy himself. Henry reveled in his heritage, not fully conscious at the beginning of its power but very much aware of its ability to gratify all his immediate desires. Always her brother's favorite, Mary shared with Catherine the privileges of their unique positions and occupied an enviable place in the Court's ceaseless pursuit of amusement which threatened, during the first few years, to engulf everything else. Pledged but still unmarried she was more eligible because already bespoken. Young and vivacious, desirable and desired, she stood on the threshold of a future that sparkled with the promise of success and happiness.

On the May morning of 1509 when his family accompanied Henry VII's funeral procession from Richmond to the City, the first shock of his passing had receded. He had been dead for seventeen days already, and others besides his son welcomed the long vigil's end. The obsequies were as Henry would have wished: regal, dignified, bidding a royal farewell to an honorable life. After a lingering illness which had quenched his spirit as it aged his body he died on the twenty-first of April at Richmond Palace, where his body lay in state until the eighth of May when it was brought up to St. Paul's Church for formal services. At London Bridge, a great crowd waited for the cortege. Countless torches and candles cast their glow on the evening mist as dignitaries of Church and State preceded the royal chariot bearing the corpse. The City officials came first, followed by the king's messengers two by two, 'with their boxes at their breasts.' Behind were minstrels, trumpeters, household ministers, and special councilors and judges; the great nobles of the realm rode abreast their peers, the spiritual lords; present too were the Knights of the Garter, standard-bearers, canons, friars, and members of trade guilds. Wealthy foreign merchants, Florentines, Venetians, Spaniards, Frenchmen, Easterlings, and Portuguese also joined the procession to pay their respects to the dead. Riding alone immediately in front of the chariot was the Lord Mayor bearing the mace, his symbol of authority.

The chariot bore Henry's coffin on which his effigy, crowned and sceptered, lay under a canopy of cloth of gold; it was drawn by five great coursers trapped in black velvet, and followed by noblemen, the Master of the Horse, the entire Guard, and innumerable other gentlemen. At St. Paul's the Bishop of London waited. The coffin was placed in the choir under a 'goodly hearse,' and after a solemn dirge by the bishop, guarded overnight by knights and heralds, while the King's household and the mourners 'reposed themselves in the bishop's palace.' In the morning Requiem Masses were said and a sermon preached by the Bishop of Rochester, and after the noon dinner the coffin was replaced on the chariot and escorted down Fleet Street and past Charing Cross to Westminster Abbey, where it was received by the two archbishops. More services were held there later in the day and Masses began before six o'clock on the following morning. That day, the tenth of May, saw the finale; offerings were made, another sermon preached—this time by the Bishop of London —and the staves of the household ceremonially broken into the vault. Henry VII was buried in the beautiful chapel in Westminster Abbey which he had had built for this purpose, in the tomb designed by Pietro Torrigiano, where, said Bacon, 'he dwelleth more richly dead, in the monument of his tomb, than he did alive in Richmond or any of his palaces.'

The cost of the funeral was almost £8,500, but with the treasure that was now his Henry VIII could pay for it with neither resentment nor anxiety. Chamber payments included £1,000 for black cloth, £500 for banners, and £3,000 in alms; 3,600 pounds of 'Poleyn **wax**' were used to light the hearse, for which an ingenious lighting fixture at the Abbey made of nine 'principalles full of lights,' was unusual enough to be recorded; over 450 special gowns and hoods were bought for the torchbearers. Mary received four new mantelets from Paris, two at 20s. apiece, and two at 26s. 8d., with six hand-kerchiefs to match at 9s. each. The saddle, pillion, and coverings of black velvet for her horse cost 17s. The horses ridden in the procession by Catherine and her ladies were similarly accoutered.

Henry VII's wishes for his younger daughter's future were set forth in his will: a bequest of fifty thousand pounds for her dot and marriage, 'over and above the cost of her traduction into the parties of Flanders, and furnishing of plate, and other her arrayments for her person, jewels and garnishings for her chamber,' was to be used for an alternative marriage if that with Charles should not materialize. In this eventuality her hand was to be at the disposal of Henry VIII and the Council, although he expressed the hope that 'she be married to some noble Prince out of this our Realm.' Henry VII spoke with characteristic foresight; in 1509 there was nothing to suggest that within five years the Hapsburg alliance would collapse, and that the 'noble Prince' would be Louis XII of France. At that time the possibility of her marrying an Englishman had not arisen. Charles Brandon, although known to be a close companion and confidant of her brother's, had then no immediate prospect of advancement.

For the moment, however, it was the King's own marriage that was the center of attention. Henry himself wished to marry Catherine, and the Council was anxious lest the gold she had brought to England as a dowry return to Spain. Moreover Ferdinand too was now urging it, offering as an added inducement to promote the union of Mary and Charles. Little persuasion was necessary, since the government was already agreed that both marriages were desirable. Henry's marriage to Catherine took place only a month after his father's funeral, with what his biographer, A. F. Pollard, called 'almost indecent haste'; it was celebrated on June 11, two weeks before the date set for Henry's coronation. They were married quietly at the Franciscan oratory near Greenwich Palace by Archbishop Warham, and after the instability of her position since Arthur's death it was a triumph for Catherine. The storms ahead cast no ominous shadow on her happiness or marred the relief she must have felt in the security of being Queen of England.

On the twenty-first of June, ten days after their wedding, they rode into London to take up residence at the Tower, where they had, according to convention, to spend the last night before the coronation on Midsummer's Day, Sunday, the twenty-fourth of June. There they rested while the commission of claims completed preparations, which were heralded by a royal order that twenty-six 'honourable persons' should join the King and Queen for dinner on the Friday beforehand. The next day they were made Knights of the Bath, having served their King by waiting on him at table 'in token that they shall never bear none [dishes] after that day.'

The coronation of Henry VIII and Catherine of Aragon is described exhaustively by Hall. After their anointing and crowning by the Archbishop and the ceremony of homage and allegiance, the assembly moved to Westminster Hall for the banquet and the ancient ritual challenge of the King's Champion. Riding the length of the hall fully armed on his courser to present himself to the King, he threw down his gauntlet as a challenge to all who questioned his sovereign's right to rule, proclaiming that he was prepared to defend it; this formal invitation meeting with no response, the Champion returned to Henry for approbation, by time-honored custom demanding a drink. Wine was offered to him in a gold cup from which he drank deeply before riding triumphantly away, retaining the cup as a reward for his service. What had originally been a simple medieval expression of loyalty from knight to liege lord had become a Renaissance symbol of a whole nation's fidelity to its new sovereign.

The feast, 'more honorable than those of the great Caesar of old,' was followed by jousts and tourneys in which Charles Brandon is mentioned as taking part. None, perhaps, watched his performance with more personal interest than the young Princess of Castile, who had played only a spectator's part in the coronation ceremony. Continuous celebrations were, however, soon halted by the death of Henry's grandmother, Lady Margaret, five days afterward. Despite the infirmities accompanying her sixty-eight years, she had remained physically active and intellectually vigorous. Her death on the twenty-ninth of June, 1509, in its way symbolized the end of the fifteenth century which she had outlived, but of which she was a product. Her patronage and charity were legendary in England, and she was greatly mourned by the people; churches and chapels were draped in black, and for six days their bells tolled a dirge for her. The final tribute came from her devoted friend and admirer, Bishop Fisher, in his funeral oration: 'enshrined in the hearts of all good men,' she represented everything 'praisable in a woman.'

Her name continued to mean something in the household she had for so long influenced. Long before she knew the value of books Mary had been exposed to Lady Margaret's library and to her grandmother's translations and general devotion to scholarship. Though she never went to Colly Weston, the Countess of Richmond's estate in Northamptonshire, she knew Cold Harbour, her London house in Thomas Street, one of the few Tudor residences with a comfortable, homelike atmosphere. The feeling of security which comes from a sense of family life may have been the greatest gift that Lady Margaret was to leave to her granddaughter. From an estate of under £18,000 Mary inherited a modest £82 8s. 4d.

Nothing seemed to mar the tranquillity of the first years of the new reign; at home and abroad affairs were serene, English merchants and alliances respected in Europe, diplomatic relations unruffled. Responding to Renaissance importations, the Court too became gayer and more expansive as it relaxed under the illusions of the changing era. It seemed to some that Henry did nothing but practice music all day and dance all night. 'He was young and lusty, disposed all to mirth and pleasure,' a visitor commented, 'nothing minding to travail in the busy affairs of his realm.' On Twelfth Night of 1512, the Feast of the Epiphany, an Italian masque was introduced to the Court for the first time; some ladies who knew 'the fashion of it' refused to dance with the disguised gentlemen of whom the King was one, because it was 'not a thing commonly seen.' Not so Mary, who shared Henry's enthusiasm for the unusual, even the bizarre; whether in the guise of rustic maiden or African princess her name always appeared somewhere in the list of masquers. On his arrival in London in May, 1515, Niccolo Sagudino, secretary to the Venetian ambassador, compared the varied English entertainment favorably with that of the French: no two such courts in Europe had 'been witnessed for the last fifty years.'

Banquets, costlier and more frequent, referred to by Catherine as 'continual feasting,' were more than feasts, they were Gargantuan exhibitions; 240 dishes were sometimes served at one meal, from platters of solid gold 'as great as men with ease might bear.' Tables were laden with most of the foods known to the century: beef, pork, veal, venison, mutton, wild game, poultry, an endless variety of fish and cheese, jellies, fruits, nuts, pastries and sweets of all kinds. Heavy and light wines from all over Europe were drunk, including the rich malmsey from Cyprus; 'a voidee of spices' might be offered to guests to take on retiring for the night. Though these gastronomic orgies shocked those who were accustomed to the restrained habits of Henry VII's Court, to the older generation of courtiers they were a familiar return to the earlier grandeur of Yorkist rule.

Henry was four times disappointed before Catherine finally delivered a baby who lived, and while waiting he spoiled his pretty young sister as he might have done his children. Warrants from the Great Wardrobe show gowns and other garments being delivered to the 'Princess of Castile' or to 'our welbeloved sister the Lady Mary,' at the same time as he perpetually demanded her presence at Court. Apparently enjoying the games and dancing, disguisings and mimicry as much as he, she was seldom separated from him for long; when Mary was spending time in the country at one or other of the royal manors, Henry would periodically send her small gifts, accompanied with a request for her return. It was in the course of these few years of irresponsible pleasure that Mary must first have become really well acquainted with Henry's childhood companion, Charles Brandon, who as a royal favorite was also one of the intimate group surrounding the King.

Until the French war broke out in 1512 the surface of domestic affairs was barely ruffled. New personalities made themselves useful to the King, among them Wolsey, who as councilor and chief minister was soon directing the entire administration, and because he was assiduous in serving those whose cause might further his own, or whose influence with Henry VIII might be conscripted in his behalf, Mary was to find him a friend. For most people the great threat was neither politics nor war but repeated outbreaks of the plague, a constant menace throughout the century. Crossing the Channel from Calais in 1509, it spread inland across England bringing terror periodically to more densely populated areas. For many years it was regularly recurrent, to which the Venetian minister bore witness in 1554: 'They have some little plague in England well nigh every year, for which they are not accustomed to make sanitary provisions, as it does not usually make great progress; the cases for the most part occur among the lower classes, as if their dissolute mode of life impaired their constitutions.' Almost all sizable towns suffered, and London most of all, during the four years before Mary left for the Continent in 1514. An Italian ambassador who had experience of the disease in both Venice and London, estimated the death rate for the English capital in 1513 at three hundred to four hundred per day. The figure is not improbable, but it represents a terrifying toll for a city of about 70,000 inhabitants.

Protected by the mantle of royalty Mary Tudor and her friends escaped even the awful pestilence, since the Court dispersed the moment it struck; when danger threatened, the King was the first to seek safety in the country. Living in the royal household, Mary accompanied its peregrinations when the plague pursued, but sooner or later always came back to Greenwich. The five years between her father's death and her marriage were happy and uncomplicated, her personal life not yet entangled in the web of European politics.

CHAPTER SIX

Exit the Princess of Castile

Everything's got a moral, if you can only find it.

Lewis Carroll, *Alice's Adventures in Wonderland*

THE new reign introduced no sudden change in England's foreign policy, which continued to revolve round her alliance with the Low Countries. No part of Henry VII's diplomacy had been more justifiable despite the two major stumbling blocks to its success, France and Spain. Although Henry VIII was now his son-in-law, Ferdinand still did not intend to promote any accord between England and the Netherlands which might strengthen Prince Charles's claim to Castile; furthermore he had every reason to question not only Henry's good faith but also Maximilian's. While plans for Mary's wedding to Charles were renewed yearly, they were taken seriously only by Henry, who for some time after his accession was too pre-occupied with the personal aspects of his new pinnacle of eminence to give undue thought to his sister's position, even had there not been another five years before consummation of the marriage was due.

Relations with the Empire and the Low Countries were outwardly cordial, though it was difficult to get either Maximilian or Margaret and her council to commit themselves to anything very definite. Ostensibly Mary's marriage contract still stood; she was the acknow-ledged Princess of Castile, and there was no reason for England to assume that the agreement would not be fulfilled. During the summer of 1511, in accordance with the terms of the treaty, Henry aided the Archduchess in her war with the Duke of Guelders, not only because of his regard for 'so noble a lady' but also 'because there was a communication hanging . . . between the young Prince Charles and the lady Marie his sister.' In response to her request the Comptroller of the Household, Sir Edward Poynings, was dispatched with fifteen hundred troops, thereby enhancing the reputation of English arms and at the same time indebting Burgundy.

The success or failure of the 'communication' was in fact to depend upon England's position in relation to the power balance which Julius II was trying to maintain in Italy. The League of Cambrai gave way to the Holy League in October, 1511, with English support still withheld in continuation of Henry VII's peace policy. Involvement implied war and its financial burdens, so Henry VIII, who himself was itching for action, was persuaded by his advisers to wait for the international situation to provide his cue. However, papal promptings, Spanish connections, and his own longing personally to share in the glories of battle finally turned the tide.

Not only was Henry a good papalist, but by rationalization he could persuade himself, as can most self-indulgent people, of the rightness of doing what he wished. What greater cause could he champion than the defense of Holy Church and her recovery of Bordeaux, lost to the French for half a century? A popular war might gain both territory and prestige for England and perhaps also the personal recognition which he coveted. When he joined the papal alliance in November it was to fight for Christendom, not in Italy as his Italian allies hoped but by an attack on France. Convinced that Louis XII would again urge Scotland to cross the border and invade England, he agreed to the first disastrous expedition to aid Ferdinand's subjugation of Navarre early the following year. Meanwhile the war parliament of February strengthened Henry's resolution to cross the Channel in person and strike at France from Calais, as, true to expectation, Louis prepared to revive the 'auld alliance' with the Scots. The Emperor was brought into the League in November, 1512; the 'man of few pence' would fight with the English for as long as they were willing to foot the bill, but in fact the fight was over four months before he actively intervened.

Meanwhile the Empire and the Low Countries had jointly reconfirmed with England the existing treaty which Henry sought to keep separate from his Spanish alliance. The distinction was little more than theoretical, for all three powers were vitally concerned with the future disposition of Prince Charles. So long as the boy was a minor his two grandfathers and his aunt constituted a triangular trusteeship in which an essential conflict of opinion was involved. As guardians, Maximilian and his daughter had a common objective, since any policy of the Low Countries, as part of the Empire, was largely determined by the commitments of the Emperor; yet in their analysis of European diplomacy they were in fundamental disagreement. More astute than he, Margaret was skeptical of French interest, more than once telling him that 'they will do you as little good as they can'; quick to perceive that in the long run the good will of England was worth more than the wayward friendship of France, she warned Maximilian that Louis XII would never keep his promises, adding that no one was in a better position than he to judge the faith and loyalty of the French. 'The other princes have mountains and the sea between them and their enemies, and are richer than this poor House of Burgundy,' she concluded, and even if Louis 'now gave us what belongs to us, he might within two or three years, on seeing an opening, take it back, and to take today and lose again tomorrow were greater shame than before. They [the French] can always find a pretext in the *loy salique* and other points of this sovereignty which they claim.'

The Emperor listened and continued opportunistically as before, unwilling wholeheartedly to accept any single ally. Later, when in 1514 he was inclined to betray England in favor of peace with France, Margaret again emphasized that his best ally was Henry, France being the common enemy of the Empire and the Low Countries, England their natural friend. '*Pour Dieu*, do not let yourself be deceived,' she protested, pointing out again that between France and Spain were great mountains and between France and England the sea, 'but between these countries and France is nothing, and you know the inveterate hatred the French bear to this House.' She urged him to look to his own honor and profit and have regard to his friendship and treaties with the king of England, from whom 'you may be assured of aid as need [be], both with person and money; for in him is no hypocrisy.'

The Most Catholic King of Spain was less optimistic than Margaret: he trusted nobody and Maximilian least of all. So long as his daughter could persuade her husband to follow Spanish leadership he anticipated no difficulty there, but while using Henry he continued to fear Maximilian's influence over him, so intent were the English on the Hapsburg marriage. As a mature ruler, Louis posed a greater problem. The strongest power in Europe, France had at all costs to be thwarted, but Ferdinand was confident in his ability to outwit her. When it was reported to him that he had twice deceived the French King, Ferdinand, whose memory was as long as a Welsh pedigree, is said to have scornfully denied it, insisting that he had done so not twice but ten times.

In 1510 Henry had sent an embassy to Maximilian hoping to further the marriage arrangements, but his ministers found it tough going. He had yet to learn what everyone else knew, that the Emperor's promises were meaningless. Again in 1512, with no better results, he dispatched three special envoys to Germany to wean Maximilian from 'the amity of the King of France,' after which it was thought the marriage would follow automatically. Since the Emperor was continually on the move, they had to work mostly through Margaret, who repeatedly found it necessary to apologize for her father's delays and assure Henry that he would come round in the end. Discussions dragged on from month to month with no forseeable improvement. A personal interview between him and Henry was suggested in the hope of agreement on the amount of money to be advanced towards war against France, if the Empire entered the League. Maximilian argued that his country was poor, that it cost money to wage war, that Louis XII was willing to pay, and moreover, that the Swiss favored the French and had to be bought off. When he made demands for more money, it was Henry's turn to hold back, conscious though he was that the French were making generous offers to Maximilian.

After a temporary settlement of 100,000 crowns was agreed to, an impasse developed over the assessment of the sum needed to woo the Swiss when Henry positively refused the extra 50,000 crowns demanded by Maximilian. Margaret, usually so 'well-disposed towards the king's cause,' spoke in sick vexation, 'a little melancholy about her stomach,' the ambassadors told Henry. Hoping perhaps to get 100,000 crowns more from Louis than Henry was willing to pay, she concluded: 'if ye be dispos[ed to] delay it [the negotiations] we shall defer it as well as you.'

So conditions stood at the end of 1512. English funds 'goeth away in every corner,' but Maximilian's 'fair promises' all expired one after the other, in 'his accustomed manner'; to the ambassadors it seemed that they were 'spending the King's money and doing him no service.' Not until the fifth of April, 1513, was a treaty finally concluded. Henry reluctantly agreed to advance 125,000 crowns to Maximilian, of which 25,000 was to be paid immediately, to take the Swiss troops into his pay, and to invade France with an army of

30,000 men. Having once joined the League the Emperor made a magnanimous offer personally to lead a contingent under the English King which Henry graciously accepted. Thus England, Germany, Spain, and the Papacy were all pledged to declare war against France within thirty days and to attack a month later. Henry and Maximilian were to invade Aquitaine, Picardy, and Normandy; Ferdinand to attack Béarn and Languedoc. At England's insistence the Low Countries were included in the agreement, though nothing was said about Mary's marriage. If the wishes of Henry and the Archduchess had been paramount the marriage would have been assured, for on that score they were in perfect accord.

Margaret had driven her father toward England in the belief that it would not only strengthen the security of the Empire, but also be in Charles's best interest. She did what she could to advance the marriage; soon after Henry VII's death, love tokens had been exchanged, Charles sending Mary a jewel and receiving a ring in return. Before the end of 1509 plans were being made for Mary to visit the Low Countries to meet her betrothed husband and become acquainted with German fashions. This was preceded in February, 1510, by the appointment of a gentleman-in-waiting to her by the Emperor, who briefly felt that his financial welfare hinged on this marriage alliance with England. The next autumn Margaret sent a Fleming, John Cerf, to serve her; he was accepted by Henry and given an annuity until such time as the marriage was solemnized.

No sooner had Mary's visit been accepted in principle than she was sent specimen dress patterns illustrating the fashions of the Netherlands Court. Thanking her 'bonne tante,' Mary replied in French that she hoped, with her ladies-in-waiting, to introduce the Flemish fashions into England. If she was curious to meet Charles there is no record of her mentioning it. No definite date was set for her journey, though it was rumored in Flanders that Henry was to deliver his sister personally when he launched his French expedition.

Preparations for the war continued. The English fleet was readied and dispatched to Calais, where the assembled army was joined by the King in the early summer of 1513. By August Maximilian had come in person to serve under his ally in the capture of Thérouanne which before the month was out had capitulated. Accompanied by the Emperor, who acceded him all the honors, Henry entered the town with 'as much pomp as he ever entered Westminster.' During the siege an attempt to relieve Thérouanne gave him his first personal taste of victory, when the relieving French force was defeated and fled in panic from Guinegate in what became known to the English as the Battle of the Spurs. Henry's army then moved on to besiege the wealthy town of Tournai, which succumbed on the twenty-first of September, a success which was marked three days later by a triumphal procession to the cathedral amid the shouts of the populace, 'vive le roi.' The following night Maximilian and Margaret came to share in the celebration, having deliberately delayed their entry lest it detract from Henry's glory. Charles, who joined them within a fortnight, received a full ceremonial welcome.

Meanwhile, from London Catherine had proudly sent the news of victory at Flodden Field: 'Almighty God helps here our part as well as there.' Henry had just reason for believing that fortune favored his every undertaking; 'indeed,' reported a Venetian, 'to everyone the King seems a being descended from Heaven.'

The days spent with Maximilian and Margaret gave Henry occasion to seek a definite agreement concerning Mary's marriage, the two rulers accepting each other's counsel in 'the most amiable and loving wise that can be thought.' It was said as they made 'good cheer together,' that the Emperor loved the King more than a son; without doubt he was deeply grateful for English money and aid against Guelders. They exchanged presents, a jewel and a great ox; some months earlier Maximilian had sent Henry a fine German crossbow which the latter assured him was not only appreciated but would also be used. After the fall of Tournai, in striking contrast to the previous interminable evasions, their discussions crystallized. Two treaties were signed in mid-October: a military one requiring joint invasion of France, with the assistance of Spain, by June, 1514, and another promising consummation of the marriage between Mary and Charles before the middle of May of the same year. Proud of what he considered his first diplomatic achievement, Henry was also relieved to have the prolonged deliberations at an end with a reasonable certainty that his allies would stand by their commitments, and felt more able to return to England with his mind free to attend to domestic problems; the Scottish war, the plague, and an approaching parliament all demanded his presence. The Master of the Rolls who had accompanied Henry noted complacently that the King had been successful in all his endeavors, even to winning the honors at the tournament held for Margaret and Maximilian. Only one note of criticism was voiced: English money which in value greatly exceeded the foreign currency 'was recklessly thrown away, thus occasioning a great loss.'

One apparently secret feature of the marriage treaty reflects the ability of its author Margaret, who extracted an oral promise from Henry that should he have no male heirs he would settle the Succession on Mary and her descendants. If this had been publicly known it would undoubtedly have evoked speculation at other European courts where the latest understanding between England and Germany was usually common gossip. She later reminded Henry of his pledge to get parliamentary sanction for this Succession regulation, but nothing was done nor was definite action taken in relation to Henry's heirs until the third Succession Act of 1543 which empowered him to dispose of the crown by will. When Henry's will was publicized by Northumberland's plot to secure the throne for his family in the summer of 1553, long after Mary's claim had become mere memory, it was found that the King had indicated a preference for the Suffolk line as opposed to the Stuart.

When the treaty was signed in 1513 it appeared to England that she and her allies had resolved all their differences; from the Continent, however, came other opinions most of which suggested a different sequence of events, as serious rifts in the unlikely marriage of interests began to appear. Early the previous May, before the agreement, the English ambassador in Spain had advised that Ferdinand was working against the union of Charles and Mary, while from Brussels it had been reported that Margaret's council was not in accord with her policy. Reconciliation with France by both Spain and Germany was in the air. Ferdinand was the first to renege, having at the beginning of April made a year's truce with France while continuing to protest his good faith to England. Knowing that a truce was simply a first step toward peace Louis set himself to the task of breaking up the Holy League as quickly as possible, confident that with proper inducement Spain would make a defensive alliance with France. His proffered bait was indeed tempting: the hand of Renée, Louis's younger daughter, for the Infante Ferdinand, with Milan, Genoa, and other towns wrested from the Venetians as her dower. Don Ferdinand was ten and Renée, to become the most engaged princess in Europe, only three years old. Ferdinand's mere entertainment of this proposal would have been a breach of faith had diplomatic promises rested upon mutual integrity; that they did not was known to everyone but the young and ingenuous Henry VIII. In Germany Maximilian was equally open to persuasion, pressed as he was on the one hand by France and Spain to join the truce, and on the other by England to prosecute the war and hasten the marriage of Mary and Charles. Louis had the obvious advantage of Spanish support, and two marriageable daughters to add conviction to his bargains. By the spring of 1514 his negotiations with Spain were waxing hot: Charles could have Renée if he wished, or her elder sister Claude, who according to the Spanish ambassador was lame and 'naturally deformed.' In March Ferdinand renewed his pledge of true with France. Betrayal was just ahead.

Henry was furious. He had returned from France eager to continue the struggle, his ardor for war unabated. The second invasion was delayed, however, by his contracting smallpox, but the bout over he rose from his bed fierce against Louis and embittered against Ferdinand who, it was said, was 'too old and crazy' to endure a war. Hurt and indignant, Henry impatiently awaited the next move, unwilling to face reality. The Spaniard, Peter Martyr, wrote of him: 'The King of England bites his lips, and will not admit the validity of the excuse; but [he] cannot help himself.'

Margaret was still as much in favor of alliance with England as she had always been, but by herself she was helpless; the policy of her father and the opposition of her own council forced her unwillingly to vacillate. She recognized in Henry the sincerity of purpose that would allow him only as a last resort to be driven into the French camp, and Louis's guile was as transparent to her as was her father's. She told the latter that France's fair offers were put forward only 'to escape the storm that would fall upon it, if every one were as ready to do his duty as the King of England, who has made incredible preparations for continuing the war. Ferdinand may desire peace, for he is old and infirm; but that is not the interest of Monsieur [Prince Charles] and his dominions.' Her protestations availed little, but though the promises she made to Henry and the admonitions she directed at Maximilian satisfied neither, preparations for Mary's journey to the Continent were still not abandoned.

By the terms of the treaty of 1513 the marriage was to be solemnized at Calais when Charles had turned fourteen, the age of majority for boys, after which plans began to take shape with that date in view. A list of temporary attendants for Mary's Flemish household was submitted to her and approved, and other arrangements made for her arrival. Earlier the Prince had written gravely to Mary from Mechlin to inform her of 'the good condition of my person and affairs'; addressing her as 'My good wife,' he solemnly inquired of her health and happiness, 'which is something I most desire, as knows the blessed Son of God, whom I pray, my good wife, to give you by his grace all that you desire.' Signed *'votre bon mari,'* the letter was undoubtedly dictated to him though stilted enough to be his own. Those closely associated with Charles must have doubted his capacity ever to be a 'good husband' to any woman; he never outgrew the ponderous gravity of his youth, throughout life seeming to lack any capability for either personal warmth or private emotion. Even Maximilian admitted him to be 'as cold and immovable as an idol.'

Regardless of the Prince's temperament the English insisted that his age was no longer reasonable cause for delaying his marriage to Mary. Anxious to have everything settled before invading France in May, Henry had determined by the beginning of 1514 on a triple marriage alliance with Germany and the Netherlands: Mary and Charles, Margaret of Savoy and the Duke of Suffolk, and his sister Margaret, recently widowed by the death of James IV at the battle of Flodden, and Maximilian. He reasoned that thrice pledged the Emperor would find it difficult to desert him even if he desired to do so. At the English Court there was as yet barely a hint of the suspicion beginning to be current all over the Continent that Mary might be repudiated entirely. Further credence was given to this by the report that the Emperor had a personal reason for freeing his grandson since he was himself seeking another wife; as long before as the previous autumn it had been rumoured that Charles would reject Mary in order that Maximilian might marry her.

If such an offer were actually suggested it cannot have been taken seriously either by England or the Low Countries, but their discrepancy in age would not have been the reason; that Maximilian at fifty-four should marry a girl thirty-six years his junior might have caused a few ribald smiles, but would have astonished few people in 1513. His second wife's death three years before had made him eligible for another marriage alliance and within the first year he was toying with the possibility, confiding to Margaret that he would consider Mary of England: 'otherwise,' he concluded, 'I will not marry at all, either for money or beauty.' He may have been repulsed by Henry, for six months later he had apparently dismissed the idea of remarrying, avowing emphatically that he would never go near a woman again.

Used to his caprices his daughter replied that she would prefer the choice of Mary to that of the Papacy, Maximilian having recently expressed his intention of seeking the pontifical chair. She seems to have been chiefly concerned lest he jeopardize Charles's chances, correctly assuming that the English would prefer the future Emperor to the present one. However, the rumor persisted in Paris and Rome that Maximilian was the favorite because Mary was thought to be twenty-four and too old for the Archduke. Her age had very likely been confused with that of her sister who was twenty-four in 1513, whereas Mary was only eighteen. Whatever his purpose then, Maximilian was certainly disposed toward her later, after her almost immediate widowhood in 1515.

Charles was fourteen on the twenty-fourth of February, 1514, only eighty days before the final date stipulated in the treaty for consummation of his marriage. Increasingly impatient, Henry again exerted pressure on the Archduchess for the wedding day to be set, but being obliged to follow her father's fluctuating policy she could still do no more than hedge. Maximilian's tactics were at this point challenged by a man whose diplomatic duplicity equaled his own; Louis XII had just become as eligible a widower as he by the death of the French queen, Anne of Brittany, in early January, and had joined the marriage carousel. Margaret herself was a possible candidate but she knew Mary to be the more probable choice. In April she was informed by her ambassador in France of its being commonly accepted there that 'the old gallant would marry the young girl' to find out if he was capable of having sons; 'but I understand,' the envoy added, 'that he is very debilitated.'

No one sensed the danger more than Margaret, who at once assured Henry's envoys that there was nothing she desired more than the English marriage, in proof of her sincerity promising an immediate proclamation for easy exchange of the two national currencies; at the same time safe conduct for Mary's passage was issued.

As preparations for her journey to the Low Countries took final shape, the English envoys there obtained all the pertinent information needed for arranging the Prince's reception at Calais: details of the size and importance of his entourage, Maximilian's retinue, and the suite accompanying Margaret. Since the English army would also be there, the adequate provision of hay and oats for the hundreds of horses expected was a considerable problem. Intending as he did to march straight off to battle as soon as his sister was married, it was imperative that Henry know for how many days the ceremonial functions would last. Luxurious furnishings were planned for everyone, except that no provision was made for beds, it being thought that 'for their better ease,' they would want to bring their own. With Mary's personal effects Henry spared no expense, hoping probably to impress her less wealthy bridegroom; for her clothes in the Flemish fashion, appropriate styles and materials had been selected by Margaret to whom a complete list of her English wardrobe, her officials, ladies in attendance, and stable equipment had been submitted for advice and suggestions. Mary was being considered on the point most dear to all women, her dress; every outfit, in color, quality, and design, was selected 'as shall best please her.'

Mary had everything even a princess could dream of: dresses and robes, bonnets, jewels and jewel cases, a mirror, gold necklaces and chains, ornate girdles of 'as goodly fashion as may be devised,' and for the wedding day a gold coronet set with precious stones. Her apartment furnishings and stable equipment were of the same regal quality; besides gold plate, china, and silver she had tapestries, wall hangings, cushions, coverings for chests and cupboards, and various-sized carpets, some for window seats and others for floors. Cloth of gold walled her bedchamber, which contained an upholstered chair and 'a large trussing bed' with celure, tester, and counterpane also of cloth of gold, and damask curtains. The two gentlewomen who were to sleep in her room had pallet beds and fustian sheets, but hers was a 'feather bed of fine down,' with linen sheets, a bolster, and two pillows. For traveling she was given a 'rich litter of cloth of gold lined with satin or damask,' chariots, three wardrobe cars for her clothing, and beautifully caparisoned palfreys and horses. Candlesticks, a silver crucifix, purple and crimson vestments, a private pew, and a missal 'of fair print' for furnishing her chapel were also part of her trousseau.

Her household personnel numbered over a hundred people. Listed were two ladies-in-waiting, five gentlewomen, twelve gentlemen of the chamber, chamberers, chaplains, an almoner, numerous yeomen and grooms, and thirty-six servants attached to the attendants. Included as well were officers to manage her personal affairs, of whom one was a tall, strong domestic employed to drive unwanted beggars from her door. The customary kitchen apartments were set up for her: larder, scullery, almonry, buttery, chandlery, acatery, spicery, bakehouse, and pantry. Everything was ready for the call that never came. In the pithy language of Hall: 'So thus the king of England retained his sister and all preparations that he had done for her conveyance, which was very costly.'

While the bride's household waited, the groom's government prevaricated, though its excuses always bore a semblance of justification and sometimes a note of sincerity: Charles had been ill; his feeble constitution was not conducive to an early marriage; Mary was too old for him; he needed a wife not a mother! It was probably this last objection that caused England to announce her age as sixteen, three years younger than she actually was. While accepting the end of May as a suitable time for the marriage, a suggestion came from the Netherlands that the place be changed to Antwerp or Mechlin since Calais was infested with the plague. In June the Prince got another fever, protracted by the moon, his doctors said. When Maximilian, laboring for more money, offered the Crown Imperial and the Vicariate as a bribe, Henry was informed by his ambassador to Germany that twenty thousand crowns monthly might persuade him to commit himself. A report that Charles had become enamored of a damsel of the Flemish Court was promptly denied; he is said to have expostulated that on his faith he desired no one but 'my Lady Mary,' and that his one hope was for immediate consummation of their marriage. The Penelopean web was spun out endlessly.

The English rallied loyally in support of their Princess; it was he and not she who had the good fortune to win both an attractive partner and a desirable alliance. Erasmus, still overflowing with praises of England, voiced the same enthusiasm when writing to his friend, the abbot of St. Bertin's. Prince Charles was thrice blessed with the prospect of such a spouse, he wrote: 'Nature never formed anything more beautiful; and she excels no less in goodness and wisdom.'

In Rome, Leo X who had succeeded Julius as Pope in February, 1513, assumed a neutral position; without scruple he shifted from one side to the other, waiting to join the victor. Fully aware of the situation he counseled Henry to dissemble, his erstwhile friends having shown themselves so fickle and inconstant. His Holiness wonders, wrote the English representative from Italy, 'how the Emperor and Aragon will dare show their faces after thus betraying Henry with a perfidy worse than that of Judas.' The Pope advised the King of England to anticipate them by offering better terms to France, and in proof of his own good will invested him with the Cap and Sword. His advice did not go unheeded; by the beginning of May Venetian merchants were sure that a special peace was brewing between England and France, and all through June and July the news spread. It was believed by everyone except Margaret who to the end refused to accept the inevitable. As the summer wore on Henry's indignation erupted. His cautious diplomacy, his expensive preparations for Mary's journey, his victories in the field had all availed him nothing. In the words of a Venetian attaché, he had been 'deceived in every direction.' His eyes opened, he resolved to trust no one while continuing to prolong negotiations; realizing at last that Maximilian intended never to keep his promise, he postponed a definite breach with Germany until after an understanding with France had been reached. From the end of April onwards England played her allies' game, making an independent treaty with France behind their backs.

Lessons in treachery are not soon forgotten. With ample justification for deserting both Ferdinand and Maximilian, Henry was becoming increasingly convinced of the rightness of his conduct and of the divine guidance which dictated it. 'Nor do I see,' he told Sebastian Giustinian, the Venetian ambassador, 'any faith in the world save in me, and therefore God Almighty, who knows this, prospers my affairs.' His belief that the infidelity of others was only exceeded by his own loyalty was not immediately shared by the rest of Europe. In the Netherlands the council, openly hostile to Margaret as well as to Henry, was selling war materials to the Scots. By the summer the English stage was set and ready for the final act of the drama; on July 30, 1514, Mary was made to renounce her compact with Charles. Immediately an English commission was appointed to treat with France, and peace was declared on the seventh of August and ratified on the twentieth. Mary future was no longer a matter of conjecture. She would go to France instead of to Germany.

Wolsey had avenged his sovereign by out-tricking the tricksters. Charles had been jilted. The frail, sedate, and melancholy lad who courted as he hunted, with stately propriety, passed out of Mary's life altogether.

CHAPTER SEVEN

Enter the Queen of France

> The Queen [Princess Mary] does not mind that the
> King [of France] is a gouty old man . . . and she
> herself a young and beautiful damsel . . . so great
> is her satisfaction at being Queen of France.
>
> Marino Sanuto, *Diarii*, Vol. XIX

LOUIS XII sought the hand of Mary Tudor as a jaded knight might enter his last tournament. Whereas his first marriage had been a travesty, from his second he had had a reasonable measure of contentment; widowed at a time when active life was behind him, he was free for a third essay in matrimony. His quest for a wife was both a dynastic and a diplomatic challenge, and if the lady were young and beautiful might also be a stimulating personal experience. In the arrangement of state marriages much had to be taken into account, but Louis's principal motivation in seeking a third wife was his need and great desire for a son. Love was not an ingredient of a royal union, the success of which was assessed by the number of offspring, especially male, that it yielded.

By some logic of masculine conceit the absence of children was always the woman's fault, the man being perhaps, as in the thinking of the great medievalist, Aquinas, a product of the harmony of faith and reason. 'As regards the individual nature,' he states, 'woman is defective and misbegotten, for the active force, the male seed, tends to the production of a perfect likeness in the masculine sex: while the production of woman comes from defect in the active force or from some material indisposition, or even from some external influence: such as that of the south wind, when it is moist, as the Philosopher observes.'

Perhaps it had been the moist south wind that had determined Louis XII's progeny, for he had begotten two daughters, Claude and

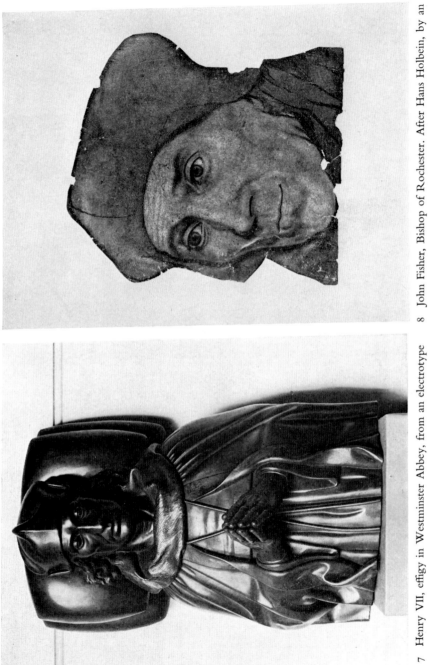

7 Henry VII, effigy in Westminster Abbey, from an electrotype

8 John Fisher, Bishop of Rochester. After Hans Holbein, by an unknown artist of the sixteenth century

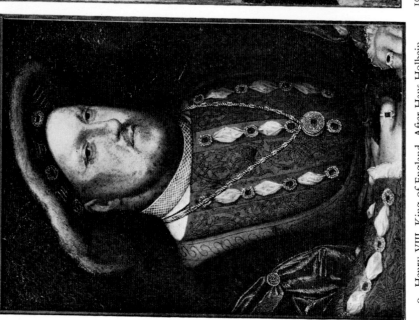

9 Henry VIII, King of England. After Hans Holbein

10 Catherine of Aragon, Queen to Henry VIII, by an unknown artist

Renée, but no sons. As conditions stood his crown would go to François d'Angoulême whose betrothal to Claude since her seventh birthday was consummated with their marriage in May, 1514, and among Louis's uncertain fears for the future was the dread that Francis with his extravagant Renaissance ideas would ruin France. His need for a son was desperate and urgent because his time was running out; premonitions of death had disturbed him since the death of Anne. 'Before the year is out I shall be with her, to keep her company,' he had sobbed over her coffin. The Pope was in agreement with French ministers that he should take a third wife, and Mary of England seemed to possess all the necessary attributes.

Towards the end of January, 1514, a papal nuncio arrived in London to labor for an expeditious reconciliation between France and England, while at the same time a secret agent of Louis was independently negotiating with Henry under the pretext of bargaining for the ransom of the Duc de Longueville, '*un très honnête jeune prince*,' who was still enjoying the hospitality of the English Court. Technically a prisoner, one of the distinguished nobles captured at Guinegate, more realistically the Duke was an unofficial envoy of France. Always more guest than prisoner, it was he who dexterously engineered the treaty from this point forward. By June informed circles all over Europe realized that peace between England and France was just a matter of time; details alone, not principles, held them apart. Louis staked everything on his eligibility and on his capacity to be both a face-saving substitute for Charles and an instrument for Henry's revenge on Germany and the Low Countries. Boasting that he could have any available lady in Europe, he expressed preference for five whose respective merits were weighed with calculating impartiality: the Archduchess Margaret, either of her nieces Eleanor and Isabella, aged sixteen and thirteen, or one of the Tudor princesses. It was believed that Margaret could not bear children, and despite the desirability of a Spanish alliance Isabella was too young, and her elder sister was said to be very slender and 'decidedly ugly' though Ferdinand assured him that her excessive thinness was no barrier, for thin women 'generally become sooner pregnant and bear more children.' Since France could always depend upon Scottish friendship without an alliance, Margaret of Scotland had little to recommend her but the fact of having recently given birth to a male child. Personally favored by Louis, the young, healthy Mary had little competition, and having studied her portrait and heard of her

D

beauty the sickly king's sluggish blood may have stirred anew. His last service to France might be an enjoyable duty.

In England haggling over the terms of the agreement began, Henry demanding 1,500,000 gold crowns in addition to Thérouanne, Boulogne, and St. Quentin, or 100,000 crowns annually if Louis were willing to take Margaret instead of Mary. Arbitration by the Papacy was suggested. Margaret, in desperate straits with the pro-French party in Scotland, was willing to cooperate, but since she was growing stout and coarse-featured at twenty-five, her age and appearance were against her. Louis was influenced too by the probability that Mary would be more acceptable to his people, and it is little wonder that he held out for her. By mid-July an understanding was virtually reached, Tournai and Mary's dowry being the last sources of contention. Henry delayed only long enough to collect the parliamentary subsidy of 160,000 pounds appropriated for the promised continuation of the war.

Before peace with France was proclaimed Mary formally repudiated her contract with Charles, the mock scene being enacted at the royal manor of Wanstead, Essex, in the presence of members of the Council summoned to witness her declaration and charged to notify Henry of it. In a rehearsed speech Mary renounced her marriage vows, charging her fiancé with breach of faith and stating that evil counsel and malicious gossip had turned him against her; thus humiliated, she was resolved never to keep her part of the bargain, and so the contract was null and void. Disclaiming any wifely affection for the Prince, she declared the severing of 'the nuptial yoke' to be entirely of her own volition, without threat or persuasion from anyone. Petitioning Henry's forgiveness, Mary concluded with an affirmation of loyalty that 'in all things she was ever ready to obey his good pleasure.'

The following week, on the seventh of August, 1514, the treaty of peace and friendship with France was signed. Its public proclamation in London a few days afterwards was accompanied by no fanfare: 'neither trumpet nor any other instrument was sounded,' the Venetian ambassador says, 'neither were bonfires burnt nor any other demonstration made for this peace.' To Wolsey and the King revenge would be all the sweeter if it came as a complete surprise to Spain and the Empire. By its terms Louis was to pay Henry a million gold crowns in renewal of the French pension formerly paid to his father, the payments to begin the following month: Tournai

and Thérouanne were to be retained by England; Scotland was included in the peace, but Milan was abandoned to Louis with England's obligations to Sforza left unhonored. Incorporated in the peace
treaty were the customary defense pact against a common enemy,
and the marriage contract which specified that Mary was to be
delivered to Louis XII at Abbeville at her brother's expense.

Charles apparently did not share the jubilation of the French on
learning the news and taxed the members of his council with having
denied him his promised wife. Louis would have appreciated their
reply : 'You are young,' they explained, 'but the King of France
is the first King in Christendom, and, having no wife, it rests with
him to take for his queen any woman he pleases.' At which, according to a Venetian account, calling for a young hawk to be brought
to him the Prince began methodically to pluck it alive, feather by
feather. When his startled councilors remonstrated he answered
bitterly :

> Thou asketh me why I plucked this hawk! he is young you see, and
> has not yet been trained, and because he is young he is held in small
> account, and because he is young he squeaked not when I plucked him.
> Thus have you done by me : I am young, you have plucked me at your
> good pleasure, and because I was young I knew not how to complain,
> but bear in mind that for the future I shall pluck you.

The story, whether true or not, illustrates the dominant traits of
Charles's character; precise, cold, callous, unemotionally correct,
indifferent to the feelings of others, none of the sensibilities of youth
were his. Some people are born old, and rigid intellectual training
added to Charles's naturally sardonic personality never let him relax
or forget for a moment that he was a prince.

It is debatable whether the Pope or Wolsey was the instigator of
the marriage treaty with France, but it was to the latter's interests
to work in its behalf. When Leo X claimed its authorship Henry
was too delighted with the treaty to quibble. Writing to His Holiness he praised it as being of the greatest significance to Christendom, since under its terms England and France could together support Rome against her enemies; in the same communiqué he incidentally divulged Mary's age as being nineteen. She has been
depicted by writers of historical fiction as either horrified at the
thought of wedding a gouty man old enough to be her grandfather, or at best as 'a most reluctant and discontented bride,' but

there is nothing to indicate that Mary was any more disgruntled by
the new marriage than she had been by the loss of the old; her
public indignation at Charles for abandoning her was no more than
diplomatic pretense. In exchanging Charles for Louis, she relinquished a singularly unappealing adolescent for a feeble, elderly
man. Louis may indeed have had the advantage in her eyes; married
to him she would be queen of the most powerful nation in Europe.

News of the *rapprochement* between England and France spread
with remarkable speed, but it took longer for the details to be veri-
fied. As late even as the middle of August Brussels was uncertain of
all the facts, though the marriage of Louis and Mary was predicted
throughout Europe. Ferdinand tried to salvage what he could: if the
report was true that Louis XII was already committed to Mary, his
envoy was instructed to press for the marriage between Renée and
the Infante Ferdinand; if not, then Louis must be persuaded to fulfill
his promise by marriage with Princess Eleanor. In Flanders the
Dutch decried the idea 'that a feeble, old, and pocky man should
marry so fair a lady'; the Emperor also pretended horror that Mary
should be sacrificed to 'an impotent, indisposed, and so malicious
a prince' as the French King. The Archduchess Margaret kept her
head as rumors of the rejection of her nephew multiplied, but took
'great thought and displeasure' therewith. If England was irretriev-
ably lost to the Low Countries, then they must 'send incontinently
into France to desire the alliance of the second daughter of the
French king and put themselves entirely into his [hands].'

While England's former allies were trying to foresee her next move,
the marriage by proxy between Mary and Louis took place publicly
at Greenwich on August 13, 1514, in the presence of the King and
Queen and all the Court. Wolsey and Suffolk were there, with Norfolk, Dorset, Buckingham, and the principal earls of the realm. For
furthering the cause of France, Wolsey and Suffolk had been rewarded by Louis with pensions, which Francis I continued to honor
for the first five years of his reign. Suffolk received 875 *livres
tournois* per year, a substantial sum for a young man without
church, family, or social connections to recommend him. Wolsey,
who received three times this sum, had the backing of the Papacy
from whom he was soon to inveigle a cardinalate. Louis had so
much faith in this form of persuasion that he assured them of his
reliance on their influence in all his dealings 'with the King his
good brother, their master.' Their earliest service to their benefactor

was to convince Henry of the advisability of an immediate marriage attended by complete publicity, before his enthusiasm could be diminished by misgivings or second thoughts.

The dignitaries assembled in the Great Banquet Hall at Greenwich early in the morning, three hours before the royal party arrived. In silk and cloth of gold, the English lords waited; around them the walls were hung with arras of gold, laced with an embroidered frieze emblazoning the royal arms of France and England. Henry and Catherine led the bridal group, Mary and her ladies immediately preceding the French delegation. The King of France was represented by Louis d'Orléans, Duc de Longueville, aided by two ministers especially sent to England for the peace conference, John de Silva, President of Normandy, and the French general, Thomas Boyer. Papal envoys were present but the Spanish ambassador, if invited, disdained to come. The Archbishop of Canterbury, William Warham, presided, assisted by Wolsey and the senior English lords. The ceremony opened with a Latin address by Warham, to which De Silva made the formal reply that his master, the Most Christian King, was desirous of taking the Lady Mary to wife. The French authorization for the proxy marriage, read by the Bishop of Durham, was followed by the espousal *per verba de praesenti*; holding Mary's right hand in his, De Longueville spoke Louis's vows in French, to which she replied in the same tongue; the ring was placed on the fourth finger of her right hand, the kiss given, and the marriage schedule signed. It was very reminiscent of her first proxy marriage six years earlier, which the same Archbishop had pronounced just as 'holy.' A bizarre symbolism, supposed to add irrevocability to the union was then enacted: Mary changed from her wedding gown into an elaborate nightdress, while De Longueville, clad in doublet and red hose to match her 'magnificent deshabille,' bared one leg to the thigh; theoretically prepared for sexual relations, they lay down together long enough for him to touch her body with his naked leg, after which Warham declared the marriage consummated.

When Mary had dressed again, this time in a checkered gown of purple satin and cloth of gold covering an ash-colored petticoat, the gathering heard High Mass in the palace chapel. Followed by the lords, the English dukes led the procession; De Longueville walked with Henry, who shone like the sun in gold and satin appliquéd with jewels. Mary accompanied Catherine, each wearing a cap of cloth of gold 'covering the ears in the Venetian fashion.' After the Court banquet, music from flute and harp supplemented by 'a certain small fife, which produced a very harmonious effect,' was played for dancing. Henry took this opportunity to display his skill, and in doublet and hose he and Buckingham danced for two hours with so much gusto that the sedate Venetian ambassador admitted to a temptation to join them. Later, the legal documents pertaining to the marriage were signed in De Longueville's quarters, where wine was served. His ransom paid, the exprisoner went home next day with ten horses and a cart bearing presents to the value of two thousand pounds, among which was the gown worn by Henry the previous evening, alone estimated at three hundred ducats.

Mary was showered with letters of congratulation and wedding presents from all over Europe, among which came a jeweled cap from Milan; but the most exquisite gifts came from Louis himself, whose bounty represented the measure of his happinness. Jean de Sains, Sieur de Marigny, arrived shortly after the wedding to serve as special attendant to his new mistress and to familiarize her with French manners and customs. With him was the artist-designer, Jean Perréal, who had been commissioned not only to paint a portrait of the 'French Queen' but also to assist in the planning of her wardrobe. Since she had never seen her husband Perréal had brought a portrait of him, to be given to Henry in exchange for that which he was to paint of her. The two men bore themselves toward Mary with all the courteous deference due to their Queen. Preceded by his attendants, the courtly Marigny respectfully presented Louis's gifts, which were borne by a handsome white horse: two coffers of plate, seals, devices, and magnificent jewelry. One of the jewels was sensational, described by an Italian merchant as a jeweled diamond as large as a man's finger, with a pear-shaped pearl beneath it 'the size of a pigeon's egg.' Sensing its worth, Henry immediately had it valued by the jewelers of 'the Row,' who assessed it at sixty thousand crowns. Known as the 'Mirror of Naples,' it was to cause Mary much trouble in the future.

No clouds darkened the horizon as each day brought auspicious news from France, whose king, excited by new reports of Mary's beauty, was said to yearn hourly for her presence. By twentieth-century standards, however, his letters to her are far too conventional to convey the warmth of feeling to which his ambassadors attested. Replying that her only desire was for his health and prosperity, she vowed diplomatically that she would love him as cordially as she could; the ending of these letters is always the same: 'Votre bien humble compaigne, Marie.' As the days passed Louis grew increasingly impatient, anxious to see his young queen.

Mary was expected in Abbeville some time in late September and arrangements for her reception took precedence over even the imminent Peninsula Invasion. The Venetian minister in Paris reported to his master that she was to be there by the twenty-ninth 'to bed with His Most Christian Majesty, so that for the present nothing was said about the Italian expedition, nor anything attended to save these rejoicings for the nuptials.'

The size of Mary's dowry and jointure were settled long before she left England, though not without some difficulty. The agreement stated that the espousals were to be performed by mutual proxies, the actual marriage to be solemnized there within two months. The amount of the dowry was a matter of economic compromise, Henry being determined to pay as little as possible, Louis to get as much as he could. The latter's avowed surprise that the English King should try to marry his sister without an adequate settlement implied such a reflection on Henry's liberality that his pride was touched, and the criticism had the desired effect. Louis afterwards admitted that his bride had come to him 'most honourably, sumptuously, and splendidly' outfitted and equipped. The total agreed upon was to the value of 400,000 gold crowns, half of it to be in plate and jewelry and half to represent the cost of her equipment. Louis's known ill-health prompted the English to insist upon a clause protecting their investment: if Mary survived her husband and returned to England, the cost of her journey to Abbeville was to be refunded and her personal belongings restored. Her jointure, a liberal one, was equal in income to that received by Anne of Brittany. The jointure lands were numerous but scattered, lying chiefly in the west-central and southeastern parts of France: the counties of Saintonge and Pezenas; the towns of Rochelle, Loudun, Roquemaure, and Chinon with its adjacent castle; the lordships of Montigny, Cessenon, and Cabrières; the profits of the small or privy seal of Montpellier; the revenues from Saintonge, St. Jean d'Angély, Rochford, Bourg, St. André, Villeneuve, and Beaucaire near Avignon; and salt profits derived from Pezenas, Montpellier, Fronlingnan, and Narbonne, valued at 10,400 *livres tournois* annually. These revenues represented a sizable income yearly, though it varied appreciably from year to year. Polydore Vergil's estimate, probably too high, was some 302,000 crowns annually. In later years, when as Duchess of Suffolk she lived in England, Mary seldom realized more than 6,150 pounds per year from her French possessions.

The remaining formality specified in the marriage contract was Louis's proxy wedding in France. Commissioners headed by the Lord Chamberlain, Charles Somerset, were sent to Paris to assist at the marriage and to act as English witnesses. As 'Queen of the French,' Mary under her own privy seal appointed Somerset, recently created Earl of Worcester, to act as her proxy, telling Louis by letter that the earl bore a special message from her *'touchant les fyansailles d'entre vous et moy en parolle de present* [that is, *per verba de praesenti*].' The ceremony took place in Paris in the church of the Celestine Order on the fourteenth of September after the celebration of a Mass. In the presence of De Longueville, the Duke of Albany, the Dauphin, English agents, and other notables, Mary was again joined in Holy Matrimony, the ritual being similar in both form and procedure to that solemnized in England. The next day at Les Tournelles in the Faubourg St. Antoine, Louis bound himself for the payment of the million crowns as contracted, under penalty of excommunication for default. Remembering the previous broken vows the English capital accepted the new alignment with reservations, but once the treaty was signed and delivered, Henry and Wolsey were more optimistic. Twice pledged and financially committed, it now seemed very improbable that Louis would change his mind.

All thought of war was forgotten in the fever of preparation for Mary's departure, and she was the distinguished guest at many entertainments and celebrations in her honor. Her trousseau was again superb, though some of the clothing and equipment bought for her abortive journey to the Netherlands must have been used. For the second time in a few months Henry provided lavishly and deliberately for his sister, the worth of her personal wardrobe being estimated at more than £43,300. Several items suggest that, where possible, support was given to home industry, as the £10 13s. 4d. for hose and the £84 19s. 6½d. paid to John Ring, the royal skinner, for the furring of a dozen gowns by order of the King's Council; since English cloth was not esteemed because the colors were poor, expensive imported fabrics were mostly used. Among the beautiful hangings and tapestries from Brussels were seven special pieces representing the story of Hercules. Sixteen of her gowns including the wedding dress were in the French fashion, six were in Milanese style, and seven in English, each with its own chemise, girdle, and accessories. Many of the accounts of workmen employed in procuring and working up the raw materials have been preserved; tailors, embroiderers, hosiers, cordwainers, 'casemakers', chariot makers, bedmakers, saddlers, painters, seamstresses, spangle workers, and gold-wire drawers all did their part in making Mary's trousseau a fitting one for the Queen of France. Her jewelry was of equally royal quality : gold chains and bracelets, carcanets of diamonds and rubies, pearled aiguillettes, golden, gem-studded frontlets, brooches, rings, medallions, and fleur-de-lis ornaments. Her servants' uniforms, her chapel fixtures, and her great seal and privy seal all proclaimed her rank while painted panels spelled out her motto in letters of gold: '*La volonté de Dieu me suffit.*' Mary Tudor was sent forth with all the trappings of royalty.

Between attending Court activities and granting audiences to ambassadors and foreign dignitaries wishing to congratulate her, Mary perfected her acquaintance with Parisian customs and the French language under the tutelage of a professional, the English schoolmaster John Palsgrave. Twenty-nine years old in 1514, he had a Bachelor of Arts degree from Corpus Christi College, Cambridge, and had studied theology in Paris preparatory to his ordination in 1512. Unable upon his return to England to find public employment as a teacher, he took work as a private tutor in order to avoid that 'horrible monster, poverty.' Linguistically his job was easy, for Mary could practice in daily conversation at Court where French was almost as commonly spoken as English. Also personal secretary to Mary, Palsgrave seems to have been hired primarily for his knowledge of French, and it may have been while tutoring the Princess that he first conceived the idea of writing a textbook; *L'Esclaircissement de la Langue Francoyse,* which he published later, is the earliest known French grammar for English pupils.

By the beginning of September everything was ready for her departure by Michaelmas. Having prepared a grand reception for her in Paris, toward the end of the month Louis journeyed to Abbeville where royal lodgings were waiting. His trip is spitefully recorded by Louise of Savoy in her journal : 'On the twenty-second of September, 1514, King Louis XII, very old and feeble left Paris, to go to meet his young wife, Queen Mary.' October arrived, however, before Mary did, the excuse being unavoidable delay. Louis suggested a meeting with Henry somewhere between Boulogne and Calais, or anywhere in Normandy to suit him, being in 'a marvellous mind' to please everybody, more especially Mary, whom he called his 'wife,' and to whom he paid constant homage. Mary sailed from Dover on the second of the month.

A few days before leaving London Mary held her last reception to which were invited merchants of every nationality to pay their respects. In a French gown of woven gold, proudly wearing the magnificent 'Mirror of Naples,' she was described as very beautiful, without equal in the realm, 'of light complexion with a colour, and most affable and graceful.' She pleased her guests by speaking a few words to them in French, but the Venetian merchant, Lorenzo Pasqualigo, was unimpressed and ended his first-hand account of the reception with the comment that her mastery of the language was by no means exceptional: 'The whole Court now speaks French and English, as in the time of the late King.'

CHAPTER EIGHT

Cloth of Gold

To furnish a ship requireth much trouble,
But to furnish a woman, the charges are double.

John Manningham's *Diary*

ON THE twenty-third of September, 1514, an embassy was organized to escort the 'Queen of France' to Abbeville. Norfolk headed the delegation, which included some of the most important lords of the Council: Dorset; Surrey; Worcester; Thomas Ruthal, Bishop of Durham; diplomatist Thomas Docwra, Prior of St. John's of Jerusalem; and Dr. Nicholas West, Dean of Windsor. Worcester, Docwra, and West were already in France, having remained there since their mission of the previous month when they presented the French monarch with an attested minute of Mary's dowry, the 'donation *propter nuptias,*' and got his acquittance and legal assurance for the jointure. They then stayed with the English party at Abbeville until after the marriage, leaving before the coronation in Paris.

Mary's attendants represented a fair cross section of the English aristocracy. Besides some seventy-five lords and gentlemen, fifty unidentified household officials also were paid twenty days' wages in advance, several receiving other financial rewards for particular loyalty. With the exception of a few indispensable household officers—secretary, chamberlain, treasurer, almoner, and physician—the ladies of the chamber and personal friends were of more importance to her, for it was upon their counsel and fidelity that she would rely in adjusting to a strange environment. The names of eighteen have been preserved, among them the Duchess of Norfolk and her daughter the Countess of Oxford, the Marchioness of Dorset, and Lady Monteagle, none of whom were among her perma-

87

nent companions. She had herself chosen them with Wolsey's approval, and the list had been submitted to Louis for his. He seems to have objected to only one of her original selection, though he later disapproved a number whose names had been added to it. This was her childhood companion, the impetuous Jane Popincourt, whom Louis rejected because of her light reputation. An old friend of Mary's, she had earned a certain notoriety by an *affaire* with De Longueville during his imprisonment in England, and it had been at his request that her name was included at all. After hearing of the scandal Louis would have no part of her; rather she were burnt alive than serve his Queen, he told the English ambassador, adding that his one concern was Mary's welfare. Jane remained behind. When she did return to her own country two years later it was with the blessing of the English Court and a one hundred pound reward for her services to the Tudor family. Chief among Mary's close associates in France were Elizabeth Grey, sister of Lord Grey of Wilton, Anne Devereux, Elizabeth Ferrers, Anne Jerningham, Lady Elizabeth Grey, sister of the Marquis of Dorset, Mary Fiennes, daughter of Lord Dacre of the South, and Joan Guildford. One of her younger maids-in-waiting was 'Nan de Boleine,' then a child of thirteen; these were coveted appointments, for the French court was thought to be the height of elegance and sophistication.

Extant are many vivid descriptions of the party that went with Mary to Dover. Everyone of importance accompanied her, '*gros princes et dames et gros personages*,' the King riding with his sister and Queen Catherine traveling in a litter because she was again pregnant. All took retainers and personal servants, but since no actual count of the train was apparently made, estimates of its number vary up to as many as two thousand. Most of them were bound only for the coast to witness Mary's embarkation, which had become so much the big social event of the year that the journey in such distinguished company attracted merchants and many others to follow solely for enjoyment. The Court on Progress was a brave sight as it proceeded with slow dignity, pausing here and there along the way to receive homage from excited country folk gathered to catch a glimpse of the royal family. The Spanish ambassador alone was unenthusiastic, since popular distrust of his sovereign had been visited upon him. Conspicuous by his absence from Mary's farewell festivities, he had kept closely to his house in London for when he ventured forth 'strange words are said to him.' Lorenzo Pasqualigo, quite overwhelmed by the pomp of Mary's departure, sent an account to his brother in Italy telling him that she was attended by the four top lords of the realm, four hundred knights and barons, two hundred gentlemen and esquires, with their wives, 'damsels,' and equippage; besides a thousand palfreys, about a hundred 'wagons' accommodated the greater ladies, who were almost as splendidly dressed as their husbands. 'There were so many gowns of woven gold and with gold grounds, housings for the horses and palfreys of the same material, and chains and jewels,' he recorded, 'that they were worth a vast amount of treasure.' Some noblemen had spent as much as 200,000 crowns on their wardrobes, he wrote; Mary in one of her new French costumes looked so pretty, that to Pasqualigo at least, her equal was not to be found in England.

Henry had planned to sail ten miles out to sea alongside her ship in his favorite vessel the *Henry Grâce de Dieu*, but inclement weather made immediate embarkation impossible and forced a delay at Dover. In the days of sailing vessels sudden squalls in the English Channel could be extremely dangerous, and in this storm, which Polydore Vergil reports as continuing for more than twenty days, the wind was so furious and the weather so foul that one of the ships of the fleet, the *Great Elizabeth*, was wrecked near Sandgate en route to join the expedition. Of the five or six hundred aboard only three hundred survived unharmed, many others being seriously injured. Though the elements could not be controlled, other precautions could be taken; the Channel had been swept by English vessels to ensure that there were no lurking cruisers that might intercept Mary's passage, and her naval escort had been carefully chosen. This flotilla of fourteen 'great ships' appointed to transport Mary and her company to Boulogne, at a 'petty and necessary' cost of £21 12s. 3d. not including wages, stood by until the storm abated. On the second of October it was decided to set sail despite threats of further high winds. Henry was never a patient man and the port of Dover offered no inducements for lingering.

The party embarked at four o'clock in the chill autumn morning, during a brief calm, to catch the early tide. After bidding farewell to Catherine at the Castle, Mary walked to the wharf with Henry, who kissed her affectionately and wished her Godspeed. Here at 'the water side,' as he was later to be reminded, she extracted from him a renewal of his promise to let her choose her second husband, for they both realized that her marriage to Louis might be of very short duration.

The sea proved more intractable than was anticipated, and after scarcely a quarter of the voyage they caught the full fury of the returning storm which scattered the convoy, dispersing the ships along the French coast from Calais to Boulogne. Only four succeeded in making their scheduled destination; one of them, the bride's ship, unable to make a safe landing, was grounded just within Boulogne harbor. Loaded into a rowing boat, Mary was brought through the perilously high breakers to within wading distance of the beach. Pale, forlorn, drenched to the bone, and prostrate with seasickness, she was caught up from the little craft by Sir Christopher Garnish, a knight in her retinue, and carried ashore in safety. Such personal gestures paid handsome dividends, and this 'strong, sturdy stallion' had already won Henry's attention as a companion-in-arms. For his gallantry at Boulogne he was given a thirty-pound annuity and half as much again in cash, awarded the following year. Mary entered her new kingdom in a pathetic condition, but even in her misery was not spared the ceremony of a royal reception. Chief among those gathered at the dock to receive her were the Duc de Vendôme and Cardinal d'Amboise.

It was several days before all the ships arrived and her full suite could be reassembled, but no lives were lost. As none of her wardrobe stuff had been aboard the *Great Elizabeth* only a minimum of plate and property was destroyed. After Louis's death the disaster was recalled by the superstitious, who interpreted it as an evil omen, boding no good to the marriage.

Mary's journey from Boulogne to Paris has been graphically described by several witnesses whose stories agree on all essentials. 'I assure you that she did not come like a lady of little consequence,' wrote one, 'for she was accompanied by great princes and ladies, and great personages.' These narrators were particularly struck with a rare tapestry she had brought with her, 'of very large dimensions, more beautiful than ever seen,' depicting the united arms of France and England. Mary traveled southward along the coast arriving at the little town of Montreuil-sur-Mer, twenty-four miles from Boulogne as the crow flies, on Thursday, the fifth of October. There she spent two nights in the household of Madame de Moncaverel, where a chamber had been prepared and decorated for her comfort and enjoyment; her next destination was Abbeville on the Somme, twelve miles inland, where she was to be married to Louis in person. There festivities were on a grander scale, a prelude to those awaiting her in Paris on the sixth of the following month. Descriptions of her reception at each of these places and the pageants presented in her honor have been minutely recorded by three French chroniclers.

She was greeted at Montreuil first with a song praising the royal marriage and the resultant peace between the two countries; the lily of France and the English rose were now united:

> Princes, try to entertain and keep
> The Rose among the lilies of France,
> So that one may say and maintain—
> Shamed be he who thinks ill thereof.

Mary and her train entered from the seaport village of Étaples. They were preceded by a delegation of *'grans seigneurs et dames'* sent by Louis to welcome her: the Duc and Duchesse de Longue-ville, the Duc de Vendôme, Cardinal d'Amboise, Francis of Angou-lême, the governor of Picardy, bishops, abbots, representatives of religious orders, local merchants, and provincial bigwigs. Official salutes over, the procession moved into the town, pausing to be entertained by five pageants at intervals along the route, all of them classically or religiously symbolic of Mary's marriage to Louis: the stories of Andromeda and Perseus, of Apollo and Diana on Mount Parnassus, of Solomon and the Queen of Sheba, of Esther and the Persian king Ahasuerus, and of the Virgin and the Annunciation. Insipid and slow-moving though such pageants usually were, the English were familiar with this form of eulogy which every triumphal procession through London had incorporated for some years. For Mary it was the first of many popular manifestations of affection, and like Henry she never tired of them, always seeming to prefer the simple awkward tributes of the common people to the elegant insincerities of courtiers.

The twenty-five miles from Montreuil to Abbeville were covered slowly, with leisure and dignity. In the early afternoon the party was met near Anders Forest by Francis and a few companions who had ridden on ahead that they might be able to inform Louis of the approximate hour of Mary's arrival. The weeks of waiting had taxed his patience and curiosity to their limits, and now that his young wife was so near he was determined to catch a glimpse of her before the official reception. Such informality was strictly precluded by Court etiquette and Louis was too conventional to flaunt prescription; their meeting must not appear to be intentional, so on the pretext of returning from a hawking expedition he arranged to come accidentally upon the procession, which in courtesy would oblige him to pay his respects to his English guests. Etiquette was placated but nobody deceived, least of all Mary who had been briefly warned by D'Angoulême to expect a surprise, and had prepared herself for just such an impromptu meeting.

The approach of the royal hunting party was heralded by two hundred guardsmen riding ahead of a group of churchmen and nobles surrounding the King. By French custom the clothes of a king and queen appearing together in public were made of identical materials, in this case cloth of gold on crimson, which Francis had reported Mary to be wearing. Mounted on a white palfrey, she pretended to be taken aback on recognizing her visitor, but doffed in salute her hat of crimson silk. The *pièce de résistance* of her costume, it was worn cocked over one eye, in a light-hearted and flippant manner. Also in a new habit Louis rode a beautiful hunter, caparisoned in gold and black. Descriptions of the animal and rider vary with the narrator: the Italian Peter Martyr has him 'perched elegantly' on a fine Spanish war-horse, a gay bridegroom in his dotage, 'licking his lips and gulping his spittle.' If the French King lives to smell the flowers of spring, the Italian snorted, 'you may promise yourself five hundred autumns.' Martyr's comments seldom flattered: 'What an old valetudinarian suffering from leprosy, can want with a handsome girl of eighteen,' he left to his readers' imaginations, predicting that she would be the death of him. Kinder with the bride, he described her as fresh, young, beautiful, radiant with health, owing nothing to artifice. An English chronicler boasted with patriotic pride that the French found their new queen so attractive that they could not keep their eyes off her, for she looked 'more like an angel than a human creature.'

As Louis approached, Mary prepared to dismount and make obeisance, but he would permit no gesture of homage. Responding to his mood she blew him a kiss from the saddle, which he returned. Possibly unfamiliar with this custom he construed it as an invitation; 'boldly,' says the Bishop of Asti, French ambassador to Venice, he 'threw his arms round her neck, and kissed her as kindly as if he had been five-and-twenty.' They chatted quietly together for a little while, Louis probably voicing his welcome and concern for her comfort and well-being. At all times he treated her with courteous deference; as on this day she was the one to be honored, and lest his presence detract from her ovation, after greeting her English companions he returned to town by a different route with a few attendants, leaving the remainder of his company with her. Among them was Francis, who escorted Mary the rest of the way, beguiling her and her lords with his charm and attentiveness as he rode at her side.

The procession moved on in full ceremonial order for the entry into Abbeville. In charge of it, Norfolk had paired the ambassadors and noblemen by rank to ride ahead of the Princess, the peers being preceded by some fifty esquires in multicolored silk uniforms who headed the long column. The lords and barons, in velvet bonnets 'some of one color and some of another,' were 'all clad either in cloth of gold or silk of various qualities.' In front of the Princess were her heralds, macers, and trumpeters, led by Garter King-of-Arms Thomas Wriothesley and Richmond Herald John Joyner. Two liveried grooms led spare palfreys, Mary riding behind them with two 'running footmen' at her stirrup. Behind were her feminine attendants, about thirty ladies and maids, clad 'in their own fashion in divers ways,' either mounted or in gaily decorated wagons. In 1514 neither the early carriage nor coach had been invented, but a cumbersome four-wheeled conveyance, covered and elaborately decorated, was used by court ladies. This carriage-like vehicle, called by the Italians a *chareta*, probably resembled the medieval char, and like it was drawn by two or more horses harnessed one before the other. Mary had several in her train, each of a size to require six horses, some of which carried her wardrobe equipment. Borne by two large horses ridden by liveried pages was the handsome royal litter, covered with cloth of gold figured with lilies, half red and half white, to symbolize the united blood of York and Lancaster that flowed in Mary's veins. Last of all marched two hundred archers in pairs, divided into three units, each dressed in a different blazing color. Never had the people of Abbeville seen such a 'brilliant and imposing' sight. 'In truth,' wrote one observer, 'the pomp of the English was as grand and costly as words can express.' Another, writing to the Bishop of Asti, excused his extravagant narrative: 'Your right reverend Lordship must not be surprised at my representing well nigh everything in the superlative degrees, for the reality exceeds my description, to the great glory of this Queen.' To a late nineteenth-century French historian, René de Maulde La Clavière, the route *'semblait une constellation d'or.'*

While they were still beyond sight of the town a delegation of the Abbeville governing body joined them, taking the lead position. The newcomers, lord mayor, chief justice, clergy, and magistrates were escorted by liveried guardsmen and a contingent of soldiers in bright red uniforms, bringing the total number in the procession to between two and three thousand. They had no sooner started on again when they were halted by an unexpected catastrophe, a sharp rainfall that continued until many were so drenched that they were compelled to change their clothing after it was over, before the journey could be resumed. Now riding under a white satin canopy supported by four of the town officials, Mary had changed into a dress of stiff gold brocade with a white gown of English design, beautiful and, for the sixteenth century, very expensive; her tiara was a new type of frontlet fashioned of jewels, two large pearls on the left side. Before reaching the little church of Notre Dame de la Chappelle in the suburbs of the town, she exchanged the palfrey for her litter as a more dignified means of conveyance. It was about five o'clock when they passed through the gates into Abbeville, where a salute of artillery fire and music from a hundred musicians greeted them. In the decorated streets those taking part in the elaborately prepared pageants were still waiting in their finery despite the rain.

The procession dispersed at the Church of St. Vulfran, where Mary heard Mass and paid homage to the patron saint of the town, after which she was taken to meet the King at his residence in the ancient Hôtel de la Gruthuse. Though this introduction was not prolonged, it was dignified by all the ceremony of a state reception. Norfolk, officiating for England, presented the bride to Louis and his diminutive Court of great peers and forty-four lesser nobles. The speech-making over, Mary was taken by Francis' wife Claude to her apartment in the Rue St. Giles, an annex to the King's lodging. The two girls were the antithesis of each other, one short and corpulent, the other slim, straight, and beautiful. Recently married, plain little Claude was immediately drawn to her stepmother, who was but three years older than she. Those who pitied Mary on her wedding eve might have saved their sympathies for Claude, whose loveless life was to be not only tragic but thirteen years shorter than Mary's. She became known as the 'Good Queen' of Francis I, bore him seven children, and died in the performance of her sole function in life: the production of heirs for as long and as often as it was physically possible.

That evening inaugurated the celebrations which continued until the Court left Abbeville. A state banquet was given by Louis and a grand ball in Mary's honor held afterwards by Francis and Claude, who as Duke and Duchess of Angoulême were frequently referred to by the English as simply the 'Duke' and the 'Duchess.' Francis was also Duke of Brittany and Valois but was mostly known to his countrymen as the 'Monseigneur.' In spite of her strenuous day Mary exceeded the highest hopes of both her husband and host that evening, delighting them with her beauty and poise. A Venetian, charmed by her grace and good manners, found Louis the envy of the world, his Mary a veritable 'paradise.'

A better opportunity for seeing the callous indifference of the privileged for those less fortunate never presented itself than on that Sunday night of royal merrymaking in Abbeville. Beyond the main section of the city, across the Somme where the poor of the town lived, a fire broke out and raged unchallenged for hours, because the ringing of the alarm bells was forbidden lest the King be disturbed at his amusements. The wind fanned the angry flames, but without help from the royal party the fighting of such a great fire seemed of no avail. On the town side of the river the thick walls and tapestried windows of the Hôtel shut out even the warning of possible calamity, and only the Italian visitors who were nearer the burning area knew and feared. They interpreted their escape as an intervention by the Almighty, who had more compassion than the King of France. The concepts of democracy and equality as visualized by later philosophies had no place in the sixteenth century. Mary's world and that of the common people were totally separated by a deep social chasm, and though the emergence of greater fluidity in the class structure was to narrow the gulf, it was never bridged. The lower orders could watch the diversions of the privileged respectfully from a distance without conscious discontent, but however great the inequity the seeds of revolution would not germinate so long as a paternalistic government gave prosperity to each estate. The breach between the two worlds provoked no antagonism in a divinely ordered system in which few governed and many obeyed. Shakespeare's words had meaning in Mary's day, when "prerogative of age, crowns, sceptres, laurels' by degree stood 'in authentic place.'

Used to the early hours of court life, which sometimes began before dawn, Mary was up early next day, the ninth of October. It was the feast of St. Denis, the patron saint of France, a seemingly auspicious date for a royal wedding. Mary's lodging was but a stone's throw from Louis's, connected by a large garden which her marriage procession was to cross. The ceremony was set for nine o'clock, allowing ample time for the bridal party to dispose themselves for their slow progress to the great hall of the Hôtel de la Gruthuse. As another display of regal ostentation whose object was to advertise English wealth, it was splendidly effective. 'If the pomp of the most Christian Queen was great yesterday at her entry . . . it was yet greater at her wedding,' wrote an unidentified witness. Twenty-six knights marching in pairs led the way; heralds, macers, and 'innumerable musicians of various sorts' followed. Mary walked between Norfolk and Dorset, behind them the English lords and ladies sent over for the wedding, and thirteen women of her personal staff, each escorted by two gentlemen. Her gown of gold brocade trimmed with ermine was of French design, and thought by some to be more becoming than her English costume of the previous day. To twentieth-century taste she was overloaded with jewelry, but while this typified Renaissance dress, her costly jewels were also worn to dazzle the French and uphold the financial prestige of her own country. Her jeweled coronet concealed none of the red-gold hair which fell in profusion over her shoulders, making her 'right goodly to behold.'

The King and his guests were waiting for Mary in the Hall; Louis, in gold and ermine to match the Queen's gown, was less extravagantly dressed than some of his nobles, all of whom had done their best to outshine the English in elegance. The Master of Horse had paid 116 crowns per yard for his cloth of gold from Italy; trimmed with sable, it was reputed to be the most splendid gown there and worth some two thousand crowns, more than four hundred pounds sterling. A Frenchman's wealth was measured by the value of his robe as an Englishman's was by his gold chain. Some of these worn at the wedding were massive, as wide as a man's hand and worn tight around the neck, 'prison fashion'; others, narrower and lighter, were long enough to double, triple, or wind even six times round the neck 'so that never was such magnificence beheld.' The hum of conversation ceased as the English entered. The King 'doffed his bonnet and the Queen curtseyed to the ground; whereupon His Majesty kissed her' and seated her beside him under a canopy supported by four of the greatest peers of France. Louis then himself clasped a necklace round Mary's neck, 'a marvellous great pointed diamond, with a ruby almost two inches long without foil, which was esteemed by some men at 10,000 marks,' as Worcester did not fail to point out in a letter to Henry. If worth less than the 'Mirror of Naples' it was still a valuable piece. The service proceeded without interruption, Francis serving the King and Claude the Queen, as custom dictated. Cardinal René de Prie, Bishop of Bayeux, performed the marriage and sang the Nuptial Mass, dividing the consecrated wafer between the bride and bridegroom. Another curtsey, another kiss, and Mary was escorted back to her own apartment. She now had a role, a short but momentarily important one, in a very small segment of history. In 'the year 1514 of human salvation,' Polydore Vergil wrote in his *Anglicae Historiae*, 'the rites were accomplished in the fullness of harmony, ceremony, tranquillity, and blessed peace.'

The marriage was immediately succeeded by a state dinner, Mary presiding at the ladies' table in her own chambers, after which everyone gathered in the Hôtel de la Gruthuse for dancing. Later in the evening was a formal ball, 'the whole Court banqueting, dancing, and making good cheer,' and Louis so proud of his bride that he would not leave her side. At eight o'clock Mary was led by Claude to the bridal bed, already blessed and prepared, 'to go and sleep with the King.' One narrator only, an unidentified Italian, comments on the wedding night: 'The next morning, the 10th, the King seemed very jovial and gay and in love [to judge] by his countenance. Thrice did he cross the river last night, and would have done more had he chosen.'

CHAPTER NINE

Louis and Mary

Wives are young men's mistresses, companions for middle age, and old men's nurses.

Francis Bacon, *Essays*, 'Of Marriage and Single Life'

LOUIS XII of France, third Duc d'Orleans, was born about 1462, the son and heir of Charles d'Orleans, the prince poet who had spent a quarter of a century in England after being taken prisoner at the Battle of Agincourt. A descendant of Charles the Wise through his grandfather, Louis was next in succession to the throne of France if the senior line of the House of Valois should die out, and his influence as Duc d'Orleans was greatly magnified when it became likely that he would indeed succeed Charles VIII as king of France. His mother was the charming Mary of Cleves who presided over the gay cultivated Court of Blois, which throughout his life was his favorite retreat from court life and political anxiety. He grew to manhood 'lusty and beautiful,' taking pride in the powerful athletic body that earned him stature and eminence in many forms of physical sport.

Louis's boyhood was marred by forced marriage to his cousin, the pitiful Princess Jeanne, whose congenital deformity was allegedly so pronounced that even her own father, Louis XI, called 'Spider Louis,' could imagine no one being more hideous. A sickly hunchback, lame and diseased, unlikely to bear children, her condition was incurable. She was eight and he fourteen when they were joined in most unholy wedlock. A marriage in name only, he could never accept her affliction though she learned both to live with it and to love the husband who was so embittered at being so. Most of the twenty-two years of their grotesque relationship were spent apart, for Louis could not bear to be with her for more than a few hours at a time. Emotional and physical frustration led him to seek adventure: to find love where he could, and excitement in political intrigue, with equally disastrous results. His father-in-law died in 1483 and was succeeded by Jeanne's thirteen-year-old brother Charles VIII, almost as deformed in body and considerably more deficient in wit than she. Louis made a bid for the regency, which culminated in the 'Foolish War,' and eventually three years of imprisonment; when he finally inherited the throne of France in 1498 he was in broken health, a prematurely old man at thirty-six.

His first act was to get a dispensation for the annulment of his marriage on the grounds that Jeanne was incapable of bearing children despite her insistence to the contrary. Always accommodating when he himself could gain thereby, the political-minded Pope Alexander VI, who needed help in Italy, was willing to grant an annulment to Louis in exchange for military aid, and a title, a fief, and a French bride for his son, the notorious Cesare Borgia. Given to God because she was 'not good enough for man,' the tragic Jeanne de France, so briefly queen, retired to a monastery and died six years later.

Louis's objective in seeking this divorce was not only repudiation of Jeanne for its own sake, but freedom to marry a woman who could give him an heir; his choice was Dowager-Queen Anne, who for six years had been the devoted wife of his brother-in-law Charles VIII. As prospective heiress to Brittany, the most important duchy of Europe, almost since birth her hand had been sought by all who aspired to possession of that rich feudatory province. The one large, technically independent state of western France that Louis XI had been unable to absorb into his centralized empire, it had been sharply watched by his daughter, Anne de Beaujeu, during her period of regency. At the age of five Anne of Britanny was betrothed to the King of the Romans in the hope of German support against French aggression, and when her father, Francis II of Brittany, died in 1488 without male issue, the pledge was reinforced by a proxy marriage which was never consummated. In fact Maximilian never set his eyes on Anne, being too busy at home to claim his wife and defend her territories. When still barely twelve she was claimed in wardship by Regent Anne de Beaujeu in the name of Charles VIII, who at eighteen had recaptured the imperialistic ambition of his father, an ambition which was to shape so many

European alliances and eventually drew even the cautious Henry VII of England into its arena. Brittany was invaded and forced to come to terms, the result being a break with the Emperor and Anne's marriage to Charles VIII in 1491. It proved to be one of the best things Charles ever did: France acquired the long-coveted Brittany, and he got an adoring wife who supported his weaknesses and accepted his deformity with motherly love and affection.

When Louis XII married Anne of Brittany in 1499, she had already borne and buried four children. Though not a celebrated beauty like Mary Tudor, in youth her regular features and charming manner had been physically appealing; but her blood had chilled with the loss of Charles, love being replaced by austerity and vindictiveness. The fire within her burnt not with passion but with the resolute awareness of duty to her family and to Brittany. After their marriage she and Louis both changed: he lost his robust health and with it his old zest for living; she became introspective, self-centered, and haughty, showing traces of the shrewish qualities attributed to her former sister-in-law, Anne de Beaujeu.

Smallish and of medium height, Anne was obviously a woman of 'virtue and merit'; one leg being slightly shorter than the other she limped, but despite Louis' strong emotional reaction to physical disfigurement for which his marriage to Jeanne was responsible, he was deeply attached to 'his Breton.' Earlier, during the forced celibacy of his first marriage, he had desired her when she was unattainable, but though the closeness of their relationship and his love for her has undoubtedly been exaggerated, their marriage was successful enough. Anne was a stimulating companion and a helpful consort, and under her guidance the Court at Blois maintained its reputation for education and culture. In only one respect did she fail in her duty: she bore him two daughters but no sons, and the succession continued to be a nagging uncertainty to them both. While their elder, Claude, could not under Salic law inherit her father's kingdom, she would acquire Brittany, for Anne had insisted in her marriage contract that the duchy revert to the second son, or barring male issue, to her eldest daughter. Recognizing the expediency of Claude's betrothal to Francis of Angoulême, Anne nevertheless fought the alliance to the bitter end, while Louis's rapidly failing health convinced him that the union was necessary to France, guaranteeing as it did her continued possession of Brittany. Though his will prevailed, Louis could not forgive Anne's opposition, nor forget that once when she thought him to be dying she had tried to send several boatloads of their plate, jewels, and best furniture to her own chateau at Nantes, in an attempt to salvage as much as she could from their marriage. But her sick husband outlived her by almost a year: she died on January 9, 1514, 'wonderfully lamented,' and twenty-two days after was given a royal burial in Paris and entombed in the church of St. Denis. Her delivery of two still-born sons had been bitterly disappointing, and she ended her life as she had lived it, suffering and unfulfilled. Her favorite poet, Fausto Andrelini, extolled her in death as he had done during her lifetime: 'Hear! All ye people. Anne was beloved of the Sun, but like a true Penelope, a true Cornelia, she was cold to his fiery love-making.' She was twice a queen and great a hundred-fold, her epitaph read: 'Never queen like her enriched all France; That is what it is to make a great alliance.'

As king, Louis's rashness had turned to caution and his prodigality to thrift. Though he still harbored the Valois dream of an empire beyond the Alps, the Italian wars did not retard France's growing internal prosperity nor prevent the administrative reforms that were contributing to her welfare. A good sovereign for the most part, he was conscientiously concerned with those domestic improvements for which he was called 'le Père du Peuple.' The financial measures of the reign were in fact those of his chief minister Cardinal d'Amboise, but both the censure and the credit for them went to Louis. When disgruntled courtiers criticized the frugality of the royal household, he replied that their sneers at his parsimony were preferable to the groans of the people at his extravagance. As is frequently true of reformers, he overemphasized his sobriety to the point where the capital began to reflect it. No one was displeased when marriage to Mary lightened the atmosphere and gaiety returned to the Court.

If Louis had been a handsome man when he married Anne, as the courtier-chronicler Pierre de Bourdeille, Seigneur de Brantôme, asserts, he had certainly ceased to be so by the time Mary first saw him. In his youth, '*très brave et très vaillant*,' time and experience had taken their toll, but that he had become a doddering old man, sickly and revolting, is unlikely. The man who had once been admired by women seems to have acquired the qualities, so often present in an older man, of graciousness, kindness, and understanding. Perréal's portrait of him, probably that presented to Henry VIII in 1514, shows a strong face, one of character and resolution. Perréal portrays a monarch of late middle age, with features distinct and even striking, the face a little heavy and sagging but in no way deathlike. The portrait is undated but was undoubtedly painted some years before being sent to England. All reliable reports of Louis's conduct after his marriage to Mary point to his being a man whom she could respect, and who might hope to win her confidence and affection.

His bodily ills are well documented, but no diagnosis of their exact nature is possible. Among other things he suffered from chronic rheumatoid arthritis, known as the 'gout' or *podagra*, which might affect the hands as well as the feet. There are numerous varieties of this disorder, which was common in the sixteenth century, and about which so little was then known. Medical science today knows a great deal about its symptoms but, like the common cold, not much more about its causes than the physicians of the seventeenth century knew when its various manifestations were so vividly described by Thomas Sydenham. While not necessarily producing gout, excessive quantities of rich food and alcohol have a recognized effect, and Louis XII had overindulged in almost everything. Medical science being what it was then, the saying 'once gouty, always gouty' was generally true.

Louis's health never fully recovered from the results of an adventurous life and three years of imprisonment. His abandonment in middle age of the pleasures he had before carried so lightly and his increased consciousness of the responsibility of a ruler originated in growing ill-health; in his later years he was constantly referred to by those who had seen him as old, infirm, and the victim of disease. Some thought he had had smallpox, others that he was afflicted with scurvy or elephantiasis; his skin condition in conjunction with attacks of gout made him appear prematurely feeble long before his third marriage. Although a few in the sixteenth century lived to old age—Burghley died at seventy-eight, the second and third Dukes of Norfolk at over eighty, Bishop Cuthbert Tunstall at eighty-five, and the first Marquis of Winchester at eighty-seven—the majority of men were spent by fifty-five or sixty. Louis was as lucky as most of his contemporaries: Ferdinand who was ten years his senior survived him by just over a year, and Maximilian by three years at the age of sixty; Henry VII had died at exactly Louis's age. Mary's generation fared no better: Charles Brandon lived to be sixty-one; Wolsey and Henry VIII, fifty-five, and Francis I, fifty-three; the sickly Charles V lived five years longer.

By 1514 Louis was resigned to his condition. More than once before Anne's death he had taken to his bed very sick, at least twice being expected not to recover. His gout grew progressively worse, confining him for days at a time, during a campaign sometimes making him incapable of remaining with his troops. When in the summer of 1513 he led them against the English, the comment was made that his heart was stronger than his legs; the same autumn he had to be brought to the field in a carriage. In the English parliament of the following January a member called attention to the 'increasing infirmities' of the French sovereign, contrasting him to Henry VIII who 'is like the rising sun, that grows brighter and stronger every day.'

It is difficult for anyone accustomed to present-day standards of beauty to conjure up an image of Mary as her contemporaries saw her. While individual taste varied then as now, the ideal female type was fairly clearly drawn. To the moralist and philosopher beauty of soul and traits of character were paramount, with form, manners, and grace playing strong subordinate roles, the whole summed up in the phrase '*honnête dame.*' To the more practical-minded physical beauty was not only admired for itself, but as the chief cause of love its essence lay in its ability to beguile the male. More men would have agreed with Malchiorre Zoppio than with the aesthetes that attraction of the sexes without the presupposition of conjugation was not really love; love as provoked by beauty, he argued, should end in embraces, 'and most lovers will be found of the same opinion.'

The most elaborate account of the physical attributes of feminine perfection in the sixteenth century comes from *The Beauty of Women*, written shortly before 1543. Its author, the Italian Agnolo Firenzuola, saw the ideal woman as 'a harmony inscrutably resulting from the composition, union, and commission of divers members, each of which shall in itself be well proportioned and in a certain sense beautiful, but which before they combine to make one body, shall be different and discrepant among themselves.' The sum total was to make her 'universally pleasing' to the eye; he presented the composite woman, and his concept of her—from the crown of her head to the soles of her smallish feet, not bony but

white as alabaster—seems to have met with little refutation at the
time.

Burckhardt's version of Firenzuola's word-picture is worth quoting at length :

He requires that the hair should be thick, long, and locky; the forehead serene, and twice as broad as high; the skin bright and clear but
not of a dead white; the eyebrows dark, silky, most strongly marked
in the middle, and shading off towards the ears and the nose; the
white of the eye faintly touched with blue, the iris not actually black,
though all the poets praise 'occhi neri' as a gift of Venus, despite that
even goddesses were known for their eyes of heavenly blue, and that
soft, joyous, brown eyes were admired by everybody. The eye itself
should be large and full, and brought well forward; the lids white, and
marked with almost invisible tiny red veins; the lashes neither too
long, nor too thick, nor too dark. The hollow round the eye should
have the same colour as the cheek. The ear, neither too large nor too
small, firmly and neatly fitted on, should show a stronger colour in
the winding than in the even parts, with an edge of the transparent
ruddiness of the pomegranate. The temples must be white and even,
and for the most perfect beauty ought not to be too narrow. The red
should grow deeper as the cheek gets rounder. The nose, which chiefly
determines the value of the profile, must recede gently and uniformly
in the direction of the eyes; where the cartilage ceases, there may
be a slight elevation, but not so marked as to make the nose acquiline,
which is not pleasing in women; the lower part must be less strongly
coloured than the ears, but not of a chilly whiteness, and the middle
partition above the lips lightly tinted with red. The mouth . . . rather
small, and neither projecting to a point, nor quite flat, with the lips
not too thin, and fitting neatly together; an accidental opening, that
is, when the woman is neither speaking nor laughing, should not
display more than six upper teeth . . . a dimple in the upper lip, a
certain fullness of the under lip, and a tempting smile in the left
corner of the mouth. . . . The teeth should not be too small, regular,
well marked off from one another, and of the colour of ivory; and
the gums must not be too dark or even like red velvet. The chin is to
be round, neither pointed nor curved outwards, and growing slightly
red as it rises; its glory is the dimple. The neck should be white and
round and rather long than short, with the hollow and the Adam's
apple but faintly marked; and the skin at every movement must show
pleasing lines. The shoulders . . . broad, and in the breadth of the
bosom [is] the first condition of its beauty. No bone may be visible
upon it, its fall and swell must be gentle and gradual, its colour

'*candidissmo.*' The leg should be long and not too hard in the lower parts, but still not without flesh on the shin, which must be provided with white, full calves. [This is one of the few attempts to include the legs as playing any part in feminine beauty.] The arms are . . . white, and in the upper parts tinted with red; in their consistence fleshy and muscular, but still soft as those of Pallas, when she stood before the shepherd on Mount Ida—in a word, ripe, fresh, and firm. The hand should be white, especially towards the wrist, but large and plump, feeling soft as silk, the rosy palm marked with a few, but distinct and not intricate lines; the elevations in it should be not too great, the space between thumb and forefinger brightly coloured and without wrinkles, the fingers long, delicate, and scarcely at all thinner towards the tips, with nails clear, even, not too long nor too square, and cut so as to show a white margin about the breadth of a knife's back.

The general impression is of order and balance, of color graduatting from white to crimson, and of form that was not to be at the expense of softness and femininity. A sensitive mouth, long, slender neck, straight and white, arched eyebrows, and '*beaux tetins,*' small and high but well rounded, appear to have been greatly admired, though the physician Jacques Ferrand states in his *Erotomania* that national preference varied. 'The Italian desires to have her [his woman] thick, well set, and plump,' he says, 'the German prefers one that is strong: the Spaniard loves a wench that is lean: and the French, one that is soft, delicate, and tender.'

Descriptions of the model woman are in inclusive detail. A French version, *De la Louange et Beauté des Dames*, lists thirty characteristics of perfect beauty, grouped into threes. With such a yardstick any damsel could evaluate her own natural assets, though she could improve on them but little:

Three things white: skin, teeth, and hands
Three things black: eyes, eyebrows, and eyelids
Three things red: lips, cheeks, and nails
Three things long: body, hair, and hands
Three things short: teeth, ears, and feet
Three things broad: bosom, brow, and space between the eyebrows
Three things narrow: mouth, waist, and ankles
Three things large: arm, thigh, and calf
Three things slender: fingers, hair, and lips
Three things small: breasts, nose, and head.

More provocative is Anthony Fitzherbert's English appraisal of the ten basic 'properties of a woman' set forth in *The Boke of Husbandrye* in 1523: the female who would snare her man must be 'hard of words' yet 'merry of cheer,' 'wellpaced' and 'easy to leap upon,' and though 'well stirring under a man,' high metal required her to be forever 'chowing on the bridle.'

Though not the extraordinary beauty portrayed in ambassadors' reports, Mary was, nevertheless, much admired. Perhaps the most objective critics, the Italians were enchanted by her gracious manners, natural dignity, and quiet behavior. The Venetians, who especially admired English woman, praised her 'splendid beauty'; Hieronymo Savorguano found them 'all extremely handsome,' more so than any he had seen except the women of Augsburg. The contrast in type between the tall, blonde English and their own Mediterranean people accounted for some of their enthusiasm. Niccollo di Favri of the Venetian embassy was struck by the unusual appearance of both the men and women of England; in particular, he thought the latter 'very beautiful and good-tempered.' Such statements can obviously not be accepted entirely at face value. Most writers describing Mary Tudor during the period 1512 to 1515 were either biased or had an ulterior motive for their poetic praise. Though later French historians are less enthusiastic, they agree that she must have merited her reputation at the time. 'A rare trait in a woman so highly placed,' wrote René de Maulde La Clavière in 1895, 'Mary of England merited her reputation. . . . She was a distinguished person . . . blonde, without being colorless, of slightly accented features, but regular, with an air of grandeur and much elegance; of a distinctly English rose-colored beauty.'

Margaret of Savoy, who before Mary's marriage to Louis had every reason to seek the truth about her, received numerous reports from Dutch agents in England. In March, 1514, Philippe Sieur de Brégilles wrote that he had seen Mary for the first time on Lent Sunday, dressed in the Milanese fashion. 'I think never man saw a more beautiful creature, nor one having so much grace and sweetness, in public and in private.' Concerning certain rumors about her, he told Margaret that she was not oversized: 'I dare say to you,' he later reported, 'that if only she were as strong as all other women, then Monsieur [Louis XII] would come to the end of it, for there are not any so small nor so sweet as she.' Ambassador Gerard de Pleine, unwilling to trust his first impressions, waited to write to the Archduchess until after he had seen Mary several times. 'I can assure you that she is one of the most beautiful young women in the world,' he wrote. 'I think I never saw a more charming creature. She is very graceful. Her deportment in dancing and conversation is as pleasing as you could desire. There is nothing gloomy or melancholy about her. I am sure if you could see her you would never rest until you had her over. I assure you that she has been well educated.' He added that she had a good figure and unusual beauty : 'I had imagined that she would have been very tall,' he concluded, 'but she is of middling height, and, as I think, a much better match for the Prince, than I had heard or could have believed before I saw her.' 'Very beautiful,' pronounced Pasqualigo, 'tall, fair, of a light complexion with a colour, and most affable and graceful'; nor did it surprise him that she seemed to the old King like a 'nymph from heaven.' An unknown critic comments that she was 'generally considered handsome and well-favoured,' though her eyebrows and eyes were too light, and her figure 'slight, rather than defective from corpulence.' Later chroniclers simply echo the admiration of Mary's contemporaries, that she was 'one of the fairest ladies of the world.' Marco Antonio Contarini, modestly admitting that he had seen many beautiful faces, described her in the early spring of 1515 before her return to England as a most beautiful and attractive person: 'The Queen widow is a very handsome woman,' he wrote from Paris, 'dressed all in black, with a white kerchief on her head and under her chin like a nun.'

The lovely red-gold hair which was her most striking asset must have attracted attention in France, where red hair was thought to be a sign of either haughtiness or passion; that these qualities were considered unbecoming in a woman may explain the fact that though the luxurious quality of her hair was noted, not a single reference was made to its color.

The Court remained at Abbeville for a full week after the wedding, its departure for Paris being delayed by a renewed attack of gout which laid Louis low. He and his nobles eventually left on the sixteenth of October, Mary staying there a few days longer, perhaps to adjust to her new position and recover from the only rift that occurred between them during her brief union with Louis. The dismissal of Mary's English attendants immediately after the wedding celebration was the cause of it. His flare-up of gout may have increased Louis's irritability at the interference of the Queen's chief lady-in-waiting, to whom he had taken an almost immediate dislike, but feelings ran high enough to threaten political repercussions in London. Although he had approved the list of Mary's personal staff, he was taken aback by the descent of several hundred of her countrymen on his Court. Even her permanent entourage of more than a hundred was large enough according to French standards to constitute an unnecessary drain on the exchequer. In addition, all her staff were English and included no trusted French personnel to counteract their foreign influence. Instinct told him that this was not a wholesome situation, but one to be corrected immediately before it developed into an impossible problem.

Louis's previous queen had earlier undermined his authority with a household of Breton attendants, and with this still rankling in his memory he summarily dismissed almost all Mary's English staff, including Lady Guildford. Sister of Sir Nicholas Vaux, Lord Vaux of Harrowden, Joan Guildford was the widow of Sir Richard Guildford, controller of the household and trusted friend of Henry VII. As a protégée of the Countess of Richmond she had served the family for a long time, first as Mary's governess and now as her chief Lady of Honor. Affectionately called 'Mother Guildford,' she was not only the senior of all the Queen's ladies-in-waiting but her mentor and bosom companion as well. Her affection for and complete dependence upon Lady Guildford, rather than anger at the King's initiative, were the real reasons for Mary's alarm.

As first related to Henry and Wolsey, this action had the appearance of a personal affront to Mary, and if such were really so was grounds for formal protest to be lodged. Mary herself was both indignant and frightened. Visions of being in a foreign country attended by no mature woman whom she could trust appalled her. Understandably she spilled out her grief to Henry, the appeal not of a queen but of a lonely, homesick sister :

My good Brother, as heartily as I can I recommend me unto your Grace, marvelling much that I never heard from you since our departing, so often as I have sent and written unto you. And now am I left most alone in effect, for on the morn after marriage my chamberlain and all other men servants were discharged, and in like wise my mother Guildford with other my women and maidens, except such as never had experience nor knowledge how to advertise or give me counsel in any time of need, which is to be feared more shortly than your grace thought at the time of my departing, as my mother Guild-

12   Marie d'Angleterre, Queen to Louis XII

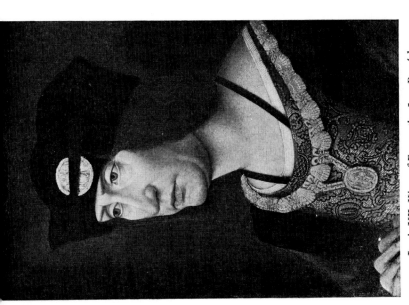

11   Louis XII, King of France, by Jean Perréal

Ouuie ſa paix entre dieu et les hõmes.
Par le moyen de la vierge marie.
ffut iadis faicte ainſy a preſet ſõmes.
Bourgoys frãcoys deſchargez de noſſõmes
Car marie auecq nous ſe marie.

13   Mary's reception in Paris, 1514, from Pierre Gringore's Pageants

ford can more plainly shew your Grace than I can write, to whom I
beseech you to give credence. And if it may be by any mean possible
I humbly require you to cause my said mother Guildford to repair
hither once again. For else if any chance hap other than weal I shall
not know where nor by whom to ask any good counsel to your
pleasure nor yet to mine own profit. I marvel much that my lord
of Norfolk would at all times so lightly grant everything at their
request here. I am well assured that when you know the truth of
everything as my mother Guildford can shew you, ye would full little
have thought I should have been thus intreated; that would God
my lord of York [Wolsey] had come with me in the room of Norfolk;
for then I am sure I should have been left much more at my heartsease
than I am now. And thus I bid your Grace farewell with . . . [letter
mutilated] as ever had Prince: and more heartsease than I have now.
[I beseech] give credence to my mother Guildford.

By your loving sister,
Mary, Queen of France
[Abbeville, October 12, 1514]

Obviously Mary was afraid that Louis might die unexpectedly,
leaving her stranded in France at the mercy of Louise of Savoy and
Francis, both of whom she was soon to have every reason to distrust. This is her first allusion to any suspicion of Norfolk's motive
for supporting Louis and thereby working at cross-purposes with
the Archbishop of York; that he had not been consulted in the
latter's selection of Mary's attendants had increased his resentment of Wolsey's growing influence.

Henry was unlikely to pay much attention to her entreaties
since his relations with Louis had never been better, and he was
ill disposed to spoil their rapport. Realizing this, Mary turned
instinctively to Wolsey, her letter to him bearing the same date
as that which she wrote to Henry. Confiding to him that Norfolk
was treating her indifferently, she affirmed that her one hope lay
in his intercession. Her chief sorrow was the loss of Lady Guildford,
the precise person who Louis was determined should go. Mary's
desolation at parting with the woman who had become almost a
mother to her was understandable; her support must have seemed
indispensable, and Mary rightly felt her to be the only person
there in whom she could freely confide.

I have not yet seen in France any lady or gentlewoman so necessary
for me as she is, nor yet so meet to do the King my brother service

as she is. And for my part, my lord, as you love the King, my brother, and me, find the means that she may in all haste come hither again, for I had as lief lose the winning I shall have in France to lose her counsel when I shall lack it, which is not like long to be required as I am sure the noblemen and gentlemen can shew you more than becometh me to write in this matter.

It is quite possible by this time that Mary had already had medical advice on Louis's condition, and been warned that he might not have long to live.

Wolsey did what he could, explaining to Louis in excellent French that Lady Guildford had been chosen for her training and experience, her knowledge of French, and her affection for the Queen. Venturing his *'simple et petite'* opinion, Wolsey diplomatically requested that she be reinstated, inasmuch as she had given up retirement in order to serve the Queen when she most needed her:

. . . and I have no doubt, Sire, [he concluded,] that when you will have known her well, you will find the lady wise, honourable, and discreet, very anxious and quick to pursue and accomplish in all things possible to her your wishes and desires, in all that you will order and commend to her, whatsoever it would profit you, or may be done to the contrary; as I have written more fully to monseigneur, your chamberlain, in order to explain it to you for my part. . . .

By the time the letter was received Lady Guildford was already in Boulogne, where she had been instructed to remain until the matter was settled.

Louis, however, remained adamant, and there was no further argument. In stating his case to Lord Worcester, he divulged the real reason for Lady Guildford's dismissal:

For in nowise he would not have her about his wife, also he said that he is a sickly body and not at all times that [he would] be merry with his wife to have any strange wo[man there] but one that he is well acquainted with [and before whom he] durst be merry, and that he is sure [the Queen his] wife is content withal for he hath set [about her neither] lady or gentlewoman to be with her for her [Mistress but her] servants and to obey her commandments.

With that, Worcester reported, 'he swore that there was never man that better loved his wife than he did, but rather than have such a woman about her he had liefer be without her.' He was sure that his good brother, the King of England, would understand his position. Worcester concluded his account of the interview with an expression of hope that the marriage would be successful: 'I pray God that so it may continue to his pleasure.'

Henry appreciated Louis's predicament, nor was Mary blind to the reasons for his objections, later admitting that however much she loved Mother Guildford she was satisfied without her and willing to abide by her husband's decision. Obedience was a wifely obligation, and so she made a virtue of necessity.

In the end Louis was generous enough, permitting his wife to retain several gentlemen, including her almoner, Dr. James Denton; her master of horse, Richard Blount; her physician, Maître Guillaume; Arthur Pole, brother of Lord Montague; and Dorset's brother, Lord Edward Grey. A few others to whom she had become especially attached stayed on: usher, grooms, pages, and minor attendants. The ladies of the bedchamber were reduced to a small staff of six: Lady Elizabeth Grey, Elizabeth Grey of Wilton, Anne Jerningham, Mary Fiennes, Anne Boleyn, and Lady Jane Bourchier, who had come over with her father Lord Berners, chamberlain to the Queen. The senior position of Lady of Honor was given to an experienced woman of the French Court, Madame d'Aumont, while among her new companions were Lady Claude, Mary of Luxembourg, and Marguerite de Valois.

Hall's indictment, that those dismissed suffered acutely before finding further employment and that some of them died or went insane on their homeward journey, is entirely without foundation. In consideration of their service most of them were given gifts before they left, the eight trumpeters receiving more than two hundred crowns apiece in cash. Mary herself spent six hundred crowns on presents for her gentlewomen, some of whom were awarded pensions by Henry VIII upon their return. Lady Guildford fared better than most; eight years widowed, she already received fifty marks annually in dower right from her former husband. To this was added a life pension of twenty pounds a year as soon as she returned to England, and another forty pounds yearly a few months later. Her second marriage to Sir Anthony Pointe was as successful as her first; she died in 1538, five years later than Mary.

In spite of the bedchamber crisis the relationship between husband and wife was close and cordial. Though gout delayed Louis's departure, it was suspected in part to be an excuse to linger with the Queen. A rather curious picture of the 'happy couple' emerges from the records, Louis lying on his couch with Mary seated nearby, singing and playing the lute to keep him amused. It was thought to be good medicine for the King, such 'wondrous pleasure did he take therein.' English agents reiterated what a good queen Mary was, and how well liked by everyone, telling Henry that she was continually with the King, who could not bear her to leave his side. As for Louis, 'he maketh as mu[ch], as she reporteth to us herself, as it is possible for any man to make of a lady.' When Suffolk first observed them together he was struck with their cordiality to each other, assuring Henry that no queen ever behaved herself better or more honorably than she, and that no man could adore a woman more than he did her, 'on account of her loving manner.'

Such misgivings as Henry may have had about French acceptance of his sister were soon removed. No hint of Tudor anger or stubbornness marred the conjugal perfection of her conduct with the King. She wrote to her brother just after arriving in Paris to thank him for his continued counsel: 'How lovingly the King my husband dealeth with me, the Lord Chamberlain, with other of your ambassadors, can clearly inform your Grace, whom I beseech your Grace heartily to thank for their great labours and pains that they have taken here for me; for I trust they have made a substantial and a perfect end.' Henry's response was to Louis:

> We have heard how she conducts herself towards you, in all humility and reverence, so that you are well content with her, and we have conceived very great joy, pleasure, and comfort, in hearing and understanding this. And our will, pleasure, and intention is, that in so acting, she should persevere from good to better, if she wish and desire to have our love and fraternal benevolence; and thus we gave her advice and counsel, before her departure from us, and we make no doubt that you will, day by day, find her more and more all that she ought to be to you, and that she will do everything which will be to your will, pleasure, and contentment.

Louis was not only a 'genteel companion' with whom Mary mostly had her way but a generous husband, lavish with his gifts to her. In a long letter to Wolsey, Worcester sent a glowing account of his largesse:

My Lord, I assure you he [Louis] hath a marvellous mind to content and please the Queen . . . and is devising new collars and goodly gear for her. . . . He showed me the goodliest and the richest sight of jewels that ever I saw. I would never have believed it if I had not seen it; for I assure you all that ever I have seen is not to compare to fifty-five great pieces that I saw of diamonds and rubies, and seven of the greatest pearls that I have seen, besides a great number of other goodly diamonds, rubies, and great pearls. The worst of the second sort of stones be priced and cost two thousand ducats. Of the principal stones there hath been refused for one of them one hundred thousand ducats. And when he had showed me all, he said that all should be for his wife. And another coffer also was there that was full of goodly girdles, collars, chains, bracelets, beads of gold, and other divers goodly jewels. . . . I make no doubt but she shall have a good life with him, with the Grace of God. . . .

Mary paid in kisses for her jewels, forgiving Louis's parsimony in dealing them out a few at a time: 'My wife shall not have all at once, but at divers times,' he told Worcester.

No one was anxious but Francis of Angoulême and his mother, Louise of Savoy. He, more objective and optimistic than she, found his chance of the throne very good: 'I am certain, unless I have been greatly deceived, that it is impossible for the King and Queen to have children.'

CHAPTER TEN

The French Queen

Women . . . are harbours of man's health,
Pleasures for night and comforts for the day:
What are fair women but rich nature's wealth?

Robert Greene, 'The Song of Arion,' *Orpharion*

MARY'S last known letter from Abbeville was written on the twentieth of October. A few days afterward she left to join Louis at Beauvais, about fifty miles outside Paris, where his gout had attacked him again, and it was there immediately upon arrival in France that Charles Brandon, Duke of Suffolk, had his first audience; the King was lying down, Mary sitting at his side. Toward the end of the month Louis was well enough to travel again, so they resumed their journey, arriving at St. Denis on the thirty-first. They had a pleasant trip during which Louis spoke of his approaching Italian expedition, and paused at each town long enough for the Queen to free all prisoners, an ancient privilege which she exercised as part of her royal prerogative; Mary was enthusiastic for the foray into Italy because Louis had promised to take her to Venice after her coronation. A friend of the Venetian Signory, who tried to keep abreast of all French news, noted that Louis was temporarily free from gout and keen on his military plans, and that he had slept with his wife two nights on the way to Paris.

The first two days at St. Denis being All Saints' Day and All Souls' Day were spent quietly. Since by custom an uncrowned Queen of France could not enter Paris, the coronation took place in this suburb just north of the city, at the abbey church there on the fifth of November, the first Sunday of the month, witnessed by a large throng of lords and ladies who had ridden out from the Court. Of all the English representatives present at the wedding, only the Earl of Worcester, Docwra, West, and Thomas Wriothesley remained in France to attend the coronation. Since then, however, Suffolk and Dorset had come from England ostensibly to engage in the jousts which were to be a major feature of the wedding celebrations, but also secretly to negotiate with Louis for a new alliance. They had ridden to Paris with Francis ahead of the King and Queen in order to make final arrangements for the tournament, and on the way had paused for a boar hunt at which their host courteously allowed them the kill. Exhibiting unusual strength, Suffolk slew one wild boar with such a powerful thrust of his sword that he bent it, while Dorset finished another with a spear. They had arrived at St. Denis with the four other Englishmen a couple of days early to discuss the meeting of the two sovereigns in the spring. Though the French were 'somewhat agreeable' the exact time and place were not definitely decided, but tentatively set for early April, somewhere between Boulogne and Calais.

The coronation itself was simple compared to the elaborate Parisian reception the following day. Francis led Mary to the altar, where she was anointed by Cardinal René de Prie, Bishop of Bayeux, who invested her with a ring, scepter, and rod of justice before crowning her. She was then conducted to a throne erected in the sanctuary, where she heard High Mass and received the sacrament. To relieve her of its weight Francis held the heavy matrimonial crown over her head during the service, after which she joined the King and their guests for dinner. That she was crowned 'right honourably' is recorded, but no mention is made of her dress or appearance. It was not Mary who immortalized the fifth of November.

Louis left St. Denis early next morning to see that everything was ready at the capital, to be followed a few hours later by Mary and her retinue. Paris in the sixteenth century was a city like no other, and Mary instinctively shared her countrymen's dislike of that center of foreign 'wickedness,' whose temptations were so well known to the English traveler. About five times the size of London, it was the chief city of Europe: big, noisy, violent, dirty Paris, a sprawling metropolis where brigandage was rife and assassination commonplace. To Charles Brandon, who had no stomach for things foreign, the town was to become a 'stinking prison,' the embodiment of all his troubles. In comparison with London's seventy thousand souls, its teeming population was a fusion of the divers elements of late medieval society: artisans and peers, bumping shoulders with merchants, vagabonds, hucksters, students, and monks, roamed its narrow, crooked streets. Danger lurked everywhere. Few individuals, whether minstrel, student, harlot, soldier, charlatan, or clerk, eschewed violence; but far more feared than they were the organized mobs, such as the '*mauvais garçons*,' who pillaged the city and terrorized its inhabitants. Paris was dominated by the Court, which visitors reported to be a gourmet's delight, with from two to four dozen different dishes of meat served at every meal. Cheek by jowl with this plenitude the town harbored within its walls between eight and nine thousand poor without visible means of support.

'*Paris sans pair*,' Thomas Platter called it at the end of the century, a world apart; not only was the air mild and agreeable but its climate wholesome and regular. The praise was not always so extravagant, but all sixteenth-century critics considered Paris unique. 'Paris is the chief town and capital of the most fertile kingdom of France,' reads a pictorial atlas of the period. Owing to its incredible size, with multitudes of nobles, merchants, citizens, and students, 'it is superior not merely to all the cities of France and Italy but also to those of the rest of Europe.' Italians admired its pomp and ostentation but hated its filth; a member of the distinguished Contarini family of Venice, Marco Antonio, described it as 'more muddy than any other town; in fact, it stinks of mud.' Then, as if in compensation, he adds: 'there is much silk; the whole Court dresses in silk; even the pages trail it on the ground.'

This was the city to which Mary was introduced on November 6, 1514. As described by the humanist Pierre Gringore, who was officially assigned to report it for posterity, her entry into Paris was magnificent. A large gathering of merchants, town officials, and university dignitaries met her at Porte St. Denis and led her into the city where the King waited at the Palais Royal. Glittering in a diamond-studded crown and riding in a beautiful litter, Mary was again escorted by Francis, who also was clad in gold and diamonds. Heralds, guardsmen, musicians, ladies-in-waiting, and virtually the whole Court rode behind them. The pageants staged along her route to the Palace were unique even among French spectacles, designed to surpass those presented to Anne of Brittany upon her entry into the city in 1504. There were seven pageants, three sponsored by the municipality and four by private organizations. In the first, wafted by the four winds of classical antiquity, a large ship represented Mary crossing the Channel; the city of Paris guided the vessel on its true course, while aloft in the rigging mariners sang the praises of the Queen:

> Noble Lady, welcome to France,
> Through you we now shall live in joy and pleasure,
> Frenchmen and Englishmen live at their ease,
> Praise to God, who sends us such a blessing!

To which an orator eloquently replied:

> Most illustrious, magnanimous Princess,
> Paris reveres and honors you
> And presents this ship to your nobility,
> Which is under the King's governance.
> Grains, wines, and sweet liqueurs are therein,
> Which the winds propel by divine ordinance.
> All men of good will
> Receive you as Queen of France.

Peace was the dominant motif:

> To Mary, who has replaced war
> By peace, friendship, and alliance,
> Between the kings of France and England.

In the last tableau in front of the Palais Royal, the angel Gabriel presided over the Garden of France, where shepherds sang of truth and justice:

> As the peace between God and man,
> By the intervention of the Virgin Mary,
> Once was made, so now we,
> The French bourgeois are relieved of our burdens;
> Because Mary has married with us.
> Through her, justice and peace join
> In the fields of France and the countryside of England;
> Since the bonds of love hold in restraint arms,
> We have acquired for ourselves, equally,
> Mary in heaven and Mary on earth.

The pageants were followed by a long reception by the University at Notre Dame de Paris, where after High Mass Mary was welcomed by the Archbishop of Paris. From there she returned to the Palais Royal for a state banquet. It was six o'clock before the diners assembled, by which time she had been subjected to the ordeal of continuous public appearance for eight or nine hours; the popular report that she fell asleep before the banquet was over and was carried to her rooms could well be true. Louis, no longer accustomed to such strenuous hours, had long since retired. The next afternoon she joined him at the Hôtel des Tournelles, where they rested until the Grand Tournament which was to begin the following Monday, November 13, 1514.

The tourney in Mary's honor was Francis' idea, originally conceived as a series of friendly jousts between French and English nobles to take place at Abbeville after the wedding. Postponed in favor of a more brilliant Parisian setting, its pristine simplicity was lost, and it grew into an elaborate Renaissance spectacle of the kind that Francis so delighted to sponsor. Resolved that it should equal anything Henry VIII could produce, he hoped also to display his own dexterity while discrediting the reputation of the English as the best jousters in Europe. As the opening date approached, public interest became excitement, the tournament having assumed the nature of an international contest in which not only sporting skill but patriotic pride were at stake. On the court calendar it overshadowed all else.

In England every effort was made to assure the success of her champions, who were carefully chosen from among the best lances of the realm : Sir Edmund Howard; Sir Edward Neville; Sir Giles Capell; Sir Thomas Cheyney; Sir William Sidney; Sir Henry Guildford, the son of Joan Guildford; Thomas Grey, Marquis of Dorset; and Charles Brandon, Duke of Suffolk. The latter two headed the group, going over disguised in gray coats and hoods to avoid recognition. Guildford as Master of Revels took over twenty-four yeomen of the guard and a dozen English horses, and he and Howard were liberally rewarded for their pains with grants of one hundred pounds each; some contestants were given money to buy coursers and equipment after their arrival in Paris, but Suffolk, among others, took his own horses and gear, having been granted an allowance of one thousand pounds to equip himself for the journey. Thomas Wriothesley, who had traveled with Mary, had remained in France to take charge of local arrangements. Francis was responsible for the French team, speaking for himself and nine other challengers when he pledged to meet all 'answerers,' both afoot and on horseback. As organized under the complicated rules of procedure, numerous courses were run by each participant over a three-day period. The jousts proper consisted of individual combat, on horse with spears and on foot with lances and swords, after which was the general tournament, or *mêlée* at barriers, in which many knights, divided into parties, engaged simultaneously. Altogether there were 305 combatants, some of whom, one chronicler dryly observed, 'were slain and not spoken of.'

Lists had been erected in the Parc des Tournelles, and a huge stage built for the spectators. The whole Court was there, presided over by the King and Queen, convalescent Louis reclining on a couch with Mary and Claude at his side. Interrupted by heavy rain, the tourney continued intermittently until the twenty-third, although there were in reality only five full days of fighting. From the beginning popular interest centered on Francis and his brother-in-law the Duc d'Alençon, the French principals, and upon Suffolk and Dorset, the leaders of the English.

The tournament opened with the introduction of all knights, each in his turn galloping twice round the lists and pausing during the second lap to bow low before the royal stand, his plumes almost touching his saddle bow. This preliminary over, jousting began, Alençon and his group leading off. He distinguished himself by running ten consecutive courses, retiring only after receiving a minor hand injury. But it was Suffolk who carried off the first day's honors, running no fewer than fifteen courses in which he was the challenger for all but two. Several horses and one Frenchman were slain. On the second day Dorset and Suffolk both did well, shivering many spears, but again it was Suffolk who received special mention: in three successive rounds he had unhorsed his antagonist. Thereafter the going was rough for everyone. Reviewing the bouts on Saturday, the eighteenth, Dorset described them as fierce, the fighting as furious as he had ever experienced,

> . . . for there was divers times both horse and man overthrown, horses slain, and one Frenchman hurt that he is not like to live. My lord of Suffolk and I ran but the first day thereat, but put our aids thereto, because there was no noblemen to be put unto us, but poor men of arms and Scots, many of them were hurt on both sides, but no great hurt, and of our Englishmen none overthrown nor greatly hurt but a little of their hands. The Dolphin himself was a little hurt on his hand.

The climax was reached on Tuesday the twenty-first, when the fighting on foot began. Unable to take his place at the barriers, Francis sent in Dorset and Suffolk, who had previously agreed to act as his special aides, to fight alone against all comers. He hoped by this means to cause the defeat of the Englishmen, particularly Suffolk, and thus disparage his reputation as a jouster; already Brandon had won both the Queen's support and the applause of many of the French Court who realized that the Englishmen were being treated unfairly. Nonetheless, most spectators were prejudiced in favor of their own candidates, refusing to recognize the superiority of the English. Determined that by fair means or foul French prestige must be preserved, Francis resorted to subterfuge: a powerful German, taller and stronger than any of the Court, was substituted for a Frenchman and sent disguised into the fray to dispatch the English champion. Brandon suddenly found himself opposing a gigantic hooded figure who came at him so fiercely that he was momentarily taken aback, but rallying he turned near defeat into victory and by sheer strength took the man by the neck 'and pommeled [him] so about the head that the blood issued out of his nose.' When it was over the German was immediately spirited away before his identity could be discovered.

It was unquestionably a victory for the English. That a younger brother of Dorset's, a boy of barely nineteen, disarmed an opponent much larger and older than he, was recorded among other exploits by English witnesses. No Englishmen were killed and few injured; Dorset and his four brothers came through unscathed, while Suffolk's only souvenir of his ordeal with the German was a slight injury to one hand. Modest in assessing his own contribution, he told Wolsey that news of their success would come from others: 'blessed be God, all our English men sped well.' Louis, secretly pleased at Francis' discomfiture, conceded that Suffolk and Dorset 'did shame all France' and richly deserved the praise of their countrymen.

The finale of the coronation festivities and Mary's last ceremonial appearance as Queen of France came the day before the removal of the Court to Saint-Germain-en-Laye. A banquet was given for her at the Hôtel de Ville by the University of Paris, at which officials vied with one another in their toasts and flowery speeches in praise of the union of England and France. One orator congratulated her for being privileged to marry a monarch whose throne was secure; she was informed that no French king since Clovis had ever been killed in battle, murdered by his own people, or driven out of his land. It was not the first time that insinuations had been made to her by foreigners that England, unlike the more stable states of Continental Europe, was 'naturally prone to revolution.' Just then, however, she must have been too pleased with her ovation to feel annoyed. The people of Paris had turned out en masse to see her and such a crowd had gathered round the banquet hall that the official party, unable to enter at the front door, had been obliged to go through the porter's lodge and up a narrow stairway to the vestibule where the cream of Parisian society waited. A special guest, the future Cardinal Jerome Alexander, who was not unused to such *'repas pantagruélique,'* was impressed with its magnificence, never having seen at a single gathering so many distinguished people in such expensive clothes! No action or comment by the Queen passed unnoticed, and it was observed with approval that after enjoying the special dessert prepared for her, she thoughtfully requested that a portion be sent to the royal nursery at Vincennes for her little four-year-old stepdaughter Renée.

The dinner closed the court season. The dazzle of pageantry and the pursuit of pleasure behind it, capital society returned to its normal routine. Congratulations over, visitors and foreign embassies left, including the English ambassadors who were glad to go home to the familiar atmosphere of London. Only Suffolk remained behind to complete his special political assignment, though he too was anxious to leave, weary of his commission and the painstaking reports it required.

It is almost impossible to determine exactly what Suffolk was trying to do, in his confidential talks with Louis, much less to measure his achievement. His mission as set forth in a secret letter was, in fact, so extremely confidential that the 'charge' so frequently alluded to was never explicitly stated for fear that the dispatches might be intercepted and the project become known in Spain and Italy. Not only did Henry want continued friendship between England and France, but he also hoped for her assistance against Spain. On the one hand he needed French support for his claim to the kingdom of Castile by right of his queen, Catherine, and on the other, military assistance in his proposed attempt to drive Ferdinand out of Navarre. The justification for such aggression was punishment of the latter's perfidy in having repudiated his promises to both sovereigns. The projects were really inseparable, as Louis assumed them to be, so he tentatively agreed to support a bona fide invasion of Spain, providing negotiations failed. His price was a loan of 200,000 crowns and Henry's help in enforcing the French claim to Milan, all of which was carefully explained to Suffolk. It was rumored in Venice that the Duke would himself join the Italian expedition with six thousand English troops.

Though it is likely that neither Henry nor Louis took the agreement very seriously, it must be remembered that overt threats of war played a prominent part in the balance of European diplomacy. Resultant action would in any case depend upon what developments the new year brought forth. There was no formal treaty, since it was arranged that Henry and Louis should again confer upon details at their suggested meeting in the early spring. Neither of them could know then that this would never take place; by January Louis was dead and Francis had no intention of honoring his predecessor's commitments.

The success of the assignment was certainly not due to any intellectual skill on Suffolk's part. Finesse was not his forte. With a soldier's inability to grasp the finer aspects of diplomatic bargaining, he was completely uninterested in international intrigue. Essentially straightforward himself he was suspicious of subtlety in others; yet he possessed a charm of personality rare among his unsophisticated peers, which made him acceptable in all circles. Although Louis was obviously predisposed on Mary's account to accept whomever Henry sent over, he genuinely liked Suffolk, enjoying the novelty of his frank, good-natured approach to all problems. When it was suggested that John Stewart, Duke of Albany, long resident at the French Court and possible claimant to the Scottish throne, might be sent to Scotland to negotiate a better understanding there, Suffolk immediately shied away, insisting that he had no authority to meddle in such delicate matters. Louis appreciated such sincerity and the staunch loyalty that produced it, traits which were lacking in his young son-in-law. 'That big youngster will spoil everything,' he had recently remarked, thinking of all that he himself had tried to achieve for France and how little it meant to Francis. In contrast, Louis repeatedly affirmed his confidence in Suffolk—a fact which Brandon's colleagues were not slow to observe; the Duke 'has behaved himself well and wisely in all his matters,' reported Dorset, 'all things goeth well and to our master's honour.' Although Wolsey had every reason to be satisfied with his choice of ambassador, he did not let Suffolk forget that further ministerial advancement would depend largely upon him.

Mary played no part in these negotiations save that of keeping her husband in a receptive mood, and this she did with grace and skill. Just how much credit should be given to her perception and how much to the ceaseless efforts of Henry's embassy is hard to say, but the result was success. The King and council accepted her, even if Madame Louise and her friends did not. In appealing to De Longueville and other councilors for advice in her marital relations, if indeed it was her own idea, she showed a tact far beyond her years. As Suffolk reported to Wolsey, she sought their counsel

> . . . how she might best order her self to content the King, whereof she was most desirous; and in her should lack no good will; and because she knew well they were the men that the King loved and trusted, and knew best his mind, therefore she was utterly determined to love them and trust them, and to be ordered by their Counsel in all causes, for she knew well that those that the King loved must love her best, and she them.

Both Louis and his council were flattered, while at home Henry and Wolsey were delighted with her conduct. On the eve of her departure from Paris, Dorset confidently reported that the Queen 'continued her goodness and wisdom and increases in the favour of her husband and the Privy Council.' She was by Louis's own admission his 'greatest jewel,' and since their first quarrel over her servants had been given her own way in everything.

On November 27, 1514, the King and Queen journeyed to Saint Germain-en-Laye, staying for three weeks at his country palace there instead of at his childhood home, the Château de Blois, because of its nearness to the capital, where Mary intended to return for the winter season. He may even have hoped for some hunting, though his wife must have known what everyone else pretended to ignore, that he was much too ill for this strenuous sport.

After their return to Paris in December, Louis was desperately ill most of the time, and realizing that his end was near, resigned himself dejectedly to the sickbed. Though normal routine at the Hôtel des Tournelles was resumed, it deceived no one. Mary spent her time from day to day sitting with her husband, now continuously in bed, and chatting with Francis, who showed too little concern for his father-in-law's condition and too much for hers. While his behavior was outwardly correct, his sophisticated conversation laced with personal insinuations disturbed her; at this point she began to sense that without Louis's protection his heir could become a problem. It is unclear exactly what overtures Francis made, though Mary confided to both Dorset and Suffolk that they had not been wanting. It may have been his importunity that additionally prompted her to seek closer understanding with members of the council lest it ever prove necessary to curb him. His amorous pursuits were well known at Court, and his unmistakable admiration for Mary led speculative courtiers to wonder if perhaps she were to share with Madame de Châteaubriant a definite place in his philanderings.

Mary appears to have had no such intention. Her attitude toward Francis would have been clear to him had he not assumed that he was irresistible to women. He was a year older than she, and his obvious interest in her was doubtless flattering. Gracious, witty, affable, the handsome heir presumptive was not to be easily repulsed and she was in no position to alienate him, for if Louis died she would be hopelessly at his mercy. Remembering the unhappy situation of Catherine of Aragon when she was left widowed in a foreign country, without friends to guide her or status to give her requests any weight, Mary must have known that her brother would be no more helpful in such an eventuality than Catherine's father had been. Awareness of all this probably made her doubly cautious. Her only course, while he continued to live, was loyalty to the husband upon whose love and respect all else depended, and she never deviated from it.

Posterity has commonly accorded her a different character, described her as flippant, light-headed, impetuous, flirtatious—one author says she could be giddy in six languages—and deliberately irresponsible. Other writers, basing their inferences on Brantôme, who delighted in good gossip, have assumed that she was unfaithful to Louis in fact as well as in spirit. That Mary regarded her marriage as a joke or made a cuckold of her husband is far from likely. Had such been the case Henry VIII or Wolsey would have heard of it, for rumors traveled fast even in the sixteenth century and would have speedily found their way to England. Mary and Louis bore the brunt of many facetious remarks about their physical relationship, the Italians in particular circulating a number of salacious stories about them in 1514. Mary was said to lament her transference from one extreme to another when she jilted the Prince of Castile to marry the French King. The French themselves were equally unkind to the 'giddy girl.' The contemporary historian, Robert de la Marck, Seigneur de Fleuranges, Marshal of France, wrote vividly of the King in his last days as valiantly plunging towards the grave he had dug for himself in an effort to satisfy his young wife:

> The King left the palace and took lodgings at Tournelles in Paris because it had the best climate, and also he did not feel very strong, because he had desired to be a pleasing companion with his wife; but he deceived himself, as he was not the man for it; . . . inasmuch as he had for a long time been very sick, particularly with gout, and for five or six years he had thought that he would die of it . . . because he was given up by the doctors and he lived on a very strict diet which he broke when he was with his wife; and the doctors told him that if he continued he would die from his pleasure.

The picture flattered neither party. Parisian gossip rumored that Louis had been tricked by the English, that the 'young filly' sent him by Henry VIII was to be his undoing: 'an old man in love hugs death,' ran a proverb.

The records are singularly silent on the happenings of Louis's last weeks. Tradition would have it that the round of parties and state functions were resumed, and that without thought for his health or regard for the advice of his physicians, Louis recklessly dissipated his feeble energies to the last. Excesses in eating, drinking, and love-making are not for a sickly old man who for years has led a careful, abstemious life, with regular hours, plenty of sleep, and restricted activities. It is said, however, that whereas before he had dined at eight in the morning, he began doing so at midday; that accustomed to retiring at six in the evening he found himself staying up until midnight or later; that plain meals gave way to rich banquets; and that sleep was replaced by the forgotten pleasures of youth—dancing, riding, and hunting. Accepting such reports of the King's behavior at their face value, Francis' mother, who believed everything that she found to her liking, told her journal that '*ces amoureuses noces*' proved fatal.

It may have been so. Brantôme says it was Mary, whose youth was 'too much for him,' who caused Louis's death, and later historians have mostly accepted his interpretation. Though his death was undoubtedly hastened by overindulgence and unaccustomed activity, the picture has been overdrawn and is not entirely in character. In the beauty and vitality of his third queen Louis rediscovered the wish to live. Age and illness had mellowed him, and to Claude, his favorite daughter, and Mary, his young queen, he became kind and generous. His attempts to please might have been at times a little pathetic, but Worcester's flat assertion of his attachment to Mary was no exaggeration. 'My lord, I assure you,' he wrote to Wolsey, 'he hath a marvellous mind to content and please the Queen.'

Christmas came and went quietly that year. Though he was growing progressively worse the King's spirit remained undaunted, and on the twenty-eighth of December he summoned his waning energy to write to his 'good brother,' the English King, of the great compensation he continued to get from his marriage. The Queen, he told Henry, 'has hitherto conducted herself, and still does every day, towards me, in such manner that I cannot but be delighted with her, and love and honour her more and more each day; and you may be assured that I do, and ever shall, so treat her, as to give both her and you perfect satisfaction. . . .' Louis ended his letter by thanking Henry for Suffolk's good services: 'I beg you to believe that, independent of the place that I know he holds with you, and the love you bear him, his virtues, manners, politeness, and good condition, deserve that he should be received with even greater honour.' Little did the Duke then know how soon this praise would stand him in good stead.

It was Louis's last letter. Three days later he was dead. It is said that Mary fainted upon hearing the news, shocked no doubt and scared by her position as a childless widow. She had been married for eighty-two days. Before the news reached London, Henry had been further beset with misfortune: Catherine's delivery of another premature child.

The death of a sovereign is no ordinary event. As the bells of Notre Dame tolled for Louis on that New Year's Day in 1515, some were sad, some were glad, but many were concerned. For Louise the waiting was over. She had bided her time at Romorantin, seeking solace in the stars, where she believed the future might be written could she but read the signs aright. For nineteen years this imperious woman had curbed her jealous impatience, living only for the time when Francis would rule and her ambitions for her Caesar be realized. With the trembling exhaustion of Louis's snuffed-out life, her waiting ended. In her exaltation the intrepid Louise forgot the anxieties of the past, forgot even the pain in her gouty fingers, and rode the hundred miles to Paris within forty-eight hours in time to witness her son's coronation. The old King had died, not in the arms of his wife but in those of his successor, but if Francis cried his tears were not of compassion but of relief. The only real grief that day was Claude's. As the new Queen she took over at Court, while Mary stepped down to await at Cluny the biological proof or denial of her pregnancy.

In London an elaborate funeral service was held at St. Paul's, with hearse, candles, black cloth for the choir, and banner rolls. Nine prelates, seven nobles to act as mourners, and five heralds were appointed to attend the ceremony; extra labor was provided for the chandlers, the coffin-maker, bell-ringers, the court painter, and many other craftsmen on the royal payroll, all because the French King was dead. For one man there, life was completely altered: Charles Brandon, who had only returned to England at the end of November, went back to France on a second embassy, to become inextricably involved with the very Queen Dowager he was sent to serve.

Chronicler Fleuranges saw forebodings of evil in Louis's death: 'On which day was the most horrible weather that ever was seen; and I swear to you on my faith, that it was for sorrow for his death. . . .'

CHAPTER ELEVEN

The White Queen

Widows so soon wed
After their husbands be dead,
Having such haste to bed,
Saw I never.

John Skelton,
'The Manner of the World
Nowadays'

Two events marked the transition to the new reign, the burial of the old King and the coronation of the new. On the day of his death Louis's corpse was disemboweled, embalmed, and laid out in state in the great hall at Les Tournelles, with crown, robes, and scepter, as befitted a 'gentle prince who had done many fine things in his time.' The long vigil by paid monks, the seemingly endless line of spectators filing past for a last curious look at death and royalty joined in final transfiguration, and the requiems monotonously intoned each day, together evoked a mournful realization of the mortality of kings. The procession to Notre Dame for the funeral eulogy passed along streets lined with black: Paris mourned. The day after at the church of St. Denis, Louis was buried with Anne of Brittany, whom he had loved so well in life and mourned so bitterly and briefly.

There was nothing unseemly about Louis XII's funeral except the haste with which it was expedited. A minor altercation took place at the church as to who should keep the pall when it was over, for when fees were involved even the clergy were venal. Francis was equally covetous: having awaited his crown for so long he was impatient to have it on his head and, a prolonged wake being expensive, the mourning period was shortened. On the eleventh day, without fuss or attention, the staves of the household ministers were struck and with them was broken the old reign: 'The good King Louis, Father of his People, is dead; long live the King!'

Kings of France were traditionally crowned in the ancient city of Rheims, where stood the statue of St. Joan and the triumphal Mars Gate. Seat of the archiepiscopal palace built during Louis XII's reign, it was known too for a famous image of the Blessed Virgin erected on the site of Clovis' baptism by St. Remigius after his victory over the Alemanni. Since that venerated Christmas Day in 496 when holy oil was said to have been miraculously brought from heaven by a white dove, the legend had persisted that French kings anointed with oil from the sacred phial at Rheims were thrice blessed. It was there that Francis was crowned on the twenty-eighth of January, shortly before the English embassy arrived to congratulate him on his accession. After the triple benediction with its sacrosanct accompaniment of recognition, prayers, blessings, anointment with oil, enthronement, and homage by princes and peers, he was as hedged with divinity as ritual and religion could make him, subject only to God and the law. Like the saintly Louis IX of crusades and miracles he could, by the authority of St. Marcoule, touch for the 'king's evil.'

While Francis wooed his public and dispersed his favors, Mary as Queen Dowager was doomed to the seclusion of her mourning chamber, a precaution which was not a custom of her own country, but one whose implications she understood and fully appreciated. It was obviously vital to Francis that any question of her possible pregnancy should be settled before he assumed the throne, for if her hypothetical baby were male it would take precedence over all other claimants to the throne. Usually, therefore, the heir presumptive postponed his coronation until the last shadow of doubt had been removed. Francis had already prevailed upon Mary to tell him the truth of her condition, but Madame Louise was suspicious, and her doubts engendered distrust in others who feared that this foreign queen was capable of producing, if not a legitimate heir, then an adulterous one, as a means of strengthening her own position. Less skeptical than his mother, Francis had accepted Mary's word when she insisted that to the best of her belief she was not pregnant, and that he was free to go on with preparations for his coronation. Despite her reassurance, however, he was still compelled by convention to wait until the acid test of time confirmed her words.

Gossip at the French Court had whispered that Mary was with

child before Louis's death, and all through January Louise was sick with worry lest Francis yet be deprived of the throne. This was her sole reason for disliking Mary, and though she maintained a pretense of cordiality, it concealed the same secret antagonism that she had felt towards Louis's second queen. When Anne of Brittany had given birth to a son Louise was in a state of frustration until the day when she triumphantly confided to her diary that the child would not 'retard the exaltation of my Caesar, for he did not live.' Now with the crown virtually within his grasp, the threat had recurred. Francis himself does not seem to have been concerned; unhampered by one woman's suspicion of another he realized what his mother did not, that the young Queen Dowager was unversed in deception. Others, however, were less sure: at the beginning of the second week of February English ambassadors still sought the truth of her condition, but by the tenth the matter was settled. Henry was informed by them that 'there is no truth in the rumour that the French Queen, that now is, is with child. Her physicians do not believe it; and also at our [being there] we saw no great appearance thereof; [and when] we showed her that your Grace was right g[lad and] joyous that she was with child, she answered that it was not so as yet.'

The term of isolation imposed on Mary was an old safeguard in France, dating back to the death of Philip the Fair in 1314, whose three successors had died before heirs expectant were born, giving rise to the so-called Salic Law and the question of female succession. For six weeks of enforced retirement the royal widow remained in mourning, usually at the Hôtel de Cluny in Paris. Clad always in white, she was known as 'La Reine Blanche,' a childless widow-queen, as distinct from 'La Reine Mère.'

Cluny Palace, originally a Cluniac abbey, overlooked the river in the Rue des Mathurins St. Jacques. Its *'chambre de la reine blanche,'* while not large by modern standards, was handsomely appointed, but to one used to constant attention and companionship it must have been infinitely depressing. Since etiquette decreed that the sun never penetrate it, the long windows were kept heavily curtained; flickering candles by the mourning bed cast weird shadows on the black wall-hangings, peopling the morbid seclusion with unnatural shapes. In this macabre atmosphere Mary lay alone all day long, her darkened chamber silent, almost airless and virtually unheated, with no friend to whom she could pour out her troubled thoughts. Her few French attendants had been carefully selected by Louise and Marguerite d'Angoulême, who as self-appointed 'curators of the womb' continued to be suspicious of her every action; if not technically spies, these servants were chosen specifically to keep watch upon her contacts with the outside world. Under their guardianship Mary grew almost neurotically irritable and melancholy: loneliness bred misgiving; apprehension became despair. Writing from Cluny to her brother she lamented that sometimes she felt so very desolate that she '[wit] not wat for to do.'

Some historians have concluded that the tension and anxiety she experienced during this incarceration led to a protracted illness. Though positive proof of this is wanting, it is likely that she was on the brink of a nervous breakdown. While mentally well-balanced, she was high-strung and emotional, given to brooding and in later life to long fits of depression. If not actually ill, she did suffer with toothache during these weeks, for she begged her brother to let his chief surgeon John Veyrye remain for a while with her, which he did. By the time Suffolk and his companions arrived from England, the conventional rules of sequestration were relaxed and they were permitted to condole with the Queen. Their presence cheered and reassured her, helping her to await with more equanimity the moment when she would be free to return to normal life.

Consisting of three ministers, the Duke of Suffolk, Sir Richard Wingfield, and Nicholas West, the English embassy was to establish amity with the new monarch and to negotiate both the safe delivery of Mary's dowry and her return to England after the expiration of her mourning. The least diplomatically experienced of the trio, Brandon nevertheless headed the delegation; his rank, his close friendship with Henry, his previous acquaintance with Francis, and his success as an ambassador to Louis all recommended him, but he was at an immediate disadvantage. Instinctively distrusting the English, Francis had no intention of making any concession to his royal brother unless he could gain thereby, and Mary's presence in France was a good bargaining point. If Henry VIII wanted her return, then obviously it was to French interest to demand compensation for surrendering her; Mary herself recognized the fact that her personal well-being was not a consideration to either king.

On first going to Cluny Mary fretted over the loss of her English

ladies, finding the Countess of Nevers and the other French women
assigned to her in their stead so unsympathetic that she freed
herself as much as possible from their ministrations. Her dilemma
seemed complete: unable to trust the servants provided for her by
Louise and Marguerite, she was at the same time not allowed to
see her own. Finally her Tudor gorge rose, and she arbitrarily dealt
with the situation herself, so that when Francis returned to Paris
he found that by her order the French women had been dismissed
and the English reinstated. Displeased though he was he took no
action, for if he were to outwit Henry in the matter of Mary's
remarriage, he needed her cooperation if not her confidence. In fact,
he had neither. As Queen Dowager she was decorous, gracious,
and respectful, as a woman quietly acquiescent to his attentions. Too
discreet to compromise herself, she worried less about his personal
importunity to her than about his constant insistence that she
remarry, even to the point of naming suitable husbands. Refusal
would keep her in France, the last thing she wanted; financially
dependent upon her French revenues, she would be at his mercy.
Even were she permitted to leave for home she might be detained
on the way, taken to the Netherlands instead of Dover, or even
bargained away by Henry. Her fears may have been magnified by
her solitude at Cluny, but they were too real to be ignored. Her
instinct was to win the confidence of the English ambassadors, and
through them enlist the sympathy of Wolsey. Before any definite
action regarding her future could be taken she must keep the good
will of the French King while remaining adamant in refusing a
second political marriage.

Francis hurried back from Rheims after his coronation in order
that its attendant state entertaining should be over before the beginning of Lent. On the thirteenth of February he made his public
entry into Paris, where, her quarantine over, Mary watched from
an upstairs window and afterwards rode with Claude to the evening banquet. Most of the foreign ambassadors were there, including
those from England, Francis having been holding audience for over
a fortnight. The new reign was under way.

A contemporary describes Francis I at the age of twenty-one
as being extremely tall, broad-shouldered, with a handsome oval
face, slender legs, and an athletic figure already disposed to corpulence. All accounts depict him as exceptionally good-looking in a
dissolute way, and sexually attractive to women. Portraits show a

self-indulgent face, callous and cynical, the sharp black eyes, dark curling beard, and mocking mouth producing a satanic effect; in all of them the predominant feature is a disproportionately large nose. 'Le Roi Grand Nez,' he was called behind his back; yet in spite of it he prided himself upon his good looks, and with women had acquired the reputation of being the devil he so much resembled. This prince—liberal, debonair, artistic, and lettered—whom Mary knew in 1515, turned out to be a Machievellian despot, a voluptuary who had too much of everything.

Because of the profound influence of women upon Francis, the earlier years of his reign were branded as a petticoat government. His doting mother and adoring sister continued to hold first place in his affections after he became king and were the first to receive a share in his wealth and power. To the former he gave outright two counties, two duchies, a barony, and the title of Duchess: on his sister he bestowed the county of Armagnac and a lucrative monopoly in the appointment of guild officials; her husband, the Duc d'Alençon, received the most important governorship in the land, that of Normandy. All the new appointments went either to his own youthful companions, not necessarily worthy, or to friends of his mother, mostly of the older generation. It did not take the Court and capital long to notice who regulated the finances, controlled the King, and generally managed all affairs. As Henry VIII had done six years earlier, Francis hunted, jousted, danced, and spent money so freely that many thought Louis's prediction was to be realized, that he would bankrupt the kingdom. But while he built chateaux, collected art, played at patronage and diplomacy, and planned his military descent upon Italy, Louise of Savoy ably supervised state policy. Not only did Suffolk write to Wolsey in early February that she was the 'best spoken princess' he had ever met, but he found her influence over the King so great that he advised Henry to write to her personally. 'Sir, [it is] she that rules all, and so may she well, [for I] never saw woman like to her.'

Indicative of her colorless, unassuming personality is the fact that no one ever spoke of Queen Claude's influence. She who had brought Brittany to Francis by marrying him had no place in either his heart or his decisions, however personally the latter might affect her; only her illnesses and her pregnancies were noted. While turning elsewhere for love, he treated his wife with respect, satisfied because she was kind and gentle but principally because she bore him children. Before her death in 1523, Claude had given him three sons and four daughters.

Francis' relationship with Mary has been highly colored by fictional conjecture based solely on court gossip and contemporary surmise. One allegation, that Mary wanted a male child so much that she was willing to take a paramour to get one, can be dismissed with the incredulity it deserves. The charge is neither logical, realistic, nor supported by fact, and merits refutation only because it has been seriously advanced as an explanation of Louise's jealous zeal in protecting her son, the prospective successor to the throne, from the supposed wiles of the Queen. In this version, Louis's wife becomes a designing English vampire ready to sacrifice her honor to her own ends.

According to Brantôme, Mary, quickly realizing that her husband, already at death's door, would be unable to give her the son through whom she could maintain her position as Queen Mother of France, decided that Francis should father her offspring, which would appear to be Louis's child. Quoting an old Spanish proverb, *nunca mujer aguda murio sin herederos*, Brantôme affirmed that a clever woman never dies without heirs; if her husband gives her none, she turns to another for fulfillment. Thus Louis would get his male heir and Francis be deprived of the throne of France by his own son. The chronicler continued by stating that their flirtation became a court scandal, that Francis, who could never resist 'making a victim of any woman upon whom he had set his desires,' was encouraged by Mary, and that Louise and her circle seeing their own interests jeopardized grew greatly alarmed. Court spies increased their vigilance, and Francis was taken to task by Jean de Talleyrand, Sieur de Grignaux de Périgord, who gave him fatherly advice about women:

> In the name of Heaven what are you about? Can't you see that this woman, who is a cunning and subtle creature, is merely trying to attract you so that you can give her a child? And if she succeeds in getting one, you are then only Count of Angoulême for the rest of your life and will never be king of France as you hoped. The king her husband is old and will never give her any children . . . you are young and hot and so is she. Good Lord! She'll snare you, just like that; she'll have a child, and you're done for! After that you may as well say: Good-bye to my kingdom of France.

If Brantôme is to be believed, 'Monsieur d'Angoulême dreamed about it in fact, and protested being good in the matter and withdrew from it; but, tempted time and again by the caresses and clever tricks of this fair Englishwoman, he rushed more than ever into it. For such is the ardor of love!' Finally, Louise herself was forced to take action.

Brantôme would have Mary later practicing deception during her quarantine at Cluny, padding herself with *'linges et drapeaux'* in a pretense of pregnancy until her devices are exposed by Madame Louise, after which Francis regains his senses in time to be crowned on the feast of the Conversion of St. Paul, while the thwarted Mary gives herself to her English lover, Charles Brandon.

In this context Louise's reaction rings true, but the behavior of the two principals in the drama is completely out of focus. In what was probably quite a superficial flirtation Francis took the initiative; he could not have intended to seduce the Queen and nothing suggests that she wished it, but even had strong mutual desire existed the disproportionate risk would have deterred both of them. Though young, Francis was emotionally mature and experienced, and here as later in his career his profligacy has been exaggerated even by qualified historians, who too frequently have accepted it without investigation. Neither the gay libertine of fiction nor the supercilious seducer of legend, behind his charming exterior was a lust for position and power far stronger than his need for women. His was the ambition of an opportunist rather than a statesman, yet this second 'father of his country' gave France more than had Louis.

What actually happened is less melodramatic. The reliable evidence all comes from Mary herself who hesitated to speak very specifically lest she turn the French King against her. Her first impulse must have been to tell her brother how rudely Francis had behaved to her not so much in deed as in word, but the implications were not easily conveyed by letter and Mary was not adept at writing. After only three months in France she was inexperienced in the niceties of flirtation as practiced at the French Court, and may have feared to overemphasize what was perhaps intended as harmless teasing. It is certain that she felt uncomfortable and disturbed by it. The French courtiers were gallant and exceedingly polite, but their haphazard morality probably shocked her. That there had been no lack of dalliance at the English Court since her father's death she knew well, but it was something with which she herself had had no familiarity. If wenching went on below stairs it was not a subject of conversation among ladies, and though sexual incontinence might be prevalent, it was nonetheless regarded as evil and not openly condoned.

The French Court was larger and gayer, its cosmopolitan society freer and more worldly. For some years before Louis's death Francis had gathered about him a coterie of distinguished young men and women to which he constantly added from the select of Europe: visitors, artists, statesmen, prelates, men of letters, celebrities, and beauties. After his accession the Court was recognized as one of the most brilliant cultural centers of the Continent; over a thousand people were said to be attached to it, and its maintenance to cost more than a million livres per year. A Venetian describing Francis' mode of living soon after his accession emphasized his great energy, calling him France's most 'ambulatory king.' Rising at eleven in the morning, he heard Mass, dined, spent some time with his mother, and then visited his 'sweethearts,' among whom Mary was not included. In the late afternoon he habitually went hunting, returning in time for the evening's gaiety; if still unwearied he might spend the rest of the night enjoying the tavern life of the town, so that it was almost impossible to obtain audience with him. 'Rejoicing and entertainment' were the rule, and nothing said about sending troops to Italy. A couple of years later when every other European sovereign was alarmed by his exploits, his boast that he would not rest until all Christendom had been brought under the banner of France was reported to Henry by Sir Robert Wingfield, the English ambassador in Germany: 'He is young, mighty, [and] insatiable, always reading or talking of such enterprizes as whet and inflame himself and his hearers. . . .' Wingfield stressed the French King's confidence of great attainment 'for his common saying [is to all] that he speaketh with, that his trust is that, by hi[s valour and] industry the things which have been lost, lettyn, [and spoiled] by his noble predecessors, shall be recovered.' When told in the summer of 1515 that Francis was idolized by his subjects, Henry scoffed: 'By God! he gives them good reason to love him, running thus at the very commencement of his reign into the toils and charges of war.'

Francis loved the royal limelight: rumors of his projected operations, stories of his gallantry and defiance of danger, and gossip about the luxury and refinement of his Court. A natural sybarite, he surrounded himself with beautiful women, declaring that it was they who set the standard: 'a Court without ladies is like a year without springtime, or a spring without roses.' Unlike England where the King inspired the behavioral patterns, in France it was the Queen who did so, though Claude was too timid and retiring to be an effective model. Mannerisms were as fashionable as changes in dress and as easily copied, and it was said that in Anne of Brittany's day every well-born lady affected a limp; so when Mary was queen they simulated English reserve, exhibiting a coolness of manner *à l'Anglaise*. It was this feminine influence, with particular reference to the style and wit of Louise and Marguerite, that the French chronicler had in mind when comparing a womanless society to a flowerless *parterre*.

While Louis lived, Francis had been publicly punctilious in his behavior to Mary, because from every point of view it was to his best interest. Through her he could reach the confidential ear of Henry VIII and thereby cultivate the friendship of England; before even meeting her he had told English ministers that he was the Queen's servant in all things, ready to aid her in every undertaking. Thereafter, in courtesy, in suggestions for her comfort, and in helping her to adjust to a new environment, he remained a dutiful 'son.' In praising the marriage, the alliance that it cemented, and the gentility of Louis's English Queen, no one appeared 'more desirous to do her honour' than he. Then Louis died: Mary was no longer queen, and as King of France he was in no further need of her brother's good will; without tactful diplomacy Wolsey's triumph might easily turn to dust. In England, Mary's future, the French treaty, the Scottish problem, and in fact the whole European situation had to be re-valuated. Despite Francis' diplomatic evasions, his antipathy to the Anglo-French alliance was well known; he had secretly opposed Louis's marriage to Mary as being a potential obstacle to his own succession, in the knowledge also that the political union of two such traditional enemies was no more popular with one than the other. Henry and Francis were rivals, and behind their outward cordiality no love was lost on either side. Against an emotional background of strong personal jealousy, each could justifiably suspect the political motives of the other. While Henry told Sebastian Giustinian in July, 1515, that the French King would not cross the Alps into Italy that year because he was afraid of him, Henry himself was fearful that Francis would increase in power by doing so. Analyzing this rivalry, the Venetian observed that the competition for glory between them was so great 'that it should be a very easy matter for this metal to become rusted !'

Wolsey's reaction, though more objective, was no less emphatic. 'The King of France never cares to ask aid of England,' he told Giustinian; 'he omits to make us the least communication of his intentions, showing in how small account he holds his Majesty.' He had just cause for bitterness, since Francis neither informed England of his plans nor expressed any willingness to cooperate with her. Treating Englishmen as enemies, he allowed his subjects to capture their ships without thought of compensation. Wolsey knew full well that Francis kept his commitments to England only to insure her neutrality when he invaded Italy; his traffic with the Scots was simply a ruse to keep England in a state of uncertainty, and it was with this in mind that Albany was sent to Scotland with French money to stir up trouble, while Richard de la Pole, the self-styled 'Duke of Suffolk,' then in exile in France, was encouraged in his claim to the English throne. These maneuverings could hardly be construed as demonstrations of close friendship. The Cardinal admitted to Giustinian that in authorizing the treaty with Louis he had overridden the objections of many of the Council who were now ready to support him in breaking it. 'We first offered our services to King Lewis to make terms between him and the Switzers,' he explained, 'and the like we did with this present King, because we have great authority with them. King Francis has never deigned to thank his Majesty. Think, Sir Ambassador, whether this is to be borne and say if these are the fashions of confederates.' The political union which had seemed so strong a few months earlier was on the point of dissolution.

Mary herself was probably unaware of the diplomatic implications of her relationship with Francis; she only knew that his attitude toward her was different. While publicly as courteous and urbane as ever, still calling her his *'belle mère,'* privately his behavior had changed. Professing his loyalty to her and his intention of paying her dower in full, he promised Henry complete fidelity, 'that he would neither do her wrong, nor suffer her to take wrong of any other person, and to be to her as a loving son should be to his mother'; to Mary he pledged continued friendship, asking her to write to her brother 'how lovingly he had behaved to her.' Just

how loving he was Mary never divulged, though she does refer
to his frequent visits to Cluny. When asked about his treatment of
her since Louis's death, she replied 'that he had been in hand with
her of many matters,' but that on hearing of Suffolk's arrival he
had promised 'that he would trouble her no more with no such
matter,' begging her to tell neither the ambassador nor her brother
of his proposals, lest Henry should take 'unkindness there in.' She
gave this explanation to the English ministers on the fifth of
February, 1515, during their first conversation with her after reaching Paris, later telling Suffolk privately that 'from the first the King
was importunate with her in divers matters not to her honour.'
The statements are Suffolk's version of what she said, and reveal
less than do her own words written to Henry ten days later:

> Pleaseth it your Grace, the French King on Tuesday night last [past]
> came to visit me, and [had] with me many divers [discours]ing
> among the which he demanded me whether I had [ever] made any
> promise of marriage in any place, assuring me upon his honour, upon
> the word of a prince, that in case I would be plain [with] him in that
> affair he would do for me therein to the best of his power, whether it
> were in his realm or out of the same. Whereunto I answered that I
> would disclose unto him the [sec]ret of my heart in hu[mility] as
> unto the prince of the world after your Grace in which I m[ost trust],
> and so decla[red unto him] the good mind [which] for divers
> consi[derations I] bear to my lord of Suffolk, asking him not only
> [to grant] me his favour and consent thereunto, but [also] that he
> would of his [own] hand write unto your Grace and pray you to
> bear your like favour unto me and to be content with the same. The
> which he granted me to do, and so hath done. . . . Sir, I most humbly
> beseech you to take this answer which I have [made u]nto the
> French King in good part, the which I [did] only to be discharg[ed
> of th]e extreme pain and annoyance I was in [by reason] of such
> suit as [the French Ki]ng made unt[o me not accord]ing with mine
> honour, [the whi]ch he hath clearly left [off]. Also, Sir, I feared
> greatly [lest in] case that I had kept the matter from his knowledge
> that he might not have well entreated my said lord Suffolk, and the
> rather [for] to have returned to his [former] malfantasy and suits.

She added in a postscript that if Henry refused her request of a
choice of husband, Francis might 'renew his suits.' Her extreme
distaste for such an eventuality was near despair: 'I would rather
be out of the world than it should so happen.'

Suffolk's account to Wolsey of Mary's interview with Francis was essentially the same, except that he excused her disclosure to Francis on the grounds that she was 'so worried and so afraid' that unless she made a clean breast of it, the French King might turn against him or imperil his position with the King and Council in England. According to Suffolk, Mary had besought Francis to let her alone and 'speak no more of the matter,' promising to tell him everything in return for his help: 'And he gave her his faith in his hand that he would keep it counsel, and that he would help her to the best of his power.'

This is the sole evidence from which so many inferences have been drawn. Were Francis' 'malfantasy and suits' an invitation to his bed in order so to compromise the Queen that she would be forced to obey him, or simply the nagging pertinacity of one whose repeated insistence that she commit herself to remarriage was exceedingly tiring? It seems probable that if Francis had ever seriously desired to make the widowed queen his mistress he would less easily have been dissuaded. Years later, his mature recollection of Mary expresses scorn for her English lack of fastidiousness; among his sarcastic comments on the court personalities portrayed in the Album d'Aix at the Bibliothèque Méjanès is the scribbled legend beneath her picture: 'More dirty than queenly.'

Her intuition may have told Mary that for all Francis' talk she was in no real danger, but she could not have failed to realize his power to make her life almost intolerable by daily nagging, restrictions on her household, financial reprisals, or, worst of all, exile at Blois or some even remoter place in the country where she would be isolated from England. Her own aim was to get home as quickly as possible, but since she could not leave without royal permission it was vital that she not alienate Francis. Unconsciously Mary used the oldest of all political stratagems, that of converting a potential enemy into an ally whose support would be serviceable. What she did not then comprehend was that by his acceptance of her attachment to Suffolk the French King was abetting her in a course of action which was as rash as it was dangerous.

If that aspect of Mary's position as Queen Dowager which concerned the Anglo-French union could be renewed and continued under the new circumstances of Francis' accession, her personal future would be straightforward; by mutual consent she would return to England as soon as the settlement of her dowry was

14 Francis I, King of France, by Jean Clouet

plus sale que
Royne

La Royne marie

15   La Royne Marie, by an unknown artist, with the inscription by Francis I:
'*plus sale que royne*' (more dirty than queenly)

arranged. It must have been the knowledge that neither Henry nor Francis was interested in her welfare or would ever consult her wishes that prompted her to the step which she finally took. The judgment was her own because there was no one to advise her.

Because they generally distrusted French motives both Henry and Wolsey anticipated foul play: the arrangement of a strategic marriage alliance for Mary would be of great political profit to Francis, and they expected him to take advantage of his control over her. Just before Louis's death, Wolsey had written to Mary advising caution and warning her of what to expect. He understood that her husband was critically ill and likely to die suddenly, he counseled, leaving her at the mercy of others. Therefore to console her in her grief, he thought it expedient to write condolences and advice, 'how your Grace shall demean [yourself], being in this heaviness and among strangers, far from [your] most loving brother, and other your assured friends and servants.' Emphasizing Henry's affection for her, he urged complete confidence:

> I most humbly beseech the same never to do anything but by the advice of his Grace, referring all things to him whether fair promises, words or persuasions shall be made to the contrary, having always a special regard to his common honour and letting nothing pass your Grace's mouth whereby any person in these parts may have [you] at an advantage. And if any motions of marriage or other [offers of] fortune to be made unto you, in no wise give hearing to the [same]. And, thus doing, ye shall not fail to have the King fast and loving to you, to attain to your [own heart's] desire [and come] home again unto England with as much honour as [ever woman] had. And for my part, to the effusion of my [blood and the spen]ding of my goods, I shall never forsake nor leav[e you]. . . .

By the time Mary received this letter Louis XII was already dead.

She must have been comforted by this unexpected proof of Wolsey's friendliness but irritated at its implications of her immaturity. She replied that as she had no one else to turn to since her husband's death, she would put her trust in those in England as she had always done. 'As it shall please the King my brother and his Council I will be ordered,' she continued, adding coldly that she had done nothing since coming to France to merit rebuke. 'And whereas you advise me that I should make no promise, my Lord, I

F

trust the King my brother and you will not reckon in me such
childhood.' With Henry she was more circumspect :

> Sir, where your Grace sends me word that I will not give no credence
> . . . for no suit, nor for no [othe]r words that shall be give[n me].
> Sir, I promise your Grace [tha]t I ever may do thy [bidding] . . . for
> I have nothi[ng in the] world that I do care for [so much] as to
> have the good and [gracious] mind that your Gr[ace] had ever
> toward me, [which] I beseech your Grace for to continue, for there
> i[s all] my trust that I ha[ve] in this world.

Neither her sarcasm to Wolsey nor her flattery to the King was of
any avail; both were too engrossed with obstructing Francis' plans
to spare time or thought for Mary's plight.

All available sources of information in England confirm the fact
that Francis intended to keep Mary in France and marry her to the
highest bidder. From Germany Sir Robert Wingfield advised that
she be brought home immediately. If the Queen were with child
she should be protected from danger, he wrote; but if she were a
'maid,' he added, 'as I think verily she is,' then the English should
get possession of her person. He does not say why, nor explain
what danger she faced, but presumably he was thinking in the first
place of the safety of a baby whose birth, if it were male, would
change the French succession, and in the second, of Francis' designs
for her marriage. The English ambassador in Flanders, Sir Thomas
Spinelly, confirmed this opinion; writing to Henry he said that the
French were resolved not to give up the Queen but to marry her
where they would. In Paris, both Nicholas West and Sir Richard
Wingfield were skeptical of the French King's intentions; only
Suffolk was taken in by his promise to let Mary decide whether she
wanted to return to England or remain in France. Part of this was
wishful thinking on Brandon's part, for he desperately needed
Francis' support in the situation that was engulfing him. He told
Henry bluntly that the French King was most desirous of cooperation and that his word could be depended upon : 'I think that you
will find him [either] a fast prince or else I will say that he is the
most [untrue] person that lives.' Regarding a French match, he
wrote that Mary had been 'sore pressed in that matter as well by
the King [that now is] as other, yet she never consented, nor never
would do, [but rather] suffer the extremity of death.' As for her
remaining in France, the ambassadors declared most emphatically

that 'she never was nor is minded thereto, for she [counts] every day an hundred till she may see your Grace.'

Theoretically Mary's position was one to excite the envy of every marriageable women in Europe. A dowager queen, young, beautiful, and well endowed, would attract even mighty and ambitious princes, who might anticipate a handsome dowry and possibly a kingdom, if Henry VIII were to die without children. All over Europe eligible males calculated their chances and at least a dozen made overtures, a few of whom had priority rating by virtue of the backing of Francis and his council. The top contenders were Anthony the Good, Duke of Lorraine, a particular favorite of the French King, and Charles III, Duke of Savoy. The latter was an uncle of Francis who at twenty-eight was the right age for Mary. From Portugal, Emmanuel the Fortunate made a bid for his eldest son John, for which he solicited papal support, while Germany put forward William, Duke of Bavaria, 'the mightiest prince of the Empire.' The Prince of Castile, too, renewed his suit, which though not favorably received by Henry, aroused speculation; certainly the Venetian ambassador in London was convinced that Henry would reconsider Charles if he could only get his sister out of France. Even Maximilian forgot his resolve never to marry again, either for money or beauty; the prospect of a substantial dowry would have been too much to resist had the woman been less attractive. The first intimation of his interest was the request that Margaret find a portrait of Mary and send it to him, which she did. He was enraptured, his secretary told the Archduchess, and kept his eyes fixed upon it for a full half-hour or more. When reassured that it was an excellent likeness of Mary, the Emperor commissioned Margaret 'to write to the king of England to get the lady into his own hands, urging His Majesty of England that if she be married in France, and were to die without heirs, his kingdom would be exposed to great hazards.' At about the same time, while discrediting the prospects of Prince Charles, the English ambassador at Brussels thought the Emperor's chance of marriage with Mary was good : 'I find no man that [has] any doubt therein.'

As usual Maximilian meditated too long and moved too slowly; while he considered, Paris reported that the Queen Dowager had already made her own choice; by the twentieth of February there was open talk of her marriage to the Duke of Suffolk.

CHAPTER TWELVE

The Suffolk Star

All kings is mostly rapscallions. . . . Look at Henry the Eighth . . . kings is kings, and you got to make allowances . . . a duke's different. But not very different.

Mark Twain, *The Adventures of Huckleberry Finn*

CHARLES BRANDON, the object of these speculations, had already attained an enviable position in English politics before this, his second embassy to the French Court. Ostensibly the idol of society as king's favorites had to be, he was also a prime target for public criticism. He had earned a reputation for being unscrupulously ruthless in the pursuit of his ambitions. He was bold and enterprising but without wealth or connections; and his phenomenal success had antagonized both the responsible, hard-working statesmen, and the nobility whose privileges were threatened by just such social upstarts as he. His enemies realized that if his marriage to Mary were indeed fact, and accepted by Henry, there would be no restraining him. By 1515, after Wolsey he was the most influential man in England. Brandon's whole career was typical of the new aristocracy that was emerging from greater social mobility, and his rise, like that of so many of Henry's companions, was meteoric. Those close to the sovereign flourished naturally, favors coming to them almost automatically and frequently unsought. Growing up in the shadow of the royal family it is not surprising, therefore, that Brandon's career was assured; only the extreme rapidity of his success was remarkable.

In the light of their later behavior, it can fairly safely be assumed that the King's younger sister also found Brandon a charming person. That she knew him early in her life is certain, for he was continually with Henry, and after his elevation to the dukedom of Suffolk early in 1514 was a prominent figure at Court.

There they were constantly thrown together in the informal social atmosphere of the royal household. Then about twenty-nine and in his prime, he was tall, charming, handsome, and athletic. Seeing him so frequently, Mary may well have been conscious of his physical appeal; her feeling for him may even have been something warmer, but it is extremely unlikely that anything more than a close friendship had developed. However cordial their association, the gulf that separated his station from hers was too great to permit real intimacy. The English nobleman of the early sixteenth century was frank and uninhibited; despite the rigid rules and elaborate ceremony that governed English court etiquette its society was less superficially fastidious than that of either France or Italy, and Continentals were frequently appalled at the seeming lack of propriety in England. The ingredients of correct behavior and good taste vary with the age and place, the line of demarcation between what is considered morally right or wrong depending largely upon social acceptability. Rough language and 'unseemly behaviour' were not strange in a Court were familiar conduct between the sexes was uncondemned, and did no more than provide spicy gossip for idle tongues. Princesses, however, were allowed no such license; no overt flirtation must smirch Mary's name, nor would Brandon have considered a secret romance as anything but a very dangerous indiscretion.

The assumption almost uniformly made by modern writers that Mary was already hopelessly in love with Brandon before she went to France and had promised to marry him is based almost entirely on conjecture. The records are quite silent on their relationship during the years preceding her departure for France in early October, 1514; though there was gossip about Brandon's philanderings with other women, his name was never linked with hers as might have been expected had their association been openly amorous. The only pertinent references made at all are vague hints of an attachment between them which they convey retrospectively in their letters to Wolsey and Henry, written from Paris after the death of the French King. Afraid that Francis I would force her into another dynastic alliance, in desperation Mary had thrown herself upon Brandon's mercy, imploring him to marry her, but by the time these explanations of their marriage were written, they were obviously trying to present a case to kindle Henry's sympathy. Mary's veiled allusions to the 'good mind' she had for

Suffolk were certainly not unknown to him, for he had noted how well she had restrained her feelings upon their first meeting in France after her marriage to Louis: it 'rejoiced me not a little,' he wrote Henry, 'your Grace knows why.' It was the nearest he came to admitting that Mary might have had an earlier interest in him.

Since much of the correspondence of Mary and Brandon from January to May of 1515 is undated and inconclusive, the few statements they make about their earlier friendship are sometimes more confusing than enlightening. Two facts and only two emerge from these letters, both of which indicate that Henry VIII knew of his sister's love for his friend, however immature it might have been. From Mary's letters to her brother it is clear that there was a bargain of sorts between them regarding her remarriage in the event of Louis's death, which at the time was commonly expected. Its actual nature is unknown, but according to Mary it gave her freedom to choose a second husband. She first referred to it as certain promises given her at Dover at the time of her departure for France: 'Sir, I beseech your Grace that you will keep all the promises that you promised me when I took my leave of you by the w[ater s]ide. Sir, your Grace knoweth well that I did marry for your pl[easure a]t this time, and now I trust that you will suffer me to [marry as] me l[iketh fo]r to do.' Again, in late April, 1515, just before her return to England, she reiterated the substance of this assurance, reminding Henry that

. . . whereas for the good of peace, and for the furtherance of your affairs, ye moved me to marry with my lord and late husband King Louis of France, whose soul God pardon, though I understood that he was very aged and sickly, yet for the advancement of the said peace and for the furtherance of your causes I was contented to conform myself to your said motion, so that if I should fortune to survive the said late king, I might with good will marry myself at my liberty without your displeasure. Whereunto, good brother, ye condescended and granted, as ye well know, promising unto me that in such case ye would never provoke or move me but as mine own heart and mind should be best pleased, and that wheresoever I should dispose myself ye would wholly be contented with the same. And upon that your good comfort and faithful promise, I assented to the said marriage; else I would never have granted to, as at the same time I showed unto you more at large.

Just what her feelings were for Suffolk when she accepted the French King she does not divulge, but she does state quite positively that she was well disposed towards him. Moreover, she assumed full responsibility for such attachment as had developed between them, assuring her brother that Brandon had pressed no suit:

> Now that God hath called my late husband to his mercy and that I am at liberty, dearest brother, remembering the great virtues which I have seen and perceived heretofore in my Lord of Suffolk, to whom I have always been of good mind, as ye well know, I have affixed and clearly determined myself to marry with him; and the same, I assure you, hath proceeded only of mine own mind, without any request or labour of my said Lord of Suffolk or any other person.

All this, of course, was reasoning after the event, when her major concern was the justification of her secret marriage to Brandon without the King's consent.

The second fact that can be clearly established relates to another promise, this time by Brandon, that he would make no personal advances to Mary during the period of his embassy to Francis I after Louis's death. Apparently Henry both doubted Suffolk's ability to resist the blandishments of an attractive woman and feared that she would try to entice him into a secret engagement that might well interfere with his own plans for them both. It is also very doubtful if he had taken his promise to Mary as seriously as she had. With no reason to question Brandon's loyalty, he proceeded on the assumption that he would keep his word, and in all his diplomatic relations with Francis and Mary conduct himself with the utmost discretion. This pledge was made to Henry at Eltham in early January, 1515, just before Suffolk left for France. He admits to having broken it in a letter dated the twenty-second of the following April, subjecting himself to the King's mercy 'to do with my poor body your gracious pleasure,' and Mary supported his plea for clemency on the grounds that he had repudiated his word because of her persuasion. As reported by Wolsey, this serious breach of faith angered Henry even more than the clandestine marriage, for his confidence in Suffolk was such 'that for all the world, and to have been torn with wild horses, ye would not have broken your oath, promise, and assurance, made to his Grace, which doth well perceive that he is deceived of the constant and assured trust that he thought to have found in you.'

That Mary was deeply in love with Charles Brandon when she married him is undeniable; what had probably started as girlish hero-worship had developed into mature feeling during their Parisian meetings when she was frightened and dependent on him. She had known him from childhood and discovered in him so many of the traits she loved and admired in her brother; his affability and virile masculinity had endeared him to many women before. He must have found her attractive, but ambitious as he was, he was not the man to consider his career well lost for love.

At least a year before the twenty-second of August, 1485, when Henry Tudor wrenched the throne from Richard III, Charles Brandon was conceived. That it was before this date is certain because his father was killed at Bosworth, but the exact day and year of his birth have never been established. During those anxious years of shifting loyalties, no importance was attached to the arrival of another child to an exiled father, whose fidelity to the Tudor cause was the baby's only legacy. It was an auspicious day for the boy's future when before his birth both his father and uncle left England to join the handful of stout-hearted men of Richmond's train, at a time when the Lancastrian cause was at its lowest ebb. Their final victory at the sleepy market town in Leicestershire brought death to one of Henry VII's most faithful followers; seeking out his rival for a hand-to-hand combat, 'King Richard set on so sharply at the first brunt that he overthrew the Earl's standard' and with a second blow the standard-bearer himself followed the dragon to the dust. The slain man was William Brandon, father of the infant Charles whom he may never have seen.

Charles could not have been less than a few months old when his father was killed, for his mother had died the previous May. She was an Essex girl, Elizabeth Bruyn, daughter and heir of Sir Henry Bruyn of South Okendon, and twice married before she wed William Brandon. The Brandon family was of sturdy yeoman stock, several of them having become substantial landowners in Norfolk and Suffolk, where tradition takes the line back to the Conquest, with a soldier of William the Bastard settling on confiscated territory in East Anglia. Shortly thereafter, this Norman established himself at the ancient flint town of Brandon on the Norfolk-Suffolk boundary, the name of which he deliberately appropriated for his family. There, on the Little Ouse, his descendants multiplied and prospered for the next four centuries, and by the end of the reign of Edward IV they had acquired considerable substance and local reputation. Charles's grandfather, another William, was Marshal of the King's Bench as well as an escheator in Norfolk and Suffolk. Enriching himself by trade he used his surplus wisely and well, investing in land in each county and apparently lending money indifferently to the Yorkist and Lancastrian factions. This William Brandon lived a long and full life, acquiring knighthood somewhere along the line and marrying rather above his station into the Letheringham branch of the Wingfield family. Thus, Charles's grandmother was the daughter of the prolific Sir John Wingfield of Letheringham, who had sixteen offspring. A number of their descendants later became closely associated with the Duke and Duchess of Suffolk. The careers of the four prominent Wingfield brothers—Robert, Richard, Humphrey, and Anthony—were all furthered in part because their cousin was brother-in-law to the King and close friend to the Cardinal.

Youngest of the Brandons, the orphaned infant Charles was probably brought up first by his grandfather and later by his uncle, Sir Thomas, who lived until the beginning of January, 1510. As he died without issue his nephew presumably inherited the bulk of his not inconsiderable estate. After his grandfather's death in 1491 the boy, then about five years old, seems to have remained with his uncle for a couple of years until a place was found for him in the King's household as a companion to Prince Arthur. In part a gesture of appreciation for the family's devoted service to the Tudors, it was also a practical arrangement, since Charles was only a year or two older than Arthur, who needed a stronger and more experienced comrade with whom to learn the physical skills whose mastery was *de rigeur* for young men of breeding. Time cheated the association of proven success, for Arthur was dead by 1502, but Henry, the new Prince of Wales, six years Brandon's junior, was more eager than his brother had been to acquire the superior sportsmanship of his older companion. So the two boys grew up in each other's company, sharing a mutual passion for hunting, riding, jousting, tennis, and indeed for all the athletic activities so necessary to a young man's stature in the early 1500's. Both matured early, tall and strong beyond their years, excelling at whatever sport they practiced, each the foremost rival of the other. This competitive association continued into adulthood, and throughout their long years of friendship Brandon remained the King's principal opponent in the tiltyard and at the net.

Brandon may have shared Henry's education to some degree, but it is unlikely that he was ever exposed to any formal program of study. Not being a scion of the nobility he was acceptable in the king's household only as the prince's companion: thus he would not have studied under the royal tutors nor been taught the same disciplines as were Arthur and Henry, though in many ways he may have come under the influence of their teachers. However his culture was achieved, in the course of growing up he had acquired polish, a cultivated bearing, and gracious manners, the principal qualities demanded of a courtier. At the same time close association at Court with such influential families as the Greys and the Wingfields eventually led him into the sophisticated legal and literary circle of professionals at the Inns of Court, where he became a member of Gray's Inn and acquainted himself with a cursory knowledge of the law to supplement his earlier training. He had a superficial familiarity with Latin, and while he spoke French passably, it was never with the fluency of one who had mastered the language. In music, which he loved as Henry did, his only gift seems to have been a fine voice, powerful and well-trained; singing together was one of the many pleasures they shared.

While Brandon undoubtedly had no great intellectual ability, at the same time he was not the mediocrity most historians describe, and his education was probably neither better nor worse than the average. Well received by foreign Courts during his various embassies, he executed his missions with as much dispatch and discernment as did most of the amateurish ambassadors of northern Europe, his greatest assets being tact, personal charm, and a frank manner. His social popularity often enabled him more easily to uncover motives and assess attitudes, for though Worcester, Norfolk, and Sir Richard Wingfield were all abler than he, they were less well liked in France by both Louis and Francis and were therefore less effective.

Brandon's star began to rise in 1509 with the accession of Henry VIII. Already in his middle twenties, he had attained no higher rank until this time than Esquire for the Body, a post in the outer chamber of the royal household which paid him £33 6s. 8d. per

annum, in addition to his keep. During the first year of the new
reign he was given the lucrative office of Chamberlain of the
Principality of Wales and appointed Marshal of the King's Bench,
a position formerly held by his uncle. In November of the following year he and Sir John Carew were granted jointly the Marshalsea
of the Household, which the latter had already held alone for
over two years. This was definitely an award of friendship, a well-
paid office with little work attached; due to his rank and seniority
Sir John undoubtedly continued to do most of the policing of the
Court. Various emoluments and sinecures followed, laying the
foundation for the jealousy and resentment which were to accumu-
late in some hearts against him. In the spring of 1512 he received
two profitable assignments, a lifetime appointment at 2d. per day
as keeper of the royal park and manor of Wanstead, Essex, and
the job of ranger in the New Forest, which he probably held by
deputy. By this time he had risen to the rank of Knight of
the Body. During succeeding months he received numerous other
tangible expressions of royal favor: stewardships, receiverships,
annuities, wardships, and license to export English commodities
for his own profit. Success begets success. Brandon was on his way
up.

It was apparent to all who watched this rapid progress that the
King would soon give him a title; in the spring of 1513 preparations were being made for the French invasion and Brandon was
to go with Henry as a major commander. Accordingly, in April he
was made a Knight of the Garter and the following month became
Viscount Lisle by virtue of his ward, Elizabeth Grey, daughter
and heir of Sir John Grey, Viscount Lisle, whose death had put a
very valuable heiress on the market; besides other possessions her
lands alone were valued at over eight hundred pounds annually.
In December, 1512, Brandon had bought the wardship and marriage
of this eight-year-old girl with the intention of marrying her when
she was old enough. After the death of his first wife, Anne Browne,
their betrothal was apparently accepted as legal marriage, for she
was acknowledged as his spouse in the patent creating his vis-
countcy, which also carried with it a stipend of twenty marks.
Their union was never consummated, however, and it has been
assumed without evidence that Elizabeth Grey was unwilling to
accept marriage; under the circumstances it was more probably
Brandon who broke the engagement, for long before consummation

would have been feasible he had his eye on bigger game. He would normally have retained her as a ward and sold her marriage at a profit had he not fallen into temporary disgrace with the King in 1515 because of his entanglement with Mary; as part of his punishment her wardship and marriage were withdrawn from him and sold to Lady Catherine Courtenay, the Dowager Countess of Devonshire, for four thousand pounds. As a result of this transaction her son, Henry Courtenay, got a wife and Elizabeth Grey disappears from history as the young Countess of Devonshire; she died at an early age without issue. Meanwhile, Brandon bore the title of Lord Lisle for almost a year, before being elevated to the dukedom of Suffolk.

As Viscount Lisle, Brandon was appointed Marshal of the English army and was chosen to lead the vanguard of the expeditionary force to Calais in June, 1513; at the end of the month he was joined by Henry with the main body of troops. This was his first real opportunity to prove himself in the field, where he felt more competent than at sea.

Several months before, he had made his debut as a naval commander with dubious success. The navy had been ordered to intercept a large French fleet thought to be heading from Brest for the English coast, and an encounter of some consequence took place on August 10, 1512, in which two English vessels, the *Sovereign* and the *Regent*, participated. When the *Sovereign*, leading the attack, was forced to fall back, the *Regent* came to her rescue, valiantly engaging one of the enemy carracks, *La Reine*, in close combat; both ships, 'fouling, were burnt and the most part of the crew in them,' it was reported. In fact, some 120 to 200 sailors out of a total of 800 were lost, among them Brandon's friend and associate in the household office, Sir John Carew, and the captain of the *Regent*, Sir Thomas Knyvet. The disaster is vividly described by Polydore Vergil, who was singularly well informed on the events of the French War:

> In the English fleet there were two great ships: one was commanded by Charles Brandon, a man of knightly rank; the other had Thomas Knyvet, also distinguished by knighthood and of great courage, as its captain. These two were first to go forth, competing with each other in their desire for glory, and they sailed in the direction of Brittany. Charles, however, went with the greater speed and was the first to spy from mid-ocean what looked to be rather a French castle than a ship,

at anchor off the port of Brest and lying at considerable distance from the other ships. Charles did not hold back, but made for it with all speed. The French, seeing the English ships coming at them, deployed and when the first came directly on they received it with a volley from their cannon in front. Charles retaliated in kind and pressed boldly on in order to join in hand to hand fighting. But in the meantime the mast of his ship had been broken by the cannon balls and he was forced to fall back. When Thomas saw from afar that Charles had turned aside, he quickly followed, accompanied by only one small ship, and made a direct and savage charge (in which he revealed more spirit than prudence) against the French ship. Grappling irons having been thrown, a fierce struggle ensued, of a character more becoming to land than to naval warfare, for it was possible to cross from one ship to the other. Many warriors on both sides were either at once cut down or cruelly flung into the sea. Meanwhile the little English vessel sailed round about and from a distance holed the French ship with cannon fire until it began to leak in several places. It would now have been only a short time before the English had the upper hand, had it not come about in the middle of the fighting, either by ruse of the enemy, to ensure that they should not perish unavenged, or by pure chance (as might well happen), that a tremendous flame suddenly spouted out of the French ship and rushed towards the English vessel. From this a terrible fire quickly rose up. Then the combatants, surrounded on all sides by flames, turned from the battle to put out the fire. But since the ships, joined by grappling irons, hung inseparably together, the flames everywhere triumphed and could not be arrested by any human agency before they had at last hideously swallowed up the two ships and all their men. Many in avoiding the fire leaped down into the sea below, of whom some were saved by the arrival of boats manned by their countrymen. Thus the engagement was melancholy for both sides.

As a demonstration of valor the honor belonged to Knyvet, despite the fact that Brandon's vessel, the *Sovereign*, whose captaincy he held with Sir Henry Guildford, carried in the crew sixty of the tallest yeomen of the King's Guard. The cause of its failure to continue fighting after the initial attack is not clear. Hall suggests that it was due either to the smoke of battle, the negligence of its Master, 'or otherwise,' but whichever it was, Brandon had no reason to be proud of this exploit. At a salary of 5s. per day, he was still with the *Sovereign* during a later naval enterprise the following year 'as well by land as water, for distressing the navy of France.' According to instructions given to the Lord Admiral, Lisle was to be in charge of operations in Brittany after a landing there had been made.

During the military campaign of 1513 Brandon established his reputation as a soldier, fighting with the King in all engagements. By the middle of August the English had regained their lost prestige by routing the French at Guinegate, followed by the surrender of Thérouanne and the fall of Tournai. It was here that Brandon distinguished himself, being the first commander to capture one of the city gates, and when the town handed over its keys the next day he was immediately proclaimed Governor. When Henry returned to England near the end of October, he left Sir Edward Poynings as Governor and Lieutenant of Tournai, with a garrison of about six hundred horse and twelve thousand foot soldiers.

Back in England early the next year, Brandon was preparing for an embassy to Germany, a special design of Henry's; on the first of February, 1514, Viscount Lisle discarded his borrowed title to assume the new dignity of Duke of Suffolk. Partially a reward for service, the elevation in rank was calculated also to make him more eligible for the hand of Margaret of Austria for which Henry was then grooming him. It has been assumed that Brandon was given the title in order that he might with less criticism marry Mary Tudor, but at no time did the King's plans include any such impertinence. His creation as Duke carried with it only a modest endowment, the Manor of Donnington in Berkshire and an annuity of forty pounds, but in addition he was given the wardship of Roger Corbett, which temporarily gave him all the Corbett estates in Shropshire. Within the year Henry granted him the first great land gift in support of his title—the estates of the executed Edmund de la Pole—which started him on the road to becoming one of the greatest landowners in England.

This sudden advancement in rank of a social nobody, with few qualifications except an agreeable personality and physical courage, was really extraordinary, particularly when compared with the honor accorded at the same time to Thomas Howard, Earl of Surrey. The restored dukedom of Norfolk, bestowed upon him in recognition of his great triumph at Flodden Field, received national approbation, but Brandon's elevation to one of the highest peerages in the realm inevitably caused resentment among the nobility. Vergil conceded as much, observing that many 'considered it very surprising.' Wolsey may have recommended it in order to counterbalance Norfolk's influence in the Council, though the King's liking for his friend and companion-in-arms was unquestionably the principal reason for the award.

The dukedom itself was not new though it had been in abeyance for some time because of its close association with the Yorkist De la Pole family. The second and last duke of that line was John de la Pole, who died in 1491: his eldest son was killed at the Battle of Stoke in 1487 and posthumously attainted, so the title became defunct with the death of the father. The second son, Edmund, always of questionable loyalty to the Tudors, nonetheless had secured the restoration of a large part, but not all, of the family property. Henry VII, however, refused to restore the rank, ostensibly on the assumption that his attenuated income was not adequate for a dukedom. So Edmund became the Earl, rather than the Duke, of Suffolk, which title he bore until 1504 when he too was attainted. Meanwhile he had support for his cause on the Continent, where as 'White Rose' he arbitrarily resumed his father's title. Returned to England by Philip of Burgundy in 1506, the ex-Earl was imprisoned in the Tower for seven years awaiting execution, and it was not until the eve of the French invasion, when Henry VIII decided that he could not afford to leave the country while a possible pretender still lived there, that Edmund was beheaded. His was the first of several De la Pole heads to be laid on the execution block.

In the end Brandon received the bulk of the forfeited lands of the De la Pole family. These extensive estates became the nucleus of his vast holdings scattered through many counties, to which well over a hundred manors were added before his death. Both the dukedom and the wealth that went with it enabled Brandon to become one of the leading councilors and noblemen of England. Considering the limited number of peerages granted by the early Tudors, the King's action was unprecedented. There was only one dukedom in 1513, that of Buckingham, held by Edward Stafford, and after the new creations of 1514 but three, two of which, Buckingham and Norfolk, represented old and outstanding English families. Brandon's elevation on the contrary, was quite different: in addition to being entrenched firmly in the King's affection he was now one of the three highest-ranking peers. Suffolk seemed to be carried on the crest of the wave from one triumph to another.

All through January, 1514, Henry VIII pretended to be on the best of terms with the Empire, which implied continuance of the

war with France and fulfillment of his treaty obligations to the
Netherlands. It was reported on the Continent that he was planning, not one, but three marriages with his allies: Mary and the
Archduke as originally agreed upon, the widowed Margaret of Scotland and Maximilian, and Lord Lisle and Margaret of Austria. It
was said that Lisle was to be given a dukedom and dispatched to
the Netherlands on a special mission to conclude the triple arrangement, though ostensibly his purpose would be the levying of troops
in the Low Countries. Before January was over the common assumption that Brandon was to marry the Archduchess had become so
widespread and annoying that she sent a special envoy to London
to investigate the matter. On no account, she instructed her agents,
must he, now Duke of Suffolk, visit her. Although great preparations had already been made for his departure, Sir Richard Wingfield, Deputy of Calais, was sent instead.

There was, in fact, sound basis for these rumors which Brandon
had done nothing to dispel, he and Henry having themselves
hatched just such a scheme some four months earlier while they
were in France enjoying their military victories. On three
different occasions then they had met Margaret of Austria after
she had joined her father's camp in Picardy during the siege of
Tournai. Brandon first saw her at Lille in September when the
agreement for the immediate marriage between Mary and Charles
was still in the final stages of negotiation. Since Margaret considered it an impropriety to call upon the English King in his own
camp, she had invited him to the little town where she was staying to meet both her and her nephew, his prospective brother-in-law.
He was greeted with parades, pageants, and feasting, but it was a
short meeting, a brief respite during the unfinished campaign. A
fortnight later, after Tournai had capitulated and there was time
for a proper triumphal celebration, Lady Margaret returned the
visit, attended by a full suite of ladies and gentlemen from her
Court; on the tenth of October Charles of Castile joined them.
Next day, despite a downpour of rain, a public tournament was
held for the guests; Henry and Brandon charged all comers, the
King excelling everyone 'as much in agility . . . as in nobleness of
stature.' Afterwards the two of them led the participants in a grand
parade round the tiltyard in homage to the ladies. A banquet, at
which a hundred separate dishes were served, followed by a masque
and dancing, finished the day. A little later Henry once more

accepted Margaret's hospitality at Lille, where for three days Brandon and the King were regally entertained in the German manner, a new kind of tournament having been devised to take place indoors where it would be unhindered by the continuing rain. A huge hall floored with black stone of marblelike smoothness was used, and to deaden the sound and give the horses better footing, felt matting covered the entire tilting area.

Except for brief exchanges of conversation and formal compliments, Brandon and Margaret can have had little chance to get acquainted until the second meeting when he, both as sportsman and cavalier, gave an impressive performance which completely captivated the Archduchess. The full story of their association is well documented, parts of it having been imparted by Margaret in strictest confidence to Wingfield, the English ambassador, in the hope of averting a scandal. All accounts, however, are short and restrained, revealing only the barest outline of a possible romance: they listened in Margaret's chamber to King Henry's solos on the lute, cornet, and cittern, and sat holding hands like lovers late into the night, making 'good cheer' together long after Henry had gone to bed.

Margaret seldom had occasion to be on such intimate terms with so charming and handsome a man, for like his sovereign Brandon made full use of his graceful figure and engaging personality. Henry's favorite, an army commander with three thousand men under him, and well on his way to becoming powerful in England, Brandon obviously felt himself in a position to pay suit to a titled lady very much more exalted than he, and in this was encouraged by his master, who was said to treat him as an equal and a brother. Margaret's discerning maître d'hôtel, Sieur de Brégilles, called him 'a second king,' one 'who does and undoes,' and from Henry's camp kept Margaret informed of all English activities: their war exploits, their leadership, and their zeal to do her service. Of Brandon and Wolsey he stated: 'there are two obstinate men who govern everything,' emphasizing that it was the former whose influence was more felt and suggesting that it would do no harm for Margaret to write to him personally, since he was most anxious to please her. With Anglo-German relations so harmonious, Margaret's encouragement of what almost became an *affaire* is quite understandable. She may even have permitted herself the luxury of a serious affection for this fashionable young Englishman who consorted with royalty, but it is highly unlikely that she considered him in terms of matrimony.

It was upon a most unusual woman—gay, sophisticated, charming, and discreet—that Brandon tried his wiles: betrothed at three, twice married, and nine years widowed before they met, Margaret was still very attractive. Despite being in her early thirties, the 'Blooming Duchess,' with the light brown eyes and wavy golden hair much admired by Continentals, captivated Brandon as she had others with her animated face and brilliant conversation; indeed, he may have felt suitably overwhelmed by this intrepid lady whose citadel had been unsuccessfully stormed by far better men than he: two kings, Henry VII and Louis XII, and the second Duke of Norfolk. He must, however, have had some more confident reason than his own arrogance for not accepting her avowed intention of remaining a widow.

The perseverance of both Henry and his protégé must have warned Margaret that she had relentless pursuers, but having worked so hard for the alliance between Charles and Mary she was unwilling to jeopardize it when success was virtually within her grasp. It was an inopportune time for her to offend the English King, and entailed being somewhat more than merely gracious to Brandon. Tact and diplomacy demanded that she be encouraging but noncommittal, a course she found no difficulty in following. Though a diplomat, as a woman Margaret loved attention, and initially was probably borne along by the pleasing affability of these two Englishmen, without foreseeing any need to take them too seriously. Henry possessed both the charm of a cultivated courtier and the spontaneity of youth, a delightful combination in any man, and one which in a king was not lightly to be disregarded even when his suit was for another. 'I hold him all good,' she wrote to Wingfield, 'and that he thinketh none evil, wherefore I have not willed to despise him. And in this business I have found myself more impeached for to know that which me seemed touched to the King than that which me touched.'

It is obvious from Margaret's estimate of the two men that in her eyes they did not compare. Brandon had no depth of learning such as had Henry, whom she considered 'much a man of virtue and wise'; his was the physical challenge of the mature male. At the same time she found him amusing, frank, courteous, a fluent conversationalist whose whimsicality with women conjured compliments from the air; she was conscious of 'the virtue and grace of his person, the which me seemed that I have not much seen [any] gentleman to approach it.' Here was the Regent of the Netherlands speaking, a woman of judgment not easily taken in yet flattered by Brandon's unconcealed admiration. Influenced in his behalf by the King's persuasion, she found it hard not to believe him sincere, 'considering the desire the which always he showed me that he had to do me service.' So she received him with the warmth that a gracious duchess would be expected to extend to a chief personage from a foreign state who came with an offer of marriage: 'All things considered by me, I have always forced me to do unto him all honour and pleasure the which to me seemed to be well agreeable unto the King his good master.'

During the crowded days at Tournai Margaret soon became conscious of the purpose behind her official reception which was becoming remarkably personal. Hall stated the opinion of impartial witnesses with his usual conciseness: 'The noise went that the Lord Lisle made request of marriage to the Lady Margaret, Duchess of Savoy . . . but whether he proffered marriage or not she favoured him highly.' Henry himself made the first move by suggesting that her 'good will' towards Brandon 'might stretch on to some effect of promise of marriage,' adding that in England it was fashionable for widows to remarry. This, she countered, was not so in Germany, explaining that her father the Emperor and all her ministers would consider a marriage with a viscount one of disparagement, and that such a *mésalliance* would cause her to 'be dishonoured, and holden for a fool and light.' She had no intention of wedding again, she said, fortune having been so unkind as to give her previous unhappiness in husbands. But Henry was persistent: returning again and again to the subject, he chided her with being too young and beautiful to stay single; ladies in his country, he said, sometimes made their last matrimonial excursion as late as fifty or sixty. Finding all her excuses of no avail, she took refuge in a final evasion, trying not to irritate him since he had the marriage 'so much at the heart.' Telling Henry that it was inconceivable that she should be driven to a hasty decision simply because of their imminent departure, she insisted on studying the matter, while assuring him diplomatically that it would give her 'much great displeasure to lose so good company.'

With that the King had to be content, although he twice

broached the subject again when Brandon was present. No John Alden ever waged a better campaign for a friend than did Henry: 'I know well, Madame, and am sure that my fellow [Brandon] shall be to you a true servant, and that he is altogether yours, but we fear that you shall not do in likewise, for [some]one shall force you to be again married; and that you shall not be found out of this country [that is, found in the country] at my return.' She replied that their fears were groundless for she would not consider marriage without her father's consent; all they could elicit from her was a promise that she would not pledge herself to anyone else until the end of the year. Brandon gave a similar pledge. Later, before leaving for England, 'after many devices and regrets, he made me to reconfirm in his hand'; also 'in my hand, without that I required him, made me the semblable, and that for always he should be to me true and humble servant; and I to him promised to be to him such mistress all my life as to him who me seemed desired to do me most of service.' Not a formal betrothal, it amounted to some degree of understanding; for Margaret what had begun in fun had ceased to be a flirtation. After his return home nothing more passed between them except 'some gracious letters, the which have been, I know, evil kept.'

Brandon's part in the drama is not as clear as Margaret's, because she was reluctant, either from reticence or from fear of jeopardizing Anglo-Dutch friendship, to reveal much of her personal relationship with him. It would seem, however, that he saw himself definitely in the role of affectionate lover, both at Tournai and during the three-day visit at Lille. They exchanged gifts as tokens of their vows of constancy, the explication of which is given in Margaret's own words:

I take none in this affair to witness but the King and him; and himself first: it is that one night at Tournay, being at the banquet, after the banquet he put himself upon his knees before me, and in speaking and him playing, he drew from my finger the ring, and put it upon his, and then shewed it me; and I took to laugh, and to him said that he was a thief, and that I thought not that the King had with him led thieves out of his country. This word *laron* he could not understand; wherefore, I was constrained for to ask how one said in Flemish *laron*. And afterwards I said to him in Flemish *dieffe*, and I prayed him many times to give it [to] me again, for that it was too much known. But he understood me not well, and kept it on to the next day that I spoke to the King, him requiring to make him to give it [to] me, because it was too much known—I promising him one of my bracelets the which I wore, the which I gave him.

Rather than offend him she permitted the ring to be taken a second time by the same tactics as before, Brandon again pretending not to understand her remonstrations. This time Henry refused to intervene on the grounds that she would be given jewels in return that were far more valuable than that which Brandon had taken. Neither he nor Brandon appeared to realize that it was the publicity and not the value of the ring that concerned Margaret; the implication of an exchange of gifts was something to which she raised no objection. She said no more and Brandon retained his love token; he obviously wanted them to keep mutual mementos, for on the following day, she told Ambassador Wingfield:

. . . he brought me one fair point of diamond, and one table of rubies, and showed me that it was for the other ring; wherefore I durst no more speak of it, if not to beseech him that it should not be showed to any person; the which hath not all been to me done. (Thus, my Lord the Ambassador, see all of this affair, and for to know my advice on all, I shall give it you more at length, which is this.)

The sequence she went on to recount can be anticipated. Instead of being discreet as he had promised, Brandon boasted of his conquest; the tale, spread by merchants, circulated through Europe and eventually reached Margaret and her father. Since the particular letter which carried the news of their secret engagement was traced to English traders, the incident became a diplomatic issue between the two countries. Personally, Margaret was 'much abashed,' because 'the bruit is so imprinted in the fantasies of people' that she was in fear for her good name; politically, she had undergone a 'marvellous sorrow,' for which she demanded state apology. She was so angry at Brandon's behavior that the episode was brought to an abrupt close. 'I am constrained to entreat him in all things like a stranger, at the least before folks, the which doeth me so much displeasure that I cannot write it, seeing that I took him so much for my good friend and servant.' In Antwerp, Spinelly, seldom wrong in his political opinions, found the Dutch much disturbed by the rumors which some of them thought to have injured Margaret's reputation. Henry apologized to her and to the Emperor, promising to hang the '*mauvais esprits*' who had caused the rift between them.

Suffolk was more cocksure than ever after receiving his dukedom, confident that Margaret was his for the taking. In the preliminary parade of the May tilts at Greenwich, before Queen Catherine and Princess Mary, he dressed as a pilgrim, carrying a long staff bearing in large bold letters the phrase: 'Who can hold that will away?' Chronicler Hall writes that this posy was dedicated to Margaret of Austria. Even if she was disillusioned and greatly vexed by his presumption, others were much impressed; but rumblings grew louder in the Council chamber where secret fears were openly expressed: was there no stopping this ambitious and arrogant young duke?

Margaret's discretion had returned; while diplomatic flirtations were not uncommon in royal circles, this one had exceeded the bounds of propriety. That she was attracted to Brandon and interested in him is obvious, but her feelings were in the end routed by hurt pride and objective judgment. Although her father and brother had each earlier urged her to take a third husband, she was not a woman to be inadvertently compromised by a situation that had already become embarrassing, and in her rejection of the English proposal she had Maximilian's encouragement. She was doubtless stating a fact in telling Henry that her father was indignant and that nothing was to be gained by a double marriage that could not be had under the existing alliance. Margaret seems to have been more upset by the gossiping that she could not control than by the occasion for it. Lord Edward Herbert of Cherbury's summary, written over a century later, was probably near the truth: the courtship 'though it took no effect was not yet without grace and favour on her part.' Her 'favour' was evidenced just before she and Brandon parted. He entrusted to her care his eight-year-old '*petite fille*' whom he had recently adopted while in France, after rescuing her from drowning. The child was Magdalen Rochester, the daughter of an Englishman living at Calais, and having saved her life Brandon had become so attached to her that he wished to provide for her future. After Margaret's possibly reluctant acceptance of his charge, he had further begged to send his elder daughter Anne to her, to be educated at the Court at Malines on the Dyle, where the palace built by her in 1507 still stands. Both girls stayed there under her tutelage for two years. It was hardly a kindness that someone in her political position would do for a mere acquaintance.

Margaret's reception of the two girls may have been partly responsible for the persistent references to a marriage contract, while the fact that Suffolk was said to have one or more wives living at the time added zest to the story. Writing to Venice from London at the end of July, 1514, Andrea Badoer spoke of it as a fact, adding significantly that the Duke, 'a very handsome man, may have had more than three wives and she more than one husband.'

The complicated sequence of Suffolk's marriages has posed a difficult problem which neither contemporary nor later writers have quite disentangled; nor is this surprising, considering how extremely involved his early matrimonial ventures were. At about seventeen years of age he had contracted, *per verba de praesenti*, to marry Anne Browne, daughter of Sir Anthony Browne, then Lieutenant and later Governor of Calais. The date of this betrothal was probably before 1505. Considering her wealth and position it was a good connection for an ambitious but impecunious young man at Court. Anne's mother was Lady Lucy Neville, daughter of John Neville, Marquis of Montagu and Earl of Northumberland, and niece of the more famous Richard Neville, 'Kingmaker'; the first marriage of Lady Lucy to Sir Thomas Fitzwilliam had brought her the support of the Fitzwilliams of Aldwark, Yorkshire. Anne herself was lady-in-waiting to Mary Tudor's mother, Elizabeth of York, when Brandon first wooed her. Young and hot-blooded, he no doubt entered into this relationship lightly enough, unaware of the difficulties it was later to cause. Common enough in England, *de praesenti* contracts were then recognized by canon law; nevertheless, they were basically unlike the 'Scotch marriages' to which they were sometimes compared, since no witnesses were required, but only the oaths of the two contracting persons who often pledged themselves secretly. A formal church ceremony was supposed to follow, but in many cases the couple, either from laxity or deliberate negligence, omitted this precaution, with the result that such unions were not infrequently rejected by the male. Since English practice accepted the husband's testimony to the exclusion of the wife's, it was relatively easy for an irresponsible man to repudiate his publicly acknowledged spouse without fear of reprisal.

This was in fact Brandon's position when he met and married Margaret Neville in 1506 or perhaps a little later. He was presumably living with Anne Browne at the time, for she had borne him a daughter, also named Anne, before he left her. His new wife was then about forty-three—more than twenty years his senior—rich, widowed, and of good family, being the third daughter of John Neville, and thus Anne Browne's aunt. Since Margaret was Anne's aunt and Brandon was a cousin of Margaret's former husband, his grand-mother having been a sister of John Mortimer's father, they were within both the second and third degrees of relationship pro-hibited by canon law, and a papal dispensation permitting the marriage had to be procured. Margaret's mother, as daughter and coheiress of Sir Edmund Ingoldsthorpe of Borough Green, near New-market, had been quite prominent in her own right. Margaret had been married twice already, first to John Horn and then to Sir John Mortimer, who had left her childless but very well endowed. Sebastian Giustinian reports Brandon as being younger than he really was in 1506-7, but even so she was enough older than he to make of their union an interesting bit of news for the Italian: 'In this country young men marry old ladies for their money and here for instance is the Duke of Suffolk, who at nineteen married a lady for her wealth . . . old enough to be his mother.' It was a sacrifice to Pluto, not to Venus.

Although in no sense a moralist, Brandon was still never accused of the gross licentiousness of his father, who had a notorious reputa-tion as a rake. Writing in 1478 Sir John Paston, a Norfolk neighbor of William Brandon, recorded how when young, the latter had 'by force ravished and swived an old gentle woman, and yet was not therewith satisfied, but swived her oldest daughter, and then would have swived the other sister both; wherefore men say foul of him,' declaring that he would have not only the hen but all her chickens as well. A ward of the king, William Brandon further blackened his career by marrying a widow without paying the accustomed fee, and it had been said at the time that he was 'like to be hanged.'

Brandon's marriage to Margaret Neville speedily proved unsuc-cessful. They were divorced in under two years on grounds of con-sanguinity, upon proof of his precontract and carnal knowledge of his previous wife, Anne. He admitted having cohabited with Anne, as the dispensation for annulment indicated, but that his conscience pricked him because of his infidelity to her is highly improbable. In an age when all important families intermarried so frequently, it was usually quite easy to obtain the dissolution of a union on the plea of its being within one of the prohibited degrees of relationship. In this case the previous dispensation was invalidated and the marriage declared null and void by the Archdeacon's Court in London, which had local jurisdiction over matrimonial causes, after which Brandon 'married the said Mrs. Anne Browne, at which all the nobility were present and did honour it.'

With a public wedding behind him Brandon was now married beyond a shadow of doubt. He lived with Anne until her death in 1512, during which time a second daughter was born. Thus, of his two children by her, Anne and Mary, the elder was illegitimate in the eyes of society though not by judicial decree, while the younger was unquestionably born in lawful wedlock. It was to be another two decades before the question of these two marriages was finally settled to Mary Tudor's satisfaction, and long after her death it arose once more to vex those concerned with the Elizabethan succession. The resolute Margaret Neville lived to marry a fourth time before her death in 1528.

Brandon's unconsummated betrothal to Elizabeth Grey in 1513 was broken off some time before his next visit to France, but his intention to marry her had been fully public. It is not surprising that Margaret of Austria advised him actually to do so, not so much out of vexation with him as to vindicate her own 'honour.' With that kind of honor Brandon was never very much engaged. His women were matters of the moment, and marriage a necessary investment. In January and February of 1515 he was once more an eligible bachelor, comparatively free of romantic complications. But not for long. He was soon to learn both the measure of Tudor love and the force of Tudor fury.

CHAPTER THIRTEEN

Duchess of Suffolk

Cloth of gold do not despise,
Though thou be match'd with cloth of frieze;
Cloth of frieze, be not too bold,
Though thou be match'd with cloth of gold.

Inscription on a label affixed to Suffolk's
lance, as recorded under the wedding
picture of Brandon and Mary

WOLSEY'S careful plans to curb the power of France and make
England predominant in Continental politics had been brought
to nought by the death of Louis XII, upon whose friendship and
cooperation everything had hinged. English success, supreme at the
end of 1514, at the beginning of 1515 was seriously threatened. Indeed all Wolsey's schemes seemed simultaneously to have gone
awry : conciliar division plagued him at home; from the Netherlands
Margaret was seeking an alliance with France for the marriage of
Prince Charles and four-year-old Renée, which England was afraid
would affect its trade; and Francis I was ready for further aggression
in Italy if England could be isolated. The skein of affairs was becoming daily more tangled.

Suffolk met Mary in Paris in early February, 1515, for the
second time as head of an official embassy. Like others of his generation he disliked any foreign assignment not of a military nature as
being both onerous and expensive : not only did it put him in debt,
but it enabled his enemies at Court to profit by his absence. To
Brandon, who never apparently accepted responsibility for the predicament in which he was to find himself, even Wolsey seemed to
be secretly opposing him.

Negotiations began immediately. Suffolk, Sir Richard Wingfield,
and Nicholas West, while in Paris to offer condolences on Louis's
decease and to congratulate Francis on his accession, had a basically

more pragmatic purpose for being there. They were to obtain possession of the gems and precious stones given to Mary by her
husband, make an inventory of all her English jewelry, plate, and
other valuables in order to secure full restitution of their value,
and finally to demand repayment of the cost of her transportation
to France. Since Francis was known to desire the return of Tournai,
its restoration was to be used as a basis for bargaining. Other matters
too were to be raised: the arrears of a million gold crowns due
from Louis's reign; French encouragement of Richard de la Pole,
the 'White Rose'; the dispatch of the Duke of Albany into Scotland; and Wolsey's ambition for the bishopric of Tournai. Much
against his will Suffolk was to lead the discussions, made easier
by his previous acquaintance with Francis, principally because his
abler colleagues carried considerably less prestige than he: Wingfield, a veteran diplomat by 1515, had been chosen to lend stability
to the mission; West, soon to become Bishop of Ely, for his ability
in Latin. Invaluable assistants though they were, it was upon Bran-
on that the burden of mediation fell.

They arrived at Senlis at the end of January, where they were
cordially received by Francis, en route back to Paris from his coronation at Rheims. After granting them formal audience, he summoned
Suffolk to his bedchamber a few days later for a private conversation
during which he accused Brandon of the traitorous intention,
reported to him on good authority, of coming to France expressly to
marry the French Queen without either his or Henry's permission.
Surprise, fear, or a combination thereof elicited a prompt denial: 'I
trust your Grace would not reckon so great folly in me to come into
a strange realm to marry the Queen of the realm without your knowledge and without authority from my Master, and that I have not
nor was it ever intended on my Master's part nor on mine.' So he
reported to Wolsey, whose sympathy he needed to enlist before
Henry heard of his alleged treachery. This was the beginning of the
'secret matter' which is so recurrent in Suffolk's personal correspondence with Wolsey.

The truth of the accusation will never be known. Brandon persisted in his story and Mary later supported it; individual thoughts,
desires, and motives are too intangible to prove. Though he must
have known that Mary favored him and that his chance of marrying
her eventually was not impossible if he could bring her safely back
to England well endowed, his personal calculations had probably

not gone beyond that point. Mary was less to be trusted, or Henry would not have extracted Brandon's promise, before he left England, that he would not make advances to her while in France. They had been on close personal terms and the King was being frank with his friend, knowing how persuasive she could be. It would seem utterly uncharacteristic for so ambitious a man even to have considered an action which could bring him only trouble, disgrace, or death if Henry so desired.

Suffolk was more abashed than ever when the French King divulged how much he knew of his and the Queen's former relationship, producing certain terms and expressions of intimacy that she and Brandon had shared before her marriage, one in particular being a secret 'ware word' or bond of endearment which he thought was known to them alone—words 'I knew no man alive could tell them but she,' Suffolk told Wolsey. He was, in fact, so taken aback that Francis pressed his advantage. 'Be not disturbed,' he reassured him, 'for you shall say that you have found a kind friend and a loving; and because you shall think no wrong of me, I give you in your hand my faith and troth, by the word of a king, that I shall never fail her or you but to help and advance this matter betwixt her and you with as good will as I would for mine own self.' The last phrase must have taken on new meaning when Suffolk heard Mary's version of her confession of the affection she bore him. When Francis had become 'importunate' with her, she had told him of 'the good mind she bear unto me' in order to be rid of him, he later wrote to Henry VIII. But for the time being he was more concerned with immediate consequences, knowing that he was 'like to be undone if the matter should come to the knowledge of the King my Master.' To allay his fears Francis promised that both he and Mary would write to Henry in his behalf as soon as he got to Paris 'in the best manner that can be devised.'

By first censuring and then championing their relationship Francis disarmed them from the start. Brandon ingenuously maintained that the French King was sincere in all his diplomatic commitments because he kept his word in this one, without apparently comprehending that Francis was acting in the interests of France. If Mary refused a husband of his choosing, as indeed she had, then Henry too should be cheated of a profitable alliance by her marriage to an English subject, which would be of no political advantage to England.

Suffolk judiciously left it to Wolsey's discretion as to how much of the 'secret matter' should be passed on to the King, and the fact that he was told everything indicates that Henry and Wolsey were both fully aware from the very beginning of the plans for marriage between Suffolk and Mary. The Cardinal's reply to Brandon, written sometime during the first week of February, refutes the theory accepted by many that Brandon's actions brought him under the wrath of the King, and that but for Wolsey's timely intercession he would have lost his head. On the contrary, not only did neither of them at this early date oppose the idea of an ultimate union, but Suffolk was actually commended for his astute handling of the affair. At the same time he was informed of the King's gift of the entire De la Pole estate and an additional settlement, 'by my pursuit,' of the lordship of Claxton, worth a thousand marks in cash, none of which would have been written to a man under suspicion of intrigue or deception. It was not the idea of their marriage or the couple's hope of achieving it that so angered Henry, but the fact that when it did take place it was done secretly and without permission. In fact, he may have considered the engagement a good ruse to deceive Francis and thereby get his permission to bring Mary home. Once back in England Henry could dispose of her as he wished.

Drafted by his secretary Brian Tuke, Wolsey's letter was full of expressions of friendship, salient portions being written in his own hand. He assured Brandon of the King's continued friendship 'in the accomplishment of the said marriage,' saying that 'his Grace marvellously rejoiced to hear of your good speed in the same, and how substantially and discreetly ye ordered and handled yourself in your words and your communication with the said French King, when he first secretly brake with you of the said marriage.' In the same letter Brandon was instructed to urge Francis to write to Henry in support of his suit for Mary's hand, 'albeit that there be daily on every side practices made to the let of the same, which I have withstanded hitherto, and doubt not so to do till ye shall have achieved your intended purpose; and ye shall say, by that time that ye know all, that ye have had of me a fast friend.' The letter concluded on a personal note:

> And whereas ye write that the French King is of no less good will towards me than his predecessor was, I pray you to thank his Grace for the same, and to offer him my poor service, which, next my Master, shall have mine heart for the good will and mind which he beareth to you; beseeching you to have my affairs recommended, and

that I may have some end in the same, one way or other. And thus for lack of more leisure I bid you most heartily farewell, beseeching you to have me recommended to the Queen's Grace.

The reference to Wolsey's 'affairs' concerned the bishopric of Tournai, which Suffolk had been asked specifically to procure for him, and during succeeding weeks it was to occupy a considerable part of his time, for he was determined that his benefactor's desire should be gratified. By March, with Francis' promise in his pocket, he could boast to Wolsey that it was forthcoming. Three years later when the city was returned to France, Wolsey received a pension of twelve thousand livres per year for the surrender of his diocesan rights.

Threatening clouds were gathering for Suffolk, but the storm did not burst until it was discovered that he had actually married Mary. His letters during this period of indecision show anxiety rather than actual fear; his relations with Francis were cordial and, barring unforeseen calamity, he was confident that his embassy would be successful. Wolsey was squarely on his side, nor could he have believed himself to have lost Henry's trust, for he felt secure enough in the second week of February to ask him for a loan of two thousand pounds to see him through the conclusion of his mission.

Suffolk's dilemma was engendered by Mary herself. Long before his arrival she had impatiently planned what to tell him and how to win him to her purpose, but as the days passed her emotional tension inevitably increased. Would he accept her story or consider it no more than feminine hysteria, born of homesickness and distress? Doubt must have vanished when she saw him, for she spilled it all out in a frenzy of tears and passion: her fear of Louise, her alarm over Francis and his persistent threats of a forced marriage, and her desire to marry Brandon, himself. Though not an emotional man, he was deeply touched. The wild torrent of words, incoherent at the time, contained a store of information, and concealed within it he recognized a desperate determination that would brook no denial. Unsure of the proper response he wrote an undated and very studied letter to the King, the composition of which may have taken a good many days. By the time it was dispatched he and Mary were married; Henry must have received it about the second week of March.

He began by thanking the King for his recent letter and his many past kindnesses. He had done the best he could to obtain all the Queen's 'stuff and jewels,' for otherwise he would have deserved death as his reward, considering that 'I find you so good lord to me that there is none thing that grieves me but that she and I have no more to content your Grace.' Mary was willing that he should have all her possessions, he continued, 'and if it comes not so much as your Grace thought, she is content to give your grace what sum you shall be content to ask, to be paid on her jointure, and all that she has in this world.' From there he proceeded to answer charges made against him that he had been pro-French in his discussions with Francis and that he had not been firm enough in regard to Tournai; this last despite the fact that most of the English Council had at one time or another 'been in hand with me and [think] it best you should depart with it.' Still, in the face of much persuasion he had 'put the French King in none hope of it.' He had striven diligently to promote amity between the two countries, whatever his enemies may have said to the contrary. It would have never occurred to him, he protested, to do anything 'that should [not] be to your contentation, but to refer it [to your] pleasure.' Stressing that his detractors at home were numerous, he implored the King not to listen to them, for he had never tried to hurt anyone in his life; 'and your Grace [knoweth] best nor I never sought other remedy [against] mine enemies but your Grace, nor never [will] : for it is your Grace that has made me of nothing and holden me up hitherto; and if your [pleasure] be so for to do, I care not for all the world. . . .'

Preliminaries over he got down to his main theme, for it was Henry's reaction to his secret marriage to Mary that he wanted. At their first private meeting Mary had confessed her love for him, he told Henry, indicating her determination to marry nobody else; sick with fear that she would be forced to accept a suitor either from France or the Low Countries, she had become hysterical at the possibility of never seeing England again. 'To which she said that she would rather be torn to pieces' than be banished from her own country, and with that she wept: 'Sir, I never saw woman so weep.' All attempts to comfort her were of no avail. Francis had already persuaded her that if she returned to England she would be sent to Flanders and married. Mary's fear of the future was so great that she half believed Brandon to have been a party to such a plot. Accusing him of enticing her back that she might be married to Prince Charles

whom she had already once rejected, Mary presented her ultimatum :
they must marry in France before their return home, and that within
four days or he could never expect 'the same proffer again.' She swore,
he said, that if he did not marry her at once, 'she would never have
me nor never come to England.'

In the face of such determination Suffolk had weakly yielded,
thinking it better to comply with her wish than to lose everything.
Shortly thereafter they were very secretly married by an unknown
priest at the Cluny Chapel in Paris, with only a handful of Mary's
personal servants attending to serve as witnesses. But ten people
were privy to it according to Brandon, though he names none of
them; certainly neither Francis and his mother nor ambassadors
Wingfield and West were present. The two latter were not confided
in because Mary had argued, no doubt with justification, that they
would refuse to cooperate.

The die was cast. Suffolk had permitted himself against his better
judgment to be led into an action so rash and so precipitous as to
imperil his whole future. On the brink of breakdown, Mary was
desperate enough to take any action rather than be forced into
another political alignment. She knew full well that marriage without Henry's consent was dangerous, but she also knew Henry : he
would threaten and fume and sulk, but would in the end give in.
She had his word that she should choose her next husband, and
though expecting his extreme displeasure, she was equally aware
that Wolsey, needing Suffolk's support in the Council, would be
disposed to help them. So while Brandon was presenting the Cardinal
with a straightforward account of their strange behavior, she under-
took the more difficult task of placating the King.

It is impossible to establish the exact date of this February marriage, since the letters of Brandon and Mary specifically mentioning
it are undated. By the beginning of March, Mary suspected that she
was pregnant, which would suggest that they were married about
the middle of February and probably not later than the twentieth.
Certainly rumors of a marriage were rife at the French capital by
the end of the month. The first definite revelation of it came from
Suffolk, who wrote Wolsey, with 'as heavy a heart as any man
living,' after Mary had divulged her fears to him : 'My Lord, so it
is that when I came to Paris I heard many things which put me in
great fear, and so did the Queen both; and the Queen would never
let me be in rest till I had granted her to be married. And so to be

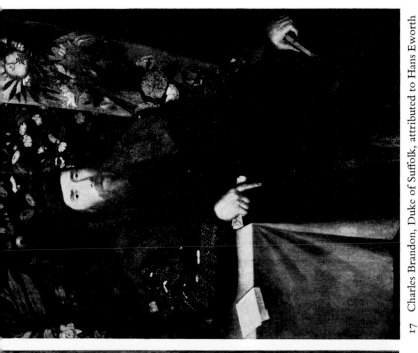

16 Charles Brandon, Duke of Suffolk, by an unknown artist

17 Charles Brandon, Duke of Suffolk, attributed to Hans Eworth

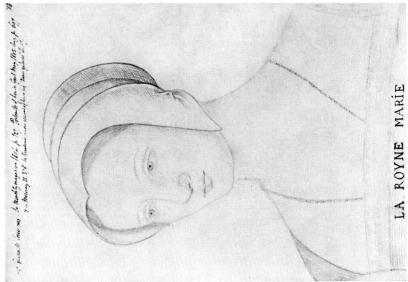

LA ROYNE MARĬE

19 La Royne Marie, by an
unknown artist

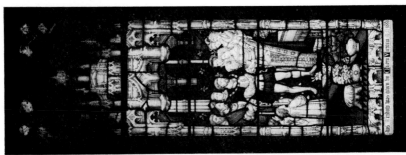

18 The secret marriage of Mary
and Brandon at Cluny
Chapel, Paris, in the
presence of Francis I.
From the panel in the
commemorative window
of St. Mary's Church,
Bury St. Edmunds

plain with you, I have married her heartily and have lain with her,
insomuch that I fear me lest she be with child.' Wolsey's reply to
this news dates Brandon's letter as being of the fifth of March. By
that time he and Mary were already considering another marriage,
a more public ceremony which would advertise their union and
prove the legitimacy of the expected offspring. They need not wait
until after Lent, he told Wolsey, for in France 'they marry in Lent
as well as out of Lent, with license of any bishop.' There were other
reasons too for wanting an open marriage; their intimacy was impossible to conceal, and the interim of waiting for permission to
return to England grew daily more embarrassing. Mary insisted on
having Suffolk with her: he visited her in her rooms; they ate together; their constant association and her obvious dependence upon
him started court tongues wagging. The Queen's honor if not his
own was in jeopardy, and even her health was endangered, causing
him to be more concerned over her state of mind than his own peril.
Tense and nervous, she was frightened by what would happen if she
became pregnant. It was paramount that their marriage be made
public, if only to avert international scandal. The sincerity of
Suffolk's plea is unmistakable: 'My Lord,' he implored, 'at the
reverance of God help that I may be married as I go out of France,
openly, for many things of which I will advertise you by mine next
letters. Give me your advice whether the French King and his
mother shall write again to the King for this open marriage; seeing
that this privy marriage is done, and that I think none otherwise
but that she is with child.'

Their fears of an immediate pregnancy proved to be groundless.
Henry, their eldest child, was not born until July 17, 1516, ten
months after their third marriage at Greenwich.

The 'open' Parisian marriage repeatedly alluded to could only have
been a second one, the date of which is nearly as uncertain as that
of the first. It took place in March, during Lent, apparently at the
end of the month. Two contemporary but conflicting dates are both
supported by manuscript documentation: March 3, as given in a
French chronicle in the Fontanieu Portefeuille, and the last Saturday
in March as recorded by Louise of Savoy in her Journal: 'Saturday
the last day of March the Duke of Suffolk, a person of low estate
whom Henry VIII had sent as ambassador to the King [Francis I],
married Mary.' Since it could hardly have occurred before Suffolk's
letter of the fifth, in which he first raised the question of a second

G

marriage, the latter is the more probable date. It was this ceremony rather than the first one that Thomas Spinelly got news of in Ghent on April 4 and warned Henry of immediately. Although it was semisecret, the second marriage was sanctioned by a bishop and public enough to bear the test of official scrutiny, if and when proof was required.

That Mary knew how to handle her brother, her letters show, though occasionally she overdid the flattery or overstepped the bounds of propriety in addressing him, so that Wolsey, who read most of her correspondence before it reached Henry, was forced to tone down some of her remarks. Mostly, however, her story supplemented Brandon's and was an appeal not so much for herself as for her husband, whose very life was at stake.

She thanked the King for sending her such able agents as Suffolk and his associates to comfort her 'in her heaviness' and assist her in obtaining her dower. To them she was the soul of meekness and cooperation. 'She said she were an unkind sister if she should not follow your mind and pleasure in every behalf,' they reported to Henry, 'for there was never princess so much beholden to her sovereign and brother as she is to your Grace.' She had no desire to stay in France; rather every day seemed to her like an eternity until she could get back to England and her brother. As for marrying a foreigner without his approval 'she never would, [but rather] suffer the extremity of death.' To Henry she kept reverting to his promise to her, on the word of a king, when they parted at Dover. The responsibility for their hasty action, she persisted in saying, was all hers and owed nothing to any persuassion on Brandon's part, her letters reflecting a natural impulse to shield the man she loved. The restraint and sincerity of her explanation are marked:

Sir, I will not in any wise deny but that I have offended your Grace, for the which I do put myself most humbly in your clemency and mercy. Nevertheless to the intent that your Highness should not think that I had simply, carnally or of any sensual appetite done the same, I having no re[gar]d to fall in your Grace's displeasure, I assure your Grace that I have never done [without your] ordinance and consent, but by the r[eason of the grea]t despair w[herein I was put]. . . . Whereupon, Sir, I put [my Lord of Su]ffolk in choice w[hether he woul]d accomplish th[e marriag]e within f[our days or else that he should never have] enjoyed me. Whereby I know well that I constrained him to break such promises as he had made to your Grace,

as well for fear of loosing me as also that I ascertained him that . . .
I would never come into England.

The direct and honest appeal for forgiveness with which she concluded this letter was likely to be effective with Henry, if not with
the Council:

> And now that your Grace knoweth the both offences of the which I
> have been the only occasion, I most humbly and as your most [sorrow]-
> ful sister requiring you to have compassion upon us both and to
> pardon our offences, and that it will please your Grace to write to me
> and to my Lord of Suffolk some [comfort]able words, for it sh[all be]
> greatest comfort for u[s both]. By your loving and most humble sister,
>
> Mary

However, the 'comfortable words' so much desired were not forthcoming. Hearing nothing from Henry, Mary then appealed to Wolsey
in the same tone, begging for news of the King's intentions, 'for I
trow there was never woman that had more need.' Once she
threatened to make an end of it all and enter a nunnery, 'the which
I think your Grace would be very sorry and your realm also,' a
gesture that must have brought a smile to the face of more than one
reader.

It was not only her brother's personal anger that Mary feared,
but the influence of Brandon's rivals in the Council who might
persuade the King to punish her disobedience by annulling her
union with Suffolk and forcing a Continental marriage upon her;
'hinderers,' she called them, for in her mind their one purpose was
to retard the Duke's further advancement. The conciliar division
was not quite as simple as that, but Mary had no interest in broader
political implications. In an effort to forestall the marriage the anti-
Suffolk faction in the Council, headed by Norfolk, had sent over
Friar Bonaventure Langley to be her father confessor, who with an
associate had tried to turn her against the Duke. Under the guise
of his office Langley sought a confession from Mary concerning her
intentions towards Brandon and failing in that warned her to beware
of him, lest she lose her own soul. Suffolk was an evil man, he told
her, in league with the Devil; it was his diabolical power that had
produced the peculiar disease 'in Compton's leg,' which Mary presumably knew all about. The reference was to Sir William Compton,
who like Brandon had grown up at Court as an inseparable companion of Henry. This ailment of Compton's was Suffolk's curse on

his rival, inflicted upon him in an attempt to checkmate his power over the prince, and when the prince became king it was 'the puissance of the said Devil' that gave Brandon and Wolsey so much control over their master. More convincingly the friar further maintained that the Council was strongly opposed to her marriage with Suffolk and would never consent to it. It was a rather childish attempt to discourage Mary and one which had no effect whatsoever except further to drive her into the secret marriage. Perhaps that was what Norfolk had really intended, for Brandon assumed him to have been the 'schoolmaster' behind the intrigue. Rejected by the Queen, the friars were recalled and reprimanded by Wolsey.

Thus far Suffolk and Mary seemed unaware of the real magnitude of their offense. English affairs in France were in good order if Francis were to be believed, and Henry appeared to be satisfied with the ambassadorial reports. The French King showed a spirit of concession on all controversial points; Suffolk had banqueted with him, jousted with him, and laid the groundwork for a personal meeting between him and Henry, all of which indicated that a desirable treaty was in the making. Before February was over he wrote Wolsey that his business in France had progressed as well as could possibly be expected. Suffolk was unduly optimistic, for within a mere fortnight all these gains seemed unimportant: by the middle of March, 1515, the fury of Henry's wrath had descended upon them.

The King's reaction, as conveyed by Wolsey after consultation with him, came as a complete surprise. The letter was a cutting reply to their confession of the secret marriage and dispelled all hope of either approval or forgiveness, stressing the extreme gravity of their offense. It was deliberately intended to dismay, and it did. With good reason to write bluntly, he was at no pains to spare their feelings, and in addressing himself to Suffolk, his censure was obviously meant for Mary as well. 'My Lord,' Wolsey began, 'with sorrowful heart I write unto you, signifying unto the same that I have to my no little discomfort and inward heaviness perceived by your letters . . . how that you be secretly married unto the King's sister, and have accompanied together as man and wife.' Considering that this action 'toucheth not only his [the King's] honour, your promise made to his Grace, but also my truth toward the same,' he had told the King all. Henry's first reaction had been one of utter incredulity; he could scarcely believe, Wolsey averred, that Suffolk would have broken his solemn promise, made 'in his hand' at Eltham, in Wolsey's presence. That he should dare to marry his sister without his permission was unthinkable! Having had such an 'assured affiance in your truth,' he wanted Suffolk to know the extent of his displeasure, 'and so his Grace would I should expressly write unto you.'

The letter was a masterpiece of implication. Wolsey wrote as if he were a close friend, reluctantly imparting a sovereign's hurt feelings and bitter indignation:

> And for my part, no man can be more sorry than I am that ye have so done, being so incumbered therewith that I cannot devise nor study the remedy thereof, considering that ye have failed to him which hath brought you up of low degree to be of this great honour; and that ye were the man in all the world he loved and trusted best, and was content that with good order and saving of his honour ye should have in marriage his said sister. Cursed be the blind affection and counsel that hath brought you hereunto, fearing that such sudden and un-advised dealing shall have sudden repentance.

Having softened his victim he dealt the final blow; he was doubt-ful if the King would forgive Suffolk under any consideration, 'for ye put yourself in the greatest danger that ever man was in.' Not-withstanding, a way out was just conceivable and 'if any remedy be, it shall be by that way.'

The remedy was of course financial. Brandon and the French Queen were to pay back, in annual installments of four thousand pounds cash, Mary's entire marriage portion, leaving her but six thousand a year to live on; and in addition, to return not only all her English plate and jewels which Henry considered as part of her original dowry, but also to surrender the jewelry that Louis had given her after their marriage. Henry wanted not a partial but a full settlement, Wolsey wrote: 'I assure you the hope that the King hath to obtain the said plate and jewels is the thing that most stayeth his Grace constantly to assert that ye should marry his sister; the lack whereof, I fear me, might make him cold and remiss and cause some altercation, whereof all men here, except his Grace and myself, would be right glad.' The price of forgiveness was to be measured in gold.

Wolsey had suddenly changed from friend to critic. He condemned Suffolk not only for commission but for omission also, rebuking him for negligence and lack of perception as an ambassador; he pointed out that by supporting his marriage to the Queen, Francis had purposely lulled him, already too willing to consider concessions, into gullibility; when he discovered that Suffolk was in disgrace he would show his true colors. On future negotiations Wolsey was even more specific: the Duke was to let the other ambassadors handle the question of Tournai and the overtures for a new confederation. 'I would not advise you to wade any further in these matters,' Wolsey told him, 'for it is to be thought that the French king intendeth to make his hand by favouring you in the attainment of the said marriage.' In all other things, particularly in connection with Mary's settlement, Suffolk was to follow Wolsey's instructions implicitly, not trusting in his own wit, which by insinuation was none too subtle. 'Thus I have as a friend declared my mind unto you, and never trust to use or have me in anything contrary to truth, my Master's honour, profits, wealth and surety.' The admonition was wisely chosen; beware of future behavior: 'Look wisely therefore upon the same, and consider you have enough to do in redressing your own causes; and think it will be hard to induce the King to give you a commission of trust, which hath so lightly regarded the same towards his Grace.'

The effect of this letter must have been shattering; Suffolk's future conduct demonstrates as much. Confidence fled, he put himself abjectly into Wolsey's hands and awaited the outcome.

Many Europeans criticized the marriage as a *mésalliance*, especially in the Netherlands where it was openly asserted that the union would do Mary no credit, but neither Henry nor Wolsey seems to have attached much importance to Brandon's social background. What must have interested them more was the gossip from Ghent, as reported by the English ambassador, that 'whatever is concluded in these matters Wolsey is the doer.' His part in the drama, however, was indirect. Politics and ambition motivated everything he did, and at that time he needed friends. His alliance with France had been unpopular, especially among members of the nobility; the Council itself was divided both on governmental policy and in composition, the older faction led by Norfolk and his son being jealous of the influence of the 'new men' who had won the confidence of the King, thereby undermining their own power. The chief offenders were Suffolk and Wolsey, whose leadership of the anti-Norfolk party and domination of the Council as well as of Henry was unassailable. The rift had begun with Wolsey's rise to power and widened as each new development in European politics inspired renewed attack upon him: the 'king's darling,' as Skelton called him, by his own admission could do whatever he liked. Unchecked, his enemies were convinced that Giustinian's prognostication would shortly become reality: Wolsey would 'have the management of the whole kingdom.'

The accession of Francis I gave Wolsey's enemies another chance to oppose him. Francis was known to be antagonistic to England and bent on resuming the Italian conquest as soon as he could protect himself against English opposition; he was therefore courting Wolsey and hence supporting Brandon, who as ambassador had been Wolsey's choice, in order to preserve Anglo-French amity and leave him free in Italy. These tactics strengthened the hand of the Norfolk clique which used Suffolk's reversal of fortune to demand his dismissal from the Council. Wolsey, in need of Suffolk's future support, stood by him, thereby placing the Duke so much in his debt that he could never afford to join the enemy camp.

The only account of the King's reaction to the marriage is Wolsey's, and according to it Henry, in his rage, was ready to listen to those of the Council who denounced Brandon's conduct. To marry the King's sister without his consent was scandalous: some demanded his dismissal, others his head. Popular opinion condemned the match as being beneath the dignity of the Queen, regretting the waste of her beauty on an upstart commoner when it might have won a profitable alliance for England; moreover Suffolk had failed the King in his charge, having compromised national interests for his own. So the stories came to him as he waited, praying for some 'word of comfort,' fearful that Henry had made up his mind, apprehensive that he had not.

Sensing the hostile attitude of the Court the couple accepted the gravity of the situation. In answer to his opponents on the Council, Brandon was quick to point out the injustice of their accusations. 'Alas, Sir, I may say that I have a hard fortune, seeing that there was never none of them in trouble but I was glad to help them in my power, and that your Grace knows best,' he told the King. 'And now that I am in this none little trouble and sorrow, now they are ready to help and destroy me. But, Sir, I can no more but God forgive them whatsoever comes to me, for I am determined.' He was willing to pay for having broken his word, but he vigorously denied all charges of disloyalty, knowing that the King would never allow him to be destroyed through the malice of others. Meanwhile, neither Henry nor Wolsey did anything to allay his fears.

The latter had, in fact, deliberately exaggerated both Suffolk's danger and Henry's indignation in order to pose as a defender. There is no question of the King's anger, but a large part of his ire was directed towards Francis, who had in effect outmaneuvered him; by encouraging the marriage of Mary and Suffolk he had deprived Henry of two political alliances, either of which might have been the groundwork for a new alignment against France if such proved necessary. Since Henry was still undecided on the question of her future, his primary concern was to get Mary home. Whatever his intentions regarding her ultimate disposition, they are conjectural; though he had promised her independence of choice, no one would have expected him to keep such a promise any more than she obviously did. Not yet the vindictive person he was to become, he was too fond of his sister and her husband to deprive himself indefinitely of their company. Quite willing, despite his great affection for them, to take pecuniary reprisals—a trait almost indistinguishable from Tudor character—he never seriously considered direr punishment. Within a few months after his return from France Suffolk had regained Henry's friendship and something of his former prestige, exercising as before an authority 'scarcely inferior to that of the king himself.' The Venetian ambassador, who always exaggerated Brandon's influence, described him as 'the first man in England' about the Court.

Nevertheless, it was clear from the beginning that Henry's leniency depended largely upon a favorable financial settlement with France regarding Mary's dowry and personal possessions. The task was not an easy one: Henry would never be satisfied with a pittance, and in practice Francis was not nearly so tractable as he had led the English ambassadors to suppose. By marrying Mary, Suffolk had turned the financial tables: Francis now had everything to gain and nothing to lose. In contrast, Mary and Suffolk found themselves alone and unsupported, with no choice but to submit to the King's demands. As intermediary, Wolsey was friendly but insistent. Just how much of the financial burden eventually imposed upon them was by his decision and how much was the result of Henry's avarice is hard to assess; probably it was a combination of both. A shrewd manipulator whose main objective was to please his sovereign, Wolsey knew they would have to pay whatever was demanded, so he gave no quarter.

In the prolonged discussions that followed, Suffolk faced the first

big crisis of his career. If he achieved all the King wanted—full
financial demands plus the renewal of a close understanding with
France—he and Wolsey would emerge from the conciliar attack
stronger than ever, while failure meant the loss of everything, including Mary. What he had at first interpreted as an easy assignment was
proving to be most taxing indeed. Negotiations floundered principally
on two points, the 'Mirror of Naples' and the restitution of Mary's
bridal expenses, estimated by the English at two hundred thousand
crowns. The former, her most cherished possession, she had given to
Henry during the first week of March as a peace offering, and his refusal to return it aroused bitter controversy. A 'star' of great price,
valued by the French chancellor at thirty thousand crowns and by the
English at even more, it had been a great mistake to send the jewel
secretly to England, especially as it was considered to be an heirloom
of the crown, traditionally belonging to the queens of France only
during their queenship. Eighteen pearls worth at least ten thousand
crowns had also mysteriously disappeared, and after it was discovered
that they too had gone to England, Francis' impatience gave way to
fury. When Mary was asked to produce the diamond and pearls
she had to confess that she had given them to her brother and could
not get them back. This looked strangely like international robbery,
and Francis was not at all polite in demanding their immediate
restoration. Suffolk promised their return, but his frantic appeals to
Wolsey were without avail. The deed was done. No Tudor ever gave
up such a treasure.

Failure to redeem himself from this initial error deprived Brandon
of any advantage he may once have had with Francis, particularly
since he had practically admitted the English demands to be unreasonable. They were indeed both excessive and irrational, including
not only the surrender of all Mary's dower lands but also restoration of her jewels and furniture, as well as financial reimbursement
for her passage expenses. On this item the ambassadors felt obliged
to demur. 'As the Queen shall have all her stuff returned,' they
insisted that it was unjust to ask also for further compensation, 'for
she may not have both the money and the stuff.' Upon the other
hand, their belief in the integrity of the French negotiators was less
realistic. 'And sithence it is likely that we shall commune with
reasonable men, we would be rather loth to demand anything out
of reason,' they wrote to Henry, despite the fact that the French
demands were equally unreasonable. Francis stubbornly held out for

the return of the 'Mirror of Naples,' though he knew that it was impossible for Mary to retrieve it, stipulating as well that she must pay all Louis's debts for which as husband and wife they had been jointly responsible, before the question of restitution would even be considered. In the end discussions shifted back to Tournai, which Francis wanted so badly that he would give Suffolk no peace. In vain the latter protested that he had no personal commission to treat on the surrender of the city, suggesting a possible exchange for Guines instead. Since Francis was willing to consider this, authorization from Wolsey was sought; the request was pointedly ignored.

Accusations were adrift that Suffolk had made a deal with Francis, promising him Tournai in exchange for support of his marriage, though both Henry and Wolsey knew the charge to be groundless, not because he might not have been desperate enough to do so but because he was not a base person. During a lifetime in Henry's service he had made many mistakes and a few serious blunders, but was never once disloyal, which is perhaps why Henry's trust in him went beyond the limits of friendship. On both the Tournai question and the renewal of the French treaty, he was rather obtuse. Too occupied with his own troubles, he found it difficult to be firm with Francis, whose support in all his personal affairs he so desperately wanted. It is hard to credit his failure to grasp the legal involvements in the controversy over Mary's jewels: 'The which is past me learning,' he wrote to Wolsey, 'and therefore as touching whether she have right or no I cannot tell.'

In part Brandon simply refused to face reality, preferring to rely upon the mercy of his benefactors for ultimate salvation. On the assumption that Wolsey would make the decisions anyway, he found a subservient attitude more effective than constructive action. He begged Wolsey to keep him informed of all developments, for he knew from friends 'what pain you take daily for my cause [and how] good Lord you are to me, for which and [all the] goodness that I find in you I heartily thank [you, as] he that shall never fail you during my life.' One in his predicament was glad of any tidings, he told the Cardinal; now as always he was resolved to follow Wolsey's advice in everything. Repeatedly assuring him that he would not forget his friendship 'to me dying day,' he added as an afterthought the wish that the King would put him on a reasonable income! With a sorrowful heart, 'I, your most poor subject, beseech you, most [dear]est lord, [for] forgiveness of mine offences,' he petitioned Henry, for 'rather than you should have me in mistrust in your [he]art that I should not be true to you as there may be accusing, [stri]ke off my head and let me not live.' Should he violate the King's faith in him, he deserved to die 'as shameful a death as ever died man.' With the love of 'so noble and so gracious' a prince, he could merit no greater favor had he 'been [master] of ten realms.' Henry must have been made conscious of a very penitent subject.

In early April the French storm clouds began to disperse: the financial settlement with Francis was virtually concluded by Easter, shortly before which Mary had been given permission to leave France. From England, however, there were still few signs of hope. Wolsey's favor had been regained but Henry appeared relentless as ever, neither expressly forbidding their return nor indicating a welcome, but rather just ignoring their request. On the eve of their departure from Paris they were to all intents still exiles.

The settlement was by no means a victory for Suffolk, who stated simply that Francis could not be compelled to 'gyf soo moche wyet howth [without] he lyst.' Nevertheless the ambassadors got more than they had anticipated. Mary was promised her jointure intact and paid two hundred thousand gold crowns as restitution of half of her original marriage portion, which included the compromise figure of twenty thousand crowns for her travel expenses to Abbeville, a sum arrived at only after a great deal of haggling. Her gold plate and most of her jewels were not retained by her, save for twenty-two diamonds, sixteen pearls, one ruby, and a large emerald which she had already appropriated as her own property. For these and the 'Mirror of Naples' she had to tender a formal receipt. This jewel remained in Henry's possession and long since has disappeared from the pages of history.

Upon her return home Mary surrendered all these jewels, later valued at £1,666 13s. 4d., to Henry, and bound herself and Suffolk in an obligation to pay him, in addition, one thousand pounds a year for twenty-four years, as compensation for the expense of her marriage to Louis. Suffolk was apologetic at having been unable to get all Mary's jewelry and furniture. 'I find you so good Lord to me,' he told the King, 'that there is nothing that grieves me, but that she and I have no more to content your Grace.'

In view of the lengthy negotiations between England and France, the new treaty of peace and amity of the fifth of April was some-

thing of an anticlimax. Full liberty of commerce and peaceful settlement of all outstanding grievances between them was pledged; the
allies of each were to be mutually respected and provisions for
assistance in case of unprovoked attack were included. More important was Francis' acknowledgment of the outstanding debt of one
million gold crowns due Henry from the previous reign. But Suffolk
and his aides had been unable to prevent Albany's return to Scotland or to stop the marriage alliance between Renée of France and
Charles of Castile; Richard de la Pole still flourished under French
protection; even plans for a meeting between the two monarchs
had fallen through. Nor were future relations improved; in fact,
Francis' hostility to England had been, if anything, intensified. Under
such circumstances all English attempts to stop the conquest of
Milan were so much wasted effort.

During her last hectic days in Paris two incidents emphasized to
Mary her change in status. The first was the loss of a beautiful
wedding present from the government of Venice, reputed to have
cost a thousand ducats or the equivalent of £225. The gift, whose
delivery had been delayed until after Louis's death by the illness of
one of the envoys, was a black silk hat in a jeweled box of black
velvet, with a pendant balas ruby and pear-shaped pearl attached to
the band. Congratulations being out of order, the Queen Dowager
was offered condolences instead. She extended 'very good greetings'
to the ambassadors, but her political importance had died with her
husband and, at her suggestion that they had brought her something,
they adroitly changed the subject. The prudent Venetians saved
their gifts for Henry VIII and the English nobles who were in a
position to shape policy 'well-disposed towards the Signory.'

The second incident, involving the last use of her official seal,
forcibly reminded her of what she was renouncing. Ironically it was
the instrument for transfer of everything she possessed to her
brother. By the authentication of this bill she rendered herself
penniless, entirely dependent upon her husband to sustain her. Only
a few other public documents sealed by her as queen have been
preserved, and may well represent the sum total of her official
activity. They are all orders to her French treasurer and receiver-
general for payments and rewards to her friends and attendants.
One, dated November 2, 1514, authorized the transfer of six hundred
crowns of *soleil* gold to London for the purchase of various jewels
given as gifts 'to some ladies and damsels of the said country of

England, nearly related to us, whom we do not wish to be named or otherwise mentioned here.' They were, of course, the English attendants who had been so peremptorily dismissed by Louis.

Since there was nothing further to detain them, the Suffolks left Paris on April 16 en route for Calais, there to remain until receiving Henry's permission to cross the Channel. Francis personally escorted them as far as St. Denis, where the recent treaty was being publicly celebrated, and as a last gesture of good will presented Mary with four rings, which Ambassador West demeaned as 'bagues of no great value'; other friends and state officials accompanied them on to Boulogne. Mary's life as queen was over. Although she retained the courtesy title 'the French Queen' for the rest of her life, she was now officially Duchess of Suffolk. The French seal, no longer of use to her, followed her home, to be filed away as a memento of past glory.

Relieved to get away from Paris, they still had no idea how long they might be compelled to stay in Calais before embarking for England: 'I am now comen out of the realm of France,' Mary informed Henry, 'and have put myself within your jurisdiction in this your town of Calais, where I intend to remain till such time as I shall have answer from you of your good and loving mind herein.' Though just a little staple town in 1515, Henry's Calais, as she chose to call it, must have been welcome to Mary, for it was at least inhabited by the English and within her brother's domain.

In doubt and indecision Mary and Brandon tarried in Calais for news from England. They were honorably entertained by the town, and the wait proved less irksome than they had expected. Despite their fears the summons was not long in coming, though the nature of the King's message is not known. Mary's last letter to Henry arrived with Suffolk's by the same messenger. In it she restated her whole case, bringing in review the King's promise to her for a free marriage and her choice of Brandon: 'And to be plain with your Grace, I have so bound myself unto him that for no cause earthly I will or may vary or change from the same.' Meanwhile she would remain in Calais, waiting for his forgiveness and the acceptance of their offer; until that came she would 'no further enter your realm.'

They set sail for Dover on May 2; Mary had been gone exactly seven months.

CHAPTER FOURTEEN

Suffolk Place

By the Mass, Master More, it is perilous striving
with princes. . . . Indignatio principis mors est.

Thomas Howard, fourth Duke of Norfolk, to Sir
Thomas More (William Roper, *Life of Sir Thomas
More*)

IN 1515 Southwark was not the flourishing London borough of
Stow's day, with 'divers streets, ways, and winding lanes, all full
of buildings inhabited,' but a sprawling agglomeration of a few
hundred houses beyond London Bridge, extending from Bankside
southward to open countryside. At the foot of Bostall Hill on the
south side of the Bridge lay the Suffolk estate, its broad terrace
sloping down to a private quay on the Thames. The house, a fine
mansion known as Suffolk Place, faced the river, long since the
principal highway linking the City to the administrative area of
Westminster Palace and its environs. Adjacent to it were two formal
gardens and a large maze behind which stretched eighty acres of
timbered woodland, filled with sturdy oak renowned for size and
beauty. From Southwark to Chelsea magnificent gardened palaces
such as this lined the river, lending dignified elegance to a city of
violent contrasts, thought by some to be the most beautiful in Europe.
Suffolk Place was built by Brandon on land inherited from his
family; a large rambling structure designed in the fashion of the
day around an inner courtyard, it was flanked by bedrooms,
nurseries, picture gallery, and a great hall. Here Mary came to live
after her return from France, and at her table from time to time sat
the King and Queen, Wolsey, the Emperor Charles, and such influential dignitaries from Court as she felt it worth her while to
entertain. Suffolk Place was her first home after her marriage and
for the rest of her life it remained her favorite.

On their arrival at Dover, Mary and Suffolk had been received by a large delegation of lords and ladies from London, sent to escort them to the capital. The party was met next day by Wolsey, who took them on to the royal manor of Barking, Essex, just outside London, where Henry greeted them privately, with none of the fanfare usually attendant upon royal reunions; yet despite the strain of their recent relationship the meeting of brother and sister was, by contemporary account, cordial and affectionate, for the King 'rejoiced greatly in her honourable return and great prosperity.' That Henry loved his sister is beyond question, and it was his pleasure at having her back at Court, increased by the profit that he hoped to derive from it, that prompted his forgiveness. The following day was spent in discussion of the financial agreement, which was drawn up and signed by the Duke and Duchess on May 11, the day after they reached London. Mary surrendered her plate and jewelry as well as all her dowry to the value of two hundred thousand pounds and agreed to pay by installments an additional twenty-four thousand for her marriage expenses in 1514, while Suffolk relinquished the estate and wardship of Elizabeth Grey. Had immediate payment been demanded it would have presented an impossible situation, for even as a long-term obligation it was an overwhelming burden, one from which they never fully recovered. 'It is hard to wive and thrive both in a year,' was for them a true saying. Despite his rank and position Brandon's fortune was yet to be made, being at this time scarcely adequate for his own maintenance without the additional strain of supporting a wife. Normal expenses were always heavy, and for a number of years their joint income was never sufficient to meet the annual payment to Henry. Chronic indebtedness, however, was not unusual among sixteenth-century peers, though it seldom represented the true financial picture. Land, not cash, was the real index of wealth, and the bulk of Suffolk's estates was not involved. In his case the debt was in the family, and once the first wave of reprisal had passed he and Mary could expect to enjoy something of Henry's former liberality. In the end their confidence was justified. While Henry VIII was never an easy creditor, with them he was not ruthless: their debt to him dragged on without foreclosure, increasing slowly but steadily year by year.

Considering the enormity of Brandon's offense the terms of the settlement were not considered excessive or immoderate at the time, either by governmental advisers or contemporary critics. From the

King's point of view the arrangement was reasonable enough, since his initial outlay on Mary's marriage, unusually large even for someone as extravagant as he, had been a political investment. That it had proved to be a poor one was no fault of his, and her subsequent union with Brandon had been deliberately entered into without his permission. Having acknowledged their guilt they expected punishment, relying upon Henry's generosity to deal out mercy rather than justice. Mercy they were given. Brandon might justly have been deprived of his offices and property and banished from Court—no small punishment in those days—and this, plus imprisonment or death, was what they had both most feared. That Brandon was getting off too easily was an opinion with which the majority of the Council seemed to concur. He was accused of the same intent as a later aspirant for power, Lord Thomas Howard, the half-brother of the Duke of Norfolk, who was so 'seduced by the devil' that he sought to marry a crown. When it was discovered that he was secretly betrothed to Lady Margaret Douglas, daughter of the Queen of Scotland and niece of the King, the poor man was attainted for treason, and not only lost the lady of his choice but died in 1536 during his period of imprisonment. Lady Margaret was sent to the Tower where she contracted fever and had to be moved to healthier confinement at Syon Abbey. Far then from mending her ways she reincurred disgrace a few years after her release by a second courtship with another member of the same family, this time the brother of Queen Catherine Howard, young Sir Charles. Again she was sent to Syon Abbey for her 'over much lightness,' until she had the good sense to 'wholly apply herself to please the king's highness.'

This was after Henry's irascibility and worry over the Succession had made him distrustful of everyone, but at no time was royal marriage to be trifled with, for princesses were not ordinary girls who might occasionally make a love match if their parents could afford it. Matrimony was for most people at best a perilous choice which Thomas More's father once likened to fishing for an eel. The hazards of chance were about seven to one, he declared: it was as if 'ye should put your hand into a blind bag full of snakes and eels together, seven snakes for one eel.' In his own case he was not easily discouraged, for he went to the bag four times with varying results.

Whether in Mary's day or later, those Tudors who tried to shirk their destiny were harshly dealt with, and as the Succession issue became more acute the danger of unlicensed unions mounted. After

1536 it was treason by act of parliament for anyone of royal blood to marry without the consent of the sovereign, a law which simply legalized a fact already virtually established. Needs of state came first, and if love perchance intervened it must be ruthlessly destroyed as inimical to the public welfare. When Mary's granddaughter, Katherine Grey, defied Elizabeth by marrying her lover, the Earl of Hertford, the Queen's fury pursued her to the grave. Despite the fact that the marriage was perfectly legal in the eyes of the Church and society, she was condemned for 'carnal copulation.' It being assumed that she and her husband had been unlawfully bedded, they were both guilty of fornication and their children branded as illegitimate. The unhappy Earl, whose crime was far less serious than Charles Brandon's, followed his wife to the Tower, and when finally sentenced by Star Chamber was found guilty on three counts: he had 'deflowered a virgin of the royal blood in the Queen's house,' had broken prison by seeing Katherine again, and had 'ravished her a second time.' The marriage was not only annulled but he was fined fifteeen thousand pounds and imprisoned during the Queen's pleasure.

In comparing the two cases it is only fair to point out the difference in the respective situations faced by the two sovereigns. In 1515 no threat to the throne was involved, though Suffolk's enemies assumed one. Henry had nothing to lose by forgiveness, and during the early years of his reign was more generous than his daughter Elizabeth. Neither Mary nor her husband was punished except financially, and Suffolk's rise continued almost without interruption. Within a few weeks he was granted a stewardship of crown lands carrying an annuity of £6 13s. 4d., and before the year was out, land and possessions worth over £500. As a further expression of good will, £5,000 of his previous debt to the King was canceled. Henry could not hold a grudge against a bosom friend for long, and Suffolk was one of the few ministers to retain his affection and confidence for an entire lifetime.

Plans for a third marriage ceremony were made immediately the couple returned to England. There were good reasons for wanting another since the previous ones had been both irregular and open to criticism. They had been secret, contracted during the Lenten season, entered into without the customary public banns, and with no record kept. Until the Succession was determined, Mary's offspring must be incontestably legitimate. She and Henry both preferred a public wedding as the simplest means of announcement, since by stopping gossip it would 'guard the King's honour and hers'; and so the banns were called and the marriage solemnized at Greenwich on Sunday, May 13, 1515, before the full Court. It was stated officially that the nation rejoiced: 'And with the same all the said estates and others of this realm be very glad and well pleased.'

The Venetians thought otherwise, since it was reported to the Signory that no public demonstrations had followed the wedding as would normally have been expected, 'because the kingdom did not approve of the marriage.' The ambassadors were undecided on the proper course to follow, doubting whether congratulations were in order. Upon learning from the Council that Mary and Suffolk had taken the step initially without the King's consent, and that Henry had concurred only because of his long friendship with the Duke, they wrote that this 'would appear incredible, but it is affirmed by the nobility of the Court.' The Venetian embassy was popular in England and, in order to avoid giving offense to the King, refrained from any mention of either Mary's return or her wedding, waiting to see if it were to be celebrated. By the end of the month 'for reason good' they had still said nothing; it was not until two months later when Suffolk was present with the King at a public audience, that they ventured to congratulate him on his marriage. The last item is interesting because it suggests that Brandon, though he did not speak of it, was at least conversant with Latin. The Venetians addressed him formally in that tongue, to which he 'answered very lovingly in English.'

Hall with his usual caution agrees in essence with the Venetian view:

> Against this marriage many men grudged and said that it was a great loss to the realm that she was not married to the Prince of Castile; but the wisest sort was content, considering that if she had been married again out of the realm, she should have carried much riches with her; and now she brought every year into the realm nine or ten thousand marks. But whatsoever the rude people said, the Duke behaved himself so that he had both the favour of the king and of the people, his wit and demeanour was such.

It was because many people 'grudged,' that Wolsey and Brandon did their best to stop all 'bruits' of the Parisian affair which were circulating over Europe. A cousin of Brandon's, Sir William Sidney, was sent to France to elicit a promise of secrecy from Francis and

Louise; the first marriage was to be hushed up altogether, the second to be kept secret by those who already knew of it, that gossip might die down. As an inducement to his consent Francis was asked to choose the date and place of his meeting with Henry, and friendship was reaffirmed with promises of English support in all French affairs. Sidney, a man of considerable ability whose relation to the Brandon family had enabled him to get an early start in public service, was determined to make this, his first major mission, a success. Not only did he obtain consent to every proposal but did some personal work for Wolsey as well, which won him the latter's confidence.

Temporary estrangement from the King brought only a brief period of relative inactivity to Brandon and Mary during the early months of their marriage. Welcome though this respite was after their agonizing anxiety in France, neither was disposed to accept social ostracism for long. At twenty Mary was full of energy and enthusiasm, and Brandon was never the man for a quiescent life. Their chief concern for the remainder of the year was to be completely reconciled with Henry and resume their normal position at Court. Like all the King's companions Brandon was an adroit time-server, clever enough not to antagonize or annoy, always receptive to his sovereign's moods and desires. Other royal favorites were cleverer, wittier, and more intelligent; yet it was he who retained first place in Henry's affection. Perhaps Giustinian's opinion that the Duke was a satellite, always reflecting the King's glory, explains Henry's acceptance of him, but in his home county of Suffolk, he was also popular in his own right: 'No one ever bore so vast a rise with so easy a dignity,' wrote an early admirer. The English had a saying, 'King Harry loved a man,' and Brandon was essentially that: proud, physical, and boastful, a mirror of everything, except intellectual ability, that Henry was himself.

Within the year Mary and Brandon had settled down in London as before, resuming again their life at Court as if they had never been away. Nonetheless, their cultural horizon had been broadened in innumerable ways, particularly in dress and manners, as a result of their Continental experiences, and Mary was delighted to bring French dances and fashions to English society. Ever intrigued with the latest foreign styles, she kept abreast of the times, never permitting herself to be outdone by ladies of fashion such as the Landgravine of Hassyn, who wore 'a head dress of pearls and rubies and a rich collar about her neck.' She liked to read the ambassadors' long recitals of banquets and balls at other Courts, of imported Venetian cloth and valuable chains, or fine headpieces worth as much as a hundred pounds sterling. Some of the German women were 'marvellous fair, well fed, and clean washed,' wrote the English ambassador from Augsburg, adding for the King's special benefit that he was still touched by the beauty of youth, though now grown prematurely old in the service of his country. Pretty, wealthy women rejoiced little in white hair and grey beard, he told the King, especially when their means were 'nearly exhausted.'

Rumors, too, and gossip scarcely to be swallowed even by the gullible brightened the days when the King was away from the capital and the social season lagged. Both Suffolk and Mary believed what they wanted to hear, thoroughly agreeing with the Pope regarding 'the ingratitude of the French' and amused by the wild report that Francis meant to get rid of his Queen by poison. News which frequently came in late was often brief and inaccurate, despite agents' instructions to write oftener and more fully. Opinions on affairs of state might be terse, but official dispatches were seldom lacking in inconsequential detail : 'First, I think the King of Hungary is sixty [years old] and is always borne in a chair,' reported Sir Robert Wingfield from the Imperial Court during the summer of 1515; he 'seemeth' to be sanguine. His brother, the King of Poland 'is not past sixty' and 'amongst big men he is of mean stature . . . and severe of cheer, for right seldom he laughs'; at his banquets the Emperor showed profuse liberality, with 'marvellous great gifts to the value of 200,000 florins in gold,' and so on. 'Nothing new in England,' wrote Henry's Latin Secretary, Andreas Ammonius to Erasmus, 'except that the King grows in excellence every day.' Ammonius had no news to relate, presumably because he was not looking for gossip. Reports, sometimes completely unfounded, spread rapidly from capital to capital across Europe and were not infrequently officially accepted as fact. As late as two months after her return from France, the Papacy, still discrediting the announcement of Mary's marriage, was interceding for her hand on behalf of the Prince of Portugal. However reliable an espionage system, it was difficult to separate fact from fiction.

Foreign ambassadors whose business it was to inform their home governments of their impressions of English ministers are strangely silent during these months on Suffolk's character and ability. It was

enough, apparently, for them to note his power and influence with
the King, a fact on which they were all agreed. When mentioned
in official dispatches he was often alluded to as a 'very handsome
man' or a 'chief nobleman of England.' Known to be ambitious, some
thought him to have 'great hopes of the crown, in the right of his
wife,' while others like the Venetian Secretary Nicolo Sagudino
called him 'a liberal and magnificent lord,' who treated ambassadors
graciously and entertained them 'most sumptuously.' He is 'very
robust and altogether not of a very noble lineage,' wrote another
Venetian somewhat later; yet as the King's brother-in-law 'much
honour and respect are paid him,' and he has 'the second seat in his
Majesty's Privy Council, which he rarely enters, save for discussion
of matters of a certain importance, passing his time more pleasantly
in other amusements.' If the chief councilor at that time was Norfolk, Suffolk was the King's principal playfellow and companion.
Until death, according to Hall, this 'noble and valiant' Duke remained
a hardy gentleman, 'yet not so hardy, as almost of all estates and
degrees of men high and low, rich and poor, heartily beloved, and his
death of them much lamented.'

Suffolk has been less generously handled, however, by modern
historians, who dub him 'shrewd' and 'intractable' with but 'mediocre
intelligence,' while to the more critical he becomes 'a man of sturdy
limbs and weak brain,' 'stupid' and 'beef-witted,' an able sportsman
who in politics and diplomacy had 'no ability whatsoever.' To
moralists, shocked by his succession of marriages, he is a 'profligate,'
a 'bad and unscrupulous man.' Judged by those who knew him well
he was neither sagacious minister nor obtuse servant. Somewhere
between the two extremes is the man the King embraced as his
nearest friend and the husband whom Mary loved and with whom
she found happiness.

Shortly after their marriage Suffolk, as was customary, made a
property settlement on Mary, designed to give her financial independence in the event of his death. Thus far Mary owned no land
save her 'right great possessions' in France which had been guaranteed to her by Francis before she left the country; even from this
the annual income, varying between six and seven thousand pounds,
was precarious, being entirely dependent upon the good will of the
French King. If England and France should war with each other her
revenues would be cut off altogether, throwing her solely upon the
generosity of her changeable brother. Since there is no accurate

record of Suffolk's estates at this time, the lands enumerated in the jointure are of some importance as indicating the extent of his possessions. Though heavily in debt and often short of actual cash, Suffolk was already a wealthy man, with widespread holdings in Suffolk, Norfolk, Berkshire, and Oxfordshire. Mary was given forty-seven manors, to revert to the crown upon her death, eighteen of which in eight counties were held by Thomas Howard, the second Earl of Surrey, inherited from his late wife, Ann, daughter of Edward IV. These were a part of the De la Pole lands, in which Suffolk had only a reversionary interest. Neither he nor Mary lived to acquire them.

The Suffolks could not afford to remain at Court for long at a time without financial assistance from Henry, which was not immediately forthcoming. The expenses of the Duke's last embassy had been exceedingly heavy, and upon his return he had been compelled to spend still more money on his wedding and on Suffolk Place, with no extra funds coming in. After a few weeks there they retired to Tattershall, one of their principal Lincolnshire manors. How long they were away is not recorded, but they were back at Court for Wolsey's honor that autumn, the reception of his Cardinal's Hat. Vergil suggests a rift between Suffolk and Wolsey about this time, due to the latter's unwillingness to intercede for the cancellation of the Duke's debt to the crown. His attitude was attributed to a desire to keep Brandon penniless and obedient: 'For just as great wealth elevates men's characters, so they are lowered by meagre resources.' Others besides Suffolk were becoming increasingly irritated by Wolsey's arrogance and ambition. Especially disliked after he received the Cardinalate, even the common folk began to turn against him. The King was indifferent to suggestions that the servant was becoming greater than the master, for Wolsey was a more effective administrator than all the others put together: the most he would promise was his word that no minister of his should get beyond control.

On the fifteenth of November, 1515, the papal prothonotary entered London bearing the Cardinal's Hat. The ceremony at Westminster Abbey the following Sunday was largely for the ecclesiastics, but Norfolk and Suffolk, heading a delegation of temporal lords, met the Cardinal at the door of the church to lead him and the procession to York Place at Charing Cross where a banquet awaited them. Everyone of importance attended, except the humanistic historian Vergil, who was imprisoned in the Tower by Wolsey's order and was not privileged to witness the ceremonies. As French Queen, Mary sat at the head table with Henry and Catherine. The palace of the Lord Cardinal, the manuscript version of the celebration says, was 'well sorted in every behalf . . . as to such a high and honourable creation belongeth.' Wolsey had now begun his own parade of power and omnipotence, using 'a golden chair, a golden cushion, a golden cloth on his table,' and, when walking he was accustomed to have the hat, symbol of the cardinalate, carried before him by a servant, 'raised up like some holy idol or other.' There was no mistaking who was Cardinal, continued Vergil, contemptuous of the proud prelate who had come to consider himself 'the peer of kings.'

The same month Mary was honored by having a ship named after her, a vessel of 207 guns, large enough to carry 800 to 1,000 troops. This was Henry's latest addition to his fleet of twenty-eight ships, of which the *Great Harry* was the largest. The King, who loved to display his knowledge of navigation, went with Catherine, Mary, Suffolk, and most of the Court to christen the vessel and personally pilot her out to sea. He wore a sailor's uniform and round his neck a gold chain, to which was attached a large boatswain's whistle with a tone as loud and clear as a trumpet. Dinner in Mary's honor was served aboard with Henry in the role of Captain. The Bishop of Durham, Thomas Ruthal, celebrated Mass, after which the galley was named *The Virgin Mary* (*La Pucelle Marie*). Better known as the *Princess Mary*, it took its place with the *Peter Pomegranate*, the *John the Baptist*, the *Katherine Pleasaunce*, and other ships both large and small, in being the nucleus of what was to become the most powerful naval force in Europe before the century closed. Other governments noted with concern that the English King was spending more on his fighting ships than they, and in vain did Wolsey assure the French envoy that this great galley and others like it had been built 'solely to give pleasure and pastime' to the two Queens. In one respect, however, Wolsey was correct: the dedication cere- mony—'the greatest cheer and triumph that could be devised'—was chiefly to please Mary. With typical royal imperiousness she had been punished by Henry and allowed to leave Court, only to be as suddenly recalled and forgiven. Her real life in England had begun again.

CHAPTER FIFTEEN

Pregnant Queens

Pastime with good company
I love and shall until I die;
Grudge who will, but none deny,
So God be pleased, this life will I
For my pastance,
Hunt, sing, and dance,
My heart is set;
All goodly sport
To my comfort;
Who shall me let?

Henry VIII, *Songs*

THE beginning of the year 1516 found the Court at Greenwich, already a favorite residence of the King. The royal couple had spent Christmas at the renovated palace of Eltham, since its nursery period frequently used for state business, but had moved to Greenwich for audiences and public receptions. The new Lord Chancellor Wolsey had accompanied them, having received the Great Seal from Warham on December 22 in London. Five times sealed by the Archbishop's signet, the seal was delivered to the King 'enclosed in a bag of white leather'; after being bestowed upon the Cardinal in the presence of Suffolk and other witnesses, it was resealed in the same bag by the new Keeper and taken to Eltham for formal presentation. There on Christmas Eve after Vespers, Wolsey took the oath of office as Chancellor of England. Having carried the burdens of the Chancery for more than a decade, Warham has been credited with giving up the position for a less strenuous life in his own diocese, but in fact he had been badgered into retirement by Wolsey. Until his downfall in 1529 when the period of great ecclesiastical chancellors ended, this Cardinal-Chancellor directed, almost single-handed, the destinies of England. Whatever his deficiencies as churchman,

196

his work as the King's 'prime' minister from this point forward was unrivaled. Giustinian considered him to be as significant as Henry himself; he was no longer simply cardinal, but another king, Richard Fox thought, 'and no one in the realm dares attempt aught in opposition to his interests.'

During the year Suffolk and Mary were at Court from time to time, depending upon the King's whim and their financial position. They remained in London over the Christmas holidays, probably reluctant to leave before the festivities were over, but left for their country estate early in the New Year. On the tenth of January Suffolk wrote to Wolsey from Norwich that he expected to be in London for eight to ten days on business, though the nature of it is not revealed. Evidently the King as well as others among the Duke's creditors was demanding a reckoning, for he was busy until the end of the month trying to straighten out his finances. Still at Court on the twenty-ninth for a sporting event at Greenwich, he competed with the King and thirty-five others in Running at the Ring, on which occasion Henry, always generous to his tilting companions, furnished clothing for everyone at a cost of £141 18s. 7d.; at the end of the contest each man was given his own outfit, the Duke getting his horse, harness, saddle, and riding coat.

While Mary stayed in the country Brandon did what he could to regain the King's favor. With her consent he sent some of her jewels to Wolsey as a manifest of their intention to pay their debt; at the same time he sought to mollify Henry by a special gift, a prized goshawk which he knew would be highly valued. If 'sche doo as wyell as I have seen her doo I dowth not boot sche schall contynt your grace,' he wrote, begging the King to have pity on them and let them know when Mary should rejoin the Court, as they desired nothing so much as the pleasure of his company. When she was finally summoned in February for the christening of her namesake, the Thames was still frozen over. The long spell of extreme cold did not break up until March, and from her own house Mary could watch the unusual sight of children sledding on the river and people crossing with their carts on the ice. She expected her own child during the second week in March.

It was a year for royal babies; Mary and Catherine were both pregnant, while in northern England Margaret Tudor, whose pregnancies during the past years they had anxiously followed, and who was now married to Archibald Douglas, had given birth the previous

October to her third daughter, Margaret Douglas, almost dying in the process. Poor Catherine, described late in 1515 as 'rather ugly than otherwise,' had at thirty-one already lost four children along with her youth, while the King was only twenty-five and the picture of radiant health. Once again the Queen failed her husband; the baby she gave England was a girl, healthy enough but not the son demanded of her. Named after her aunt, the French Queen, the future 'Bloody Mary' was born at Greenwich Palace on February 18, a fine Tudor redhead, a baby who 'never cries,' her father boasted. Henry successfully concealed his disappointment from the public, confident that since he and Catherine were still young, sons would follow. The christening took place on the twenty-first at the little Franciscan chapel near the Palace, where the child's parents had been married almost seven years before. Special for the event was a beautiful silver font brought from Canterbury, later to be used by Suffolk and Mary for the baptism of their third child. Although she was in London there is no record of Mary's having attended the christening, her own advanced state of pregnancy presumably accounting for her absence. Brandon represented the family, giving to the baby her New Year's Gift of a gold pomander. Worn suspended from the girdle it was a practical piece of jewelry for women of all ages, a scented bauble to be sniffed when confronted with unpleasant odors.

Financial difficulties must have been partly responsible for the semiretirement of Suffolk and Mary from Court during the summer of 1516, but current diplomatic developments may have furthered their temporary estrangement from the King. The French victory, the 'Battle of the Giants' at Marignano near Milan the previous September, had been a great triumph for Francis I, who then pressed his advantage by breaking up the alliances formed against him. Henry fumed, threatened, and squandered good money on Swiss mercenaries, all to no avail, while in Scotland all efforts failed to stay French intervention. Wolsey was blamed for everything, especially for wasting good English cash. In the Council even ministerial changes were not enough to bridge the widening rift, as Wolsey, supported by the new Lord Privy Seal, Thomas Ruthal, rode roughshod over all. English allies in Europe were lukewarm and undependable; Ferdinand had died in January, 1516, and his grandson the seventeen-year-old Charles, now King of Castile, had yielded to French influence the following summer with the Treaty of Noyon, which bound him among other things to marry the daughter of the French king, not yet a year old, or in case of her death to take a sister 'not yet born.' Wolsey, who was seeking to maintain what Giustinian termed the role of 'arbitrator of the affairs of Christendom,' had no choice but to accept this agreement, recognizing its probably ephemeral nature. It was the most 'slanderous alliance that ever was heard of,' he stated, more piqued at the eighty thousand pounds he had squandered than at the impropriety of the match.

Ensuing months witnessed no improvement. Maximilian, with promised financial support, had made a fiasco of his military expedition against Francis, about which English ambassadors in Germany did not mince words: the Emperor, 'continually in necessity and need,' would sell his very soul for money, they told Wolsey, advising that English funds would be better spent in strengthening Tournai or in attacking the Scots. In Italy things were no better: 'The Pope is French and all [everyone else] from Rome to Calais,' wrote the minister from Brussels. In the face of this situation Wolsey may well have encouraged ill-feeling between the King and any member of the Council who might oppose his own policies, to the point of suggesting that Henry turn a cold shoulder to his sister and brother-in-law until their financial relationship with him was more satisfactory. As matters stood Mary could hardly anticipate any revenue at all from her French possessions until the Continental situation improved.

Meanwhile, the birth of their first-born took precedence even over the mounting debt which eventually had to be faced. The child, a healthy boy, was born on Tuesday, March 11, between ten and twelve o'clock at night, at Wolsey's house just outside Temple Bar, then called Bath Place. In contrast to Catherine's latest failure to produce a male child, Mary had every reason to be elated, having, in the language of Marcellus Paligenius, vindicated her existence. In addition to her sense of personal achievement she and Brandon were quite aware, as was everyone at Court, that barring a male heir by the King, this son of theirs might one day succeed to the throne of England.

The christening of the child, named Henry after the King, marked the beginning of a reconciliation. Henry, who could never resist children, was immensely pleased at having Mary's first child named after him. John Fisher, Bishop of Rochester, who had known Mary since birth, officiated, assisted by the Bishop of Durham. The King

and the Cardinal were godfathers, the former giving the name; Lady
Catherine, Countess of Devonshire, daughter of Edward IV, was
godmother, and the Bishop of Durham sponsor at the confirmation.
The presence of Wolsey and the King made it a state function
enriched by all the pomp and trappings of royalty, which must have
pleased Brandon and Mary. The contemporary manuscript account
describes the appointments of the Hall at Suffolk Place where the
font filled with lukewarm water stood : fires blazed in the corners,
and twenty-four torches lit up the wall-hangings and bench cushions,
with their motif of red Tudor and white Yorkist roses. Everyone of
importance was there except Mary herself, who waited in the
nursery to receive her baby and his presents. The walk from the
nursery to the hall door had been well graveled and sweetened with
rushes of 'a meetly thickness,' and edged with a fancy railing and
flaming torches; outside the hall 'was a goodly porch of timber work
substantially builded . . . hanged without with cloth of arras and
within with cloth of gold.' The christening procession moved down
this artificial aisle, basin, taper, salt, and chrisom borne by members
of the Suffolk household; Lady Anne Grey, attended by Lord Edward
Grey and Mary's chamberlain Lord Thomas Dacre, carried the young
lord. Four squires acting as their torch-bearers were dressed in the
livery of the Duke, whose financial embarrassment had in no way
curtailed his taste for extravagance. Sir Humphrey Banaster, vice-
chamberlain to the French Queen, carried the infant's train.

After the ceremony spice and wine were served by Norfolk and
other lords. Each of the sponsors' gifts was presented separately, Lady
Catherine giving two pots of silver and gilt, the King a saltcellar
and cup of solid gold. No prince could have had a more auspicious
start than this child of royal stock, whose future was the envy of all
those who disparaged the Suffolk line.

Despite the heavy outlay entailed by the birth of their son, the
Suffolks tarried at Southwark for several weeks after this. While the
Duke could ill afford the expense of a social season in London, he
could hardly deny Mary the long anticipated reunion with her sister
Margaret, who was expected to visit the Court sometime after April,
and the gaiety that her coming would occasion.

Margaret, Queen of Scotland for ten years and Queen Regent for
two, had since the previous autumn been living quietly in northern
England where she had fled from quasi-imprisonment at Edinburgh.
Neither her brother nor sister had seen her since she left London in

1503 to become the bride of James IV, but they had followed her colorful and intrepid career with both interest and alarm, beset as it had been by the division and intrigue surrounding her. Turbulent Scotland had not been kind to its alien queen, giving her no public peace and little private happiness. After the death of James at Flodden in 1513 her position as Regent had grown increasingly insecure, rendered even more so by the arrival of the Duke of Albany, cousin and possible successor to the infant James V, to lead the French faction. With civil war imminent her imprudent marriage to the handsome Archibald Douglas, sixth Earl of Angus, had aggravated national discontent, and by August, 1515, having lost both her regency and her children, Margaret was virtually a political prisoner of the anti-Douglas faction. Her escape to England in September was timely, for by then she was ill and heavy with child; her third daughter, Margaret, future Countess of Lennox, was born at Harbottle Castle in Northumberland on October 8. Margaret Tudor was childless for the first four years of her marriage to James; after that babies had come to her with a frequency that pleased him and prematurely aged her. After the birth of her seventh child she had lost whatever charm she had ever had; neither beautiful like Mary nor cultured like Catherine of Aragon, she retained little of her youth but her heavy golden hair and passionate nature.

The wilful Margaret whom Mary had known as a child was changed less in character than in appearance. Still vain, selfish, and inconsiderate of others, she was more like her brother than her father, with Henry VIII's 'great twang' of temper and the same callousness that characterized so much of his later behavior. She shared his inordinate fondness for finery and ostentation, and this Tudor love of pomp, pageantry, and luxurious clothing was about the only thing she had in common with her sister. This love for apparel was almost childlike, for it had become more important than personal relationships. It was reported to Henry that the gifts and dresses he had sent to her in Northumberland after the birth of Margaret Douglas were a greater restorative to good health than all the medical attention she had received. For days at a time she showed no interest other than in the new gowns, over forty of them, which she had collected for her visit to the English Court. During her illness in 1515 she was removed from Harbottle Castle to Morpeth, Lord Dacre's Northumberland estate, to await recovery; while there she was nobly entertained, but her one desire was to be off to the capital where once again she might enjoy the privileges of royalty.

Margaret arrived in London with a company of English noblemen on May 3, having spent Ascension Eve with the Duke of Norfolk at Enfield. The King met her near Tottenham and escorted her to Baynard's Castle where she was temporarily lodged; later she was given permanent quarters just below Charing Cross in Scotland Yard, where of old the kings of Scotland had resided. Her reception by her family seems to have been spontaneous and genuine, Mary and Catherine in particular welcoming a sister with whom they could discuss past experiences and intimacies. Besides the pleasures of a family reunion their infants must have provided a common meeting ground inspired by mutual affection and interest, not only for the three queens but also for Henry. Politically the situation in Scotland was still hopelessly involved, though there were indications that it might improve to England's advantage if Margaret could in the future behave with more tact and discretion. Neither the King nor the Cardinal expected her marriage with Angus to last, and if she were free a new political alliance was not unthinkable; scarcely had she arrived in London than Wolsey was suggesting such to the Imperial ambassador. Although he had been chief among those who caused the break-up of the previous marriage alliance with the Netherlands, he now vowed that he would willingly renounce his Cardinal's Hat or sacrifice a finger of his right hand, 'if he could effect a marriage between [Margaret] and the Emperor.'

Reception of the King's sister began with a state dinner at Lambeth, followed by a series of entertainments during succeeding weeks either at Westminster or Greenwich, the highlight of which was a Grand Tournament on the nineteenth and twentieth climaxed by a big banquet for her. The King, with Suffolk, Essex, and young Nicholas Carew, were the challengers. From the royal grandstand Margaret, Mary, and Catherine reviewed a procession of thirty-five gorgeously dressed contestants and forty footmen; 'every man did well, but the King did best and so was adjudged.' The next day Henry and Suffolk 'ran volant at all comers, which was a pleasant sight to see.' Almost immediately after this tournament Mary and her husband departed for their Suffolk estate, leaving Wolsey in full command of the Council. It was noted that the Cardinal and Sir William Compton were 'marvellous great' in their control of policy, since a number of councilors for one reason or another were absent from Court; Norfolk was ill and Buckingham, like Suffolk, had retired to the country, while Dorset, Surrey, and Lord Abergavenny had been banished from the council chamber, 'whatsover that did mean.'

The meaning was clear enough : Wolsey was directing foreign policy alone, supported only by those who were willing to take his directions. In July Giustinian observed that Suffolk had lost favor, while Sir Thomas Lovell, long a trusted friend of the crown, interfered but little in public matters. 'The whole direction of affairs rests (to the dissatisfaction of everybody) with the Right Reverend Cardinal, the Bishop of Durham, and the illustrious Lord Treasurer,' he wrote, referring to Wolsey's main allies, Thomas Ruthal and Thomas Howard, second Duke of Norfolk. Ignored by both the King and Wolsey Suffolk was forced to bear his vexation with as good grace as possible, remaining in the country for the rest of the year, afraid or unwilling to return to Court until actually summoned. Mary wrote a pathetic letter to her brother from Letheringham, Suffolk, in September, thanking him abjectly for permitting her husband to see him when he was in Berkshire earlier that month, and adding that their one hope was to be with him again soon which she desired more 'than all the honour of the world.' She desperately wanted to be recalled to London : 'I account myself as much bounden unto your Grace as ever sister was to brother; and according thereunto I shall, to the best of my power during my life, endeavour myself as far as in me shall be possible to do the thing that shall stand with your pleasure.' Before the end of the year Suffolk had re-established himself with Henry, and had been chosen to lead the army against France in the event of war. Malicious tongues again indicted Wolsey and Suffolk for the power they wielded over the King. One indiscreet critic in Lincolnshire was publicly brought to task for his words : they 'do rule him in all things even as they list . . . whether it be by necromancy, witchcraft, or policy no man knoweth.'

With his wife's French revenues withheld, Brandon had as yet very little income beyond the rental from his estates, usually slow in coming in. In addition to Mary's debt to her brother, Suffolk had been forced to borrow an extra six thousand pounds since his return from England, so that his obligation to the King totaled twelve thousand by the end of 1516. Their reconciliation included a new financial arrangement by which jewels were accepted in lieu of Mary's yearly payment, and Suffolk was given an extension of time, his debt to be paid off gradually by regular installments terminating on or before 1531, the date to be dependent upon the state's financial need in case of war. Other creditors, like George Talbot, Earl of Shrewsbury, he stalled indefinitely, without pretense of repayment.

Some relief came the following spring when Brandon was given the wardship of the sons of Sir Thomas Knyvet, which brought in an appreciable income from their holdings in Norfolk and Wiltshire, but it was far from adequate for his needs. Despite this he never seemed to be unduly worried by his precarious financies, nor is there any evidence of his having curtailed expenditure during periods when money was short. While still in doubt about the renewal of his notes he imported tapestry from the Continent, presumably on credit. Such optimism was not unusual for Tudor noblemen, many of whom were heavily indebted to the crown. They shared with Suffolk full confidence in the King's leniency, knowing that if they could avoid repayment long enough a large portion, and perhaps all, of the debt might be canceled.

While Brandon and Mary were in Norfolk in the spring of 1517, Catherine made a pilgrimage to the celebrated shrine of Our Lady at the Austin Priory at Walsingham to pray for a son, a practice common to all classes. They met her at Pickenham Wade in Norfolk and accompanied her to the Priory; on her return journey, according to Suffolk, they entertained her with 'such poor cheer as we could make her Grace,' but with such graciousness that the Queen felt obliged to return their hospitality the following month. During Catherine's brief visit an incident occurred which Suffolk rightly feared might re-arouse Henry's hostility. Meddlesome Anne Jerning-ham, formerly an English attendant in Paris, had taken advantage of his hospitality to contrive the betrothal of a young ward of the King, then in Suffolk's custody, to Lady Anne Grey, one of Mary's ladies-in-waiting. The lad was John Berkeley, son and heir of Sir Maurice Berkeley, for whose welfare Brandon was responsible. Suffolk knew that this could be serious if the King chose to take offense and blame him for the clandestine engagement. He hastily wrote to Wolsey, expressing his 'no little displeasure' over what might prove to be a new and unforeseen catastrophe: 'I had lever have spent a thousand pounds than any such pageant should have been within the Queen's house and mine.' Disclaiming all responsibility, he advised the Cardinal to make Mistress Jerningham an example to anyone else who might in future take such a liberty

20 Mary and Brandon, wedding portrait, Greenwich, May 13, 1515, by an unknown artist

22 Acknowledgment of the receipt of 'le Mirouer de Napples,' with a large pearl attached, and twenty diamonds, April 16, 1515

21 Letter from Princess Mary to Louis XII, undated, written by a scribe, but signed by Mary in her own hand, with her seal

'within any nobleman or woman's house hereafter, and in especially with one of the King's wards.' Since the unlicensed engagement had been nipped in the bud, no issue was made of it and the foolish woman went unpunished.

For the rest of the year the Suffolks divided their time between the country and the capital. Like all landed nobility they needed to spend a portion of each year on their estates, but neither of them was willingly absent for long from Court, unless indeed the King chose to ignore them. Forced exclusion could be a great punishment, for it implied royal disapproval; when the monarch's support meant success or failure, a frown might spell disaster. Mary and Brandon were no longer in any danger of that dimension, but because of their nearness to the throne their absence was noticeable. Besides being loved by both Henry and Catherine, Mary was an ornament to the Court and her courtesy title of French Queen gave her status subordinate only to the English Queen; loveliness among women of the nobility was then, as it still is, unusual enough to cause a stir. She would not soon forget the rare compliment of the French Lord Admiral, Guillaume Gouffier de Bonnivet: 'Madame, you are the rose of Christendom. You should have stayed in France. We would have appreciated you.' Brandon's presence was equally desirable; after his reinstatement as the King's bosom companion he was on constant call for participation in jousts and revels, which since Henry's accession were becoming famous. Thus no couple was more in demand than they, and it was not until Mary's health began to fail that she remained for months at a time in the country, months made even longer and more lonely by Brandon's absence. Seldom did a month pass when he was not called to London or elsewhere to join the King.

In late April, 1517, they visited Henry at Richmond, whither the Court had removed itself to avoid the plague which was rapidly spreading across London. While there, its seclusion was interrupted by an alarming demonstration of artisans and apprentices, known as the Evil May-Day Riots. The chroniclers' narratives of these dramatic outbursts differ considerably, so that the parts played by the King, Wolsey, the queens, and others have been variously interpreted.

The source of the rising discontent among the London workers in the winter of 1516-17 is not fully established, but high prices, the presence of foreign merchants, and general economic dissatisfaction were contributing factors; foreigners had increased in number to

H

such an extent that they were said to dominate the City's commerce. To the 'utter undoing' of the natives, merchant strangers were accused of taking over practically all retail trade, so 'that no man almost buyeth of an Englishman.' While Londoners starved, foreigners were reported to be living 'abundantly in great pleasure.' Pent-up indignation at this state of affairs had been released by a certain Dr. Beale, a canon of St. Mary's Hospital, who incited the populace to action by a fiery sermon at St. Paul's Cross on Easter Tuesday. To a large audience he harangued against all the strangers who had been favored by the King and his ministers. He accused them of behaving scandalously, maltreating those who gave them a livelihood, mocking and oppressing Londoners, and added that not only had they deprived the English of their rightful living but had actually disgraced homes by the seduction of wives and daughters. 'The heaven is the Lord's and the fullness thereof; but the earth He has given to the children of men,' he misquoted as his text, arguing that under God's law it was right for any man to fight against aliens in defense of his country. England belonged to the English, he entreated, and 'as birds would defend their nest, so ought Englishmen to cherish and defend themselves and to hurt and grieve aliens for the common weal: *pugna pro patria.*'

Confusion and rumor grew steadily, and it was whispered that all foreigners would be massacred indiscriminately on May Day or soon thereafter. Precautions were taken but not before an inflamed mob of some two thousand rioters had sacked the houses of French, Flemish, and Italian artificers during the night of April 30. Troops were called out to protect the citizenry; Beale and other ringleaders were arrested along with about seventy followers, some no more than children. After a summary trial a baker's dozen were condemned to be hanged, drawn, and quartered on the seventh of May, but at the appointed hour the sentence was remitted for all but one of them. John Stow's story that the pardon was granted by the King at the plea of the three queens may be so, for Mary and Margaret were both at Richmond with Catherine at the time. If their compassion was aroused and prompted concerted intercession, the King could hardly have ignored it; Catherine and Mary were both pregnant again, and Henry, hoping once more for a male heir, may have been inclined to leniency.

The queens can have had little influence on the hearings that followed the first prosecutions. To the Howards, Surrey, and Norfolk fell the task of ruthlessly stamping out the insurrection, which they did with all the unfeeling brutality of the sixteenth century. Vergil deplored the fact that of the 275 or more culprits rounded up for trial—priests, farmers, laborers, even children—many were innocent victims from outside the town: 'Those whose lot was indeed worse were those who had fallen in with that rabble of abandoned men by sudden chance rather than by any set plan and who yet shared the punishment.' One ringleader and four of his associates were speedily executed and their dismembered bodies impaled on the gates of the City where they remained for fifteen days. Hall narrates that Norfolk came a second time with two thousand armed men to picket the streets; again prisoners were arraigned, summarily found guilty of high treason, hanged, drawn, and quartered. To many spectators the whole procedure must have smacked of 'Jedburgh justice,' the proverbial Lydford law 'how in the morn they hang and draw and sit in judgement after.'

In the days following all suspects were rounded up as quickly as possible and gallows erected at prominent centers in London for their immediate execution; even 'the poor younglings' among them received no mercy. An eye-witness described the public impression created as the hangings and mutilations continued; by the middle of May at least forty had been executed and hundreds imprisoned. 'At the city gates one sees nothing but gibbets and the quarters of these wretches, so that it is horrible to pass near them.'

The final act of the drama was played at Westminster Hall later in the month. Wolsey, the Council, the chief magistrates and citizens of London, and other prominent men were called together to witness the sentence of over four hundred delinquents, including a few young boys, eleven women, and a handful of hardened criminals who had managed to join them in the hope of a general pardon. There is no mention of Catherine or Mary being present, though Henry presided and Brandon sat with the Council. Margaret had already left the Court. The King, the Cardinal, and their attendants sat on a dais at the end of the Hall, and the culprits were brought before them 'all in their shirts and barefoot, and each with a halter around his neck.' It was too smoothly enacted not to have been pre-planned. Whether or not the queens had earlier persuaded him, Wolsey recommended mercy, and a royal pardon was granted to all the prisoners: 'It was a fine spectacle and well arranged, and the crowds of people present were innumerable.' The Cardinal, with tears in his eyes admonished future loyalty and obedience; the prisoners 'making such signs of rejoicing as became their escape from such peril,' shouted in unison, many of them leaping into the air from sheer relief, throwing their halters to the ceiling. Hall, anxious to give all the credit to the King, adds an undocumented conclusion: 'Then were all the gallows within the city taken down and many a good prayer said for the king, and the citizens took more heed to their servants.'

There is no proof that on this occasion Catherine and Mary knelt before the King, joining Wolsey in an appeal for leniency. If such a touching scene occurred at all, as some writers have implied, it must have been earlier at Greenwich Palace, when about May 9 the Lord Mayor and aldermen of London formally waited on Henry, petitioning his pardon of all offenders. Margaret was still there, and the three of them may well have added their supplication to that of the City delegation. This, however, was not the occasion mentioned by Stow, for Henry had definitely refused to grant this particular request.

On May 18 Margaret departed for Scotland to rejoin her arrant husband, who had preferred to cast his lot with Albany rather than remain in England with his wife. This was not surprising to Henry, although in the language of chronicler Hall it 'much made her to muse.' Having been entertained by her brother for more than a year at a cost of well over two thousand pounds—and no one was more conscious of the lavish expenditure of the English Court than she— she returned to her normal frugal life laden with gifts, 'albeit she came into England with much poverty.' As a parting gesture Henry had given her two gold cups, gear and trappings for the horses, and bales of cloth of gold and velvet so that she might re-enter her adopted country in state, in exchange for her promise that she would take no part in the current administration of the government; but the capricious Margaret was incapable of abiding for long by any commitment and, utterly unable to remain free of intrigue, in a few months she was as unhappy as she had been before leaving. 'I had liever be dead than live my life in Scotland,' she wrote to Thomas Dacre, Lord Dacre of the North, but Wolsey and Henry found it cheaper and less complicated to keep her there than to grant her another asylum in England. Mary heard from her occasionally but never saw her again. Although considerably older Margaret survived her sister by eight years.

Suffolk and Mary stayed away from London for most of the summer of 1517, recouping their finances and avoiding the 'sweat' or sweating sickness of which London was full. Like most noble families they deliberately sought the 'purer air' of the country or small towns where the population was less congested. Besides the King, Brandon had other creditors who were not reluctant to demand payment, and in the country he could avoid those he owed rather than face their embarrassing questions in London.

Meanwhile, Mary's French income remained in jeopardy. It was, therefore, with considerable misgiving that Suffolk added his signature to the treaty of friendship with Spain and joined in the hospitality extended to the diplomatic delegation from Charles and Maximilian that arrived early in the summer, for by alienating Francis in so doing, Mary might irrevocably lose her revenue. In reality he had no choice, his welfare being so dependent upon the King that he could never afford openly to oppose royal policy. Moreover, domestic happiness dictated that he do nothing to endanger their personal relationship with Henry. Thus they participated fully in the reception of the Burgundian ambassadors at Greenwich at the beginning of July, 1517.

No expense was spared in entertaining the envoys, who arrived with a large retinue of a hundred horses and twenty-four wagons of luggage. Not to be outdone, Henry sent four hundred nobles to meet them and escort them to Greenwich. At their first audience the members of the Court, including Catherine and Mary, were dressed in cloth of gold, their jewels conspicuously displayed. The King himself was the most magnificent 'in the Hungarian fashion,' with a heavy collar of 'inestimable value' round his neck. 'Everything glittered with gold,' wrote the Venetian minister. Henry's intention to impress succeeded beyond his expectation, the foreigners being dazzled by English wealth and culture. They were banqueted daily, and diverted with pageants and concerts, exhibitions and jousts; the King was the focal point of it all, whether he was tilting or showing off his musical talent at the banquet table. On St. Peter's Day, after Mass, the terms of the accord were read and discussed.

The culmination was a joust held in front of fifty thousand spectators, for which a special walled tiltyard had been built, stated by the Venetians to be three times larger than the Piazza di San Pieto at Mantua, with stands for guests and 'two special tents of cloth of gold' for contestants. The King and Suffolk led off at the lists; Henry had wanted to fight the whole array of jousters alone, challenging each individually, but in order to limit the tournament to six courses, each to be finished in one day, he was persuaded to content himself with a single competitor, Suffolk. Sagudino was extravagantly enthusiastic; throughout 'they bore themselves so bravely that the spectators fancied themselves witnessing a joust between Hector and Achilles.' They tilted eight courses, 'shivering their lances at every time, to the great applause of the spectators.' When the King arrived in the lists, reported another, he presented himself to the queens and other ladies, 'making a thousand jumps in the air, and after tiring one horse, he entered the tent and mounted another . . . doing this constantly, and reappearing in the lists until the end of the jousts.' The contest lasted for four hours.

Many doubted whether the money lavished on this embassy was well invested, while Wolsey complacently waited for the next turn of events. A defensive league, composed of the Papacy, the Empire, Spain, and England was proclaimed, and the ambassadors left with a loan of £13,333 6s. 8d. to be repaid in yearly installments. Gifts valued at one to three thousand ducats were distributed at parting; to one was given a fine horse with all its trappings and a sabled gown of gold brocade alone worth 700 ducats. A tribute to the English and their King was paid by the papal nuncio, Francesco Chieregato:

> In short, the wealth and civilization of the world are here; and those who call the English barbarians appear to me to render themselves such. I here perceive very elegant manners, extreme decorum, and very great politeness; and amongst other things there is this most invincible King, whose acquirements and qualities are so many and excellent that I consider him to excel all who ever wore a crown; and blessed and happy may this country call itself in having as its lord so worthy and eminent a sovereign, whose sway is more bland and gentle than the greatest liberty under any other.

The Court broke up immediately after the ambassadors' departure. Henry took a 'pleasure progress' through the country, while Mary, en route to Walsingham Priory, was forced to stop and accept the hospitality of her old friend Nicholas West, the Bishop of Ely, at Hatfield, where she gave birth to her second child. Seventeen miles north of London, Hatfield, then known as Bishop's Hatfield, had been the seat of the Bishops of Ely since the Middle Ages, but the Palace

had been leased to the King's farriers early in Henry VIII's reign
and was considered virtually crown property, which it did in fact
become after Mary's death. A quiet place surrounded by orchards
and gardens, it proved ideal for Mary's confinement. There her first
daughter was born between two and three o'clock in the morning on
St. Francis' Day, the sixteenth of July and was called Frances, ostensibly after the saint; the choice of name may have been in part a
gesture to the King of France. The baby was christened two days
later at the local parish church before about seventy-five people, the
ceremony illuminated by eighty torch-bearers. The godmothers,
Queeen Catherine and the infant Princess Mary, were represented
by 'Lady Boleyn' and Elizabeth Grey; the former was probably Lady
Anne Boleyn, aunt of Henry's second queen, who was the wife of
Edward Boleyn and a favorite of Catherine. The Abbot of St. Alban's
was godfather. The christening lacked the regal formality of that of
Mary's first-born, for the King was not present; nor did the later
birth of a second Suffolk daughter attract any national attention.
If any of Brandon's children were then considered dynastically significant, it could only have been Lord Henry.

The 'sickness' kept most of the nobility in the country for the
rest of the year. In the towns the casualties were increasingly
alarming, especially to the King, who had withdrawn himself to
some distance from London, wrote the Venetian ambassador: 'This
[sweating] sickness makes very great progress, proving fatal in
twenty-four hours at the furthest, and many are carried off in four
or five hours; the patients experience nothing but a profuse sweat,
which dissolves the frame, and when once the twenty-four hours are
passed all danger is at an end.'

Brandon and Mary spent the winter in Suffolk in comparative
peace: Westhorpe had escaped the epidemic, a financial crisis had
been averted, and they were once more restored to the King's favor.

CHAPTER SIXTEEN

Westhorpe

> Good bread and good drink, a good fire in the Hall,
> Brawn, pudding and souse, and good mustard withal.
> Beef, mutton and pork, shred pies of the best,
> Pig, veal, goose and capon, and turkey well drest,
> Cheese, apples and nuts, jolly carols to hear,
> As then in the country is counted good cheer.
> What cost to good husband is any of this?
> Good household provision only it is:
> Of others the like, I do leave out many,
> That costeth the husbandman never a penny.
> At Christmas be merry, and thankful withal,
> And feast thy neighbours, the great with the small;
> Yea, all the year long, to the poor let us give,
> God's blessing to follow us, whiles we do live.

Thomas Tusser, 'Christmas Husbandly Fare,' in
The Suffolk Garland

SUFFOLK owned extensive property in East Anglia, including numerous estates in several eastern counties. While his principal residences were in Suffolk, he and his wife spent shorter periods at their other houses, in particular at Castle Rising in Norfolk, Donnington in Berkshire, and Ewelme and Hognorton in Oxfordshire. The bulk of his holdings in Lincolnshire, 119 manors, was acquired by Brandon after Mary's death, as were the Dissolution spoils which multiplied his wealth within a few years. The greater part of the possessions that came to him by virtue of his last marriage to Catherine Willoughby were in the same county; to these were added grants of monastic lands and gifts from the King in recognition of his services in putting down the Lincolnshire rebellion in 1536, making him one of the wealthiest landowners there. But it was in Suffolk that most of his estates lay in the 1520's, with substantial

houses at Haughley, Cravens Lordship, Thorndon, Wingfield, Letheringham, Henham, Ipswich, and Westhorpe.

Westhorpe Hall was the actual country seat of the family and it
was here that Mary spent most of her time when not in London. This
and Suffolk Place were the only real homes of her own that she
knew. Lying in the heart of the country near the village of Finning-
ham about twelve miles from Bury St. Edmunds, Westhorpe parish
was rural Suffolk at its best. Green, quiet, peaceful, somnolent, it
was in striking contrast to the hustle and bustle of London. Although
Westhorpe was only seventy-five miles from the capital as the crow
flies, it was then a four- or five-day journey depending upon the
mood of the traveler and the condition of the roads. Ipswich, incorporated in 1464, was the largest town in Suffolk in Mary's day with
a population of less than six thousand. Starting early in the morning the family made the trip from London unhurriedly, the little
train of carts and horses passing up St. Martin's Lane, through
Clerkenwell and up the great north road to St. Alban's—the old
Watling Street of Roman times—where the travelers would spend
the first night; the next two would be at Baldock and Cambridge, the
last at Bury St. Edmunds. Mary and the children probably rode in a
small char or carriage with the nurse, as was customary then, the
others on horseback, while the servants attended to the packhorses
and carts loaded with clothes and household stuff in the rear.

In many ways Brandon enjoyed returning to the country, to his
hunting and the prize herds of horses and mules in which he took
great pride. Among the most valued were Wolsey's mules, which
Suffolk acquired upon the Cardinal's downfall in 1529, some of
which were worth fifteen pounds a span. All his parks were well-
stocked with red deer, and if he was at Westhorpe during the summer
'grease season' when the buck was fat for slaughter, he hunted with
his friends in Haughley Park nearby, or in the Huntingdon estate
lying along the River Blyth which came into his possession in 1531.

Once Mary was established in Suffolk, her life was not disagree-
able. Westhorpe Hall was a stately enough building for a country
manor house, with a cloistered court, a private chapel beautifully
lit by lofty stained glass windows, and appropriate outbuildings, the
whole surrounded by a mossy moat crossed by a three-arched bridge
of Tudor brick. An account of the house when it was pulled down in
the eighteenth century gives some indication of its former size and
dignity. It was never rebuilt, but the bridge remains, and the pedi-

ment bearing Mary's coat-of-arms is inserted above the doorway of the farmhouse that now stands near the site of the original building. Within walking distance was the fourteenth-century parish church which still contains the royal pew where Brandon and Mary sat during Sunday worship. West Suffolk was picturesque, its windmills and dovecotes nestling half-hidden in the rolling landscape, and produced excellent cheeses and the sweet butter for which the county was famous. Every year at 'Edmunsbury,' which John Leland, the antiquary, styled the most 'neatly-seated' town the sun ever saw, there were three regional fairs which demanded the presence of the local nobility when they happened to be in residence. The Easter Fair and Market was frequently attended by the Suffolks; in a tent of cloth of gold the French Queen held court, receiving guests and greeting friends from the country gentry. Homage was paid her wherever she went; the people of Suffolk did not forget that she was a Dowager Queen and the King's sister. As well as entertaining the county with picnics, feasts, and hunting parties, Brandon and Mary made pilgrimages to local shrines, and when food was scarce or boredom unbearable, short progresses to their adjacent manors where different problems and new faces relieved the monotony of country life. Sometimes they went farther afield in search of supplies, to Norwich or more often to the cloth market at Ipswich, and occasionally spent weeks at a time at some monastery where hospitality to the nobility was always graciously bestowed. Mary was certainly not idle during the periods of her residence at Westhorpe. When not otherwise engaged her hours were filled from morning to night with the endless routine of managing a large household. For both mistress and servant in the sixteenth century the day began early. In this respect Mary was probably not so different from her successor, Catherine Willoughby, who wrote to William Cecil from Grimsthorpe, at six o'clock in the morning, 'like a sluggard in my bed.'

Not much is known about the Suffolk establishments, but they were presumably similar to those of other noble households of the period, about which ample evidence is available. Before the suppression of the monasteries from 1536 to 1539, when almost every lord acquired a share of the booty, the Tudor nobility was neither as wealthy nor as numerous, but to use the phrase of a modern scholar, it demonstrated the same 'spreading taste for conspicuous waste' as the Elizabethans were to do. As a result of increasing Renaissance extravagance, Nemesis was overtaking the English aristocracy, and

Brandon was not alone in always spending as much and usually far more than he could afford. All nobles maintained similar standards of living at Court, and even when in the country, their habits continued to be governed by the same high criteria. Locally the great lords dominated the counties in influence and politics, in social leadership, and sometimes in philanthropy, although their charitable contributions in education and patronage were insignificant. While less wealthy during earlier years than some other peers, Brandon's financial and managerial problems were no different from theirs and frequently more acute; until after Mary's death he lived on a more modest scale than they, but his appetites and his economic aspirations were the same. Skelton's characterization of the fourth Earl of Northumberland applied equally to many a poorer but no less haughty nobleman:

> So noble a man, so valiant lord and knight,
>   Fulfilled with honour, as all the world doth ken;
> At his commaundement, which had both day and night
>   Knights and squires, at every season when
> He called upon them, as menial household men.

No regular household accounts of the Suffolk family have been preserved, and isolated documents relating to their personal activities yield only the barest suggestion of the size and extent of the household unit. In the subsidy assessment for 1526, Mary's servants at Westhorpe are listed as forty-three men and seven women, including two knights, one esquire, and a Frenchman. The total wages for this little group amounted to only £327 yearly, which suggests that most of those assessed must have been domestics rather than more highly paid officials. The figure is in any case unreliable since many were included in that particular assessment who escaped taxation altogether. In comparison with these numbers, Princess Mary was credited with 65 servants and Wolsey with 429. The latter figure is definitely incorrect; his biographer, A. F. Pollard, reckoned the Cardinal's servants at almost a thousand.

The number given in the subsidy roll did not include the Duke's personal retinue, which must have been considerable. Unlike Queen Elizabeth, the early Tudors kept a careful check on the number of these liveried retainers, the size of each band being strictly regulated by statute. While the restrictions were not always enforced, penalties could be invoked as shown by the not infrequent indictments for willful violation. In 1516 Henry Algernon Percy, the fifth Earl of Northumberland, was imprisoned for having too many, and others were expelled from the Council for the same offense; at his trial in 1521 the Duke of Buckingham maintained that his position in society required him to retain a bodyguard of three to four hundred men. The days when mighty barons threatened the power of the crown with their own private armies were still within living memory, and the King had no intention of permitting any peer to forget that he kept any retainers at all by royal sufferance. However, Suffolk undoubtedly maintained as many as his rank allowed. The keeping of many servants was a practice common to all peers: Northumberland kept 166, including men, women, and children, though most of them were not retainers; Derby had almost as many, while Oxford's liverymen were seldom fewer than two hundred. It seems therefore to have been usual for the first lords of the realm to retain between one hundred and two hundred men in addition to their other servants. This custom promoted rivalry, which in turn encouraged extravagance and the incurrence of large debts: 'as well be in for a pound as a penny.'

The household of the Tudor nobleman was a status symbol, commensurate with his wealth and position, and as such varied in size and prestige. The same Earl of Northumberland was waited upon by twenty attendants in the morning, eighteen in the afternoon, and as many as thirty at supper and afterwards. His smaller houses each supported at least forty-two persons, and when he traveled he was attended by a riding household of fifty-seven. He regularly maintained a small orchestra, fifteen chapel attendants, twenty grooms, footmen, falconers, a painter, carpenter, huntsman, and almoner, besides the menials in the kitchen and stable, and the four chief officers of the household: chamberlain, steward, treasurer, and comptroller, employing ten clerks to keep the accounts tallied and in order. The Household Books for 1512-13 show the consumption of provisions to have been inordinately large even for so many people: 16,923 bushels of wheat, 124 'beeves,' 667 sheep, 25 hogs, 60 lambs, 28 calves, 942 salt fish, 144 stock fish, 19 barrels of herring, 5 kegs of eels, and 2,080 salt salmon. Other staples, including sugar, salt, pepper, vinegar and verjuice, rice, nuts, spices, and sweetmeats, were too numerous to detail; 4,087½ pounds of wax, 29 pounds of rosin for torches, and over 1,000 Parisian candles were used to light the premises. The beer, 27,594 gallons or an average of about 138 gallons

apiece, was mainly for the servants; for the family and guests between 4,580 and 4,900 gallons of wine, domestic and imported, were
drunk, the number depending upon the size of the hogsheads. All
this cost a total of £933 6s. 8d. in what seems to have been a not
untypical year. The good Earl died some £17,000 in debt.

The Northumberland estates were valued at about £3,000 to
£4,000 per year, those of Henry Courtenay, Marquis of Exeter, at
slightly less; Buckingham, reputedly the wealthiest nobleman in
England, boasted a landed income of over £6,000 per year. Suffolk's
was probably less than half that in 1521, although no safe valuation
is available; Giustinian estimated it at 12,000 ducats, or about £2,700
annually, the same as that of the Duke of Norfolk.

The only extant inventory of Suffolk Place is a fragmentary one
of the chapel in 1535. In addition to the usual chapel furnishings—
altar pieces, vestments, missals and breviaries, candlesticks, crosses,
chalices, altar basins, censers, pyx, and sacring bell—six gilt images
of saints, each weighing sixty to seventy ounces, and plate to the
value of £193 12s. are listed. The inventory specifies other plate at
Suffolk Place worth approximately £1,181, some of which Mary
may have been allowed to keep at the time of her financial settlement with the King.

Though operational expenses of the lesser manorial houses were
lower, even there demands upon the purse were considerable. Gifts
and rewards were expected from the Lord and Lady wherever they
resided, and local contributions at Easter, Christmas, and New Year
were equally mandatory. Cash offerings, as well as gifts of candles
and shrine 'stuff,' had to be made to the local church, while doles to
the poor on holy days were an established custom. The 'alms tub,'
especially to the aged and indigent of the community, represented the
measure of the family's charity, just as the entertainment of strangers
signified its liberality. Travelers stopped for a meal or so with the
great lord as a matter of course, and, like proverbial relations,
sometimes outstayed their welcome. Around the turn of the sixteenth
century an Italian guest expressed his astonishment to the Venetian government at the prevalence of English hospitality; they take
great pleasure in serving large quantities of 'excellent victuals,' he
told the Senate, and remain at the table for long periods. Struck with
the amount of food they ate, he remarked on their preference for ale
and beer rather than wine. Being great epicures and avaricious by
nature, the English 'indulge in the most delicate fare themselves,

and give their household the coarsest bread, and beer, and cold meat baked on Sunday for the week, which, however, they allow them in great abundance.' The Dutch and Germans, themselves connoisseurs of good living, also had their comments. Nicander Nucius branded them as crude 'flesh eaters,' a nation 'insatiable of animal food, sottish and unrestrained in their appetites.' Local people as well as transients took advantage of this 'open house' hospitality. In 1512 Northumberland reckoned to feed an average of fifty-seven strangers every day for the entire year at an estimated daily cost of a halfpenny per head. There were 244 people at Norfolk's house in Framlingham at the end of December, 1526, of whom 30 were servants, 14 were guest strangers, and the other 200 'persons of the country.' The great hall of the Duke of Buckingham at Thornbury, Gloucestershire, fed at least one hundred daily and on holidays a great many more. The Duke's accounts for Christmas, 1508, show that he entertained 294 people at both dinner and supper, of whom the majority were guests foreign to the community; twelve days later on the feast of the Epiphany he banqueted 519 at dinner and 400 at supper.

Most English landowners enjoyed being in the country, but might not have agreed with Antonio de Guevara, the Spanish author of 'A Looking-Glass for the Court' that 'the rustical life' was less demanding than that of the court. Visits to even remote estates were necessary to prevent their deterioration, and they involved considerable work and attention. It was the nobleman's neglect of estates that contributed to the decay of manors in the sixteenth century about which so much has been written. Protracted absence might incur spoliation of woods, loss of deer and livestock, and general breakdown of discipline. Suffolk's more distant properties suffered in this way from the hurried and infrequent visits which he sandwiched between political assignments. When he was not on an embassy or military service his time was occupied by commission investigations, Council deliberations, and personal business for the King, to the exclusion of his own needs. Prior to selling Ewelme and Hognorton to the crown in 1538, Brandon had spent £2,500 on them; yet these houses were still in a run-down condition and badly in need of repair. When land sales were made to the crown, royal agents had to be cautious lest the estate was stripped of deer and timber before it changed hands. In the Hognorton transfer it was stipulated that Suffolk should leave eighty deer in the park, though it does not say what number, if any, the Duke was permitted to keep and move to other land.

The sweating sickness, regularly recurrent in 1517 and 1518, kept most of the nobility in the country where the chances of infection were less acute. The King was deadly afraid of the disease and fled from it in mortal terror, as one by one members of his household succumbed. The Court, closed to all but the few whose presence official business necessitated, was continually on the move, fleeing from place to place before the spreading epidemic. Not even Brandon and Mary were permitted to join the King save occasionally, when out of fright or boredom he sent for them. From Greenwich to Eltham to Richmond, the Court ran from the sickness, and farther away to Farnham, Reading, Wallingford, Abingdon, and Woodstock, while Wolsey, undaunted, remained at his desk and fought off four separate attacks. This was the third wave of the disease which first struck England in 1485, to reappear in 1508, 1517, 1528, and again in 1551. Because it began in England and seemed to thrive on the English people, Europeans referred to it as 'the English sweat.' Unlike the plague, it was if anything less fatal to the poor than to the rich, and was even more alarming to the upper classes that sought most to avoid it. The closest modern parallel to this infectious disease which resembled malaria is miliary fever or the 'Picardy sweat,' which paradoxically does not appear in the United Kingdom. Characterized by violent inflammatory fever, prostration, depression, profuse perspiration, and general internal disorders, the sweating sickness struck suddenly and killed quickly. 'Multitudes are dying all around us,' More wrote to Erasmus in August, 1517, 'almost everyone in Oxford, Cambridge and London has been ill lately,' observing that 'no one dies except on the first day of attack.' Another account reads: 'All either died or escaped within the twenty-four hours.' Completely baffled by the pestilence, the medical profession was helpless; the most that was accomplished was a series of new prescriptions for the treatment of patients, the effectiveness of which may be measured by the following 'King's medicine' for the 'foul sickness':

> Take a handful of sage of vertue, a handful of herb grace, a handful of elder leaves, and a handful of red briar leaves, and stamp them together, and strain them in a fair cloth with a quart of white wine, and then take a quantity of ginger, and mingle them all together, and drink of that medicine a spoonful every day, nine days together, and

after nine days ye shall be whole, for the whole year, by the grace of God. And if it fortune that one be sore taken with the plague before he hath drunk of the same medicine, let him take the water of scabies, and a spoonful of betony water, and a quart of fine treacle, and put them all together, and cause the person to drink it, and it shall put out all the venom; and if it fortune that the botch do appear, then take of leaves of briars, elders, and mustard seed, and stamp them all together, and make a plaster thereof, and lay it to the sore, and it shall draw out all the venom, and the person shall be whole.

In the absence of medical protection, faith and divine guidance seemed to the righteous to be the best safeguard. A nostrum of 1561 illustrates this point of view:

Take a pound of good hard penance, and wash it well with the water of your eyes, and let it lie a good while at your heart. Take also of the best fine faith, hope and charity that you can get, a like quantity of all mixed together, your soul even full, and use this confection every day in your life, while the plagues of God reigneth. Then, take both your hands full of good works recommended by God, and keep them close in a clean conscience from the dust of vain glory, and ever as you are able and see necessity to use them.

This sour medicine was guaranteed to be of such strength and virtue as to purge the sick 'through the grace of Almighty God' from all 'pestilent infection.'

Brandon and Mary spent most of the critical months in Suffolk with friends and family. Both his daughters by Anne Browne were with them at Westhorpe Hall, and probably his adopted daughter, Magdalen Rochester, whom he had brought back from France. She was about thirteen in 1518, while Mary Brandon was only eight; little is known of this Mary save that she married Thomas Stanley, second Baron of Monteagle, shortly before her stepmother's death, and died in 1544. Anne, Suffolk's eldest child, was a handsome girl of sixteen, old enough to be companionable to Mary during her husband's frequent absences. She had been sent for at her stepmother's insistence, Suffolk having apparently intended to leave her permanently with Margaret of Savoy.

In March, 1518, the Suffolks welcomed a summons to spend Easter with the King and Queen, who at the time were in Abingdon. They were so pleased that Brandon sent a special letter to find out the state of the Court there and how the French Queen should be 'ordered.' They arrived on April 1 and remained until after St.

George's Day, going with Henry and Catherine to the royal manor of Woodstock at the end of the month. Buckingham and other members of the Council had been sent away earlier, but Suffolk was allowed to tarry because Mary was loath to leave. Henry, who had intended to return to London, changed his mind upon learning that it was still infected with the sweat: 'he was at ease here [Abingdon], where no man cometh [to] tell him of the death of any person, as they are wont daily.'

Secretary Richard Pace, who reported this conversation to Wolsey, told him of another episode which had occurred the same April. Various councilors, still suspecting Suffolk of disloyalty, accused him of favoring the restoration of Tournai to the French as part of his obligation to Francis for supporting him at the time of his marriage to Mary. Taken aback by the charge, on Easter Day after Mass Brandon had sworn to Pace that such accusations were entirely without foundation. There is no reason either to doubt his sincerity or to question his fidelity, since he was fully aware that his stand on the new accord with Francis I was bound to be liable to misinterpretation, if only because his wife's income hung in the delicate balance of the French King's pleasure. The treaty with France was pending and Suffolk was in close touch with the ambassadors, while at the same time his relations with Wolsey were strained, partly because the Duke had acquired advance information about the treaty negotiations. The Cardinal's coldness may have been further increased by a recent misunderstanding between them over Mary's French revenue, which Suffolk felt he had neglected. Wolsey may even have sought to turn the King away from Brandon again, for he warned him against the influence of such 'great personages' as Suffolk and Buckingham, who had free access to their sovereign. If not afraid of Suffolk's closeness to the King, Wolsey was not anxious to further it, and Giustinian's observation that Brandon was not 'so much in favour' as before may have been accurate. In speaking so succinctly to Pace the Duke was seeking a reconciliation with Wolsey, confident that his words would reach him. If it came to a choice his influence was worth more than the French income. Few had better reason than Brandon to respect the old saying, 'better is a friend in Court than a penny in the purse.'

Suffolk made another attempt to improve their relationship two months later at Woodstock, when he affirmed to Pace still more strongly his continued support of Wolsey. Avowing fulsome pledges of friendship, in 'most humble manner' he solemnly swore his 'faithful love and servitude that he intended to use toward your Grace, in all manner of things touching your honour,' the Secretary wrote. Next to the King he bore him a true heart 'planted and set without dissimulation, craft, or untruth,' protesting that if Wolsey continued to find fault with him he would 'renounce for ever his favour and good will and all honour in this present life.' With the King, whose faith in him was unshaken, he had less difficulty in maintaining his position. At the end of July he attended Wolsey at Westminster because Henry had demanded his presence in the Council.

Mary remained longer at Woodstock than she intended, for she was stricken with a severe attack of fever. Each day she was expected to recover, but when he finally realized that she was too ill to be moved, Suffolk wrote Wolsey an almost apologetic letter explaining why they were detained. The French Queen was unable to 'depart the Court so soon as was appointed,' he told him, 'for, Sir, it hath pleased God to visit her with an ague, the which has taken her Grace every third day four times very sharp, but by the grace of God she shall shortly recover.' He added that she was constantly attended by the Court physicians who, with the King's kindness, took away 'a gryth par of her payne.'

It is tempting to associate this ague with the sweating sickness, which had been joined in areas round London by measles and smallpox. It was undoubtedly a malarial fever with symptoms similar to the sweat, but less fatal. Many suffered from it, including Pace, but it caused no deaths in London though some were reported in the vicinity of Woodstock. In despair the King and Queen moved on with Mary and Brandon to Ewelme and thence to Bisham in Berkshire; the Court considered most places to be infected, 'for they die in these parts in every place, not only of the smallpox and measles, but also of the great sickness.'

The Court had to be back in London for the reception of the French ministers in the autumn, and with it went Suffolk and Mary. She may not have been with him at the state audience and reception of the papal nuncio, Cardinal Campeggio, at Greenwich in early August of that year, but was well enough to be present at the court entertainments of October. The French embassy arrived on September 23, with three objectives: to arrange for the delivery of Tournai, to sign a general peace between England and France, and to celebrate the marriage between Princess Mary and the Dauphin which had been arranged during the summer. It was a large and imposing delegation of over eighty noblemen and hundreds of attendants, with a train of six hundred horses, seventy mules, and scores of baggage wagons. Mary's old friend and admirer, the dashing Bonnivet, Admiral of France, headed the company of nobles and 'fresh young gallants' from the French Court. In the extravagant program of hospitality that accompanied the signing of the treaty and agreements, the Suffolks played a prominent part, as Masses, pageants, banquets, and dancing filled their days to the exclusion of anxiety about health or finance. Henry himself became so engrossed as momentarily to forget his fear of the sweat. Though Mary was not a hostess, she helped Catherine and the other ladies of the Court to entertain the large group of ambassadors who were not actively engaged in formal negotiations. The signing of the general peace took place on October 3 at St. Paul's, followed by a dinner given by the King and a supper by Wolsey at Durham House, which the Venetian ambassador thought must have surpassed the ancient feasts of Caligula and Cleopatra. Afterwards Suffolk and Mary led in a mummery, and later in the evening she paired with the King, improvising on new dances from the Continent; feasting, dancing, and gambling continued until after midnight.

Mary relished days like these when with Queen Catherine she was the center of attention. Amused by the antics of the French as they rode around town on their mules, to the astonishment of the London crowd unused to such foreign ways, she must have laughed as well at the efforts of the courtly French gallants to follow Bonnivet's instructions to 'warm up those cold ladies' of England. Also, there was fascinating talk of new Parisian styles to listen to; among the innovations in masculine dress was a new type of garment called a 'shemew,' described by Chronicler Hall as 'a gown cut in the middle.' Actually, this 'shemew' was a loose coat or gown worn open, which soon was to become popular in England. Henry himself was to set the style for his people when he wore one given him by the French King at the Field of Cloth of Gold two years later.

After two days the Court went to Greenwich by barge for the espousals of the Princess. There in the Queen's Great Chamber the two-and-a-half-year-old child was plighted, gowned in stately cloth of gold topped by a little black hat adorned with jewels. Long formal speeches were made, consent was begged and given, and the little girl, big-eyed with wonder, was lifted up to receive the matrimonial ring. In it was set a very large diamond, far too heavy for the tiny fourth finger of her right hand on which it was placed by Cardinal Wolsey, but Bonnivet, proxy for the Dauphin, pushed it firmly down over the second joint. The bride was blessed and Mass was sung, 'every possible ceremony being observed.' Far away in his French cradle the infant bridegroom, younger still than Lady Mary, was blissfully unaware of the commotion he was causing. Though he never became king, he lived long enough to learn that dynasties must be perpetuated. Catherine was eight months with child, the whole country anxious again for a prince, 'the sole fear of this kingdom being that it may pass into the power of the French through this marriage.'

Further diversions were organized for the ambassadors before their departure; over £2,600 was distributed in rewards and £1,000 spent by the King in 'playing money,' the over-all cost of entertaining the embassy for the month being £9,600. While such magnificence impressed Henry's subjects as well as his foreign visitors, some were critical of its inordinate cost, while others deplored another alliance with the French. Henry himself welcomed it as a necessary safeguard : he had been paid handsomely for Tournai and was looking forward with pleasure to his meeting with Francis in the spring.

Again Wolsey had his way. England and France were once more united in a defensive marriage alliance, to be expanded by the end of the year into a general league of peace for all Europe known as the Treaty of London. A few, with Richard Fox, Bishop of Winchester, felt it to have been 'the best deed that ever was done for England'; he told Wolsey that 'no one was gladder than he' of it, and the credit was all the Cardinal's. The country as a whole was more skeptical, since national anti-French sentiment and a growing commercial attitude had produced strong pro-German leanings. The Council was as divided as the Court, and Catherine's kinship with Spain and the Netherlands made an alliance with France distasteful to her though she offered no overt objection to her husband's decision. Supported by a younger group, she found herself opposing Suffolk and Mary with whom she had always been in close accord. For her there was no choice : if a summit meeting were to be held, it ought not to be with Francis but with Charles.

As Catherine approached the end of her sixth and last pregnancy the kingdom waited hopefully, but the baby was a still-born daughter, 'to the vexation of everybody,' the Venetian ambassador declared. The future now depended upon the Princess Mary, so lately betrothed to the heir of France. Speculation was making a vital issue of the Succession problem, especially to ambitious men like Suffolk and Buckingham, both of whom had personal stakes in its outcome.

After Catherine's confinement Mary retired to the country for the winter and the following summer of 1519. She probably spent most of her time at Westhorpe, though there are glimpses of her at Butley Priory and at Letheringham Hall where Wolsey called upon her and Brandon more than once. Butley Priory must have been one of Mary's favorite religious houses, for she visited it four or five times, the last one a couple of years before her death. The Suffolks had both been received into the Augustinian Order the previous year, probably in the hope of their patronage, but it seems to have had a contrary effect; instead of acting as generous patrons they became beneficiaries. Butley was one of several Austin priories in Suffolk and conveniently near Westhorpe; in the eastern part of the county near Orford, it was one of the few prosperous priories that could still afford to provide well for distinguished guests. A sizable community of a prior and twelve canons, it had a gross income of some four hundred pounds a year and an establishment of about seventy-five, which included an estate surveyor and thirty-six workmen. The higher nobility frequently stopped for a day or so to enjoy its hospitality, but none took such long vacations there as did Suffolk and his wife. At one time the Duke even parked his entire chapel staff on the house for a period of several months, thereby saving himself the expense of their support.

It probably flattered the canons to have royalty descend upon them, and in Mary's case it was surely an agreeable experience, for she could be gracious and charming. Her visits are fully recorded in the priory's chronicle, which is still preserved. She and her husband were provided with an apartment within the main building where they could be alone if they so wished, though in warm weather they took their meals with the canons in the sacrist's garden, just north of the church. Sometimes on warm days they fox-hunted in Staverton Park or Scuttegrove Wood nearby until late in the afternoon, staying out for a picnic supper afterwards. On the last recorded visit in 1530 they remained for almost two months, from September 20 to November 16, hunting, riding, and gaming. At other times they broke the monotony of the country by trips to such local centers as Yarmouth and Norwich where they were royally received. At Yarmouth they were so delighted with the cordiality of their welcome that they promised its citizens to persuade the King to visit the city.

On intimate terms with Henry again, Brandon and Mary were in and out of Court intermittently during these months, he more often than she. When there at special summons they stayed in the royal household and ate at the high table; otherwise they lived at Suffolk Place where the King would now and then spend a family evening with them. It was during this period that Brandon was awarded various fees and annuities in Wales by Henry, and given a fine 'black bald horse bought at the Hague,' a gift which meant something to both of them. Suffolk's relations with Wolsey had improved, the Cardinal taking advantage of the Duke's intimacy with Henry to keep himself informed of happenings at Court. His letters to Wolsey contain odd bits of news and brief accounts of any pertinent developments since their last meeting. The King was dissatisfied with the hostages left by the French delegation as guarantee of fulfillment of the recent treaty, Suffolk wrote from Greenwich in 1519, for they were not important personages in France nor held in great favor by their own sovereign. He suggested that the Cardinal should attend the Council debates on the matter. Their presence at Court had incidentally involved Henry in heavy gambling losses, for his ruffled feelings did not prevent him from fraternizing with them at cards and dice to the tune, it was said, of six to eight thousand ducats a day. The fact that they were better gamblers than he did not improve public relations.

The interest of the Court now centered around the coming meeting with Francis I in the spring; it was impossible then to foresee that practical politics would finally reject the French agreement in favor of one with the Emperor.

CHAPTER SEVENTEEN

Guines and Gravelines

Till this time pomp was single, but now married
To one above itself. Each following day
Became the next day's master, till the last
Made former wonders its.

Shakespeare, *King Henry the Eighth*, I. 1

AS THE YEAR 1520 progressed London buzzed with talk of the impending meeting between Henry and Francis. By his death on January 12, 1519, doughty old Maximilian had caused one of the sudden shifts in Continental power which inevitably upset the *status quo* of European calculations. The new King of Spain, Charles I, as Hapsburg heir was first in line for the Holy Roman Emperorship; in spite of both the opposition of France and the Papacy and Henry's puny bid for candidacy, the result was a foregone conclusion. No amount of bribery could stay the unanimous choice of Charles at the Imperial Election in June, which thereby united Spain and the Empire. Abruptly the political balance on the Continent was radically changed: three young monarchs, eager, impatient, and ambitious, directed the destinies of Europe. Mary's onetime suitor, the youngest of the three, now a grave, hatchet-faced Emperor of nineteen, was a person to be reckoned with. Francis was twenty-five, Henry almost twenty-eight, and unsure of their new ground they jockeyed for position, seeking to turn this potentially formidable enemy into a powerful friend. Since Charles's first move was unpredictable, both kings were anxious to woo him. While mutually pledging more love and conformity 'betwixt them than in or amongst all other Christian princes,' each was privately making overtures to the new Emperor. Henry suggested the hand of his daughter to Charles, it not mattering to either that she was betrothed to the Dauphin or that Charles himself was pledged to the Dauphin's sister.

As a further precaution Wolsey arranged a hurried meeting between them, that Henry might be better equipped to dicker with Francis at Calais.

The French conference had been postponed so many times that by the summer of 1520 it could be put off no longer. Henry and Francis both wished their queens to attend, and because of Claude's pregnancy the date could not safely be later than early June. Under Wolsey's meticulous direction the Court was alive with preparation, while he himself selected the nobility and personnel to accompany the King and Queen and determined the size of their entourages. In March he asked Suffolk how many attendants and servants the French Queen intended to take with her, at the same time requesting a roster of them. Although he could impose limits on the others lest any retinue exceed his own, no precedent existed to govern the number of Mary's attendants. Suffolk sent him the list, informing him also that his wife was ill again, suffering from the 'old disease in her side' which was to plague her to the end of her life. Writing from Croydon where he and Mary were staying temporarily at the house of Sir Nicholas Carew, he apologized for his absence from recent Council sessions:

> The cause why hath been that the said French Queen hath had, and yet hath, divers physicians with her for her old disease in her side, and as yet can not be perfectly restored to her health. And albeit I have been two times at London only to the intent to have waited on your lordship, yet her Grace at both times hath so sent for me that I might not otherwise do but return home betimes. Nevertheless her Grace is now in such good advancement that upon Tuesday or Wednesday next coming I intend, by God's grace, to wait upon your lordship.

The prospect of a formal visit to France in the reflections of Henry's glory seems to have put her on her feet again, as on later occasions some approaching social function was to serve as a temporary stimulant to her ailing health. As long as she could face the rigorous journey to Court she let pass no summons to attend.

Catherine and Mary were both busy during April and May preparing for the French and German discussions. The former was to be in early June, while in response to Wolsey's negotiations, Charles had promised to visit England sometime that spring on his way from Spain to Aachen where he was to be crowned on October 23. Delayed by bad weather, he did not actually reach Dover until late May, just

as Henry was about to embark for France. The interview was, therefore, a hurried one of only four days, but long enough to satisfy
Catherine's desire to see her nephew, which she had hoped to do ever
since he had become King of Spain. Aided by Wolsey, who had his
eye on the pontificate and wanted Imperial support, she had her wish.
She is reported to have wept when she embraced him. Everything
was done to make a success of this brief visit, the King being very
conscious of the fact that no Emperor had deigned to come to England
since Sigismund's meeting with Henry V in London in May, 1416.

Wolsey and a retinue of fifty men met Charles at Dover on the
evening of the twenty-sixth; hard upon their heels Henry with a
select group of nobles arrived the same night to welcome him long
after he was abed. Undaunted by the lateness of the hour the King
insisted upon waking the Emperor for a chat, exchanging with him
'embraces and other loving compliments.' The next day, Whitsunday,
they all rode to Canterbury for his formal reception by Catherine,
Mary, and the entire Court; all those going to France with the King
were already there to celebrate Pentecost before leaving England.

The three days that followed had their own significance for
Mary: for the first time she saw the man to whom she had been
pledged in marriage for six years, and instinctively she must have
tried to shine in front of him, if only that he might be made aware
of what he had missed. Accounts of the preparations for the two
conferences show her as having a completely new wardrobe for
herself and, to a more limited extent, for all her personal attendants.
Great shipments of stuff were also bought for Catherine and her
household, including large quantities of imported dress materials
ranging from 2s. 4d. to 46s. 8d. per yard. Royal permission for unstinted expenditure furnished an excuse for 'great provisions to be
made at every hand,' Hall states, 'for these noble meetings of so
high princes: and especially the Queen of England and the Lady
Dowager of France, made great cost on the apparel of their ladies and
gentlemen.' The Venetians report that a third queen was present,
Germaine de Foix, who was internationally known for her loveliness.
Formerly the second queen of Ferdinand of Aragon, in 1520 she was
Margravine of Brandenburg, and by far the most distinguished of
the 'many fair ladies' in the Imperial party. It was alleged of her
that like Mary she had sent an aging husband to the grave by his
efforts to beget an heir of her; unlike her, she lived to marry and
bury a third. In the first procession to the church, Mary, dressed

in silver lamé trimmed with pearls and gold cord, walked with Catherine immediately behind the Emperor and the King; in the procession the following day, when the women went separately, she was paired with Germaine; at the three-hour state banquet for about two hundred people, all three queens sat at the royal table, afterwards enjoying 'much revelry' until daybreak. At one point the younger visiting gallants entered into the spirit of the entertainment rather too lustily, according to the Venetian ambassador. Enamored with the role of foreign suitor, one of their number 'made love so heartily that he had a fainting fit' and had to be carried bodily from the room. Mary danced with Henry and Suffolk, but the Emperor ungraciously declined to take the floor. Legend has it that he was so thunderstruck by Mary's beauty that he was morose, and refused to dance so that he could silently watch the lovely creature whose perfection had been denied him. In fact, it is very unlikely that he cared or even noticed whether Mary was fascinating or not. Always unemotional, even as a child, at nineteen he had accepted his place in power politics and would marry as expedience dictated. Charles V was hardly one to suffer romantic regrets.

His most recently proposed bride was there too, for his inspection, pretty and demure in her best finery, but he must have known that no more than the first Mary Tudor was the second one to be his. At that moment marriage was not uppermost in his mind: all he sought from this visit was friendship with England, which he hoped would elicit the military assistance he might soon need. Henry, who had initiated the interview, had more reason to search the Emperor's mind as he rode with him five miles beyond the town limits before their farewell. What they said is not known, but enough understanding of future cooperation may have been reached to enable Henry to meet Francis with the assurance that if he decided on a reversal of policy, an alliance with Charles would be a possible alternative. They parted on the best of terms on May 29 about an hour after sunset. Wolsey took Charles and his train to Sandwich, while Henry and the main body of the English company proceeded directly to Dover. To guarantee their safe crossing five ships scoured the Channel; a few days after disembarkation at Calais they moved on to Guines, arriving there on June 4.

While Charles was hesitating between friendship with France or England, Henry and Francis proceeded with their elaborate pretense of accord. A French alliance was really Henry's second choice, but one with Germany seemed for the moment more remote, and failing in both England might hope to balance power on the Continent to her ultimate advantage. Though dubious of its real value both kings were stirred by the prospect of such high-level negotiation, conscious of the increased prestige that it would promise. Francis, since Maximilian's death more anxious than Henry, had pressed for this meeting, the last thing he wanted being an Anglo-German alliance against him. As an earnest of mutual sincerity the two kings had vowed to wear their beards until they met, but though Henry had weakened and shaved his off, Louise of Savoy dismissed his breach of faith lightly, declaring that the love they bore each other was not in their beards but in their hearts.

All arrangements had been made months in advance by Wolsey, whose penchant for detail and exactitude was already famous. Plans for the talks with Francis had been brewing for five years, and in anticipation Henry had imported great quantities of silk and cloth of gold and silver in order to meet his Most Christian brother with honor, immediately beforehand buying an extra 1,050 yards of velvet at 12s. 8d. per yard. Local preparations in France had been under way for a considerable time, directed by Sir Edward Belknap, Sir Nicholas Vaux, and Sir William Sandys, who were responsible for the English palace at Guines and for the food and lodging required. A total of £4,079 1s. had been spent on the extravaganza before it started, £8,839 2s. 4d. afterward. The best materials available went into the English buildings, the main structure—the work of more than two thousand skilled English and Flemish artisans—being called by contemporaries a fabulous 'Palace of Illusions.' The finest timber and glass procurable were used, with the decorative work designed and executed by the King's sergeant painter, John Brown, assisted by More's brother-in-law, John Rastall; Clement Urmyston, 'famous designer of pageants'; and probably the Neapolitan Vincent Volpe, who was then a court painter in England. This was an undertaking for everyone.

Made of stone, brick, and wood, covered with cloth or boards painted to resemble brick, this Gothic edifice was an imitation castle of four equal quadrants 328 feet square, with a gatehouse, round corner towers, and battlements. A secret passage connected it with the old castle at Guines as a safeguard against possible French treachery. Inside this palace Renaissance decorations included gilt cornices, the arms of both countries, tapestries of all designs interspersed with silk relief in the English colors of green and white, and everywhere a profusion of Tudor roses. The chapel contained gold shrines and images, a silver organ, and 'an incredible quantity' of jewels. One Italian affirmed that the palace would have done justice to Leonardo da Vinci, while Erasmus' friend, the French scholar William Budaeus, accustomed to extravagant display, thought he had never seen such magnificence: 'The house of the king of England, run up in a few months for temporary use, and ornamented with incredible skill, might occupy the eyes and attention, for some days, of the least excitable man accustomed to such spectacles.' Lying across the plain beyond, the gilded tent of the French King 'astonished everyone with its cloth of gold and other precious textures, and was never surpassed.'

The gateway of the English headquarters was guarded outside by four huge golden lions, a naked winged Cupid hovering above them, supposedly symbolizing this love feast between England and France. On the broad green in front of the many-windowed palace, presided Bacchus, bearing the inscription *'Faicte bonne chere quy vouldra.'* From the concealed conduits beneath his fountain ordinary red, white, and claret wine spouted unendingly for the poorer folk, so that day or night they might console themselves for their inferior status. Since neither the town nor the 'Crystal Palace' was large enough to house everyone, the English overflow had encamped in the fields a half-league from Guines, where twenty-eight brilliant-hued tents sparkled in the June sun, transforming a drab common into a *'Camp du Drap d'Or.'* On the Ardres side lay the French counterpart, a little town of flashing tents of cloth of gold and silver. In its center was the big royal marquee, sixty feet square, 'a house of solace and sport,' lined in blue to represent the heavens and set with stars of gold foil. Here, under the golden statue of St. Michael the Archangel, Francis entertained Wolsey and Henry, until one day the flimsy tent succumbed to the strong winds that sometimes sweep the Picardy plains and collapsed. After this catastrophe the French headquarters moved to Ardres, where borrowed capital provided new halls and pavilions and even a Roman theater.

By the time Henry and Francis arrived the construction was all finished, a monument to Renaissance splendor and a backcloth for lingering medieval pageantry. The national pride of both countries was vindicated, though the English lodgings were judged even by the impartial to be *'trop plus belle'* and more expensive than the French.

Wolsey and Henry had set the standard: more cloth of gold for the glory of England! With such a precedent, ministers and nobles had little choice but to spend exorbitantly when exhorted to attend 'in their best manner, apparelled according to their estate and degrees' to uphold the English reputation for opulence. All of them had long since laid in supplies of silk and cloth of gold lest they fail to fulfill Henry's command. The royal bodyguard was composed of two hundred of the 'tallest and most elect persons,' each with two outfits; Wolsey's dignity needed the support of three hundred servants and fifty mounted horsemen; Buckingham and Suffolk were ordered to equip seventy retainers and thirty horses apiece, the latter in addition being required to lend his valuable collection of batons and coats of arms for the 'furtherance of the King's business.'

In France, Louise had bought an 'emporium' of cloth of gold, 'in which to array the whole Court pompously.' The ambassador from Paris wrote that nothing else was thought of, since the French King and his ministers were concerned 'solely on bedecking themselves.' Determined to outrival their visitors, some French noblemen spent as much as a whole year's income on their costume; one commentator, Martin du Bellay, states that many 'carried on their shoulders their mills, their forests, and their meadows.' Foreign ambassadors in England demanded extra allowances from their home governments to pay for their finery, while wealthy peers like Buckingham justly decried the pointless exhibitionism. In Shakespeare's words, many 'broke their backs with laying manors on 'em for this great journey.' In gloomy retrospect men were to deplore the emptiness of diplomatic protestations, hollow as the shell of St. Michael's golden image in the French pavilion, which had purported to justify this orgy of spending. Vanity had transcended reason.

> To-day the French,
> All clinquant, all in gold, like heathen gods,
> Shone down the English; and tomorrow they
> Made Britain India—every man that stood
> Show'd like a mine. Their dwarfish pages were
> As cherubins, all gilt: the madams too,
> Not us'd to toil, did almost sweat to bear
> The pride upon them, that their very labour
> Was to them as a painting.

Though contemporaries vied with each other in describing the Field of Cloth of Gold, all are in remarkable factual agreement on points of detail. As both monarchs appointed historians and artists to attend and record their impressions for posterity, numerous versions are available; the official narrative by Hall is the most widely accepted, but the French accounts by Du Bellay and De Fleuranges, while less detailed, are substantially just as trustworthy. The familiar Hampton Court painting of the English encampment, wrongly attributed to Vincent Volpe, was done by an able but unknown Flemish artist.

Almost everybody of any significance in both countries was present. Not only was it something of a command performance, but no one wanted to miss the spectacle of the century, and only a few, like the Duke of Norfolk, remained in England to carry on the business of government while Henry played at diplomacy with Francis. Estimates of the number of those actually there vary somewhat, but Wolsey's official list provides for more than 5,000, not including Mary's escort, over which he had no control; 2,865 horses were brought from England, though their fodder was provided locally. Accommodation for them, as for the 2,200 sheep, 1,300 chickens, 800 calves, and 340 'beeves' to be slaughtered must have constituted a major problem for the purveyors and caretakers. The French train was about the same size, though Francis' staff had perhaps emphasized personnel rather than equipment, the country having been scoured for 'the fairest ladies and demoiselles.' Sir Richard Wingfield, observing these efforts, urged that similar care should be taken in the selection of English beauties, apprehensive that their reputation for loveliness might be imperiled. Leading the ladies were Catherine, Mary, Claude, Francis' mother, his sister Marguerite, and Françoise de Châteaubriant, then his favorite mistress. Rivalry among the women was as great as that among the men, declared Hall, nor could ten men's wits adequately describe them, 'their rich attire, their sumptuous jewels, their diversities of beauties.' The Duchess of Suffolk and Madame de Châteaubriant seem to have been the two outstanding belles among the high-ranking ladies; clad in a Genoese costume of white satin with headdress and flowing veil, Mary led a procession of lords and ladies to the French camp, 'scintillating in her saddle.'

Mary and her ladies were lodged in a temporary house at Guines, her apartment of three large rooms lying between that of the Queen and the Cardinal's suite. As Duchess of Suffolk, ex-Queen of France, and sister of the English King, she took a prominent part in everything, valuable in knowing all the principals from both countries. She had acquired a cosmopolitan taste in dress, and whether in Genoese or French costume, Milanese or English, she was always described as 'superbly arrayed.' She found no immodesty in the new garb borrowed from the bolder ladies from the French Court, which Vergil declared to be 'singularly unfit for the chaste.' John Fisher's objective account, which gave proper eulogy to all the queens and due credit to the French for their many contributions to the entertainment, should have impressed his London audience more with the sights they had missed than by the moral lessons to be deduced from them :

> And every of them [the queens] accompanied with so many other fair ladies in sumptuous and gorgeous apparel—such dancings, such harmonies, such dalliance, and so many pleasant pastimes, so curious houses and buildings so preciously apparelled, such costly welfare of dinners, suppers, and banquets, so delicate wines, so precious meats, such and so many noblemen of arms, so rich and goodly tents, such joustings, such tourneys, and such feats of war. These were assuredly wonderful sights as for this world. . . . Nevertheless, these great sights have a far difference from the joys of heaven, and that in five points....

No narrators mention the governmental cost of the enterprise : despite war and unending extravagance, English wealth seemed unlimited. The food bill alone at Guines and Calais was almost £7,500.

Notwithstanding all the suspicion and uneasiness the twenty-day program from June 4 to June 24 unfolded as planned. If not exactly cordial, all meetings were formally correct, restrained, and dignified. The first time that 'the most noble and puissant Henry the Eighth, King of England and France,' met the Most Christian King personally, their initial purpose was apparently to dazzle each other with their courtliness of mien and elegance of dress. Henry had grown his beard again, as shining as the bright gold collar about his neck, 'the most goodliest Prince that ever reigned over the realm of England.' Though the reception took place near the French pavilion it was in the pale of Calais, still within English territory. Francis, courteous and debonair, was profuse in his welcome.

'Twixt Guynes and Arde.
I was then present, saw them salute on horseback;
Beheld them when they lighted, how they clung
In their embracement, as they grew together;

Which had they, what four thron'd ones could have weigh'd
Such a compounded one?

On the tenth of June they visited each other's queens, Mary riding
with her brother to the French camp at the head of an English
escort of nineteen lords and ladies. Tourneys and other contests of
strength occupied the next fortnight, and though Henry and Suffolk
excelled, Hall in his account magnanimously concedes that the
French King did run 'valiantly' and 'brake spears mightily.' Masses,
banquets, and impromptu meetings punctuated these exhibitions of
physical skill until Midsummer Day, when fond farewells were said
and gifts exchanged as tokens of future cooperation. Only one
incident capable of jarring the fellowship and harmony had arisen,
and that was glossed over by the intervention of the queens: Henry
had confidently challenged the wiry Francis to a wrestling bout only
to find himself thrown flat on his back for his pains. English records
are discreetly silent on the subject.

Adieux made, the French Court left for Abbeville while Henry
and his party returned to Calais for another diplomatic rendezvous
with Charles. Drunken stragglers lay along their respective routes,
as hundreds of hangers-on and spectators who had enjoyed the surplus of hospitality from two kingdoms also turned homeward. So
great was the number of onlookers from West Flanders and Picardy
that knights and ladies who could afford accommodation had been
unable to find any; yet determined not to miss the fun, they 'were
fain to lie in hay and straw and hold them thereof highly pleased.'
Francis had earlier turned back ten thousand of the populace who
sought vicariously to brighten their drab days by watching royalty
in action. Once back at Calais, half the English retinue was sent
home in a belated effort at economy, while waiting for the Emperor.
On July 5 Henry went to meet Charles at Gravelines, for a continuation of the talks that they had begun at Canterbury.

Modern historians, with a hindsight denied the contemporary
writers, have condemned the Field of Cloth of Gold as valueless
diplomatic hypocrisy, and most of their criticism is legitimate. Discerning minds even then were not completely deceived by the superficial signs of concord between Henry and Francis, aware that beneath the geniality ran a strong current of suspicion, distrust, and
personal jealousy. Du Bellay observes that in the gay festivities
people saw signs of complete and enduring amity, 'but these were

23 Letter from Mary, Queen of France, to Henry VIII, March 6,
1515

24 Letter from the Duke of Suffolk to Henry VIII, April 22,
1515

25   The Field of Cloth of Gold, by an unknown Flemish artist

vain hopes, which instantly vanished,' he adds. 'These sovereigns are not at peace,' remarked an unidentified Venetian; while they adapt themselves to circumstances 'they hate each other very cordially.' All this was too true. Rumor circulated that Francis was secretly preparing for war; that a French army lurked nearby in case of need; that the surrender of Calais was in the offing; in fact, that the display of French-English cordiality had been one vast deception. It had, nevertheless, not been altogether futile. Each sovereign was groping his way toward a policy, taking determined measure of his opponent's intentions and capabilities. For Henry the way had been cleared for his second and more important meeting with the Emperor at Gravelines, just as his first meeting with him had been a prelude to seeing Francis. As Wolsey had anticipated, political ties remained inconclusive: the marriage of Princess Mary to the Dauphin did not take place, Anglo-French accord was not cemented, and Francis' hopes of English neutrality came to nought. Only as an unequaled exhibition of Renaissance pageantry was the Field of Cloth of Gold unique among the important conferences of the period.

Socially the interview with Charles V was anticlimactic, though politically it was infinitely more significant. Having met the Emperor at Gravelines in Flanders, Henry brought him back to Calais for a short visit terminating on July 14. If Francis had hoped for a triple interview, he was disappointed; it was not even considered. Alone together Henry and Charles were free to look solely to their own interests.

There was a minimum of entertainment, for the party spirit of Guines was worn out. The English were tired and sated, restless to return to normal life and less concerned with the impression they were making upon their guests; but Charles V neither expected nor desired protracted sociability. Not an exhibitionist like Francis, he was interested only in political results and, aware of his temperament, Wolsey arranged everything to his liking. He must not be pushed nor persuaded to any premature commitment. Under the Cardinal's guidance all went smoothly: Henry was enthusiastic, Charles amenable, the ladies charming. A treaty of amity was signed, pledging cooperation in the event of open hostilities with France. More specifically, the matrimonial alliance between the Dauphin and Princess Mary was severed, and her hand offered to her cousin, the Emperor Charles, subject to papal dispensation. This entailed the repudiation of his betrothal to Princess Charlotte of France, broken

I

with the same aplomb as his earlier ones with Mary, Claude, Renée, Louise, and others. He finally married none of them. The understanding arrived at between Henry and Charles might not have been very conclusive, but its implication was clear : England had joined the Imperial camp. It justified the extra £1,042 12s 7d. expended.

At Calais Mary was brought face to face for the first time with Margaret of Austria, an erstwhile contender for both her husband's and her father's affections, who but for the turns of fortune might have become either her stepmother or, through Charles, her aunt. Whatever her unrecorded impression of that first lady of Europe, time had flowed in her own favor; her father had been spared a domineering queen, and Margaret's rejection of Suffolk had enabled him to make an even more ambitious marriage.

Friendly relations with the Empire proceeded steadily but slowly, as the widening breach between France and England led to open hostilities. Wolsey, hoping to serve as arbitrator in a conflict that developed into war, pushed negotiations forward until a more definite commitment was achieved at Bruges and Calais in 1521. The plans for consummation of the marriage between Charles and Princess Mary developed into a full-dress military alliance for the invasion of France in the treaty at Windsor on June 19 the following year, when Charles came a second time to England. During his lengthy visit Mary and Brandon again took a prominent part in the formalities, entertaining him and Henry to dinner at Suffolk Place, with a hunt in the park afterwards. It was the last time Mary was to see the Emperor.

CHAPTER EIGHTEEN

Final Years

For though the day be never so longe,
At last the belles ryngeth to evensonge.

Stephen Hawes,
The Pastime of Pleasure (1506)

THE last decade of Mary's life is obscured by silence, except for
occasional references to her family activities and brief appearances at Court. After 1523 the latter were progressively infrequent,
chronic ill-health making her either unwilling or unable to endure
the rigors of travel from Westhorpe to London. As Suffolk's star
rose to new heights, she increasingly receded into the background of
his life, at times spending weeks or months in the country without
him. The last public function that she attended was at Greenwich in
the spring of 1527, when the treaty of 'perpetual peace' with France
was signed and Princess Mary contracted to Francis I.

In the upheaval of Henry's divorce from Catherine and his break
with Rome, Mary played no part, and though the English Reformation began before her death, involving all around her, no comment
of hers has survived. In their preoccupation with the 'secret matter'
of Henry's conscience Wolsey and the King ignored her, as in
apparently unprotesting silence she watched her former maid Anne
Boleyn drive her friend Catherine from the throne; neither did she
speak out with conviction when the doubtful validity of her own
marriage rose again. Her lack of pronouncement on these and other
problems about which she must have felt strongly leads to the
assumption that she confided her thoughts and feelings only to her
husband, who in his own interest suppressed them from public knowledge. Any known opinion of hers on matters of such national concern would inescapably have been noticed and reported by some
among the foreign ambassadors; yet after 1527, except for recurrent

references to her French revenues and her standing debt to the King, Mary as an individual disappears from the pages of history.

When in London together the Duke and Duchess now habitually lodged and ate at Court on the Queen's side of the royal household. If alone Brandon stayed at the 'King's house,' where meals were served daily from ten to eleven in the morning and four to six in the afternoon. With others of the household they enjoyed the usual allowances for the 'King's honourable house,' the weekly 'bouche of Court' providing supplies for lighting and heating their own rooms and extra food and drink for their private consumption; judging from the liberal amounts provided for everybody, no one enjoying Henry's bounty could ever have experienced hunger unappeased or thirst unassuaged. The size of the allowance varied appreciably with the degrees of nobility. Dukes and Duchesses were presumed either to have greater appetites than their social inferiors or to entertain more lavishly, for in addition to their regular meals each received two cheat loaves of bread and three manchets, three gallons of ale and a pitcher of wine per day. Including candles, lights, wood, and coal, the yearly allotment was estimated at £39 13s. 3d. per person. Though this free board was extended to all those privileged to reside at Court, the King could withdraw it when he chose. Mary and Brandon once experienced Henry's parsimony in the form of a bill for six hundred pounds for back diets.

For as long as her health permitted, the French Queen complied with requests for her presence in London. Mary was the head of a small clique of younger nobility and foreigners, and her familiarity with Parisian culture gave her and her young devotees a distinct role in the official life of the English Court. It is quite likely that French-trained Anne Boleyn was one of this group after her return to England in the 1520's, and this being so her first acceptance at Court may well have been due to Mary's influence. At one of Wolsey's revels at York Place in the spring of 1522, she and Anne and six other ladies participated, afterwards being given their gowns of yellow satin decorated with twenty-four 'resuns' each, and cauls of Venice gold.

In comparison with earlier years Mary's part in Court hospitality during the late 1520's and early 1530's was small. She helped Catherine to entertain Charles V's sister, the Queen of Denmark, in May, 1523, when Christian II came to England, but returned to the country almost immediately; the German ambassador noted with surprise that 'La Reine Blanche' was given precedence at the dinner table over the Danish queen. Two years later Mary returned to London with Suffolk to be present when a peerage was conferred upon their son, Henry. The investiture, at which the King's natural son by Elizabeth Blount, Henry Fitzroy, also became a peer, took place at the new Bridewell Palace on June 18. The two boys, aged nine and six respectively, were among several others honored, but the elevation of Fitzroy to the earldom of Nottingham and the dukedom of Richmond and Somerset overshadowed them all. However much Catherine may have resented the public honor to her husband's illegitimate child—for he would take precedence not only over all the nobility but also over her daughter—she had no choice but to acquiesce. Neither were Brandon and Mary in a position to criticize: their own son, now Earl of Lincoln, was still a possible future heir to the throne of England.

Again at Court in 1526, Mary was principal guest at the great banquet at Greenwich in honor of the French and Italian ambassadors, and in 1527 was present at the celebration of Princess Mary's most current engagement. Already jilted by the Emperor, she was now courted by Francis I, who was notorious throughout Europe as a philanderer. Widowed for less than a year, he was considering every matrimonial possibility, though he was thought to prefer a German alliance. He was reported as being so keen on an agreement with Charles V that he was willing to marry any woman, though she be a hundred years old—'even Caesar's mule'—if no other presented herself. In fact, Charles's sister Eleanore, Queen Widow of Portugal, while she did not in the least appeal to Francis was none the less available. Obedient to her brother as she had always been, she 'cast off her widow's weeds,' even calling herself the French Queen. Without batting an eyelash Francis took solemn oath on his honor as a king and gentleman to keep the troth, while simultaneously giving his royal word to the English that he was free of all commitments and desired nothing more than to marry their young princess, being well aware of 'her manifold virtues and other gay qualities.'

Knowing of these dual negotiations Wolsey redoubled his efforts, pointing out that Madame Eleanore was thirty, too old for Francis, too mature to be molded into the perfect lover, and of an age where there could 'not be found, peradventure, so much good nature and humility in her as in my lady Princess.' With an eye to Francis' vanity he suggested 'that a lady of more tender years and nature, and of better education, beauty, and other virtues' would be more suitable. In support of this, Mary's accomplishments were exhibited during a banquet for the French delegation, at which she displayed her skill in music and dancing, and conversed with the commissioners in four languages. The Venetian ambassador was struck with 'her great and uncommon mental endowments,' but warned that her body was 'so thin, spare, and small' that marriage would be impossible for a few years. Wolsey also realized this, and it was agreed that the marriage would not take place until Mary was fourteen.

The treaty of betrothal was signed at the end of April, 1527, after much feasting and entertainment. Francis promised an annual tribute of salt, two million gold crowns, and a personal pension to Henry of fifty thousand gold crowns, in exchange for a bride. Even if neither nation took its promises seriously, the treaty would undoubtedly give the Emperor pause.

Suffolk's private fortune continued to grow. After 1529 he received one thousand gold crowns a year from Charles V, while at the same time revenues from new offices and more land steadily augmented his previous income. Upon Buckingham's attainder in 1521, Brandon acquired a liberal portion of his forfeited estates in Suffolk, to which had been added the manor of Ewelme, Oxfordshire, a few years later. Minor awards from the King included stewardships, constableships, and a rangership in the New Forest, and after 1526 the honorific position of Earl Marshal in the King's household, which he had held in reversion since 1523.

Despite his bungling of various assignments, the Duke remained the King's chief favorite, attending him regularly and accompanying him on progresses. As he grew older and less vigorous, Henry turned more to hunting and tennis for exercise than to jousting, which had earlier been his principal sport, but he still played bowls and found long nights spent in gambling more exciting than his daytime routine of dictating letters and signing documents. While Wolsey controlled state administration Henry amused himself with a younger set of cronies who, with the exception of Suffolk, were beginning to replace his older friends. Sir William Compton, Sir Francis Bryan, Sir Henry Norris, Sir George Boleyn, and Sir Gilbert Pickering among others were in this group, all reckless and 'light of morals' in the opinion of More and Elyot, who were shocked by the frivolity and extravagance of the King and his companions. Brandon, however, had no reason to fear their rivalry or to resent the greater influence of older and more distinguished councilors; not even the powerful Buckingham, with all his birth and breeding, had ever been a serious contestant for Henry's affections. Only Norfolk aroused his jealousy; superior to Suffolk in everything save physical skills, he outshone him both on the field of battle and in the Council chamber. His success was a cross which Brandon had to bear, refusing always to admit that it was due more to Norfolk's native ability than to his noble birth.

Suffolk had won his first military laurels in the Continental campaign of 1513, and ten years later in late August, 1523, an opportunity to win more presented itself. England fulfilled her commitment to aid the Emperor in his struggle against France by sending Suffolk to Calais with an army of over fourteen thousand, which Wolsey boasted to be the largest invading force for over a century. No one in authority wanted another expensive and useless war except the King and the Cardinal; much less did the people want to pay for one. Neither were they impressed with the latter's desire to 'recover France' for his sovereign. The best justification for the war that Wolsey could present to Parliament was a plea for the repayment of 'many injuries' done by Francis to Henry and Mary, especially his withholding of her dower. The expedition proved to be unhappy for Brandon from the beginning, despite its accompanying fanfare and trappings of chivalry : the shining arms and armor, standards, banners and guidons made a brave show, as did the 'parcels of stuff' designed by John Brown, the King's painter, for the 'high and mighty prince Charles Duke of Suffolk . . . Leftenant general of [the] King's Royal Army,' but they bore no relation to success. As the imposing array slowly worked its way southward into France, all were agreed that Suffolk's 'courage and forwardness' were commendable. Between long intervals of rest there were military encounters, towns besieged and taken, and prisoners captured. Though wine was in 'great plenty' for everybody, the foul winter of 1523 brought with it grumbling and discouragament; by December the army had capitulated to the cold and rain, and Suffolk had dispatched a messenger to England requesting permission to bring it home. His troops, deep in French territory, 'abode much misery,' he told the King, for the weather was wet, the going difficult, and the nights long; great journeys and little victuals 'caused the soldiers daily to die.' Disgruntled with Suffolk, Henry expressed willingness to send reinforcements and supplies, but enjoined him that under no circumstances must the army disband. The order was disobeyed, and mid-December found the Duke and his officers back at Calais, 'sore abashed' at their sovereign's displeasure. Though Suffolk's arbitrary return bordered on insubordination, he was fairly confident of Henry's forgiveness. In Hall's words, 'at last all things were taken in good part and they well received and in great love, favour and familiarity with the King.' Wolsey was probably the instigator of his pardon and warm reception.

Not long after his return from the French campaign the domestic tranquillity of Suffolk's household was upset by an appeal for assistance from his former wife, Margaret Mortimer, who after her separation from him had taken a third husband. Her only daughter by that union, Anne Downes, encouraged by an unscrupulous husband, was trying to get possession of both a pension held by her mother from the national exchequer and her property in Suffolk and Worcestershire. The sordid dispute had got into the courts, and the aged Margaret had turned to Suffolk as the only person she knew with enough influence to rescue her from the clutches of her tormentors. His intercession through Wolsey and the technicalities of the case do not concern the story of Mary Tudor, but the episode does. It forcibly recalled to her the sequence of Brandon's early marriages, the questionable validity of her own, and the haunting doubt of her children's legitimacy. The fact that her brother's son Henry Fitzroy had been born out of wedlock, though he was officially acknowledged by the King the following year, and the recent report of the scandalous adultery of her sister with Henry Stewart must have worried her and made her brood on the legal status of her own children. The rumblings of the Divorce issue between Henry and Catherine in 1527 and the death of Margaret Mortimer early in 1528 probably agitated her forebodings to such an extent that Suffolk was finally prodded into a clarification of his marital status.

Mary's concern about her own marriage during these years probably dictated her attitude towards Henry's matrimonial problem, forcing her to remain aloof from the controversy lest Suffolk's appeal to the Papacy be endangered. Fortunately she was in the country a great deal and saw little of either the King or Catherine during the long period when his troubled conscience preoccupied everyone. Even before the 'great matter' which he had tried so long to keep secret became public knowledge, people had taken sides, and as the annulment of his marriage progressed it was quickly apparent that popular sympathy was with the Queen. So too was Mary's; she had accepted Henry's 'night crow' as a plaything and a social ornament, but not as a future queen of England. Mary's reaction must have been the only one possible to her: she instinctively disliked indiscretion, and Henry's and Anne's behavior was scandalizing all England. Her friendship with Catherine was close and of long standing, but her loyalty was also engendered in part by objection to the injustice of the situation. The Queen had done no wrong, yet her whole private life was to be laid bare for prying eyes and nasty gossip to dissect. Mary's natural sense of decency must have rebelled, and the fact that Anne was officially given precedence over both the Queen and herself accentuated her resentment. Despite this it was obvious that Brandon sooner or later would become involved, obliged to uphold the King wherever his own sympathy lay. Consequently, however strong her own feelings on the divorce, Mary could afford to take no public stand in support of her friend. Assuming that neither the Duke nor the Duchess, though privately favoring Catherine, would openly oppose the King, the Imperial minister, Chapuys, realized the position they would have preferred to assume: 'Suffolk and his wife, if they dared, would offer all possible resistance to the marriage,' he wrote Charles V. When Henry insisted on taking Anne to France to meet Francis I in 1532 Mary positively refused to accompany them, albeit her poor health was a legitimate excuse for the refusal. Emboldened by his wife's stand, Suffolk remonstrated privately with Henry, speaking so plainly that the King 'insulted him several times,' the ambassador related. His indignation, however, proved to be weaker than his ambition, and he accompanied his sovereign to the meeting, where he received the Order of St. Michael from Francis.

Perhaps the most operative reason for the Suffolk's neutrality was the fact that they were dependent upon Henry's intercession with the Papacy in their behalf. The official pronouncement upon the validity of their marriage was pending in Rome, and the decision they sought—the revocation of a dispensation granted by a previous pontiff—was precisely what Henry himself desired. The legality of both unions rested in each instance on the adequacy of an original authorization for marriage, in Brandon's case a papal bull permitting him to marry Margaret Mortimer, a dispensation which in 1507 had been declared invalid by an English court. In view of his son's possible candidacy for the Succession it is curious that Suffolk had not attempted earlier to clarify his first two marriages; possibly the reason was his known reluctance to face any situation until forced to, especially when it involved points beyond his understanding, such as the fine distinctions of canon law. Without political assistance he may have felt incapable of surmounting the difficulties which an appeal to the Papacy involved, and furthermore feared lest the initiation of such a step be construed in some quarters as a buttress to his dynastic ambitions. Now, however, the King supported him in the hope that Clement VII, who had already granted a divorce to Margaret of Scotland on grounds far less substantial, might establish a precedent in a case so closely parallel to his own.

Confident of his influence in Rome and of another proof of His Holiness' cooperation, Wolsey foresaw no difficulty. Everything went as he had anticipated; since Lady Margaret Mortimer was deceased, the issue was also dead as far as the Church was concerned. The bull, dated May 12, 1528, at Orvieto, recounted in detail the sequence of Suffolk's relations with Anne Browne and Margaret Mortimer, finding the dispensation to marry the latter insufficient, and Brandon's divorce of her valid. In spite of a few factual inaccuracies it ratified his subsequent marriage to Anne Browne, which made his contract with Mary Tudor after her death completely legal. The next year, on August 20, notorial attestation was given to the decree before the Bishop of Norwich at his manor house of Hoxne in the presence of several witnesses. Mary was a lawful wife according to the highest pronouncement of Christendom, and anybody who impugned her relations with Suffolk was subject to the ecclesiastical censure of the Supreme Pontiff. The bull incidentally cleared the name of Anne Brandon, Suffolk's elder daughter by Anne Browne, who for years had faced accusations of bastardy. Suffolk's house was in order if Henry's was not.

By the time papal ratification of his marriage was published, Suffolk had completed an embassy to Francis I for general discussion of his alliance with England, but more specifically to persuade him to support Henry's divorce of Catherine. Upon his return he joined Norfolk in an effort further to undermine Wolsey's already waning influence. By prejudicing the King and Council against him they hoped to weaken his position and themselves assume much of the routine business of state. At the end of October, 1529, Chapuys reported to the Emperor that his downfall was imminent, Norfolk and Suffolk in complete authority, and no one in the King's confidence who was not 'saturated with French money.' After Wolsey's failure to obtain Henry's divorce his enemies launched their attack: 'A staff is soon found to beat a dog'. He had lost the race against time and his adversaries, and his days were numbered. 'Formerly no one dared say a word against the Cardinal,' Chapuys wrote, 'but now the tables are turned and his name is in everybody's mouth.'

By October 20 the Great Seal had been surrendered, and until a new custodian was appointed Norfolk and Suffolk sat together as judges in Star Chamber interpreting, one suspects rather clumsily, the 'new law' with which the Cardinal had become so closely identified. There was much speculation as to who would be appointed to the Chancery. Those who apparently expected Suffolk to be chosen had not reckoned on the power of Norfolk, who had no intention of playing second fiddle to another upstart. His objection to the Seal going to 'such high hands' carried weight, and the chancellorship was given to Thomas More. Norfolk, who had been most instrumental in effecting the downfall of that 'Ipswich fellow,' claimed and received the Presidency of the Council and Suffolk had to be content with its Vice-Presidency.

Meanwhile, the Divorce trial had proceeded without a hitch, everyone obediently falling in line to give prearranged testimony, not for fear of Wolsey but to maintain their favor with the King. Though Suffolk had always shared Mary's respect for Catherine, he was no exception, and his testimony added no luster to his name. His wife was not called as a witness. Suffolk's evidence that Arthur had carnally known his bride on the marriage night was affirmed by Norfolk and others: 'Furthermore, he added that the Shrovetide following the Marriage (which was in November preceding) the said Prince began to decay, and grow feeble in body; which grew, as the said St. John related [Maurice St. John, one of Arthur's attendants], by reason the said Prince lay with the Lady Katherine.'

The Court's decision seemed certain until it became clear that the two judges were working at cross purposes. When Clement VII had commissioned Wolsey and a special Italian agent, the eminent cardinal and jurist Lorenzo Campeggio, to try the case in London, ostensibly with full powers to proceed in a bona fide manner and arrive at an impartial judgment, he had secretly instructed Cardinal Campeggio to procrastinate as much as possible. Regardless of the evidence presented, he was in no circumstances to permit a decree favorable to the King. Knowing that the weak Clement was completely under the domination of Charles V, Wolsey and Henry strove for a successful verdict before Catherine's appeal, supported by the Emperor, to the papal tribunal in Rome, won acceptance.

Thus the issue stood the third week in July, when the trial was nearing conclusion. Unable to stall proceedings further, on July 23, 1529, Campeggio arbitrarily adjourned the hearings of the Legatine Court at Blackfriars, on the pretext that the summer holiday for Roman ecclesiastical courts had begun. Entangled as it was with English foreign policy and Imperial opposition, the possibility of an annulment of the King's marriage was now dead, and with its death came the downfall of its instigator. Wolsey's failure sealed his fate. For once, Suffolk's anger was unrestrained, an indignation which he shared with the majority of the Council. 'By the Mass! now I see that the old said saw is true,' he expostulated, pounding the table; 'there was never legate nor Cardinal that did good in England!' Wolsey must have been astonished at such a violent outburst from the one person he had generally supported throughout the years. His reply, if indeed he deigned to make one, rests entirely upon the word of George Cavendish: 'Sir, of all men within this realm, ye have least cause to dispraise or be offended with Cardinals; for if I, simply Cardinal, had not been, ye should have had at this present no head upon your shoulders, wherein ye should have a tongue to make any such report in despite of us.' He advised Brandon to behave like a gentleman and keep quiet, 'for ye know best what friendship ye have received at my hands, the which yet I never revealed to no person alive before now, neither to my glory, ne to your dishonour.' Since the King had already left the chamber, only Suffolk could refute the charge of base ingratitude. He followed Henry from the room in silence.

Suffolk's bitter repudiation was colored no doubt by two highhanded acts of Wolsey's which he had never forgotten. The first concerned the forced loan of 1525, called an 'amicable grant,' levied on the land and goods of everybody, which the Duke had been called upon to collect in his home county. Open resistance to it necessitated the use of force, and Suffolk had found himself under criticism in the execution of an unpopular policy for which he was in no way responsible. Wolsey's other offense was more direct: the seizure of land for the furtherance of his pet project, the founding of a college at Oxford and a preparatory school for it at his native town of Ipswich. Funds for these two educational memorials entailed the hitherto unprecedented suppression, between 1524 and his downfall in 1529, of twenty-nine small religious houses, preceding the general Dissolution by almost a decade. Since qualified papal permission had been construed as a blanket approval for 'uncanonical' annexations far in excess of the amount originally authorized, confiscation of property proceeded without the consent of either the monasteries or the heirs of their founders. Not only had a few of Brandon's and Mary's friends been affected, but they themselves had been required to forfeit title to three valuable properties towards the support of Ipswich College: Snape Priory in Suffolk and the manors of Sayes Court and Bickling at Deptford in Kent. Though Wolsey had favored them in many ways, particularly in securing their French revenues, they both realized that it had been to his advantage to do so. Wolsey never gave something for nothing, and Suffolk may have felt, with some justification, that he had paid his debt in full. It was not, however, until the problem of these revenues had been resolved that they could break with the Cardinal without fear of retaliation.

During the twenties when Mary's dower was hanging fire, Wolsey was constantly reminded by her and Brandon that the successful outcome of the negotiations with Francis depended entirely upon his assistance. They sought his good will in every way possible, indicating by their letters how cordially they felt; writing in August, 1525, Mary told Wolsey that 'in this and in all others I evermore have and do put mine only trust and confidence in you,' with the full assurance that he would support her cause.

> And by the same I trust my said causes shall be brought to such good conclusion and order now, that I shall from henceforth enjoy my estate there [in France] in as ample use as I have heretofore. . . . And thus my Lord I am evermore bold to put you to pains without any recompense unless my good mind and hearty prayers, whereof ye shall be assured during my life to the best of my power, as knoweth the Lord.

Shortly thereafter the Duke added his appreciation to that of his wife for 'the great kindness that your Grace doth daily shew unto the said French Queen and me, by the which you bind us during our life to do your Grace such pleasures as shall lie in our powers'.

A 'good conclusion and order' were not so easily established as Mary had hoped, and the matter remained a bone of contention for a number of years. The original dispute over her movables was re-opened and the old issue of English right to the 'Mirror of Naples' raised once more. Since all payments had lapsed during the war, arrears had mounted, but even when installments of back revenues were promised, Mary's agents were unable to collect them. It was not until after the Treaty of 'The More' in 1525, signed at Wolsey's palace at Moor Park near Harrow, that final settlement was guaranteed, with the first five thousand crowns paid in September of that year. In 1531 the annual payments of arrears were increased from seventeen thousand to twenty thousand livres, and from that time onward she regularly received her French income. Thus Wolsey was responsible for the full restitution of Mary's jointure, as if in compensation for his earlier acquiescence in saddling her with an impossible debt to the King as a condition of royal forgiveness for her rash marriage.

Since 1518 Mary and Brandon had paid on their debt to the crown by regular installments, though these were waived when she was without her French revenues; but with her attenuated income Suffolk was not always able to meet the current payments, and occasionally had to borrow from friends to keep going. In 1521 their total obligation to Henry stood at £23,900; by 1526 it had risen to £25,853, including £19,333 still owed by Mary as the unpaid balance of her original debt. An indenture of that year bound them to meet semi-annual payments of £500 each until the principal was paid, with the provision that in the event of Mary's death her portion of it would be liquidated. In reality Suffolk had to wait an extra two and a half years for the fulfillment of this clause. He also had to assume another liability of Mary's to Sir Thomas Wyatt for £2,000. Meanwhile, he resorted to extreme methods for reducing his encumbrances and restoring his credit, including a frantic, if futile, search for gold on his Hognorton estate. Pawned jewels raised some £700 in cash, and the surrender of valuable lands and property to the King greatly relieved his financial straits. Both Westhorpe and Suffolk Place were relinquished a few years after Mary's death, in return for which the Duke was provided by act of parliament with the Bishop of Norwich's residence near Charing Cross, known for some years thereafter as Suffolk House. Even when Mary's debt to her brother had been canceled, Suffolk still owed Henry £8,722 which remained pressing for the rest of his life, but was commuted to £4,000 after his death for the benefit of his widow.

During her last lingering months of illness Mary was unable to give much attention to their pecuniary difficulties, problems which the Duke, however good his intentions, was never quite able to solve. He had always lived beyond his income, and his expenses in the early thirties were increased by the marriage of two of his daughters and by the unforeseen outlay of Mary's expensive funeral. Heavy indebtedness, as much as anything else, prompted him to look for a profitable remarriage almost immediately.

CHAPTER NINETEEN

Not without Honor

Even such is Time, that takes in trust
Our youth, our joys, our all we have,
And pays us but with age and dust;
Who, in the dark and silent grave,
When we have wandered all our ways,
Shuts up the story of our days.
But from this earth, this grave, this dust,
My God shall raise me up, I trust!

Sir Walter Raleigh, 'Even Such Is Time'

MARY'S last years were spent at Westhorpe. Her own three children and her two stepdaughters, Anne and Mary, were with her, but the family was beginning to break up shortly before her death. In 1531 Anne Brandon married Edward Grey, Lord Powis, for which Suffolk collected a feudal aid of twenty shillings per knight's fee. The only son of Baron John Grey of Powis, Wales, and a personal friend of the family, Edward Grey had accompanied the Duke on his expedition to France in 1523 and received knighthood at his hands during the campaign. Two years after Anne's marriage, Mary summoned her last energies to go to London for the wedding at Suffolk Place of her elder daughter Frances to Henry Grey, Marquis of Dorset, of the Greys of Groby, Leicestershire, who though only seventeen years of age held a high position at Court, having inherited his title and wealth three years before. Young Dorset was well known to Suffolk through his father, Thomas Grey, the second marquis, who had served with him during the French war in 1513, and had joined him the next year in leading the English team in the Parisian tournament celebrating Mary's marriage to Louis XII. After his death, union of their families naturally suggesting itself, Brandon, with an eye to his daughter's future, sought and obtained the wardship and marriage of Thomas Grey's heir in March, 1533. The ceremony took place, with Henry VIII's consent, as soon as Dorset had bought his way out of an earlier betrothal. For the Suffolks it had a double significance, for their younger daughter Eleanor was promised at the same time to Henry Lord Clifford, eldest son of the Earl of Cumberland, whom she married three years later. Frances' wedding must have been a grand one for it cost her father £1,666; immediately it was over the sixteen-year-old bride went to her new home at Bradgate in Leicestershire, while Mary returned to Westhorpe to die. Suffolk had to stay in London to help Henry arrange for the coronation of his 'goggle-eyed whore,' and was unable to accompany her; as Earl Marshal he had more business than 'English ovens at Christmas time,' and Mary and Eleanor made the slow journey home alone.

Notwithstanding Brandon's and Mary's objection to Anne Boleyn, there had been no break between them and the King over the issue which was dividing the Court. If the Imperial ambassador was correct in his statement that Suffolk had warned Henry as early as 1530 that Anne had had questionable relations with Sir Thomas Wyatt, it was his nearest approach to a positive stand; but if this was the cause of his temporary banishment from Court, he soon repented of it and was speedily reinstated. New Year's gifts to the King in 1532 consisted of writing tables and a gold whistle from Mary, a 'gold ball for fume [pomander]' from Suffolk, in return for which they were given several pieces of silver gilt; the next year they received more plate from Henry. At his request Mary had also lent jewels to her brother for Anne to wear at the French meeting in October, 1532. Catherine had been compelled to do the same, though not without expressing her indignation. Probably the last time Mary saw Henry was at her daughter's marriage; being in London then he must have been present.

Her correspondence declined during the last two years of her life. One of her few surviving letters for this period, written in the wavering hand of a very sick person at the end of March, 1533, is to her friend Arthur Plantagenet, Viscount Lisle, Lieutenant of Calais, in behalf of one of her servants for whom she was trying to help get a position as a soldier at the garrison there. Her last to Henry, composed a few years earlier, shows her utter discouragement all too clearly. 'My Most Dearest and Best Beloved Brother,' she wrote:

I humbly recommend me to your Grace. Sir, so it is that I have been very sick and ill at ease, for which I was fain to send for Master Peter

the Fesysyon [physician] for to have holpen me of this disease that I
have; howbeit, I am rather worse than better, wherefore I trust surely
to come to London with my Lord. For an' if I should tarry here I am
sure I should never assperre the sekenys [asperge—i.e., scatter, the
sickness] that I have. Wherefore, Sir, I would be the gladder a great
deal to come thither, because I would be glad to see your Grace, the
which I do think long for to do. For I have been a great while out of
your sight, and now I trust I shall not be so long again. For the sight
of your Grace is the greatest comfort to me that may be possible. No
more to your Grace at this time, but I pray God [to] send you your
heart's desire, and surely to the sight of you.

By your loving sister,
Mary, the French Queen

In early May of 1533 Suffolk made a hurried journey home to see
her, the last time he was to do so. The exact length of his visit is
unknown, but he was back in London before the end of the month
preparing for the coronation of Queen Anne, whose hasty and unexpected elevation to the throne had been almost too ridiculous to
be real. Emerging out of the shadows of the Court as a mere maid-
in-waiting to the Queen, she had inch by inch usurped her mistress's
position, with land, jewels, and public honors showered upon her in
rapid succession. On January 25, 1533, Henry secretly married her;
it then remained only for Thomas Cranmer, the new Archbishop
of Canterbury, to nullify his union with Catherine so that the new
marriage might be openly proclaimed. This was done on May 23, after
which the secret contract, together with Anne's exultant pregnancy,
was pronounced valid. On June 1 she was crowned. People close to
the throne were surprised not so much by Henry's *affaire* with Anne
as by his insistence upon marrying her in the face of public disapproval. 'Even those who took her part,' wrote Chapuys, 'know
not whether to laugh or cry.'

Though Henry ordained the usual show he discovered that while
he could enforce outward obedience, inward acceptance was not within his control. Few of the Court dared to brave his anger by absence
from Anne's coronation. One blessing at least accrued from Mary's
sickness: unable to be there, she did not have to watch her husband
preside over a ceremony that must have been repugnant to them
both. High Constable for the coronation and Steward of the feast
that followed, he was forced to pay homage to a woman who possibly
still wore his wife's jewels, one whose unborn child would supersede

his own son. He showed no trace of disapproval, accepting the honor of the stewardship and the new gown of crimson velvet that went with it, but his heart was not in the ceremony, an event which Chapuys called a 'cold, meagre, and uncomfortable thing.'

Mary's death on June 25 attracted no attention in the capitals of Europe and not much in England. A noteworthy event in Suffolk, in London it was eclipsed by other things. In the summer of 1533 the 'King's cause' was still uppermost in the public mind; despite rumors of lovers' quarrels between the King and Anne the fact remained that she carried his child in her body, a child which physicians and astrologers assured him would be a son. The 'infinite clamours' against the church by parliament had raised new apprehension in men's minds. Thomas Elyot voiced the alarm of many : 'We have hanging over us a great cloud, which is likely to be a great storm when it falleth.' Soon to use it to his own and the King's advantage, Thomas Cromwell had grasped the situation accurately enough. Even before Mary's death his capable hand was to be seen at work. After the Statute in Restraint of Appeals and the Act in Absolute Restraint of Annates had been passed, eventual break with Rome and royal supremacy in ecclesiastical affairs were inevitable. No sooner was Anne's coronation over than the official propaganda campaign against the Papacy was launched with the anonymous tract, *A Glass of the Truth*; 'truth' in England was fast becoming a matter of governmental pressure. Excommunication of Henry and his supporters followed, while at home rumblings of the coming Dissolution explosion were becoming audible. Even the King was too preoccupied to grieve noticeably over the loss of his favorite sister, the person who with Brandon had longest held first place in his affections. None of the women with whom Henry was infatuated during the course of his life ever quite captured the same spontaneous love and esteem which he had for Mary. She was never repudiated.

By the 1530's Mary's prestige in England had faded and her name was all but forgotten in diplomatic circles. Socially she belonged to a passing generation that had little in common with the audacious Boleyn clique. She had never had any political influence over Henry, and her position at Court had been usurped first by the Princess and then by the new Queen. Writing to the Emperor, Chapuys spoke of the French Queen's death as an afterthought, his chief concern lying in the fact that Francis I stood to gain '30,000 crowns a year of dower.' The French ambassador mentioned it to his sovereign because they had both known Mary so well, adding that she was 'much beloved in the country and by the common people.' Francis replied from Auvergne that he was 'grieved.'

Since no account of Mary's last illness has survived, it is fruitless to speculate on the nature of the 'old disease in her side' occasionally mentioned. Her constitution, never strong, must have been weakened by childbirth and recurring fevers. Like her niece, Mary Tudor, she was of nervous temperament, subject to periods of melancholy at times bordering on hysteria—'fits of the mother'—which may have aggravated her sickly condition and a possible pulmonary weakness. Chest diseases were well known in the sixteenth century, though their diagnosticians gave more attention to symptoms than to treatment; the physician's function, wrote Nicholas Breton in 1616, was 'most in feeling of pulses, and his discourses chiefly of the nature of diseases.' Like her father and her eldest brother, both of whom are considered probably to have died of consumption, Mary had long suffered from delicate health, but there is no record of her having a critical illness before 1533. The Spanish *Chronicle* attributed her death to grief over Henry's divorce: 'When the King left the blessed Queen Katherine, the Queen Dowager of France, wife of the Duke of Suffolk, was so much attached to her that the sight of her brother leaving his wife brought on an illness from which she died.' Physical maladies were regarded by most as an expression of God's inexplicable will, to be borne patiently without complaint. Varied interpretations were given of those diseases about which little was known, and serious sickness or death could be accredited to melancholy, ennui, sadness, or 'mental vexation'; Sir John Cheke, it was said, died of a broken heart. The humoral theory derived from Galen, which fixed the 'temperament' of the human system, still obtained:

> Four humors reign within our bodies wholly
> And these compared to four Elements,
> The *Sanguine, Choler, Phlegm,* and *Melancholy,*
> The latter two are heavy, dull of sense,
> Th'other two are more jovial, quick, and jolly.

Uniformity of temperament being the ideal state, correction of imbalance of the humors would restore health, and since bleeding was accepted as the best method of doing this, it became the standard treatment. Medical science was even vaguer on the relationship of mind to body, so that nervous disorders were totally misunderstood.

Remedies for hysteria varied from complex prescriptions to simple recipes: 'Stir a couple of ounces of powdered buck's horn in a quart of old ale, boilt to a pint and take at a single dose.'

It is understandable that Mary lacked confidence in the local medical skill. County physicians and apothecaries habitually prescribed more superstition than medicine, and were less effectual than the country housewives with their herbal draughts. 'Physic without astrology is like a lamp without oil' was a premise with which few then disagreed. Mary probably had the Duke's physician with her at Westhorpe, but nothing is known of his competence.

The tolling bell was death's crier, and throughout England it rang from the parish church of the deceased. Mary's 'passing bell' was heard just before eight o'clock on the morning of her death. Her bier lay in state in the chapel at Westhorpe Hall for over three weeks before burial, since convention dictated that no one of consequence should be buried in indecent haste; only lesser folk were interred immediately. Noble families used death as an occasion for displaying their wealth and importance, but in all classes funeral customs, including dress and precedence, were a matter of strict social formula. Much of the court etiquette governing death and burial had originated from Margaret of Richmond's passion for order and discipline. Under her guidance specific rules and regulations had been laid down for all possible eventualities, from the proper procedure for making the royal bed to births, christenings, marriages, and deaths. In the 'Orders for Precedence' drawn up by her in 1503, dictating the correct dress for public mourning, not only was the quality and form of the ladies' costumes ordained but also the length of their trains. A countess might wear a double train, one 'before and another behind,' though the first was not to be over eight inches in width, while a baroness was denied such ostentation. Similarly, ladies of high degree could wear mourning cloth of fine linen over the chin, but the wives of knights must wear it underneath, and the wives of esquires beneath the throat.

As in medieval times the mysteries of life and death were most meticulously served. Death represented the individual's final appearance in the society in which he had lived, and his last rites were a reflection of his erstwhile position. Responsibility for upholding class traditions was taken seriously as a social and even moral duty, class-consciousness existing at all levels as proper recognition of the structure of society. Suffolk conformed automatically to the credo of conventional behavior and, as one of royal blood, Mary was buried in impressive accordance with her exalted station. Discerning thinkers like Erasmus and Vives might criticize the useless financial outlay incurred by such insistence on the pomp due to high-born corpses, but the majority accepted it as part of the safely established pattern. Only once did Brandon himself raise his voice against this extravagant practice of his class, when he who had complied all his life defied conformity in death. More concerned with the financial status of his family and creditors than with the magnificence of his funeral, he requested to be buried quietly at the College Church at Tattershall in Lincolnshire 'without any pomp or outward pride of the world.' It was the King's pride that insisted on Brandon's body having formal burial at Windsor at royal expense.

The science of embalming was well understood in northern Europe, and the bodies of the aristocratic were frequently kept for quite long periods before interment. Henry VII was buried eighteen days after death, Henry VIII nineteen days after. Queen Mary's burial was postponed for almost a month, that of Edward VI somewhat longer. A century later the funeral of Oliver Cromwell was put off for over two months, from September 3 to November 23, owing to a delay in preparations. In Mary's case the elapse of twenty-seven days seems to have been due to the late arrival of the French deputation, but despite the interval neither Henry nor Brandon was present to bid her farewell. On July 22 when she was committed to the earth, the King was staying at Windsor and Suffolk at Ewelme.

The symbolism and pageantry of sixteenth-century funerals were fascinating to the common people. Curiosity and superstition produced in them an inordinately morbid interest in all aspects of death, from the last anguishing hours of struggle to the often ludicrously mournful obsequies at the grave. Occasionally an entombment developed into a hazard, flames from the huge tapers and torches threatening the safety of the bystanders. During the Norfolk funeral of John Paston in 1466, the smoke during the Dirge was so overwhelming that the windows of the building had to be removed to save the mourners from suffocation. Turgid imagination gave credence to tales of supernatural duels between God and the Devil for possession of the departed soul, after which there was vicarious rejoicing in the triumph of the Almighty. Great weeping and wailing were believed to drive away the evil demons who hovered ready to drag the dear departed into the fiery torment of hell, so that the larger the number of mourners the better the chances for the soul's ultimate deliverance. For the humbler people fees were to be earned as hired mourners, gowns provided for those who took part in the funeral procession, free wine and ale, alms, and a cash reward for those who persevered to the bitter end and were present at the graveside. The refreshments served both before and after the funeral, the quality and quantity of which varied according to the wealth and social prominence of the deceased, were an added attraction. Among the higher nobility these wake feasts, often punctuated by dancing and entertainment, sometimes went on for days and included even parishioners of other local churches. The bounty of the dead surpassed the hospitality of the living.

For all sections of society death had an absorbing attraction; few were permitted the luxury of dying in either privacy or peace, as those at bedside watch shared silently with the sufferer in the greatest of all human experiences. Death did not distinguish between the rich and the poor: at the last all were mute before it, acknowledging with Raleigh in his *The Historie of the World* 'their deformity and rottenness.'

> Oh eloquent, just and mighty Death ! whom none could advise thou hast persuaded, what none hath dared thou hast done, and whom all the world hath flattered thou only hast cast out of the world and despised. Thou hast drawn together all the farstretched greatness, all the pride, cruelty and ambition of man, and covered it all over with those two narrow words, *Hic jacet*.

A detailed account of the funeral of the French Queen, 'A Remembrance for the buryall of the Right Excellent prynces Mary,' is preserved among the records of the Royal College of Arms. It reflects clearly the practices of the period: the preoccupation with preliminaries, the studied plans for the funeral procession to the church, the number and order of mourners, the minutiae of banners, decorations, and dress, and the liturgical ritual of Dirge, Matins, Requiem, and interment. Mary's coffin lay in state for twenty-five days in Westhorpe Chapel. The complete technique by which her body was embalmed is not explained, but it was probably the same as that employed for her mother, whose embalment required, in addition to various chemicals, seventy-five yards of Holland cloth three and three-quarter yards in width, gums, spices, sweet wine, and wax. The cerecloth treated with the perfumed melted wax was wrapped round the body, which was then sealed in a leaden box covered with black velvet and adorned by a cross of white damask. Mary was treated similarly: 'the wax chandler did sere and trammel the body with cloth, spiced, leaded [and] chested, with all other things thereunto appertaining.' In the Chapel the coffin was covered with an embroidered pall of blue velvet, many tapers burning day and night beside it and elsewhere round the shrouded room, while continuous vigil was kept by appointed attendants.

English heralds, accompanied by a pursuivant sent from France in deference to her rank of Queen Dowager, arrived from London. By July 20 preparations were complete, the official party equipped with black gowns and hoods for the lords and trains for the ladies. Mary's children and Suffolk's married daughters by Anne Browne, the Ladies Powis and Monteagle, were present, and his young ward Catherine Willoughby, whom he was shortly to marry. In the royal delegation from London was Frances Brandon's husband, Dorset, representing the head of the family in his absence. The ceremonies began with the solemn chanting of the Dirge in the chapel, where the following morning the funeral party heard Mass before departing for Bury St. Edmunds. As chief mourner Frances was escorted by her husband and her brother, the Earl of Lincoln. The offerings for the day went to the poor, as was the custom.

For the journey the coffin was transferred to a hearse draped in black velvet embroidered with Mary's arms. Over the coffin hung a pall of black cloth of gold, frizzed, on which was designed a large white cross; on this lay Mary's effigy representing her as Queen of France. The effigy was clothed in robes of state, with coronation rings and a gold crown, and in its right hand a golden scepter as the symbol of Mary's erstwhile authority. This effigy has been lost or destroyed, but could have been executed by one of any number of heraldic painters such as Richard Rownangre; the Italians, Bartholomew Penne and Anthony Toto; or the Frenchman, Nicholas Lizard, who designed the effigy of her niece, Queen Mary of England, which has survived. It could have been made of painted wax and wood similar to that of Edward IV by Nicholas Bellin. Direct evidence from the accounts of the Great Wardrobe exists for only one person. The King's Sergeant Painter, Andrew Wright, was paid £5 6s. 8d. for four pieces of decorative design: 'Large baners with Images beten golde with 11 schochoyns [escutcheons] in every baner.' These were carried at each corner of the hearse, proclaiming the high estate of the deceased. The hearse, or funeral car as it was commonly called, was drawn by six great coursers trapped in black cloth; over it was a canopy supported by four knights, while on either side were more standard-bearers carrying the insignia of the family arms and genealogy.

The cortege wended its slow way down the narrow parish road to Bury St. Edmunds led by a hundred torch-bearers, local country folk in hooded clothing of coarse black cloth, glad to earn a few pence while honoring one who had often befriended them. The clergy carrying the chapel cross were next, followed by household staff, heralds, officials, and mounted knights and nobles; in the middle was the hearse, with another hundred taper-bearing yeomen behind it. After them came Frances and her husband, her horse caparisoned in black velvet to indicate that she was chief mourner. The ladies, also on horseback, rode behind them, each attended by a running footman. Two mourning wagons or 'coaches' preceded those on foot: Mary's waiting women and all Suffolk's yeomanry and servants. Along the way others joined, 'all other that would.' Organized delegations from each parish met the column at intervals to pay their tribute to the dead queen and to receive their torches and money allotments. The procession reached Bury St. Edmunds at about two o'clock in the afternoon, to be received ceremoniously by the local clergy and the Abbot and monks from the Abbey.

At the great Abbey church the coffin was placed on a catafalque which stood before the high altar surrounded by mourners whose stations were governed by protocol. After the singing of the Dirge the French pursuivant chanted: 'Pray for the soul of the right high excellent princess and right Christian Queen, Mary, late French Queen, and all Christian souls.' Whereupon everyone moved to the refectory for a supper 'prepared plenteously' and served in as 'goodly order and sort as could be devised, with all manner of delicacies.' Free food was provided elsewhere for those of lower station and for the less privileged guests. Eight women, twelve men, thirty yeomen, and a number of priests and clerks were appointed to 'watch about the corpse' during the night.

Early next day breakfast was served in the monastery to the important visitors and in other places for all those who cared to come. A Requiem Mass was sung between seven and eight o'clock and offerings of cloth of gold palls made by the six leading mourners—the four Suffolk daughters, Catherine Willoughby, and her mother—

each being presented in order of precedence. William Rugg, the Abbot of St. Bennet's at Hulme, Norfolk, who was soon to become Bishop of Norwich, delivered the funeral oration, of which no record is extant; nor is it known exactly why Rugg was chosen except possibly that since St. Bennet's was a mitred abbey, as a spiritual peer he had sat in the House of Lords with Suffolk and become a friend of the family. It is likely that through her influence Mary had helped him to his abbacy three years before, as she had many other times aided people in Norfolk and Suffolk. That the discourse was long is testified to by the fact that Frances and Eleanor were too exhausted by the end of it to attend the service at the grave. They had had two physically wearying days, and must also have been overwrought from grief and emotional tension; sent to rest, they were spared the ordeal of the breaking of the staves of office by the household officiary and the 'great weeping and lamenting.'

On July 23 the funeral party dispersed, the family returning to Westhorpe. The catafalque remained in the church awaiting its disposition by the Duke, who was expected to arrive within a fortnight, its cloth of gold pall gleaming under the flickering light of four candles.

Mary was soon forgotten in London, but the memory of her kindness lingered on in the country, where stories continued to be told of the gentle queen who had lived there. Gratefully remembered was the 'great dole' distributed after the final funeral dinner, when from four places in Bury St. Edmunds meat and drink were available to all. The bells were still that evening and the town quiet, but from the largesse of the grave every poor person received four pennies.

While Mary's body was still lying in state at Westhorpe an official funeral service was solemnized at Westminster Abbey on the tenth and eleventh of July, as a public gesture of honor by her husband and brother. In tribute to her rank it was conducted with all the ostentatious formality accorded to royalty; the Earl of Essex was the chief of seven designated mourners, with the king-of-arms, herald-of-arms, and royal pursuivants performing their official duties. Henry and Suffolk were both too busy establishing a living queen to have time to go to Suffolk to honor a dead one. Three years later when it was suggested that a similar service be held at St. Paul's to commemorate Catherine of Aragon's death, the King refused. Mary 'was a Queen' he observed, deserving of such expenditure, but for his former spouse, 'it should be more charge than was either requisite or needful.'

In the absence of preserved household accounts for the Duke of Suffolk, the total cost of Mary's funeral is not known. Crown officials and their servants were paid by the King, five shillings per day for the heralds, and two shillings and sixpence for the pursuivants, for the ten days of their services. Most of the cloth, the major decorations, the palls, and the heavy black material used for the hearse seem to have come from the royal wardrobe. The rest of the expense, which must have been considerable, was presumably borne by Suffolk. Over and above the money spent on the food, wine, and beer consumed by so many people were the fees to hired laborers, priests, torch-bearers, bell-ringers, and extra servitors. Even for the middle classes death was financially crippling, as witnessed by the Paston funeral when fourteen bell-ringers and ninety-four servitors were employed, and eighteen barrels of beer and a proportionate quantity of wine drunk; somewhat later Thomas Stoner paid seventy-four pounds for a simpler interment. In 1579 Sir Thomas Gresham was buried at a cost of eight hundred pounds. Funerary ostentation seems to have reached its peak in the latter half of the sixteenth century, when the price of aristocratic funerals varied between one thousand and two thousand pounds, the Earl of Leicester's even amounting to three thousand.

Suffolk could afford to be lavish for he might expect reimbursement if Henry were pleased. In this he was not disappointed: within two months he was granted the fruits of the vacant see of Ely, a sum of more than twelve thousand ducats, to help him over his financial crisis. At the same time a crown debt of one thousand pounds was remitted. Sir Edward Baynton, one of Henry's favorite courtiers who knew Suffolk well, made the sardonic comment that Brandon was 'loth to let fall a noble unless he took up a royal for it.' Within three years he had obtained remittance of all Mary's crown debts and refinanced his own.

The cost of Mary's ornate alabaster monument at Bury St. Edmunds may have been shared by Suffolk and the King. Both the tomb and the record of its construction were destroyed during the Dissolution, but the coffin itself was saved and removed without ceremony to the monastic church of St. Mary's within the precincts of the former Abbey, where it still is.

Mary's death left Suffolk heavily in debt, with a large household, a young ward, and two unmarried children to support. It was expected that a widower so placed would remarry as soon as a woman with good financial prospects presented herself. Brandon had not far to look: his ward, Catherine Willoughby, having just reached the marriageable age of fourteen, was attractive, young, titled, and wealthy. Daughter and heir of Lord William Willoughby by his second wife, Maria de Salinas, Spanish lady-in-waiting to Queen Catherine, she was a baroness in her own right endowed with an annual income of fifteen thousand ducats. He had bought her wardship for £2,266 13s. 4d. five years earlier with the idea of marrying her to his son as soon as he was old enough. They were in fact betrothed and ready for marriage when Mary's death intervened, but to Suffolk it seemed unrealistic to waste her on his son when he himself was eligible, especially since the boy could without trouble be mated equally profitably elsewhere. So Brandon wed his son's intended, which prompted the remark of a Spanish chronicler that the young man was 'so sorry that he died.' Henry Brandon did indeed die shortly thereafter, though almost certainly not of a broken heart. Anne Boleyn, who had little cause to malign the Duke of Suffolk, is reported as having encouraged the rumor: 'My Lord of Suffolk kills one son to beget another.'

Charles Brandon and Catherine Willoughby were married on Sunday, September 7, 1533, a few hours before Elizabeth Tudor was born. Mary had been in her grave less than seven weeks. While almost immediate remarriage by both widows and widowers was not uncommon in England, it frequently caused suspicious eyebrows to lift. Henry VIII's last queen, Catherine Parr, married Thomas Seymour so soon after Henry's death that the birth to them of even a full-term child would have caused speculation as to when the child had been conceived. However, Brandon's marriage attracted no particular attention despite its almost indecent haste. The mortality rate was so high that a man had need of more than one son, since death was continually interrupting the continuity of family lines. Suffolk was forty-nine, and if he were to sire more sons it was recognized that he could not afford to wait. A man had not only to seek a woman who would 'bring with her meat in her mouth to maintain her expense'—the words are Henry Percy's—but also youth in her limbs and fertility in her womb. Sixteenth-century society accepted these common-sense facts, and respected matrimony with its total lack of modern romance as an honorable estate.

To take a wife, it is a glorious thing,
And namely when a man is old and hoor;
Then is a wife the fruit of his tresor.
Then should he take a young wife and a fair,
On which he might engender him an heir,
And lead his life in joy and in solas.

Commenting on the union to Charles V, Chapuys noted not the discrepancy in age but the zeal with which Suffolk hastened from the bier of one wife to the bed of another: 'The Duke will have done a service to the ladies,' he observed laconically, 'when they are reproached, as is usual, with marrying again immediately after the death of their husbands.' The marriage proved eminently successful. Brandon had grown fond of Catherine since she entered his household. An intelligent spirited girl who could be both a lover and a companion to him, she in her turn acquired not only position and prestige, but a distinguished husband of vigor and experience. They spent twelve happy years together and were blessed with two sons, the first of whom was born just over a year after their marriage when Catherine was fifteen. Henry, his son by Mary, having died in March of that year, 1534, Suffolk was pleased to have another boy, and again named the baby Henry, requesting the King to 'make a Christian soul of him.' Infidelity was not among Brandon's faults: he was as good a husband to Catherine as he had been to Mary.

The highest compliment Brandon ever received was paid him by the King just after his death in 1545, when Henry told the Council in open meeting that for as long as the Duke had served him he had never betrayed a friend or intentionally taken unfair advantage of an adversary. He then challenged the lords to silence, with the avowal that none of them could say as much. Once Suffolk was dead the King in his loneliness forgot everything but that he had been deprived of his last genuine friend, as with Mary's death he had lost his only disinterested love.

Only a few times more was Mary temporarily to evoke public interest. Shortly after her death a strange story was circulated about her by a pathetic Yorkshire girl, the eighteen-year-old daughter of Thomas Baynton of Bridlington, who claimed to be the Royal Princess helplessly cast out by her father, Henry VIII, by whose cruelty 'she was put forth into the broad world to shift for her living.' She described the compassion of her aunt the French Queen who, she said, had once prophesied her sad fate and urged her to appeal to the Emperor for assistance. 'Niece Mary, I am right sorry for you, for I see here'—reading from a book—'that your fortune is very hard,' the Queen was quoted as having told her: 'You must go a-begging once in your life, either in your youth or in your age.' And so tragic Mary Baynton had set out upon her wanderings, resolved to cross the sea for help from her cousin in Germany. The story, though apocryphal, emphasized Henry's known and sometimes wanton cruelty to members of his family, a fact which lent a certain credibility to the tale.

Not even in death did Mary's body remain undisturbed. Twice her leaden coffin was dug up, and once opened by curious souvenir seekers who unscrupulously clipped from her head locks of its long hair, still golden-bright and shiny.

In 1784, two and a half centuries after her death, her coffin was removed to a new resting-place in the chancel of St. Mary's church, where the plain slab of Petworth marble which had originally marked her altar tomb now covers the grave. It is simply inscribed: 'Sacred to the Memory of Mary Tudor, third daughter of Henry VII of England, and Queen of France.' The sermon delivered by the Reverend Arthur Hervey, Bishop of Bath and Wells, at the dedication ceremony of the Mary Tudor Memorial Window in the Lady Chapel of St. Mary's Church at Bury St. Edmunds in 1881, summed up her life in a glowing, if conjectural, tribute: 'We may well conclude that she was a follower of godly and quiet matrons; that her home was the centre of her affections, the sphere of her duties, the scene of her activity, the theatre on which she shone before the loving eyes of husband and children.'

THE House of Suffolk might quickly have ceased to be of any particular significance had the last testament of a dying sovereign not once again inspired this ambitious family with dynastic hopes. Brandon was scarcely cold in his grave when Henry VIII sought to guarantee England's security by a peaceful and uncontested Succession. One legitimate male heir was not enough: the line of descent must depend on more than a sickly boy and two unwed daughters who might die childless.

The first of a long series of Succession Acts came in 1534, a year after Mary's death, supplemented by the royal will in 1546 bequeathing the crown to the descendants of the King's two sisters in the event of his own children dying without issue. Preference was given to the Suffolk line of Henry's younger sister Mary, as against the Stuart line of his elder sister Margaret. What prompted this personal discrimination on Henry's part in opposition to the normal principle of inheritance is not known. Possibly he was motivated by national distrust of the Scots or by the common-law rule that foreigners could not inherit English land. John Strype, however, may have more nearly touched the truth when he said that since the King loved Mary and Brandon, nature influenced him, while 'heirs of the Scottish queen, you know, he did cease to love.' The will was given parliamentary sanction in the second and third Succession Acts of 1536 and 1543, and further confirmed in the first Edwardian Treason Act of 1547, which also made it treason to alter it, thereby lending support to the Suffolk claim for another half-century. While their chances of inheriting the throne were never strong, the blight of Tudor blood was, nevertheless, visited upon Mary's descendants to the third generation. Her nearness to the throne and the love her brother had had for her were to cause grief, imprisonment, and death to certain of her posterity whose lives might otherwise have been quiet and constructive.

Henry and the Council had been growing increasingly uneasy long before the Succession, toward the end of his reign, became a pertinent issue. More than one English noble privately flirted with the thought of possessing the crown of England, including the three senior peers, Norfolk, Buckingham, and Suffolk. As Henry grew older their pretensions became less inconceivable, especially when it became obvious that Catherine of Aragon would not provide the kingdom with a male heir. Buckingham was both the strongest and most likely contender, and many deemed his chances excellent in the event of Henry's untimely death. After the birth of the Queen's last baby, still-born, in 1518, foreign capitals watched the critical situation closely, as indeed they were to do for decades to come. The Venetian government was informed by its representative in England the following year that were the King to die without male issue at that time, it was believed that the Duke 'might easily obtain the crown.' Henry evidently concurred, for he felt compelled to blot out this source of apprehension. Buckingham's execution in 1521 allayed but did not remove the nagging fear of later dissension unless a definite settlement were made. The death of Henry's illegitimate son in 1536 and the birth of his legitimate one in 1537 did little to change the ultimate fact that specific provision for the future was imperative. This was recognized by the nation when in the Succession Act of 1536, expanded in 1543, parliament authorized the King arbitrarily to choose his successors should his third queen, Jane Seymour, bear him no issue. The gravity of the situation was emphasized by Henry VIII's biographer, A. F. Pollard, when he suggested that civil war would inevitably have ensued had the King died in that year. His case is overstated, but the danger was there. The birth of Edward VI postponed the eligibility of the Suffolk heirs for another ten years.

When Charles Brandon died in August, 1545, he was survived by two of his three children by Mary Tudor. Their son, Henry Brandon, Earl of Lincoln, had died in 1534 and his death had been the occasion for some comment. 'I have been told that the Scottish ambassador considers the death of the son of the Duke of Suffolk a piece of good fortune for his master,' the Emperor was told, 'as, though of the younger sister, his being a native would have made him a formidable competitor to the Scotch King.' Frances and Eleanor, Suffolk's daughters by Mary, both outlived their father, the former still being alive when Edward VI made his 'Devise' for the Succession. Eleanor lived until 1547, her descendants continuing as possible claimants to the throne long after her sister's line had died out. It was, however, on the three daughters of Frances Brandon, as favored by the King, that the Suffolk claim immediately depended.

The Succession as arranged in Henry's will was clear in intent, providing that 'immediately after our Departure out of this present Life our said Son Edward shall have and enjoy the said Imperial Crown,' then the heirs of Edward's body or, if he failed in issue, the heirs of Queen Catherine Parr or any later wife of the King. That much was straightforward and acceptable, but the remaining provisions were more controvertible. Princess Mary and her heirs were given next preference, provided she had had the consent of the Privy Council to her marriage, followed by Princess Elizabeth on whom similar restrictions were imposed, and lastly by the grandchildren of the French Queen, that is the heirs of the body of the Lady Frances and Lady Eleanor, in that order. Finally, there were 'the next Rightful Heirs,' presumably the Scottish line through Margaret Tudor. Thus priority was given to the Suffolks' grandchildren, their daughters being passed over on the assumption that they would die before Mary and Elizabeth. Obviously by slighting the Scottish claimants and by the safeguards designed to guarantee suitable mates for Henry's daughters, the King hoped to exclude the taint of undesirable foreign blood from the English throne.

This arrangement remained unchanged and uncontested until the end of the next reign, when Edward VI was persuaded by the Duke of Northumberland, Lord President of the Council and at the time real ruler of the state, to alter the provision of Henry's will so as to deprive his half-sisters, Mary and Elizabeth, of their inheritance. Both princesses were declared illegitimate and hence ineligible for the crown, which by Northumberland's new 'Devise' was to go not to Lady Jane Grey's male heirs, as originally intended, but rather 'to the Lady Jane *and* her heirs males.' Frances Brandon was again passed over in favor of her eldest daughter Jane, not yet sixteen and already conveniently married to Northumberland's son, Guildford Dudley; this ensured the descent, first to Jane, and second to any sons born to her, in case her mother, Frances, who was only thirty-six, should still have sons who would take precedence over any of her grandsons.

The result of this foolhardy attempt to deprive Catholic Mary Tudor of her right of succession is as well known as is the tragic fate of the 'nine-day Queen,' the 'hope of Protestantism.' Worthiest of the Suffolk posterity, Jane was guilty only of her royal blood. Fair of face and freckled, with arched eyebrows, even white teeth, and the bright reddish hair of the Tudors, she bore a distinct resemblance to her grandmother. Her offense against her country was no crime

K

before her God, 'in that being in so royal estate as I was, my enforced honour never mixed with mine innocent heart.' The same curse of birth was to affect still others after her: 'Mercy to the innocent!'

Her rash father, Henry Grey, Marquis of Dorset, of whom it was said people 'neither misliked nor much regarded,' suffered a similar doom. His widow, Frances Brandon, lived to marry a second time, but her two children by this marriage died in infancy, thereby escaping the hazards of kinship to the throne. The two younger Grey girls, Katherine and Mary, were in a different way as unjustly victimized as was their sister, though their persecution was precipitated as much by their own indiscretion as by the incident of their birth. Their folly in marrying secretly without royal consent was no more impetuous or unreasonable than the clandestine marriage of their grandmother had been, but the dangers attendant upon such action were far more acute in the Elizabethan period, when so long as the Queen refused to take a husband the surety of the realm was in jeopardy. No less than Lady Jane, Katherine and Mary were hapless pawns in this matter of heredity, which in Burghley's words was 'so deep' that neither he nor parliament could 'reach into it.' The whole country had become concerned, and joined with him 'in praying God to send it a good issue.' Katherine and Mary suffered years of imprisonment, both for their presumption in marrying without permission and in Katherine's case bearing claimants to the throne, but also simply because, being Tudors, they were an inherent threat to the crown. No one seemed greatly concerned with their lot, though the Queen's conscience prompted her to give Katherine a burial which cost over a thousand pounds. Thirty-five years afterward when Katherine's eldest son, Edward Seymour, Lord Beauchamp, was mentioned to the dying Elizabeth as a possible successor, the Queen's earlier wrath was rekindled: 'I will have no rascal's son to succeed me.' In 1610 the union of the Suffolk and Stuart lines in the marriage of William Seymour, second Duke of Somerset, to Arabella Stuart met with a like end. She was sent to the Tower and died insane four years later.

The misdemeanor of dwarfish Mary Grey in marrying without Elizabeth's permission was less serious because she left no issue, but Cecil records that the offense was 'very great.' Her husband, Thomas Keyes, spent the remainder of his life in prison, while she, after seven years in close custody, lived to die a natural death in 1578.

Less favored for the Succession were the descendants of Eleanor

Brandon, who had borne two sons and a daughter by her husband Henry Clifford, second Earl of Cumberland. Both boys died in infancy, but her daughter Margaret Clifford grew to maturity and married Henry Stanley, fourth Earl of Derby. Of Margaret's five sons three lived to perpetuate the Suffolk house. Although Margaret's claim was inferior to that of her cousin Lady Jane Grey, in that she represented the younger branch of the family, it had the advantage in 1553 of directness, her mother having died in 1547. During Elizabeth's reign the Stanleys were only indirectly involved in Succession plots, since Derby was discreet enough not to advance his wife's claim, and their sons wisely followed his example. For a short while only, upon his father's death in 1593, Ferdinando, the fifth earl, was the subject of a Catholic scheme to revive the family's pretension to the throne, on the grounds that through Margaret Clifford's Tudor blood the Stanleys 'were next in propinquity of blood' to the Queen. The fact that he was one of the richest peers in the country raised the hopes of exiled English Jesuits, who were then working through Richard Hesketh, an English refugee adventurer sent back to England with the promise of Spanish aid.

The Earl had the good sense to reveal the plot to the government, and Hesketh was apprehended and executed. Ferdinando died the following year, and was succeeded by his brother William Stanley, whose remote claim to the throne was never emphasized.

After the failure of the Lady Jane Grey plot, it was apparent that the Suffolk claimants had no real chance of success. Not only was the legal position of Margaret Tudor's Stuart line sounder, but the arguments in support of her younger sister's descendants were problematical at best. Did Henry VIII have the constitutional right to dispose of the crown at his own discretion, even if so authorized by parliament? Was his will a valid instrument when merely signed by dry stamp and not with his own hand, as required by statute? After Mary's reign serious doubts of its authenticity were voiced. Even assuming its validity, had it been Henry VIII's desire to exclude the Scottish line completely? There was much quibbling over the intent of the phrase 'and if it so happen that the said Lady Eleanor die without issue, then we will that the said Imperial Crown shall come to our next rightful heirs,' not 'right heirs' as stated in the first Act of Succession.

Finally under Elizabeth the legality of Mary Tudor's marriage to Suffolk and the contingent legitimacy of their children was again questioned. In the end time defeated the Suffolks, as with each succeeding generation their connection with the throne became further removed. 'You know them all,' Queen Elizabeth once remarked of that unhappy breed; 'Alas! what power or force has any of them, poor souls?'

Mary's Birth, Death, and Exhumation

THOUGH the year of Mary's birth has been variously chosen by biographers and historians as one between 1485 and 1500, the only two possible are 1495 and 1496. The fragmentary evidence available points to the former as the most probable. The claim for this year rather than 1496 was clearly stated over half a century ago by Mary Croom Brown (*Mary Tudor, Queen of France*, London, 1911) and need not be repeated here. Likewise uncertain are the month and day of her birth. I have accepted the date, March 18, as given in the calendar to the Psalter belonging to Mary's mother, now in Exeter College Library, Oxford, which also verifies the year as being 1495. Only in the interest of historical accuracy is the exact date of any value, because it is not significant in relation to the events of her life. Writers have tended to assume that she married Louis XII at an earlier age than the facts warrant, but whether eighteen or nineteen at the time, she was certainly not a child bride.

There is also disparity of opinion about the day of her death in June, 1533. The Bailie of Troyes, Jean de Dinteville, writing to Francis I on June 30, mentioned that she had been dead for three days, though not explicitly stating that she died on the twenty-seventh; Chapuys, hearing of her death on the twenty-eighth, wrote to inform Charles V immediately. The Venetian ambassador reported it as being on the twenty-sixth, while Hall's *Chronicle* gives Midsummer's Day, the twenty-fourth of June, as the date of her death. The more specific account of her funeral in the College of Arms, however, states that she died at Westhorpe, between seven and eight o'clock on the morning of June 25 ('A Remembraunce for the buryall of the Right Excellent prynces Mary . . .').

The exhumation of her body in 1731, in 1758, and again in 1784, aroused considerable interest in its state of preservation after the lapse of two centuries; it also threw light on the embalming technique of the period. The condition of the corpse in 1784 is quite well documented, with several extant descriptions of its appearance at that time.

On the leaden coffin, six feet two inches in length, had been traced a crude likeness of the face; over the breast a portion of the encasement, smoothed and polished, bore the inscription: 'Mary Quene of Fraunce, 1533. Edmund H.' Whether artist or embalmer, the identity of Edmund H. is not known. The corpse was still in excellent condition, although it had become very moist from exposure to the air a quarter of a century before. When examined the cerecloth showed about ten thicknesses of material, already broken at the stomach. The body was not opened up for critical examination, but it appeared to have been filled originally with calcareous material after the brain and viscera had been removed; the eyeballs had also been taken out and the sockets filled with a preservative. The hair was almost two feet long and still retained its reddish gold color.

Most surprising was the soundness of the teeth, which were even and complete, with little evidence of such decáy as might have been expected in a woman of thirty-eight. It was thought that the tiny perforations in the enamel of certain crowns were post-mortem, and probably made by insects hatched from eggs deposited during the previous exposure in 1758. The phenomenon of a sound set of teeth is an enlightening commentary on a generation of English people whose teeth were considered by contemporaries to be proverbially bad.

It was during the examination of the body in 1784 that tresses of the French Queen's hair were cut off and acquired by several people, including Horace Walpole and the Dowager Duchess of Portland, Margaret Bentinck. A lock of it can still be seen in the local museum at Moyse's Hall at Bury St. Edmunds. The resealed coffin was moved to the northeast corner of the church, where it lies just below the level of the chancel floor. In 1904 Edward VII authorized the original altar slab covering the grave to be enclosed by a marble curb.

APPENDIX II

Note on Portraits of Mary, Brandon, and Their Family

IN A historical appraisal of early English Renaissance portraiture it should be remembered that often it is extremely difficult to identify either the artists or the dates of their paintings. In fact, most of the surviving portraits for the period before Holbein the Younger are of dubious authenticity, both as to subject and artist; with definite proof lacking, it is seldom possible to determine authorship prior to 1525. In England, during Mary's lifetime, 1495-1533, most of the productive portraitists were foreign and, since little is known of their life there, identification of their work is, at best, but a shrewd guess. Furthermore, it is questionable if any of these early portraits bear more than an imaginary resemblance to the subject. Certainly costume was greatly emphasized and to the artist details of dress and jewelry were as professionally significant as a faithful reproduction of the face. Even when it is known that he had access to his subject, it cannot always be established whether the finished portrait was done from life, from earlier sketches, or from memory. A reputable painter like Holbein seems to have had limited access to some of his sitters: it is said that Christina of Denmark sat for only three hours for the famous 'Duchess of Milan,' the actual portrait being painted in the studio. Consequently, it is not surprising that various likenesses of the same individual are often quite dissimilar, none of them perhaps conforming closely to contemporary descriptions of the subject. Word pictures probably produced more accurate images than did the finished products of artists, impressive though these could be. Until the advent of photography, no medium existed for the reproduction of an exact likeness.

Although renowned for her charm and beauty there are no portraits of Mary Tudor that support her universally acknowledged loveliness. In fact, only vaguely do they resemble each other in

275

any specific sense. The few that appear to be original differ appreciably in the impression they convey, and of these none can really stand the test of searching inquiry regarding date and identity. Numerous iconographs exist—drawings, engravings, etchings, illustrations—mostly copies of earlier portraits themselves of questionable originality, or imaginary representations designed to portray some colorful episode in her life. Among those passing for genuine likenesses of Mary, only a few can be positively identified as authentic.

The best known portrait of her is the controversial one at Sudeley Castle attributed to John Corvus, probably completed some time late in life, a few years before her death (see facing page 32). Apart from his being one of the few identifiable foreign artists in England before Holbein the Younger, little is known about this naturalized Fleming and his English paintings. Sometime early in Henry VIII's reign a certain Jan Raf or Rave came to the English Court; a native of Bruges, he painted under the Latinized name of Joannes Corvus. Among the portraits attributed to him is that of Richard Fox, Bishop of Winchester, now at Corpus Christi College, Oxford. Alleged to date from about 1518, it represents the churchman as blind, and though more distinctive than the Sudeley picture of Mary, the style of painting is similar. Originally both were set in like frames bearing the legend, 'Johannes Corvus Flandrus Faciabat.' Assuming Mary's age to have been thirty-four as was recorded on the lost frame, the picture must have been painted in 1529; but there is no positive proof either of that or of its being an original. It could be a copy of an earlier one, executed by Corvus or some other Flemish portraitist at some time after her death.

This painting is a half-length one showing her seated at a red-covered table or desk in front of a tapestry of cloth of gold. Her arms are reposing on the table, an apple in her right hand. Her dress is richly jeweled in the style worn by noble ladies of the Henrician Renaissance, its close-fitting grey bodice cut in a low square neckline trimmed with pearls, the long full undersleeves of white material delicately embroidered in gold, black, and silver, with turned-back cuffs. Her hair is completely hidden by a diamond-shaped chevron hood of cloth of gold, framing the face with nun-like severity, a long black veil falling low over the back. A lengthy necklace embellished with precious stones twice encircles her neck; from it hang two ornate pearl pendants. Her hands are so placed upon the table as to display their six rings of precious stones. Mary's face is pale and slightly drawn, the eyes unsmiling, but the pain she suffered during the chronic ill-health of her last years had probably left its mark upon her beauty.

The earlier so-called wedding picture of Mary and Charles Brandon is usually attributed to Jan Gossaert, who may have come to England from the Low Countries about 1500. He is better known now as Jan Mabuse or John of Maubeuge, the small town in Hainault where he was born. Traditionally he has been accepted by some authorities as a pioneer of English portraiture during Henry VIII's reign, one to whom a number of English portraits have been ascribed. An artist of some standing on the Continent, his connection with England is so uncertain that recent scholarship has inclined to be skeptical of certain Mabuse items. Though the bridal portrait purports to have been painted at the time of Mary's marriage at Greenwich in May, 1515, it may have been done later.

Now in the Woburn collection of the Duke of Bedford, this portrait (see facing page 224) shows the pair sitting side by side, with left hands joined. In her right hand Mary holds an orb, the symbol of majesty and authority, curiously shaped like an artichoke. It is surmounted by a caduceus or Mercury's wand instead of the commoner cross, perhaps because the marriage had been solemnized in May, the month of this pagan god's festival. Her costume is quite similar in style to that of the Sudeley portrait, the neckline almost identical. The one striking difference is in headdress, which perhaps shows the influence of her months in Paris. She wears the more sophisticated French hood and bongrace to the shoulders, exposing the front of her hair, which is combed straight and parted in the middle. Neither the hood and its trimming of nether and upper billiments garnished with jewels, nor the court bonnet with halo brim and medallion over the left temple worn by Brandon, seems to have come into general use in England until the latter part of Henry VIII's reign. Despite the discrepancy between the dates of these two pictures of Mary, their resemblance to each other is unmistakable.

Various copies of the original wedding picture were made, one of which includes the figure of a jester, presumably Brandon's, whispering to him derisively the stanza which Suffolk is supposed to have written about his presumptuous and unequal marriage to a queen:

Cloth of gold do not despise,
Though thou be match'd with cloth of frieze;

Cloth of frieze be not too bold,
Though thou be match'd with cloth of gold.

Of the various reproductions of the painting, that engraved by
George Vertue in 1748 is the best (No. 3 of Vertue's set of Tudor
prints).

There are several pictures of Mary by unknown French artists,
which though mostly not flattering, all bear a striking resemblance
to each other. The most engaging are those of her as Queen of
France (see facing page 128), and a simple but sympathetic study of
about the same period, portraying her as a demure young lady.
Seven portraits of her are also preserved among the extant album collections of drawings and paintings of prominent persons at the Court
of Francis I, of which a delicate drawing probably done in 1515, included in the Album Fontelle of the Ashmolean Museum, Oxford,
is the most attractive (see facing page 193). The others, all in the
manner of Jean Clouet, are found in albums at the Louvre, Aix-en-
Provence, Chantilly, Lille, and Florence.

Finally, there is a very doubtful and much disputed portait of a
young girl believed by some art critics to be Mary at some point
before she went to France to marry Louis XII in 1514. Against a
background of flowered damask, the sitter faces the spectator with
her head slightly turned, in an ornately decorated dress of cloth of
gold with a semi-low square neckline, its slashed white sleeves
trimmed at the wrists with bands of jewels. She wears a single-
strand necklace of large pearls with a larger pearl drop, rings, and a
collar of knotted gold cord set with jewels and pearls from which
hangs a pendant of the same pattern. The uncovered head reveals
long hair, parted in the middle and held in place by a simple narrow
jeweled bandeau, falling in thick waves over the shoulders. The girl
holds a covered silver pot, possibly intended as an emblem of Mary
Magdalen. The face is so completely expressionless as to be almost
anybody, but the nose and chin, high forehead and small mouth, do
bear a distinct resemblance to pictures of Mary Tudor (see facing
page 32). The authorship of this portrait is also unknown. If it is of
Mary, it may be a copy of one painted by Jean Perréal of Paris, royal
painter at the French Court from about 1483 to 1528. That Louis XII
sent him to England to paint her is a matter of record, and though
he presumably returned to Paris with a portrait which the French
King found pleasing, proof of this is wanting. Whether by Perréal

or not, the original did not survive, but a copy can be seen in the vestry of St. Mary's Church at Bury St. Edmunds.

The stained-glass window in the Lady Chapel of the same church shows scenes from Mary's life, both as Princess and Queen. This memorial window, the work of Clayton and Bell, London, was presented to the church by Queen Victoria in 1881 (see facing page 193). Two of the panels depict Mary and Brandon together, one in the Hôtel de Cluny during her seclusion as 'White Queen' and the other being secretly married before their return to England. At the top of the window are likenesses of Henry VIII, Louis XII, and Charles of Castile, as well as of Suffolk and Mary.

Of the etchings and engravings allegedly of Mary, a number are of questionable authenticity. Those from the Sudeley Castle and the Woburn Abbey have been frequently reproduced. Variations occur, as in the engraving by an anonymous artist which shows Mary holding a book in her left hand instead of the apple; while differing in detail the pose is the same as in the Sudeley portrait from which is was apparently copied. Another, 'Mary Tudor Duchess of Suffolk,' engraved by Edward Hargrave, presents a full-length view of her in long gown and angular hood; if it is she it bears only a vague resemblance. A woodcut by C. A. Hebert of 'Marie Tudor' in a large rising collar set in a highly decorative oval frame, is obviously false. Prints of these and others of Mary and Brandon are to be found in the Print Room of the British Museum.

The portraits of Charles Brandon, Duke of Suffolk, are fewer in number but no less difficult to appraise. The best and most acceptable one, by an unknown painter, is no longer extant; formerly in the possession of the Norbert Fischman Gallery, it was destroyed during World War II. However, a photograph of it at the National Portrait Gallery clearly reveals the bold design and superb quality of the original. It was a half-length, full-face, life-size portrait of a courtier, elaborately dressed in black beret, coat, and surcoat. Seated in a large chair, he wears the collar of the Order of the Garter with the emblem of St. George and holds a small bunch of flowers in his ungloved left hand. A very large man, the strong face, sharp eyes, Roman nose, and hard mouth, suggest a powerful dominant character. The full, square-cut, grey-white beard dates the picture as sometime after 1535, when Henry VIII reintroduced and popularized the fashion. The general expression of the face, plus the broad shoulders and obvious height of the man, add up to such a marked likeness to

Henry VIII that the picture has often been mistaken for a portrait of him. As early as 1513 when they were in France together, the similarity was pronounced enough for Brandon to be referred to as the King's 'bastard brother.' Excellent copies of this, differing slightly in detail, are held by the National Portrait Gallery and by the Duke of Bedford at Woburn Abbey.

Brandon lived to be at least sixty, so the portrait could have been painted at any time between 1535 and 1545, the year of his death, when he was in his fifties and getting progressively heavier. On insufficient evidence it has been described by Paul Ganz as a Holbein, whose style had by then influenced most other portraitists. Ganz is correct in stating that the miniatures of Brandon's two sons by Catherine Willoughby, now at Windsor Castle, are by Holbein, but there seems to be no basis for his assertion that this artist made a sketch for a commission to do a Suffolk family group.

A second portrait of a gartered nobleman, possibly of the 1520's, purports to be either Suffolk or Edward Stafford, Duke of Buckingham. It portrays a large man of about thirty years of age dressed in black coat and brown fur collar, his French bonnet adorned with a gold medallion bearing the motto, '*Je tiens en sa cord*,' the broad face mostly concealed by moustache and heavy, wavy dark brown beard. While the portrait is impressive, it has little similarity to Brandon as shown in the wedding picture when he would have been about that age. Ganz's attempt to identify the painter of this portrait as an unknown 'Master of Queen Mary Tudor' is surprising; if Mary had such a sergeant-painter no record of him exists. The painting was shown in the Tudor exhibition at the New Gallery in 1890 as being of Buckingham; later it was acquired by the Fischman Gallery and is now in the possession of Mrs. Norbert Fischman (see facing page 208). There is an identical portrait in the collection of the Marquis of Bath at Longleat House.

Another unauthenticated portrait of the Duke of Suffolk is in the possession of the Marquis of Northampton, and hangs in 'Henry VIII's Bedroom' at Compton Wynyates. It is attributed to the Flemish painter, Hans Eworth, who came to England about the time of Suffolk's death (see facing page 208).

There are numerous engravings of Brandon, based on his various portraits, or from the picture of him and Mary, by Vertue, Trotter, Harding, Scriven, Mote, Bertie, and others. The best is by Vertue. An anonymous one copied from an original at Strawberry Hill carries

Suffolk's autograph. A Cottonian manuscript drawing of a head, said to be that of the Duke, cannot be authenticated.

Painted portraits of Mary's children are extremely scarce. None exists of her son or of her younger daughter Eleanor. There is, however, an excellent Holbein drawing in the royal collection at Windsor of Frances Brandon, mother of Lady Jane Grey, as Marchioness of Dorset. That of Frances most commonly reproduced is by Hans Eworth, with her second husband Adrian Stokes, dated 1559, the year of her death. An engraving by Vertue of Lucas de Heere's painting, is also of Frances and Adrian Stokes.

APPENDIX III

Genealogical Tables

THE HOUSE OF TUDOR

Notes

* Margaret Tudor's third husband, Henry Stuart, Lord Methven, by whom she had no offspring, survived her.

† Frances Brandon married Adrian Stokes, by whom she had two sons and a daughter, after Dorset's execution in 1554; they all three died in infancy, as did her first two children by Dorset.

‡ The dukedom of Suffolk was vacated by the deaths of Henry and Charles Brandon on July 16, 1551. It was awarded to Dorset the following October.

§ Arabella Stuart, daughter of Charles Stuart, Earl of Lennox, was the great-granddaughter of Margaret Tudor, Queen of James IV of Scotland.

THE HOUSE OF SUFFOLK

Notes

* Brandon's granddaughters (by his daughter Mary)—Elizabeth, Margaret, and Anne—all had issue.

† After Suffolk's death, Catherine Willoughby married Richard Bertie, by whom she had a son, Peregrin Bertie (the 11th Lord Willoughby), and a daughter, Susan Bertie (Countess of Kent).

‡ Henry and Charles Brandon, Suffolk's sons by Catherine Willoughby, both died of the sweating sickness in July, 1551, Charles surviving his elder brother by about half an hour. Consequently, Charles is sometimes also styled Duke of Suffolk. The dukedom became temporarily extinct but was recreated and given to Henry Grey, 2nd Marquis of Dorset and husband of Frances Brandon, later in the same year, 1551.

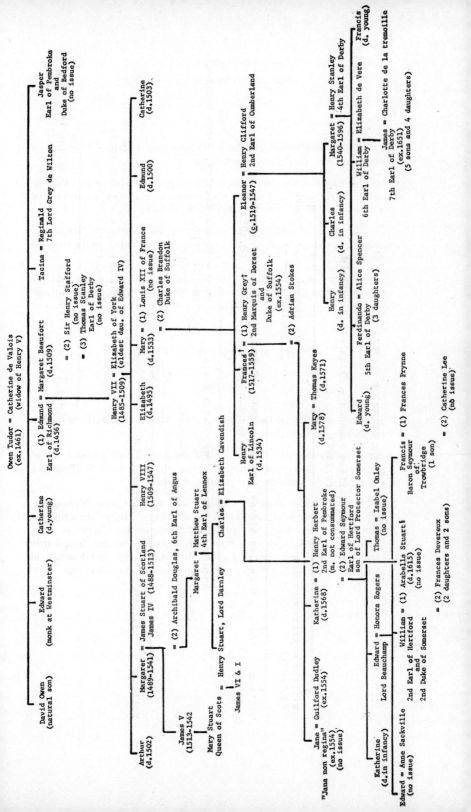

THE HOUSE OF SUFFOLK

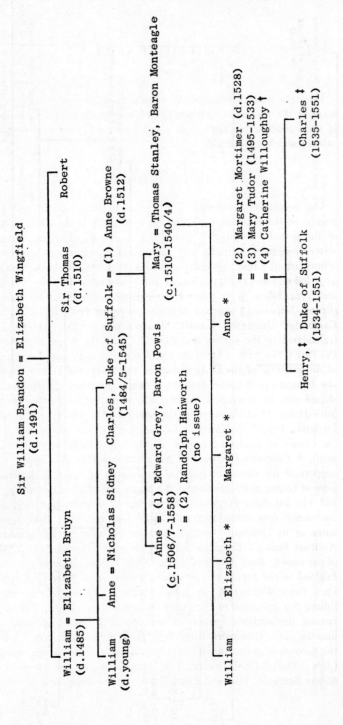

BIBLIOGRAPHY

This is a selected bibliography of major works from which quotations occur in the text and important references that illuminate various aspects of the narrative. No attempt at a full listing of either pertinent or consulted books has been made.

SPECIAL REFERENCES

The Succession Question: The literature, both modern and contemporary, on the Succession is abundant; in addition to the standard histories of the period a number of specialized studies give detailed accounts of sixteenth-century attitudes and implications. Several unpublished manuscripts are of value, especially: (British Museum) Harleian Manuscripts 419, folios 150–51v., 555, 849 (a folio volume containing two tracts), and 4314, folios 59–71 (John Hales's defense of the Suffolk claim), and (British Museum) Cottonian Manuscript, Julius F. vi, folios 431–44; the Cambridge University Library Manuscript 172, Dd. III. 85, No. 18 (calendared in the *Letters and Papers . . . of the Reign of Henry VIII*, IV, Part I, No. 738: a Latin tract presenting an argument for the validity of the marriage of the Duke of Suffolk and Mary, the French Queen, and the legitimacy of their daughter, Frances Brandon, by Robert Beale), should also be mentioned. Among the more pertinent early tracts are: John Hales, 'A declaration of the succession of the crown imperial of England,' 1563 (reproduced in George Harbin, *The Hereditary Right of the Crown of England Asserted*, 1713); Robert Parsons (pseud. R. Doleman), *A Conference About the Next Succession to the Crown*, 1594 (in support of the claims of Isabella, the Infanta of Spain, a descendant of John of Gaunt; the succession of the House of Suffolk is treated, pp. 54–55 and 130–40); John Hayward, 'An answer to the first part of a certaine conference concerning succession published not long since under the name of R. Doleman,' 1603; a tract by Nicholas Bacon, in answer to Anthony Brown's 'Discourse upon certain points touching the inheritance of the crown,' later published as *The Right of Succession to the Crown of England in the Family of the Stuarts, Exclusive of Mary Queen of Scots*, 1723; Peter Wentworth, 'A pithy exhortation to her majesty for establishing her successor to the crown, whereunto is added a discourse containing the author's opinion of the true and lawful successor to her majesty,' 1587 (published Edinburgh, 1598); John Harington, 'A tract on the succession to the crown,' 1602, edited by R. C. Markham (Roxburghe Club, 1880); John Hayward, *The Right of Succession Asserted*, 1603; Robert Brady, *A True and Exact History of the Succession of the Crown* of England, 1681; William Atwood, The Fundamental Constitution of English Government, 1690 ('Allegations' concerning the claims of the Suffolk House and those of Mary Queen of Scots is printed in the Appendix, pp. 1–19); George Harbin, The Present Constitution of the Protestant Succession Vindicated, 1714; Nathaniel Booth, The Right of Succession of the Crown of England in the Family of the Stuarts (contains the Hales' tract and one supporting Mary Queen of Scots by John Leslie), 1723 (but written in 1569); Alfred Bailey, The Succession to the English Crown, 1879, the best general account; and Roger Edwards, 'Castra Regis, a treatise on the succession to the crown of England, addressed to Queen Elizabeth,' originally written in 1568, edited by Philip Bliss and Buckley Bandinel, Historical Papers, Part I (Roxburghe Club, 1846).

Excellent modern studies of the problem are found in: William L. Rutton, 'Lady Katherine Grey and Edward Seymour, Earl of Hertford,' English Historical Review, XIII (1898), 302–7; John H. Pollen, 'The Question of Queen Elizabeth's Successor,' The Month, CI (1903), 517–32; J. E. Neale, 'Parliament and the Succession Question in 1562–63 and 1566,' English Historical Review, XXXVI (1921), 497–520; Mortimer Levine, 'A Study of the Elizabethan Succession Question circa 1558–1568, and especially of the Suffolk Claim' (particularly Parts III, pp. 278–315 and IV, pp. 316–58), an unpublished doctoral dissertation presented at the University of Pennsylvania, 1954 (in revised form this thesis is now available as The Early Elizabethan Succession Question, 1558–1568, Stanford, Cal.: Stanford University Press, 1966); Mortimer Levine, 'A Letter on the Elizabethan Succession Question, 1566,' Huntington Library Quarterly, XIX (1955), 13–38; Leo Hicks, 'Sir Robert Cecil, Father Persons [Parsons], and the Succession, 1600–1,' Archaeological Historical Society Iesu, XXIV (1955), 95–139; and J. Hurstfield, 'The Succession Struggle in Late Elizabethan England,' in Elizabethan Government and Society, edited by T. S. Bindoff, J. Hurstfield, and C. R. Williams (London: Athlone Press, 1961). A critical evaluation of Henry VIII's will is found in Lacey Baldwin Smith, 'The Last Will and Testament of Henry VIII, a Question of Perspective,' The Journal of British Studies, II (November, 1962), 14–27. Modern biographies of Mary Tudor's granddaughters, the Grey sisters, are available in Hester W. Chapman's two recent studies, Two Tudor Portraits (London: Jonathan Cape, 1960) and Lady Jane Grey (London: Jonathan Cape, 1962).

Portraits and Artists: For a full interpretation of the portraiture of the early Tudor age, with special reference to portraits of the Suffolk family, the following sources are suggested. Excellent general surveys may be found in: C. H. Collins Baker and W. G. Constable, English Painting of the Sixteenth and Seventeenth Centuries (New York: Harcourt, Brace and Co., 1930); Louis Dimier, *French Painting in the Sixteenth Century* (London: Duckworth and Co.; New York: Charles Scribner's Sons, 1904) and *Histoire de la peinture de portrait en France au XVI⁰ siècle* (Paris et Bruxelles, G. van Oest et cⁱᵉ, 1924–26); Carl Winter, *The British School of Miniature Portrait Painters*, Annual Lecture on Aspects of Art, British Academy, 1948 (London: Oxford University Press, 1949); E. K. Waterhouse, *Painting in Britain, 1530–1790* (London: Penguin Books, 1953); A. M. Hind, *Engraving in England in the Sixteenth and Seventeenth Centuries*, Part I: *The Tudor Period* (Cambridge: Cambridge University Press, 1952); Sir Matthew Digby Wyatt, *On the Foreign Artists Employed in England during the Sixteenth Century* (London, 1868); John Woodward, *Tudor and Stuart Drawings*, edited by K. T. Parker (London: Faber and Faber, 1951); Horace Walpole, *Anecdotes of Painting in England*, edited by J. Dallaway and R. N. Wornum, 3 vols. (London, 1888); Henry M. Hake, *The English Historic Portrait: Document and Myth*, Annual Lecture on Aspects of Art, British Academy, 1943; James Lees-Milne, *Tudor Renaissance* (London. B. T. Batsford, 1951); David Harrison, *Tudor England*, 2 vols. in 1 (London: Casswell and Co., 1953); Erna Auerbach, *Tudor Artists* (an authoritative study; London: Athlone Press, 1954); J. H. Plumb, *The Horizon Book of the Renaissance*, ed. Richard M. Ketchum (New York: American Heritage Publishing Co., 1961); A. B. Chamberlain, *Hans Holbein the Younger*, 2 vols. (New York: Dodd, Mead and Co., 1913); Paul Ganz, *The Paintings of Han Holbein* (enlarged editions, London: Phaidon Press, 1956); C. R. L. Fletcher and Emery Walker, *Historical Portraits, 1400–1600* (Oxford, 1909).

Among the innumerable special articles on individual painters, several are of particular interest to this study: Erna Auerbach, 'Holbein's Followers in England,' *The Burlington Magazine*, XCIII (1951), 44–51, and 'Early English Engravings,' *The Burlington Magazine*, XCIV (1952), 326–30; A. E. Popham, 'Hans Holbein's Italian Contemporaries,' *The Burlington Magazine*, LXXXIV (1944), 12–17; George Scharf, 'Additional Observations on Some of the Painters Contemporary with Holbein,' *Archaeologia*, XXXIX, Part I (1862), 47–56; W. A. Shaw, 'An Early English Pre-Holbein School of Portraiture,' *The Connoisseur*, XXXI (1911), 72–81, and 'The Early English School of Portraiture,' *The Burlington Magazine*, LXV (1934), 171–84; F. Gordon Roe, 'Portrait of an Ancestress,' *The Connoisseur*, LXXXVI (December, 1930), 365–72; Paul Ganz, 'Holbein and Henry VIII,' *The Burlington Magazine*, LXXXIII (1943), 269–73, 'A Rediscovered Portrait of Charles Brandon, Duke of Suffolk, by Holbein,' *The Burlington Magazine*, LVII (1930), 58, 65, and 'A Portrait of Charles Brandon, Duke of Suffolk, by "the Master of Queen Mary Tudor,"' *The Burlington Magazine*, LXX (1937), 205–11; M. H. Goldblatt, 'Jean Perréal,' *The Connoisseur*, CXXIII (1949), 3–9.

For portraits and illustrations used in this book, consult: C. H. C. Baker, *Catalogue of the Principal Pictures in the Royal Collection at Windsor Castle* (London: Constable and Co., 1937); C. H. C. Baker, *Catalogue of the Pictures at Hampton Court* (Glasgow: printed for the Lord Chamberlain, 1929); *Catalogue of the National Portrait Gallery, 1856–1947* (London: National Portrait Gallery, 1949). *Supplement, 1949–1959* (London: National Portrait Gallery, 1960); *Catalogue of Prints and Drawings in the British Museum*, edited by Frederic George Stephens (London, 1870–83); F. M. O'Donoghue and H. M. Hake, *Catalogue of Engraved British Portraits Preserved in the Department of Prints and Drawings in the British Museum*, 5 vols. (London: British Museum, Department of Prints and Drawings, 1908–22; VI, *Supplemental Index*, 1925).

An account of the collection of the Duke of Bedford is available in George Scharf, A *Descriptive and Historical Catalogue of the Collection of Pictures at Woburn Abbey*, 2 Parts (London: privately printed, 1877–78). The problem of the portraits of Lady Jane Grey and her family is briefly presented in Richard Davey, *The Nine Day's Queen* (London: Methuen and Co., 1909), Appendix, pp. 359–63.

GENERAL REFERENCES

Archival Collections: Public documents and private letters relating to the life of Mary Tudor and the history of her times are located primarily in three major depositories: the British Museum and Public Record Office, London, and the Bibliothèque Nationale in Paris. Most of the bibliographical data, particularly plentiful for the years 1514–17, are contained in her own letters to the various principals in the story; but this correspondence is liberally supported by ambassadorial reports and accounts of European events by contemporary observers, many of whom were official agents either of England or Continental powers. Most of the English letters are preserved among the Cottonian Manuscripts in the British Museum, but those of Louis XII, Francis I, Charles of Castile, Louise of Savoy, Margaret of Austria, and some of Mary's are found predominantly in the French archives. The bulk of this material has not been published, although a small portion of it is now available, either *in extenso* or in abstracted form. Especially pertinent are: *Letters and Papers, Foreign and Domestic, of the Reign of Henry VIII*, edited by J. S. Brewer, James Gairdner, and R. H. Brodie, 21 vols. in 33 parts (London: Stationery Office, 1862–1932); *State Papers During the Reign of Henry VIII*, 11 vols. (London: published under the authority of His Majesty's Commission, 1830–52, printed in full); Mary Anne Everett [Wood] Green (ed.), *Letters of Royal and Illustrious Ladies of Great Britain*, 3 vols. (London: Henry Colburn, 1846); Sir Henry Ellis (ed.), *Orginal Letters Illustrative of English History*, 3 series, 11 vols. (London: Richard Bentley, 1824, 1827, and 1846); *Lettres de Roy Louis XII et du Cardinal Georges d'Amboise, avec plusieurs autres lettres, mémoires et instructions (1504–14)*, edited with notes, by J. Godefroy, 4 vols. (Brussels: F. Foppens, 1712); *Lettres de rois, reines et autres personages des cours de France et d'Angleterre*, edited by J. J. Champollion-Figeac, 2 vols. (Paris, 1845–47), especially Vol. II for Anglo-French relations from 1485 to 1515; and the Journal of Louise of Savoy, edited by Samuel Guichenon, in his *Histoire généalogique de la Royale Maison de Savoye*, 2 parts (Lyon, 1660; nouvelle édition, avec des suppléments, 4 vols., Turin, 1778–80). Vol. IV contains the Journal of Louise of Savoy, pp. 457–64.

Among the valuable unpublished English manuscripts are numerous letters and other items from the Caligula, Galba, Vitellius, and Vespasian divisions of the Cottonian collection in the British Museum, the accounts of the Chamber and the Great Wardrobe in the Public Record Office, and the original record in the Royal College of Arms, London, of Mary's burial in 1533. Pertinent miscellaneous material from foreign archives relating to Mary and Brandon is available in the *Calendar of Letters, Dispatches, and State Papers, Relating to the Negotiations between England and Spain*, edited by G. A. Bergenroth *et al.*, 11 vols. (London: Stationery Office, 1862–96), Vols, I, II, and the *Calendar of State Papers and Manuscripts Relating to English Affairs, Preserved in the Archives of Venice*, edited by R. Brown *et al.*, 9 vols. (London: Stationery Office, 1864–98), Vol. I.

Printed Sources: The life of Mary Tudor has been variously interpreted by fictional writers, ranging from the seventeenth-century French version of Jean de Préchac (1677) to the recent novel by Molly Costain Haycraft in 1962, but straight historical accounts are less numerous. Since the nineteenth-century studies of the lives of the Tudor princesses by Mary Anne Everett Green and Agnes Strickland, only one serious biography of her has been attempted, that of Mary Croom Brown in 1911. Although presented as a full-scale biography it is quite unsatisfactory and not always accurate. Parts of it are based on inadequate research, with practically nothing on Mary's later years; nor is the career of her second husband, the Duke of Suffolk, clearly delineated. With the single exception of Mark Noble's unpublished sketch of Brandon, no life of Suffolk has been written. The several biographical items now available are listed separately in the following selection of printed books.

The subsequent list of reading suggestions is intended as a guide to readers interested in the background history of the age and in the colorful commentaries of Tudor contemporaries. Further references on particular topics may be found in the standard bibliography of the period: *Bibliography of British History, Tudor Period, 1485–1603,* edited by Conyers Read (2nd ed.; Oxford: Clarendon Press, 1959).

BIOGRAPHICAL

Brown, Mary Croom. *Mary Tudor, Queen of France.* London: Methuen and Co., 1911.

Burke, S. H. *Historical Portraits of the Tudor Dynasty and the Reformation Period.* 4 vols. London: John Hodges, 1879–83. See Vol. I.

Cleland, Mabel [Mrs. Kenneth Widdemer]. 'The Laughing Princess,' *American Girl* (September, 1932–February 1933.) Fiction.

Ford, Francis. *Mary Tudor, A Retrospective Sketch.* Bury St. Edmunds: E. L. Barker, 1882.

Garnier, Russell Montague. *The White Queen.* London and New York: Harper and Brothers, 1899. Fiction.

Green, Mary Anne Everett [Wood]. *The Lives of the Princesses of England.* 6 vols. London: Henry Colburn, 1849–55. See Vol. V.

Haycraft, Molly Costain. *The Reluctant Queen.* Philadelphia and New York: J. B. Lippincott Co., 1962. Fiction.

Holt, Emily Sarah. *The Harvest of Yesterday: A Tale of the Sixteenth Century.* Boston: Bradley and Woodruff, 1892. London: J. F. Shaw and Co., 1893. Fiction.

Lussan, Marguerite de [attributed also to Claude Joseph Chéron de Boismorand]. *Marie d'Angleterre, Reine-Duchesse.* Amsterdam, 1749. Fiction.

Major, Charles [pseud. Edwin Caskoden]. *When Knighthood was in Flower.* Indianapolis, Ind.: Bowen-Merrill Co., 1898. Theater edition, New York: Grosset and Dunlop, 1907. Fiction. Dramatized by Paul Kester in 1901; adapted to the screen by Luther Reed in 1922, with the same title; and again in 1953, by Walt Disney in *The Sword and the Rose.*

Noble, Mark. 'An History of the Illustrious House of Brandon' (1807). Unpublished manuscript in the Bodleian Library (MS. Top. Suffolk. d. 16), 33 pp.

Préchac, Jean de. *La Princesse d'Angleterre, ou la Duchesse Reyne.* Paris: Chez Claude Barbin, au Palais, sur le second Perron de la S. Chapelle, 1677. Fiction. Trans into English by the author, 1678.

Strickland, Agnes. *Lives of the Tudor Princesses, Including Lady Jane Grey and her Sisters.* London: Longmans and Co., 1868.

Woodward, Ida. *Five English Consorts of Foreign Princes*. London: Methuen and Co., 1911. Part II, 'Mary Tudor, Queen of France and Duchess of Suffolk, Third Daughter of Henry VII, 1496-1533,' pp. 73-112.

BACKGROUND

Adamson, J. W. 'The Extent of Literacy in England in the Fifteenth and Sixteenth Centuries: Notes and Conjectures,' *The Library*, 4th Series, X (1929-30), 163-93.

Agrippa, Henry Cornelius. *A Treatise of the Nobilitie and Excellencye of Woman Kynde* (1529), trans. David Clapham. London: Thomas Berthelet, 1542.

————. *The Commendation of Matrimony* (1540), trans. David Clapham. London: Thomas Berthelet, 1545.

————. *The Glory of a Woman; or a Looking-Glasse for Ladies*, trans. Edward Fleetwood. London: Robert Ibbitson, 1652.

Alberti, Leon Baptista. *The Art of Love, or Love Discovered in an Hundred Severall Kindes*. London: P. Short for William Leake, 1598.

Allen, Don Cameron. *The Star-crossed Renaissance: The Quarrel about Astrology and Its Influence in England*. Durham, N.C.: Duke University Press, 1941.

Allen, P. S. *The Age of Erasmus*. Oxford: Clarendon Press, 1914.

————. 'A Sixteenth-Century School,' *English Historical Review*, X (1895), 738-44.

Allen, P. S. and H. M., and H. W. Garrod (eds.). *Opus Epistolarum Des. Erasmi Roterdami*. 12 vols. Oxford: Clarendon Press, 1906-58. For an English translation of most of these letters, see Nichols, F. M.

Anglo, Sydney. 'Le Camp du Drap d'Or et les Entrevues d'Henri VIII et de Charles Quint,' *Fêtes et Cérémonies au Temps de Charles Quint*. Paris, 1959.

————. 'The Court Festivals of Henry VII: A Study Based upon the Account Books of John Heron, Treasure of the Chamber,' *Bulletin of the John Rylands Library*, XLIII, No. I (September, 1960), 12-45.

Ascham, Roger. *The Scholemaster, or Plaine and Perfite Way of Teaching Children* (London, 1570), ed. Edward Arber. London: Muir and Patterson, 1870.

————. *Toxophilus, the Schole of Shootinge*. London: Edward Whytchurch, 1545, 1571, 1589. For the best edition of the *Toxophilus*, see Wright, W. A. (ed.)

Auton, Jean de. *Chroniques de Louis XII*, ed. R. de Maulde La Clavière. 4 vols. Paris: Renouard, 1889-95.

Bacon, Francis. *Historie of the Raigne of King Henrie the Seventh* (London, 1622), ed. Joseph Rawson Lumby. (Pitt Press Series.) Cambridge: Cambridge University Press, 1875.

Ballard, George. *Memoirs of Several Ladies of Great Britain*. Oxford: W. Jackson, 1752.

Bansley, Charles. A *Treatyse shewing and declaring the Pryde and Abuse of Women now a dayes* (c. 1550), ed. J. P. Collier. London, 1841.

Barclay, Alexander, *The Myrrour of Good Maners*, trans. from the Latin of Dominicus Mancinus. London: R. Pynson, c. 1523.

Baskervill, Charles Read (ed.). *Pierre Gringore's Pageants for the Entry of Mary Tudor into Paris* (from the Cottonian Manuscript, Vespasian B. ii, in the British Museum). Chicago, Ill.: University of Chicago Press, 1934.

Batiffol, Louis. *Le Siècle de la Renaissance* (Paris, 1909), trans. Elsie Finnimore Buckley. London: William Heinemann, 1916.

Beaute of Women [anonymous]. London, c. 1525.

Bearne, Catherine Mary. *Pictures of the Old French Court*. London: T. Fisher Unwin, 1900.

Becon, Thomas. *The Worckes of Thomas Becon*. 3 vols. London: John Day, 1560–64. See especially *The Golden Boke of Christen Matrimonye* and *An Homely against Whordome*.

Belloc, Hilaire. 'Casual Papers. Charles Brandon, Duke of Suffolk,' *New Statesman*, XXXV (July 12, 1930), 443–44.

Bennett, H. S. *The Pastons and their England: Studies in an Age of Transition*. 2nd ed. Cambridge: Cambridge University Press, 1932.

——. *English Books and Readers: 1475–1557*. Cambridge: Cambridge University Press, 1952.

Bercher [Barker], William. *A Dyssputacion off the Nobylytye off Wymen* (London, 1559), ed. R. Warwick Bond. London: Roxburghe Club, 1904.

Besant, Sir Walter. *London in the Time of the Tudors* (1904). Vol. II of *The Survey of London*. 10 vols. London: A. and C. Black, 1902–12.

Borde [Boorde], Andrew. *The Fyrst Boke of the Introduction of Knowledge* (London, 1542), ed. F. J. Furnivall. (Early English Text Society, Extra Series, Vol. X, 1870.)

——. *A Compendyous Regyment or a Dyetary of Helth* (London, c. 1542), ed. F. J. Furnivall. (Early English Text Society, Extra Series, Vol. X, 1870.)

Brantôme, Pierre de Bourdeille, Seigneur de. *Recueil des dames*. Vol. III of *Oeuvres complètes*, ed. Ludovic Salanne. 12 vols. Paris: Librarie de la Société de l'Histoire de France, 1864–96. See Translation by Wormeley, Katherine Prescott.

Brandi, Karl. *The Emperor Charles V*. (Munich, 1937), trans. from the German by C. V. Wedgwood. London: Jonathan Cape, 1939.

Brewer, J. S. *The Reign of Henry VIII from his Accession to the Death of Wolsey. Reviewed and Illustrated from Original Documents,* ed James Gairdner. 2 vols. London: John Murray, 1884.

Bridge, John S. C. *A History of France from the Death of Louis XI.* 5 vols. Oxford: Clarendon Press, 1921–36. See Vols. IV, V.

Brook, Roy. *The Story of Eltham Palace.* London: George Harrap and Co., 1960.

Brooke, Iris, and James Laver. *English Costume from the Fourteenth through the Nineteenth Century.* New York: Macmillan Co., 1937.

Bruto, Giovanni Michele. *The Necessarie, Fit, and Convenient Education of a Yong Gentlewoman,* trans. W. P. London: Adam Islip, 1598.

———. *The Mirrhor of Modestie,* trans. Thomas Salter. London: Edward White, 1579.

Buchon, Jean-Alexander C. *Choix de chroniques et mémoires relatifs à l'Histoire de France.* (Panthéon littéraire.) Orléans: H. Herluison, 1861.

Bunny, Edmund. *Of Divorce for Adulterie, and Marrying Againe.* Oxford: J. Barnes, 1610.

Burckhardt, Jacob. *Die Kultur des Renaissance in Italien* (15th ed., 1860), trans. S. G. C. Middlemore, *The Civilization of the Renaissance in Italy.* London and New York: Oxford University Press, 1929.

Burke, Maurice. 'Charles Brandon, Gentleman Adventurer,' *Contemporary Review,* CLXXIX (1951), 111–16.

Burton, Robert. *The Anatomy of Melancholy.* Oxford: John Litchfield and James Short, 1621, 1624, 1628, 1632, 1638. London: J. M. Dent and Sons, 1932. New York: E. P. Dutton and Co., 1932.

Busch, Wilhelm. *England unter den Tudors.* Band I, *Konig Heinrich VII* (Stuttgart, 1892), trans. Alice M. Todd. London: A. D. Innes and Co., 1895.

Bush, Douglas. *The Renaissance and English Humanism.* Toronto, Ont.: University of Toronto Press, 1939.

———. 'Tudor Humanism and Henry VIII,' *University of Toronto Quarterly,* VII (1938), 162–77.

Camden, Carroll. *The Elizabethan Woman.* Houston, Texas, New York, and London: Elsevier Press, 1952.

Cambridge History of English Literature, ed. Sir A. W. Ward and A. R. Waller. 15 vols. Cambridge: Cambridge University Press, 1907–32. Vol. III, *Renascence and Reformation.*

Campbell, W. E. 'Erasmus in England,' *Dublin Review,* CCXI (1942), 36–49.

Carmelianus, Petrus. *Solennes ceremoniae et triumphi or the solempnities & triumphs doon & made at the spouselles and mariage of the kynges daughter, the ladye Marye to the Prynce of Castile, archduke of Austrige* (London, 1508), ed. Henry Ellis. London: Roxburghe Club,

1818. Also ed. James Gairdner. London: Camden Society, *Miscellany*, New Series, Vol. IX. No. 53 (2), 1893.

Castiglione, Baldassare. *Il libro del cortegiano* (Venice, 1528), trans. Thomas Hoby, *The Courtyer*, London, 1561. Also trans. W. Raleigh. London, 1900.

Cavendish, George. *The Life of Cardinal Wolsey* (London, 1641), ed. S. W. Singer, 2 vols. London, 1827. See also Sylvester, Richard S., and Davis P. Harding (eds.).

Caxton, William (trans.) *Le Grande's Boke of Good Maners* (translated from the French of Jacque le Grande). Westminster, 1487.

Chambers, Sir Edmund K. *Notes on the History of the Revels Office under the Tudors*. London: A. H. Bullen, 1906.

Chambers, R. W. *Thomas More*. London: Jonathan Cape, 1935. Paperback edition, Ann Arbor Paperbacks, University of Michigan Press, 1958.

Chapman, Hester W. *Lady Jane Grey*. London: Jonathan Cape, 1962.

———. *Two Tudor Portraits*. London: Jonathan Cape, 1960.

Charlton, Kenneth. *Education in Renaissance England*. London: Routledge and Kegan Paul, 1965.

Chartrou, Josèphe. *Les Entrées solennelles et triomphales à la Renaissance (1484–1551)*. Paris: Presses universitaires, 1928.

Cheyney, Edward Potts. *Social Changes in England in the Sixteenth Century, as Reflected in Contemporary Literature*. (University of Pennsylvania Series in Philology, Literature, and Archaeology, Vol. IV, No. 2, 1895.)

Cocheris, Hippolyte. *Entrée de Marie d'Angleterre, Femme de Louis XII, à Abbeville et à Paris*. Paris, 1859. See also Baskerville, Charles Read.

Comper, Frances M. M. (ed.) *The Book of the Craft of Dying, and Other Early English Tracts concerning Death*. London: Longmans, Green and Co., 1917.

Cooper, C. H. *Memoir of Margaret [Beaufort], Countess of Richmond and Derby*, ed. J. E. B. Mayor. Cambridge: Deighton, Bell and Co., 1874.

Copeman, W. S. C. *Doctors and Disease in Tudor Times*. London: Dawson's of Pall Mall, 1960.

Cripps-Day, Francis Henry. *The History of the Tournament in England and France*. London: Bernard Quaritch, 1918.

Cunningham, J. V. (ed.) *The Renaissance in England*. New York: Harcourt, Brace and World, 1966.

Cunnington, C. Willett and Phillis. *English Costume in the Sixteenth Century*. London: Faber and Faber, 1954.

Davey, Richard. *The Nine Days' Queen*, ed. with an Introduction by Martin Hume. London: Methuen and Co., 1909.

————. *The Sisters of Lady Jane Grey and Their Wicked Grandfather.*
London : Chapman and Hall, 1911. New York : E. P. Dutton Co., 1912.

Dayot, Armand. *L'Image de la femme.* Paris : Hachette, 1899.

Dekker (Decker), Thomas. *The Batchelars Banquet* (trans. of Antione de
la Sale, *Les quinze joyes de Mariage*, London, 1509). London : Printed
by T. C., 1603.

————. *The Seven Deadly Sinnes of London* (1606), ed. H. F. B. Brett-
Smith. Oxford : Basil Blackwell, 1922.

Dictionary of National Biography, ed. Sir Leslie Stephen and Sir Sidney
Lee. 63 vols. London : Smith, Elder, and Company, 1885–1900. Supplements; Index and Epitome.

Drummond, J. C., and Anne Wilbraham. *The Englishman's Food: A
History of Five Centuries of English Diet.* Rev. ed. London : Jonathan
Cape, 1957.

Du Bellay, Martin. *Mémoires . . . de plusieurs choses advenues au royaume
de France depuis MDXIII jusques au trépas du roy François premier . . .*
(Paris, 1569). Standard edition by V. L. Bourrilly. 4 vols. (Société de
l'Histoire de France.) Paris, 1908–19. Jean Du Bellay, brother of the
author, was an ambassador in London during the period of the Divorce.

Edwards, Ralph, and L. G. G. Ramsey (eds.). *The Tudor Period.* Vol. I of
The Connoisseur Period Guides. 6 vols. London, 1956–58. New York :
Reynal and Co., 1956.

Einstein, Lewis. *The Italian Renaissance in England.* New York : Columbia
University Press, 1902.

————. *Tudor Ideals.* London : G. Bell and Sons, 1921.

Elyot, Sir Thomas. *The Boke Named the Governour* (London, 1531). Best
edition by H. H. S. Croft. 2 vols. London : C. Kegan Paul and Co., 1880.
Also Everyman's Library edition. London, 1907.

————. *The Education or Bringinge up of Children.* London, *c.* 1530–35.

————. *Of the Knowledge which Maketh a Wise Man* (1533), ed. E. J.
Howard. Oxford, Ohio : Anchor Press, 1946.

————. *The Castel of Helth* (1534), ed. S. A. Tannenbaum. New York :
Scholars' Facsimiles and Reprints, 1937.

————. *The Defence of Good Women* (London : Thomas Berthlet, 1545),
ed. E. J. Howard. Oxford, Ohio : Anchor Press, 1941.

————. *A Preservative Agaynste Deth.* London, 1545.

Emmison, F. G. *Tudor Food and Pastimes.* London : Ernest Benn, 1964.

Erasmus, Desiderius. *Opera*, ed. J. Le Clerc (*Des. Erasmi Roterdami Opera
Omnia*, curavit J. Clericus). 10 vols. Leyden, 1703–6. See also Allen,
P. S. and H. M., and H. W. Garrod (eds.).

————. *Epistles*, from his earliest letters to his fifty-first year, trans.
F. M. Nichols. 3 vols. London and New York : Longmans, Green, and
Co., 1901–18. New York : Russell and Russell, 1962.

Evans, Joan. *Magical Jewels of the Middle Ages and the Renaissance, particularly in England*. Oxford: Clarendon Press, 1922.

Ewald, Alexander Charles. *Stories from the State Papers*. 2 vols. London: Chatto and Windus, 1882.

——. 'An Historical Love Match,' *Living Age*, CXLVII (October 30, 1880), 290–301.

Ferrand, Jacques. *Traité de l'essence et guérison de l'Amour, ou de la mélancholie érotique* (Toulouse: J. and R. Colomiez, 1610, 1623), trans. E. Chilmead, *Erotomania, or A Treatise Discoursing of Love*. Oxford: L. Lichfield, 1640, 1645.

Fetherstone, Christopher. *A Dialogue Agaynst Light, Lewde and Lascivious Dauncing*. London: T. Dawson, 1582.

Firenzuola, Agnolo. *Dialogodella bellezze delle donne* (1548; also in prose, 1552, 1562, 1622; French translations, 1578). Vol. I of *Opere di Firenzuola*. Milano, 1802.

Firth, Charles H. 'The Ballad History of the Reigns of Henry VII and Henry VIII,' *Transactions of the Royal Historical Society*, 3rd Series, II (1908), 21–50.

Fisher, H. A. L. *The History of England From the Accession of Henry VII to the Death of Henry VIII, 1485–1547*. (Political History of England Series, ed. William Hunt and R. L. Poole, Vol. V.) London: Longmans, Green, and Co., 1928.

Fisher, John. *The English Works of*, ed. J. E. B. Mayor. (Early English Text Society, Extra Series, Vol. XXVII, 1876.)

Fitzherbert, Anthony. *The Boke of Husbandrye* (London, 1523, 1532, 1548), ed. W. W. Skeat. (English Dialect Society, Vol. XIII, 1881.)

Fleuranges, Robert de la Marck, Seigneur de. *Histoire des choses mémorables advenues aux règnes de Louis XII et de François I*, ed. l'Abbé Lambert. Paris, 1753.

——. *Mémoirs*, in *Choix de chroniques et mémoires relatifs a l'Histoire de France*, ed. Jean-Alexander C. Buchon. (Panthéon littéraire.) Orléans: H. Herluison, 1875.

Furnivall, F. J. (ed.). *Manners and Meals in Olden Times*. (Early English Text Society, Vol. XXXII.) London: Oxford University Press, 1868. Reprinted, 1931.

——. (ed.). *Child Marriages, Divorces, and Ratifications*. (Early English Text Society. Vol. CVIII, 1897.)

Gairdner, James. *Henry the Seventh*. London and New York: Macmillan Co., 1889. London: Macmillan and Co., 1920.

——. (ed.). *Memorials of King Henry the Seventh* (Rolls Series). London: Longman, Brown, Green, Longmans, and Roberts, 1858. Contains: Bernardi Andreae, *Vite Henrici VII*; 'Report of Ambassadors touching the Queen of Naples'; 'A Narrative of the Reception of Philip, King of

Castile in England in 1506'; 'The Twelve Triumpths of Henry VII'; and 'Journals of Roger Machado.'

————. (ed.). *The Paston Letters, 1422–1509.* 6 vols. London : Chatto and Windus, 1904.

Giustinian, Sebastian [Sebastiano Giustiano]. *Four Years at the Court of Henry VIII,* trans. R. Brown. 2 vols. London, 1854.

Goff, Cecilie. *A Woman of the Tudor Age.* London : John Murray, 1930. A biography of Catherine Willoughby.

Gosson, Stephen. *The Schoole of Abuse.* London, 1579.

————. *Pleasant Quippes for Upstart Newfangled Gentlewomen, or a Glasse, to View the Pride of Vainglorious Women.* London : Richard Jones, 1596. Verse.

Gosynhill, Edward. *The Prayse of all Women, called Mulierum Pean.* London : Wyllyam Myddylton, c. 1542.

————. *Here Begynneth the Scole House of Women: Wherein Every Man may reade a Goodly Prayse of the Condicyons of Women.* London : John Kynge, 1560. For an answer to the *Scole House* see Edward More, *A Lytle and Bryefe Treatyse, called the Defence of Women, and especially of Englyshe Women, made agaynst the Schole Howse of Women.* London : John Kynge, 1560.

Grafton, Richard. *Chronicle* (London, 1569), ed. Henry Ellis. 2 vols. London : G. Woodfall Printer, 1809.

The Great Chronicle of London, ed. A. H. Thomas and I. D. Thornley. London, 1938. Chronicle for the period 1189–1512, written in the late fifteenth or early sixteenth century, probably by Robert Fabyan; valuable for the years 1503–12.

Gringore, Pierre. 'De la réception en entrée de la illustrissime dame et princesse Marie d'Angleterre . . . dans le ville de Paris le 6 Novembre 1514.' British Museum, Cottonian Manuscript, Vespasian B. ii. See also Baskervill, Charles Read.

Guichenon, Samuel. *Histoire généalogique de la Royale Maison de Savoye* (2 parts, Lyon, 1660), new edition, with supplements. 4 vols. Turin, 1778–80. Vol. IV contains the Journal of Louise of Savoy, pp. 457–64.

Hall, Edward. *Chronicle* [*The Union of the Two Noble Families of Lancaster and York*] (London, 1542), ed. R. Grafton. London, 1548. Standard edition by Henry Ellis. London : G. Woodfall Printer, 1809.

Halsted, C. A. *Life of Margaret Beaufort.* London : Smith, Elder and Co., 1839, 1845.

Hannay, Patrick. *A Happy Husband: Or, Directions for a Maide to chose her Mate; As also a Wives Behaviour towards her Husband after Marriage.* London, 1619.

Harrison, William. *Description of England in Shakespeare's Youth,* edited from the first two editions of Holinshed's *Chronicle* by F. J. Furnivall. 3 vols. London: N. Trübner and Co., 1877–81.

Hentzner, Paul. A *Journey into England in the Year of 1598*, trans. from the German by Richard Bently. Strawberry Hill, 1757.

Herbert, Lord Edward [of Cherbury]. *The Life and Raigne of King Henry the Eighth*. London: Printed by E. G. for Thomas Whitaker, 1649.

Herman, V. [von Wild]. A *Brefe and Playne Declaratyon of the Dewty of Maried Folkes* (London, c. 1553), trans. from the German by Haunce Dekin [Hans Dekyn]. London: by J. C. for Hugh Singleton, c. 1588.

Hexter, J. H. 'The Education of the Aristocracy in the Renaissance,' *Journal of Modern History*, XXII (1950), 1–20.

Heywood, John. *The Proverbes in the English Tongue, Compacte in a Matter Concernyng two Maner of Mariages*. London: T. Berthelet, 1546.

Heywood, Thomas. *How a Man May Choose a Good Wife*. London, 1602.

Himes, Norman E. *Medical History of Contraception*. Baltimore: Williams and Wilkins, 1936.

Hole, Christina. *English Home Life, 1500–1800*. London: B. T. Batsford, 1947.

Holinshed, Raphael. *Chronicle of England, Scotland, and Ireland* (2 vols. London, 1577), ed. Henry Ellis. 6 vols. London: G. Woodfall Printer, 1807–8.

Holt, Emily Sarah. *Memoirs of Royal Ladies*. 2 vols. London: Hurst and Blackett, 1861.

Jacqueton, Gilbert. *La politique exterieur de Louise de Savoie*. Paris: E. Bouillon, 1892.

Jerdan, William (ed.). *Rutland Papers: Original Documents Illustrative of the Courts and Times of Henry VII and Henry VIII*. Camden Society, XXI (1842). Contains: 'The Marriage of Mary, Daughter of Henry VII to Louis XII of France'; 'The Field of the Cloth of Gold'; 'Meeting of King Henry VIII and the Emperor Charles V at Gravelines'; and 'The Visit of the Emperor Charles V to England, A.D. 1522.'

Jones, Paul Van Brunt. *The Household of a Tudor Nobleman*. (University of Illinois Studies in the Social Sciences, Vol. VI, No. 4.) Urbana: University of Illinois Press, 1917.

Kelso, Ruth. *The Doctrine of the English Gentleman in the Sixteenth Century*. (University of Illinois Studies in Language and Literature, Vol. XIV.) Urbana: University of Illinois Press, 1929.

———. *Doctrine for the Lady of the Renaissance*. Urbana: University of Illinois Press, 1956.

Kendall, Paul Murray. *The Yorkist Age*. London: George Allen and Unwin, 1962.

Kingsford, Charles L. *Prejudice and Promise in XVth Century England.* Oxford: Clarendon Press, 1925.

——. *English Historical Literature in the Fifteenth Century.* Oxford: Clarendon Press, 1913.

Knox, John. *The First Blast of the Trumpet against the Monstrous Regiment of Women* (Geneva, 1558), ed. Edward Arber. (The English Scholars Library, No. 2.) London, 1878.

Lawrence, Margaret. *The School of Femininity.* New York: Frederick A. Stokes Co., 1936.

Leland, John. *Itinerary* (ed. Thomas Hearne. 9 vols. Oxford, 1710–12, 1745–47, 1770), ed. L. T. Smith. 5 vols. London, 1906–8. This material, along with that of his *Collectanea,* was collected by Leland during the years 1535–43, but not published until the eighteenth century.

——. *De Rebus Britannicis Collectanea,* ed. Thomas Hearne. 6 vols. Oxford, 1715.

Lewis, C. S. *English Literature in the Sixteenth Century.* Oxford: Clarendon Press, 1954.

Lodge, Edmund (ed.). *Illustrations of British History, Biography, and Manners.* 3 vols. London, 1791. Best edition, 1838.

Louandre, F. C. *Histoire d'Abbeville.* 2 vols. Paris: Joubert, 1844–45. See especially II, 13–17.

Louise de Savoie. Journal, in Jean-Alexander C. Buchon's *Choix de chroniques et mémoires relatifs à l'Histoire de France.* See also Guichenon, Samuel.

Lupset, Thomas. *A Treatise of Charitie* (1533), *A Compendious Treatise, teachyng the Waie of Dieyng Well* (1534), and *An Exhortacion to Young Men* (1535), in *The Life and Works of Thomas Lupset,* ed. John Archer Gee. New Haven, Conn.: Yale University Press, 1928.

Lyly, John. *Complete Works,* ed. R. Warwick Bond. Oxford: Clarendon Press, 1902.

McConica, James Kelsey. *English Humanists and Reformation Politics under Henry VIII and Edward VI.* Oxford: Clarendon Press, 1965.

Mackie, J. D. *The Earlier Tudors, 1485–1558.* (The Oxford History of England, ed. G. N. Clark, Vol. VII.) Oxford: Clarendon Press, 1952.

MacNalty, Sir Arthur S. *The Renaissance and Its Influence on English Medicine, Surgery and Public Health.* (Thomas Vicary Lecture, Royal College of Surgeons.) London: Christopher Johnson, 1945.

Markham, Gervase. *Country Contentments, or The English Huswife.* London, 1623.

'Mary Tudor and Brandon, Duke of Suffolk' (unsigned article based on Brewer's *Calendar of State Papers,* published under the direction of the Rt. Hon. Master of the Rolls), *The Edinburgh Review,* CXXIII (January, 1866), 248–63.

L

Mattingley, Garrett. *Catherine of Aragon*. Boston, Mass.: Little, Brown and Co., 1941.

———. *Renaissance Diplomacy*. Boston, Mass.: Houghton Mifflin Co., 1955.

———. 'A Humanist Ambassador' (Eustache Chapuys, ambassador of Charles V to England, 1529–45), *Journal of Modern History*, IV (1932), 175–85.

———. 'The Reputation of Dr. Puebla,' *English Historical Review*, LV (January, 1940), 27–46.

Maulde La Clavière, Marie Alphonse René de. *Histoire de Louis XII*. 6 vols. Paris: E. Leroux, 1889–93.

———. *Les Femmes de la Renaissance* (Paris: Perrin et Cie 1898), trans. George Herbert Ely, *The Women of the Renaissance: A Study of Feminism*. London: S. Sonnenschein and Co., 1900; reprinted 1901, 1903, 1911.

———. *Louise de Savoie et François Ier*. Paris: Perrin et Cie, 1895.

Morpurgo, J. E. (ed.). *Life Under the Tudors*. (Falcon Educational Books.) London: Peregrine Press, 1950.

Mulcaster, Richard. *Positions wherin those Primitive Circumstances be examined, which are Necessarie for the Training up of Children, either for Skill in their Booke, or Health in their Bodie*. London: Thomas Vautrollier, 1581.

Niccholes, Alexander. *A Discourse of Marriage and Wiving, and of the Greatest Mystery therein Contained: How to Choose a Good Wife from a Bad*. London, 1615.

Nichols, F. M. (trans.). *The Epistles of D. Erasmus*. 3 vols. London and New York: Longmans, Green, and Co., 1901–18. New York: Russell and Russell, 1962.

Nichols, John Gouge (ed.). *Illustrations of the Manners and Expenses of Ancient Times in England in the 15th, 16th and 17th Centuries*. London: 1797.

———. (ed.). *The Chronicle of Calais in the Reigns of Henry VII and Henry VIII to the Year 1540* (by Richard Turpyn). (Camden Society, Vol. XXXV.) London: J. B. Nichols and Son, 1846. The documents include the letters of Margaret of Austria to Sir Richard Wingfield concerning her relations with Charles Brandon, Duke of Suffolk (pp. 68–76).

———. (ed.). *The Diary of Henry Machyn, Citizen and Merchant-tailor of London, 1550–1563*. (Camden Society, Vol. XLII.) London: J. B. Nichols and Son, 1848. See especially pp. xx–xxxii: 'Note upon Funerals.'

Nicolas, Sir Nicholas Harris (ed.). *The Privy Purse Expenses of Elizabeth of York, Queen of Henry VII, with a memoir of Elizabeth of York and Notes*. London, 1830.

————. (ed.). *The Privy Purse Expenses of Henry VIII from November 1529 to December 1532*. London, 1827.

Notestein, Wallace. 'The English Woman, 1580–1650,' *Studies in Social History: A Tribute to G. M. Trevelyan*, ed. J. H. Plumb. London and New York: Longmans, Green, 1955.

Nucius, Nicander. *The Second Book of Travels of Nicander Nucius of Corcyra*, ed. and trans. from the Greek by J. A. Cranmer. (Camden Society, Vol. XVII.) London, 1841.

Nugent, Elizabeth M. (ed.). *The Thought and Culture of the English Renaissance, 1481–1555*. Cambridge: Cambridge University Press, 1956.

Palgrave, John. *Lesclarcissement de la langue francoyse*. . . . 2 parts. London: J. Haukyns, 1530.

Pardoe, Julia. *The Court and Reign of Francis the First*. 2 vols. London: R. Bentley, 1849. Also 3 vols. New York: J. Pott and Co., 1901.

Paul, John E. *Catherine of Aragon and Her Friends*. London: Burns and Oates, 1966.

Pearson, Lu Emily. *Elizabethans at Home*. Stanford, Calif.: Stanford University Press, 1957.

Platt, Sir Hugh. *Delights for Ladies, to adorn their Persons, Tables, Closets and Distillatories: with Beauties, Banquets, Perfumes and Waters* (London, 1602), with Introduction by G. E. Fussell and Kathleen Rosemary Fussell. London: Crosby Lockwood and Son, 1948.

Pollard, A. F. *Henry VIII*. London: Goupil and Co., 1902. Illus. edition, London: Longmans, Green and Co., 1951.

————. *Wolsey*. London: Longmans, Green and Co., 1929. Illus. edition, Longmans, Green and Co., 1953.

————. *Factors in Modern History*. London: Constable and Co., 1907. Paperback edition, Beacon Paperbacks, Boston: Constable and Co., 1960. A collection of essays; see especially 'The Advent of the Middle Class'.

Read, Evelyn. *Catherine, Duchess of Suffolk*. London: Jonathan Cape, 1962.

Resch, Wolfgang. *The Vertuous Scholehous of Ungracious Women* (c 1550).

Robson-Scott [William Douglas Robson], W. D. *German Travellers in England, 1400–1800*. Oxford: Basil Blackwell, 1953.

Roper, William. *The Life, Arraignement and Death of . . . Syr Thomas More* (Paris, 1626), best edition by E. V. Hitchcock (Early English Text Society, Original Series, Vol. CXCVII, 1935). See also Sylvester, Richard S., and Davis P. Harding (eds.).

Röslin [Roesslin], Eucharius. *The Birth of Man-Kinde; Otherwise Named, The Womans Booke* (c. 1513), trans. from the German by Thomas Raynold, 1545.

Routh, E. M. G. *Lady Margaret. A Memoir of Lady Margaret Beaufort . . . Mother of Henry VII.* London : Humphrey Milford, 1924.

Rye, W. B. *England as Seen by Foreigners.* London : J. R. Smith, 1865.

St. Mary's Church, Bury St. Edmunds: An Illustrated Description. Gloucester : British Publishing Co., n.d.

Salmon, J. H. M. 'Francis the First: le roi chevalier,' *History Today,* (May, 1958), 295–305.

Salter, Emma Gurney. *Tudor England through Venetian Eyes.* London : William and Norgate, 1930. Compiled from the reports and correspondence of the Venetian diplomatic and commercial agents in England, mainly between 1498 and 1558.

Salter, Thomas. *A Mirrhor Mete for all Mothers, Matrones, and Maidens, intituled the Mirrhor of Modestie* (1579), in John Payne Collier (ed.), *Illustrations of Old English Literature.* 3 vols. London : privately printed, 1866. See Vol. I.

Salzman, L. F. *England in Tudor Times.* London : B. T. Batsford Co., 1926.

Sanuto [Sanudo], Marino. *Diarii,* 58 vols. in 59, ed. R. Fulin, F. Stefani, *et al.* Venice, 1879–1903. Covers the period 1496 to 1533 with remarkable fullness.

Scarisbrick, J. J. *Henry VIII.* London : Eyre and Spottiswoode, 1968.

Schoell, F. L. *Études sur l'humanisme continental en Angleterre à la fin de la Renaissance.* (Bibliothèque de la Revue de littérature comparée, Vol. XXIX.) Paris, 1926.

Sichel, Edith. *Women and Men of the French Renaissance.* London : Archibald Constable and Co., 1901.

Siegel, Paul N. 'English Humanism and the New Tudor Aristocracy,' *Journal of the History of Ideas,* XIII (1952), 450–68.

Simons, Eric N. *Henry VII: The First Tudor King.* New York : Barnes and Noble, 1968.

Smith, Henry. *The Wedding Garment* (London, 1590), in *The Sermons of Mr. Henry Smith* [minister of St. Clement Danes]; *also the Life of the Author,* by Thomas Fuller (1675).

———. *A Preparative Mariage.* London : J. Charlewood for Thomas Man, 1591.

Smith, H. Clifford. 'Jewellery in Tudor Times,' *Illustrated London News,* July 9, 1949.

Smith, Lacey Baldwin. *A Tudor Tragedy.* London : Jonathan Cape, 1961.

Sneyd, C. A. (ed.). *A Relation . . . of the Island of England about the Year 1500, with Particulars of the Customs of these People and of the Royal Revenues under . . . Henry VII.* (Camden Society, Original Series, Vol. XXXVII.) London, 1847. A description of England by an anonymous Italian.

Spanish *Chronica del rey Enrico Ottavo de Inglaterra* (by an unknown contemporary Spaniard, published in Madrid, 1874), trans. M. A. S. Hume, *Chronicle of King Henry VIII of England.* London: George Bell and Sons, 1889.

Staars, David [Prince Serge Yourievitch]. *Études sur la femme anglaise et son évolution psychique* (Paris: A. Moloine, 1907), trans J. M. E. Brownlow, *The English Woman.* London: Smith, Elder and Co., 1909.

Stone, Lawrence. 'Marriage Among the English Nobility in the 16th and 17th Centuries,' *Contemporary Studies in Society and History*, III (January, 1961), 182–206.

———. 'The Nobility in Business, 1540–1640.' pp. 14–21 in *The Entrepreneur.* (Papers presented at the annual conference of the Economic History Society at Cambridge, England, April, 1957.) Cambridge, Mass.: Research Center in Entrepreneurial History, Harvard University, through the courtesy of the Economic History Society, n.d.

Stow, John. *The Annals of England* (based upon his *Chronicle* of 1580). London, 1592. Susequent editions in 1600, 1601, 1605 (the best edition), 1614, 1615, 1631.

———. *A Survey of London* (London, 1598), ed. C. L. Kingsford. 2 vols. Oxford: Clarendon Press, 1908.

Strutt, Joseph. *A Complete View of the Manners, Customs, Habits . . . of the Inhabitants of England.* 3 vols. London, 1775–76.

Strype, John. *Ecclesiastical Memorials.* 3 vols. London, 1721–1733. In *Works.* Oxford: Clarendon Press, 1820–40. Contains many original documents.

Stubbes, Philip. *The Anatomie of Abuses* (1583), ed. F. J. Furnivall. 2 vols. London: N. Trübner, 1877–79.

———. *A Christal Glasse for Christian Women . . . of a Right Vertuous Life and Christian Death.* London: R. Jhones, 1591.

The Suffolk Garland: or a Collection of Poems, Songs, Tales, Ballads, Sonnets, and Elegies, Legendary and Romantic, Historical and Descriptive, Relative to that County. London, 1818.

Swinburne, Henry (lawyer, c. 1590). *A Treatise of Spousals, or Matrimonial Contracts.* London: S. Roycroft for Robert Clavell, 1686, 1711.

Sylvester, Richard S., and Davis P. Harding (eds.). *Two Early Tudor Lives: The Life and Death of Cardinal Wolsey*, by George Cavendish, and *The Life of Sir Thomas More*, by William Roper. New Haven, Conn., and London: Yale University Press, 1962.

Terrasse, Charles, *Françoise I*er*: le roi et le Règne.* Paris, 1945.

Thomson, Mrs. A. T. [Katherine Thomson]. *Memoirs of the Court of Henry the Eighth.* 2 vols. London: Longman and Co., 1826.

Thomson, Craig R. 'Schools in Tudor England,' pp. 285–334 in *Life and*

Letters in Tudor and Stuart England, ed. Louis B. Wright and Virginia A. LaMar. (The Folger Shakespeare Library.) Ithaca, N.Y.: Cornell University Press, 1962.

Thornton-Cook, Elsie. *Royal Marys: Princess Mary and her Predecessors.* London: J. Murray Co., 1929.

Tilley, M. P. A *Dictionary of the Proverbs in England in the 16th and 17th Centuries.* Ann Arbor: University of Michigan Press, 1950.

Tillyard, E. M. W. *The English Renaissance: Fact or Fiction?* (The Turnbull Memorial Lectures for 1950–51.) Baltimore, Md.: Johns Hopkins Press, 1952.

Tremayne, Eleanor E. *The First Governess of the Netherlands, Margaret of Austria.* New York: G. P. Putnam's Sons, 1908.

Tusser, Thomas. A *Hundredth Good Pointes of Husbandrie* (1557); later expanded to *Five Hundreth Pointes of Good Husbandry,* with a poem, 'The Ladder to Thrift,' ed. Dorothy Hartley. London: London Country Life, 1931.

Tyler, Royall. *The Emperor Charles the Fifth.* London: Allen and Unwin, 1956.

Vaughan, Robert. A *Dyalogue Defensyve for Women, agaynst Malycyous Detractoures.* London: Robert Meyer, 1542.

Vergil, Polydore. *Anglicae Historiae Libri xxvi* (Basel, 1534; by Antonius Thysius, Basel, 1546; Leyden, 1651), trans. and ed. Denys Hay. (Camden Society, 3rd Series, Vol. LXXIV, 1950.) The first and second editions cover the period 1485–1509; later editions to 1537.

Vives, Juan Luis. *Joannis Ludovici Vivis Valentini de Institutione Feminae Christianae, ad Inclytam d. Catharinam Hispanam, Angliae Libri Tres* (Basel: Robert Winter, 1538), trans. Rycharde Hyrd, A *Very Frutefull and Pleasant Boke called the Instruction of a Christen Woman.* London: Thomas Berthelet, 1540.

——. *Joannis Ludovici Vivis Valentini de Officio Mariti Liber Unus. De Institutione Foeminae Christianae Libri Tres . . .* (Basileae, 1529), trans. Thomas Paynell, *The Office and Dutie of an Husband.* London: John Cawood, 1553(?).

——. *Linguae Latinae Exercitio* (c. 1539). An English translation was published in 1908. See Watson, Foster, *Tudor School-Boy Life.*

Walpole, Horace. *Anecdotes of Painting in England, with Some Account of the Principal Artists* (4 vols. Strawberry Hill: Thomas Farmer, 1762–71), ed. J. Dallaway, with additional notes by R. N. Wornum. 3 vols. London: Henry G. Bohn, 1849.

Watson, Foster (ed.). *Vives and the Renascence Education of Women.* New York: Longmans, Green and Co. London: Edward Arnold, 1912. Includes extracts from J. L. Vives, Richard Hyrde, Sir Thomas More, and Sir Thomas Elyot.

———— (ed. and trans.). *Tudor School-Boy Life* (a translation of Vives, *Linguae Latinae Exercitatio*, 1539). London: J. M. Dent and Co., 1908.

Weiss, R. *Humanism in England during the Fifteenth Century.* 2nd ed. Oxford: Clarendon Press, 1957.

Wiley, W. L. *The Gentleman of Renaissance France.* Cambridge, Mass.: Harvard University Press, 1954.

Williams, C. H. *The Making of Tudor Despotism.* London, Edinburgh, and New York: Thomas Nelson and Sons, 1928.

Williams, Neville. *The Royal Residences of Great Britain.* London: Barrie and Rockcliff, 1960.

Williams, Penry. *Life in Tudor England.* London: B. T. Batsford, 1964. New York: G. P. Putnam's Sons, 1964.

Wirsung [Wirtzung], Christopher. *Praxis Medicinae Uniuersalis*, or *A Generall Practise of Physicke*, trans. J. Mosan, 1598, 1617. London: George Bishop, 1617.

Wormald, Francis. 'The Solemn Entry of Mary Tudor to Montreuil-sur-Mer in 1514,' pp. 471–79 in *Studies Presented to Sir Hilary Jenkinson*, ed. J. Conway Davies. London: Oxford University Press, 1957.

Wormeley, Katherine Prescott. *Famous Women.* London: A. L. Humphreys, 1908. Translation of Pierre de Bourdeille, Seigneur de Brantôme, *Recueil des dames.*

Wright, Louis B. *Middle-Class Culture in Elizabethan England.* Chapel Hill: University of North Carolina Press, 1935. Ithaca, N.Y.: Cornell University Press, 1958.

————. 'The Reading of Renaissance English Women,' *Studies in Philology*, XXVIII (1931), 671–88.

Wright, W. A. (ed.). *English Works of Roger Ascham.* Cambridge: Cambridge University Press, 1904.

Wriothesley, Charles. *A Chronicle of England*, ed. W. D. Hamilton. 2 vols. (Camden Society, New Series, Vols. XI, XX.) London, 1875, 1877.

Yarwood, Doreen. *English Costume from the Second Century B.C. to 1952.* London: B. T. Batsford, 1952.

Yonge, John [Somerset herald]. *The Fyancells of Margaret, Eldest Daughter of Henry VII*, in John Leland, *Itinerary*, ed. Thomas Hearne. 9 vols. Oxford, 1710-12. See Vol. IV.

INDEX